*Real Estate Syndicator's Handbook*

**Other books by Charles Klotsche**

*The Real Estate Revolution*

*Real Estate Investing: A Complete Guide to Wealth-Building Secrets*

# Real Estate Syndicator's Handbook

Charles Klotsche

Prentice-Hall, Inc. Englewood Cliffs, NJ

Prentice-Hall International, Inc., *London*
Prentice-Hall of Australia, Pty. Ltd., *Sydney*
Prentice-Hall of Canada, Inc., *Toronto*
Prentice-Hall of India Private Ltd., *New Delhi*
Prentice-Hall of Japan, Inc., *Tokyo*
Prentice-Hall of Southeast Asia Pte., Ltd., *Singapore*
Whitehall Books, Ltd., *Wellington, New Zealand*
Editora Prentice-Hall do Brasil Ltda., *Rio de Janeiro*
Prentice-Hall Hispanoamericana, S.A., *Mexico*



**Library of Congress Cataloging in Publication Data**

Klotsche, Charles
Real estate syndicator's handbook

Includes index.
1. Real estate investment—Syndication I. Title.
HD1382.55.K56 1985 332.63'247 85-8319

ISBN 0-13-766452-4

PRINTED IN THE UNITED STATES OF AMERICA

# Dedication

Only a few in each generation achieve the spiritual integrity to share the future, irrespective of their fields of endeavor. Those avant-garde bearers of the torch, swimming against the current without suffocating the flames, are truly at peace with those who elevate life to its true meaning, a definition that escapes all but a select few. To one such centenarian achiever, Annette J. Roberts.

# Contents

# Acknowledgment

I want to express my gratitude to my brother John, a practicing attorney in Chicago, who has contributed significantly to the development of many of the chapters in this book, particularly those touching on the tax and other legal ramifications of real estate syndication, and to Joan M. Krage, for her editorial assistance.

# What This Book Offers Investors and Syndicators

Timing, leverage, and the inflationary process have combined to enhance real estate to the point where it is now an unparalleled investment vehicle. Syndication has contributed enormously to this enhancement and constitutes the most promising and lucrative segment of the real estate industry. This book presents the advantages and practical consequences of syndication, substantiating them with examples and documentation that permit you as a syndicator or investor to anticipate, long before they arise, problems that could occur in syndications. With the help of this comprehensive reference volume, you can analyze and avoid mediocre investments characterized by the risks—high leverage; negative cash flow; hyperinflated appraisals; tax avoidance schemes; and accrued, deferred, and often unrepayable interest obligations—that can produce a toxic environment for investors and syndicators alike.

The time-tested concepts in this volume reflect the knowledge I have gained through involvement in more than $100 million worth of real estate ventures. You'll find syndicated investments from the perspective of an active real estate developer and with input from a counsel in corporate law. This book offers grassroots advice to the self-reliant investor who is currently engaged in or contemplates syndicated activities, whether as an active syndicator or as a passive investor. A comprehensive explanation of a variety of syndication forms is also offered. I demonstrate the means to compare and analyze those most appropriate to your investment needs and the practical techniques most effective in marketing various syndicated offerings.

This book emphasizes private offerings, in contrast to syndications publicly promoted by individuals who tend to inflate property values and undercut investor returns. Private offerings are geared toward semisophisticated investors, often of substantial means, who demand respectable and documentable values structured by informed and knowledgeable investment advisors. Syndicated offerings cannot afford to entice investors in the 50 percent tax bracket into offerings with 50 cents after-tax investment dollars that are not fully repayable at a predetermined point in time. Private syndications have the potential for destroying or tarnishing the syndicator's credibility as well as subjecting him to significant financial exposure. They must therefore also be carefully structured for conformity to the securities laws and for solid standing under Internal Revenue Service (IRS) scrutiny.

The important ramifications of the securities laws and how they are interpreted and enforced by the Securities Exchange Commission (SEC) are fully explored and amplified in layman's terms. The undefined areas of IRS rulings are also explained. The potential for dramatic changes in the Internal Revenue Code (IRC) is considered in light of the retroactive applications that can be so disastrous to tax-oriented offerings.

## FORMING, STRUCTURING, AND PRICING THE SYNDICATE

The first three chapters of this book set forth the complete framework of the syndication, a profile of the typical investor and definitions or guidelines of investors' often illusory objectives. Offering workable formulas for structuring and pricing real estate syndications, this section offers such practical pointers as

- how you can effectively balance tax-deferred benefits, cash flow, and appreciation factors in order to maximize your offering;
- how you can determine the feasibility of the essential economics and structure them into your syndicated offering;
- how you can temper the investors' exposure by adequately diversifying a syndication;
- how you can ascertain the typical returns you must tender to your investors;

- how you can utilize leverage, depreciation, and your syndication fees to enhance the amount of your offering;
- how you can be the recipient of large-scale economic returns of massive or multiple real estate syndications; and
- how you can insulate or safeguard yourself by structuring in the appropriate reserves for contingencies.

Even during periods of tight money, excessive and fluctuating interest rates, and adverse economic conditions, these and many similar ideas will enable you to conceive syndications creatively for maximum returns to both you and your investors.

## NEGOTIATING THE PROPERTIES AND QUALIFYING THE INVESTORS

Developing and fine-tuning an overall acquisition strategy is an essential ingredient in capitalizing on opportunities as they arise, and often demands decisive action in a matter of days or hours. Chapters 4 and 5 concentrate on these interrelated techniques. As a partial overview, this section will show you

- how to find and procure properties where a strong investor demand exists;
- how to facilitate the screening of properties and option the appropriate one for your offering;
- how to structure tax-oriented vehicles in order to maximize the value of your syndication;
- how to systematically determine what holdings will have the most useful economic and tax-sheltered lives;
- how to plan the appropriate time frame necessary to structure and close your offering;
- how to learn why the investors' income, net worth, and investment objectives are so significant to you as syndicator;
- how to determine and calculate the minimum regulatory requirements for your potential investors;
- how independent investment advisors can assist you in dealing with unsophisticated investors; and
- how and when you should function as a principal or commissioned broker in the syndicating process.

The mechanisms of property acquisition and investor qualification detailed in this section give a methodical approach to accumulating a vast, diversified, and relatively risk-free personal fortune.

## MARKETING SYNDICATIONS, STRUCTURING COMPENSATION, AND JOINT VENTURE ARRANGEMENTS

The third section of this book consists of three chapters concerned with leverage and the return on investors' equity. Many syndicators have come to realize that by increasing their own fees and commissions they can simultaneously maximize their investors' tax deductions. Some of the highlights of this portion of the publication will

- summarize the proven techniques for merchandising the various and specific types of real estate investments;
- demonstrate how the fees you can command are based on your past reputation;
- approach the location of potential prospects methodically and use outside marketing organizations effectively;
- offer ways to convey formats of realistic projections of income and values to your investors;
- explain the pros and cons of merchandising a firm commitment (guaranteed) versus a best-efforts (unguaranteed) type of offering;
- delineate the industry norms or ranges of syndication fees in accordance with the appropriate disclosure procedures; and
- emphasize the types of compensation you can justifiably command, such as underwriting fees, syndication and real estate commissions, and equity participation interests.

These and other potentially lucrative techniques, when used creatively, help explain why real estate syndication is a more than $10-billion-a-year industry for its participants.

Chapter 8 explores the advantages of side stepping the syndication process by means of equity joint venturing with sophisticated institutional lenders.

## OWNERSHIP, LEGAL, AND MANAGEMENT ASPECTS OF SYNDICATIONS

Chapters 9 through 11 review the choices of vehicles for syndication open to you, then explore your legal obligations proceeding from those choices, and, finally, discuss your alternatives in performing and monitoring the often monotonous reporting activities of syndications. The far-reaching ramifications of both asset and property management are explored in the light of assistance available from specialized professionals. As a partial overview, this section includes the

- appropriate vehicle tailored to fit your syndication goals, combined with the ramifications of choosing a partnership, a corporation, or a real estate investment trust;
- factors affecting your choice of vehicles, including personal financial resources and exposure, investment requirements, and taxable consequences to investors;
- parameters for estimating the income, losses, and economic life of an offering;
- guidelines, legal requirements, and backbone documentation for managing a syndication's affairs;
- formulas for effectively dealing with troubled syndications;
- techniques for organizing and maintaining the syndication's financial records and how to allocate the profits and losses; and
- aggregate approach for filing the required financial reports, while remaining in compliance with securities requirements.

These chapters outline proceedings for controlling a syndication, with emphasis on the legal, moral, contractual, and fiduciary aspects of real estate offerings.

## SECURITIES LAWS AND THE IMPORTANT TAX ASPECTS THAT AFFECT SYNDICATIONS

While real estate syndications are highly regulated in terms of boilerplate investor documentation, little of the substantive financial material comes under close scrutiny except in large public offerings. Much of the equity is raised through tax-deferred deductions supported by costly and often misleading legal opinions and accountants' projections that are preemptively qualified for IRS purposes. As we will discuss in the concluding chapter of this book, Congress is under pressure to close tax loopholes to ease federal government deficits. Syndications structured without economic substance will be the first to be in nonconformity to the stricter IRS guidelines and thus will suffer their retroactive consequences.

The fifth section, Chapters 12 through 15, will position you as syndicator soundly for the future, putting a respectable distance between you and the regulatory bodies that will eventually have to police the industry. Specifically, this aspect will illustrate and support

- how to allocate maximum tax writeoffs disproportionally to those who benefit most;
- how the deductibility of prepaid or accrued interest combined with syndication fees can enhance the value of your offerings;
- how to restructure an overleveraged and unworkable syndicated venture;
- how to pass the investment tax credits, excess loss carry-overs, and long-term appreciation benefits to your investors;
- how to liquidate your syndication on the most appealing basis to you and your investors;
- how to extend the tax benefits when other investor expectations fail to materialize; and
- how the broker-dealer registration requirements interrelate with your syndication activities.

Incorporated are the full and limited registration requirements for dealing with securities laws, the recognized exemptions from registration, the elementary restrictions placed on marketing, and the acceptable parameters for syndication compensation and offering expenses. The increasing effect of the interaction of "blue sky" legislation is also covered.

## FULL DISCLOSURE PROVISIONS AND THE PRIVATE-PLACEMENT MEMORANDUM

Two chapters in the final section deal with the Private–Placement Memorandum. This critical document is illustrated with a typical format, a Subscription Agreement, and Limited Partnership Agreement, all of which are normally included in the offering package. Understanding and utilizing these documents will preclude the need to participate in future seminars on real estate syndication, since these documents are preceded by the all-encompassing background information. You will more easily understand the composite legal and ethical ramifications of syndicated offerings through the sample documents that meet the full disclosure requirements, with additional explanations of the

- salient risk factors and important fiduciary responsibilities required by full-disclosure provisions;
- requirement for accurate disclosure of capitalization and the investors' suitability requirements;
- need to air potential conflicts of interest between you and your investors;
- integral procedural and legal documentation for marketing syndicated real estate interests; and
- full disclosure provisions of general-partner compensation and the need to report on the use of syndicated proceeds.

Most syndicated investors have little comprehension of what their passive investments will be worth when the property is disposed of or when mortgages become due. As a syndicator, you must forearm yourself by conforming to the disclosure provisions required by securities laws if you are to survive unscathed in a climate of increasing regulation of this industry. At a critical time, when many syndications are tainted by overpricing, by structuring to yield excessive fees, and by overleveraging, this book is designed as a practical and comprehensive guide for the professional real estate syndicator and his or her investors. These concepts are presented to reflect what is happening in real estate today and the sophisticated trends and legislative controls being projected to counteract abuses.

**Charles Klotsche**
Santa Fe, New Mexico

# 1

# How Syndications Work and What Investors Look For

Syndication is a matching of money and talent, in which a passive and relatively unsophisticated group contributes the financial resources, and another entity, usually the instigator of the project, injects the expertise and needed managerial capabilities. The latter usually acquires, develops, and manages the affairs of the syndication, intending eventually to maximize the investors' return by successfully disposing of the syndicated asset at a substantial profit to all parties concerned.

As it relates to real estate ventures, syndication can be the ultimate refinement of the art of using other people's money. Due to the extremely unpredictable conditions prevailing in the debt-financing markets during the late 1970s and early 1980s, syndications have recently taken on unparalleled importance. People who formerly were able to acquire major real estate assets exclusively through conventional debt-related financing now find it difficult to accomplish their objectives due to the

- high and constantly fluctuating interest rates that often produce unacceptable mortgage constants;
- relatively short-term financing commitments obtainable from the majority of lenders, and
- substantially decreased loan-to-value ratios achieved through newer conventional financing.

These changing and adverse financial conditions in the long-term debt markets have affected not only the small investors, but the sophisticated real estate professionals as well. Both groups are finding that the more desirable properties usually available to them have far outdistanced their financial reach with the prevailing conditions in the 1980s. In order to continue acquiring these leveraged investment assets that were so profitable in the past, they now are compelled to pool their investment capital with others less sophisticated than they through one of the recognized forms of syndication.

The purpose of this book is to describe the most current, up-to-date types of syndicating activity designed specifically to meet the objectives of a wide range of potential real estate investors and to offer proven methods for attracting and retaining these highly sought-after individuals.

## STRUCTURING A SYNDICATION TO MEET YOUR INVESTORS' OBJECTIVES

Investors intend through their portfolios to substantially increase their equity positions. The primary difference in their investment goals is *when* that gain materializes:

- *now,* to produce ordinary income, or
- *later,* to appreciate capital and provide tax shelter.

Syndications can be designed to achieve either goal singly or in a combination of the two.

A syndication designed or structured to provide a steady cash flow initially will attract a relatively conservative type of investor. The intention of such an offering is to assure a positive, realistic, and, more important, predictable income to the passive investors—amounting to an almost irrevocable guarantee of a fixed rate of return. Real properties suitable for achieving such goals are normally blue-chip-type investments involving

- long-term high-grade leases;
- sale and leaseback arrangements;
- investments involving uncomplicated management activities;
- conservatively leveraged holdings; or
- properties offering little downside risk potential.

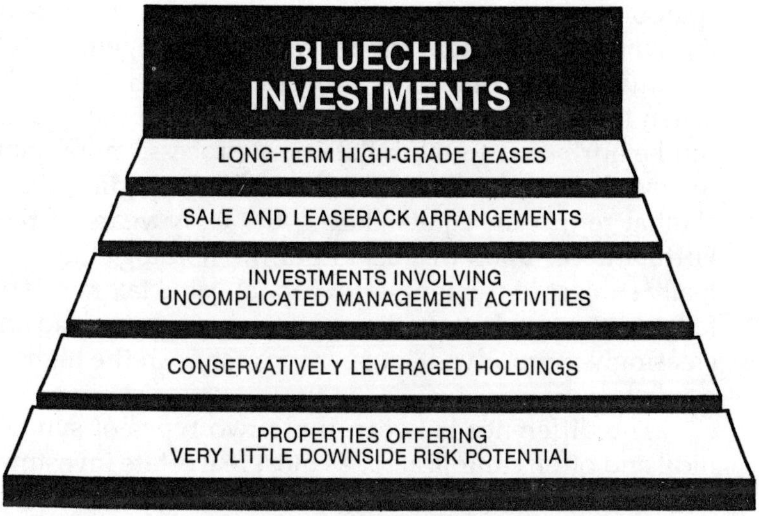


**Figure 1.1** Desirable qualities in real estate properties chosen to provide cash flow.

Income-oriented syndications concerned with the *now* aspect of cash flow can, nonetheless, often provide tax-shelter benefits. These tax-sheltering advantages vary with the type of property, its current or eventual use, the nature and extent of the improvements placed thereon, and the amount of financial leverage that accompanies the syndicated venture. Whatever the nature or degree of this variation, the tax-shelter ramifications are an important aspect of merchandising an income-oriented syndication. At a minimum, the cash-on-invested-cash return offered to investors on an income-oriented syndication should generally be increased 50 percent by the noncash benefits derived from the after-tax-related considerations. Herein lie the inherent advantages that will lure many conservative individuals from the more conventional common stock-and-bond-portfolio investments to the less liquid field of real estate offerings.

Syndications designed for long-range generation of profits through the vehicle of appreciation offer less of a guarantee of fixed cash returns on invested equity. These investors rely on the syndicator's ability and willingness to manage the property so as to substantially increase the income it generates over the years. The investment life is directly governed by the predictable period of stabilized cash flow and terminated when it fails to provide the substantial tax shelter required by members of the syndicate. During the fixed span of years over which the property generates tax-shelter benefits, the syndicator provides the appropriate management vehicle designed eventually to maximize the property's appreciation at the time of sale. When the asset is disposed of, the eventual proceeds, much of which can be attributed to the inflationary process, more than compensates the syndicating investors for the lack of liquidity, cash flow, or substantial return on equity during the early years of their ownership. Furthermore, upon disposition of the holding, the investors are normally subject to the long-term capital-gains tax rate. This treatment is far more favorable than the ordinary income-tax rate and becomes increasingly more advantageous to investors in the higher individual tax brackets.

The difference between these two types of syndications is technical and often complicated, as most real estate investments offer some of the advantages of both:

- a relatively predictable cash flow, generated at some predetermined point in the investment;
- an understandable, predictable, and generally lucrative package of tax benefits; and
- an appreciation and leverage factor that is in many respects unparalleled in any other investment field.

## THE MAJOR DRAWBACKS FOUND IN REAL ESTATE SYNDICATIONS

The most common catastrophic events adversely affecting any real estate investment can usually be traced to three attributable situations:

1. acquisition price well in excess of the current market value of the property;
2. undercapitalization or overleveraging combined with corresponding lack of financial reserves; and
3. lack of professional management necessary to oversee the day-to-day operations.

One or a combination of these shortcomings is inherent in any marginal business venture and occurs to some degree even in the most sophisticated of offerings.

Well-funded syndications can often eliminate the need to pay

**MAJOR PITFALLS**

1. AN ACQUISITION PRICE WELL IN EXCESS OF CURRENT MARKET VALUE OF PROPERTY.
2. UNDERCAPITALIZATION OR OVERLEVERAGE AND CORRESPONDING LACK OF FINANCIAL RESERVES AND STABILITY.
3. LACK OF PROFESSIONAL MANAGEMENT TO OVERSEE DAY-TO-DAY OPERATIONS.

**Figure 1.2** Causes of most catastrophes in real estate investments.

more than the market value when acquiring real estate. The pooling and duplicating of funds found in major syndications almost always assures the syndicator a position of tremendous bargaining strength. Sellers are generally impressed and often intimidated when dealing with individuals or groups with substantial means, and they are normally willing to negotiate major price concessions and financing terms with well-capitalized, sophisticated principals or agents. Even the most experienced syndicator needs sufficient time to confirm the financial ramifications of any specific investment purchase. The syndicator must have the means to buy that time with large earnest money deposits or substantial down payments, which give credibility to his or her contractual contingencies.

Many real estate projects have or subsequently develop complications not easily recognized at the time of the acquisition that often require financial reserves and staying power far beyond the ability of the majority of most single investors. Many older properties need major infusions of capital often equal to and even exceeding the initial equity contribution to continue to generate a fixed, constant, and predictable cash flow. Such potential expenditures can be grossly underestimated when the property is initially acquired, contributing to the downfall of many a well-conceived venture. Undercapitalization is particularly prevalent when purchasers seek out older, more seasoned quality properties that may not produce the anticipated rapid appreciation expected. I have found that some of these top-of-the-line holdings can come to the market at the apex of their income stream. Any underlying weakness in the market following their purchase could entail a substantial need for future expenditures or reserves. I found this to be the case in a large-sized apartment complex that I had under option several years ago. Initially, I had thought the project would have made an outstanding conversion; however, upon further analysis, the market was too thin and the absorption period too extensive. In attempting to salvage the option, I looked at the income potential, which was realistic for the age of the building. In order to increase the income substantially, however, major uneconomical renovations would have been required that would not have produced the desired return on equity that the additional injection of capital would or should have warranted.

## CONDITIONS THAT CAN JEOPARDIZE REAL ESTATE SYNDICATIONS

Sometimes unpleasant financial pressures can surface through unpredictable economic changes that are often unrelated to the specific property, such as:

- a shift in employment away from a given area causing an unusual vacancy factor or reduction in rental rates;
- a major increase in interest rates, shortened amortization schedules, or other problems related to financing that are not fixed by nature; or
- unsettled economic conditions prevailing on a national or international scale that can be disruptive to an otherwise healthy local economy.

Any of these situations can quickly drain adequately budgeted cash reserves, jeopardize a project, and threaten its investors.

Syndications can also have the benefit of reducing your exposure as they relate to first-mortgage financing. A well-conceived, highly leveraged syndicated offering can normally be financed on a nonrecourse basis to the managing general partner through most conventional lending institutions. This arrangement conveniently minimizes exposure, also providing the syndicator the ultimate degree of leverage in renegotiating the terms and conditions of an existing loan should financial complications arise.

Another area frequently overlooked and underestimated is the necessity for a qualified management team to effectively operate the partnership affairs on a daily basis. Many syndicators, including myself, find that the management aspect of real estate acquisition or development is far less lucrative than the fees involved in the up-front offering process or in deriving an equity position at the tail end. For that reason, many professional syndicators look exclusively to outside management firms, preferring to utilize their own creative abilities in different and more rewarding areas. All adequately prepared pro forma projections provided to investors inevitably include a category to compensate professional management, thus relieving the syndicator of this often neglected responsibility. The more active the syndicator, the more likely he or she will be able to assure respectable and reliable management to his investors, since independent professional groups are always eager for association with a constant source of new projects, assuring them reliable current and future income. The farsighted syndicator will, in fact, search out the most professional management group in his or her geographic area before completing the first offering, since this assumed association can provide credibility in the eyes of potential investors who are familiar with the capabilities of the time-tested management team to be retained. The first venture that I syndicated, a 50-unit condominium, was a success primarily due to the retention of a major independent marketing firm. Many of my investors' initial reservations were immediately resolved when I introduced them to the principal owner of the firm, whose status in the community was second only to his enthusiasm for the project.

## CHARACTERISTICS OF A TYPICAL SYNDICATED INVESTOR

Most people involved in real estate syndications are generally preoccupied with the time-consuming activities of their own professions. Many are knowledgeable of the advantages of acquiring and holding real estate assets but have limited firsthand experience, usually confined to the ownership of their residence or business-related facilities. Already educated to the fact that a sound real estate holding is a proper place to invest a portion of their assets that are not required for immediate liquidity, these relatively passive investors desire to be associated with a sophisticated investment group in which they have access to firsthand knowledge of the property and the syndicating group. These professional individuals tend to shy away from large, mass-marketed real estate securities where the only contact with the general partner is through the annual corporate or partnership report with limited conversations through an obscure stockbroker. Professional individuals generally are more comfortable with small- to medium-sized syndications where they can specifically relate either to a given entrepreneurial-type person or to a specific real estate property.

This desire for individual eye contact also extends to their preference for properties. The investing public generally have preconceived concepts about what types of investments will provide the quickest appreciation with the least amount of potential risk of exposure. These so-called fashionable properties are the easiest and often the most desirable to syndicate to investors, since they have achieved a built-in market recognition. In fact, an experienced real estate syndicator with an eye on a given prime investment property can readily structure and predict the profile of a syndicate of investors and will almost be assured of acquiring their interest.

Often, the key to initiating a syndication can be locating the appropriate property. Once the investment holding is isolated and optioned, the balance of the syndicating venture can be relatively simple, as the securities laws generally standardize the type of format and the attendant investment presentation that can be advanced to the prospective purchasers. The major underlying reason for the success of the majority of local or regional syndications is that their offerings zero in exclusively on fashionable properties whose predictable rate of return is known and can therefore be easily tailored to a diverse group of potential passive investors.

This favored approach to acquisition or development also has obvious limitations. Desirable properties must often be acquired at premium prices, leaving the syndicate a limited up-side potential, at least initially. Selecting these attractive holdings also inhibits the creative ability of the syndicator to pick and choose among the properties that can provide the longest-range appreciation potential. The creative individual should attempt to associate with investors who can, sooner or later, be educated away from these stereotyped investment vehicles, relying then exclusively upon the syndicator's time-tested judgment.

In some respects this close judgmental concept is changing, as the major stock brokerage houses continue to escalate their mass-market real estate securities, substantiating their choices of properties by their proven track records. Still, the creative local entrepreneur has the often irresistible and irreplaceable advantage.

## DETERMINING YOUR OBJECTIVES AS A REAL ESTATE SYNDICATOR

Since major syndicating efforts are relatively new to the real estate profession, few individuals have long-standing, professional careers or established track records in organizing partnerships for real estate acquisition or development. Many of the most successful and active syndicators have switched to real estate ventures from such varied backgrounds as marketing, finance, or the legal professions. Many bring their own unique professional talents to these real estate offerings, where substantial numbers of individuals inevitably lack the expertise to recognize the pitfalls unique to holding real estate assets, as real estate syndications are forever ongoing, extremely complicated, and management-intensive ventures.

Once the initial funds for acquisition or development are raised, the offering entity must be prepared to adequately manage the project during the life expectancy of the syndication. Many people, including some real estate brokers, are accustomed to terminating their obligations or activities upon the acquisition of the asset by the syndicate and the subsequent distribution of the brokerage commissions. Those entering the field of real estate syndication from backgrounds relating to marketing, legal, financial, or other specialties are often ill prepared to wrestle or deal with the day-to-day complications associated with managing the affairs of a complicated syndication.

In offerings that are oriented toward specific performance objectives, management is extremely important, so much so that the syndicator must often continue to monitor the progress of the partnership's holdings. The sponsor is usually compensated with a percentage of gross income reflecting the anticipated increased net profits generated to the investors through his or her management efforts. Performance-oriented syndications generally have the longest-lasting value in terms of potential appreciation. The syndicator-manager well deserves the high percentage of profits he or she receives, as his or her continuing managerial talent is the key to the successful achievement of the partnership investment goals. We were recently involved in a syndication of a $30-million condominium that was to be phased over a multiyear period in which five investor shares were sold at $200,000 per share. The increments were marketed through a certified public accountant who had not set foot in the municipality in which the condominium was located, relying exclusively on the prior performance or track record of the general partners. Based exclusively on the seasoned reputations of the developers, this nontax-shelter-type syndication attracted some prominent and well-heeled investors from the eastern part of the United States.

## HOW SYNDICATING ACTIVITIES CAN DIFFER SUBSTANTIALLY

Syndications that are not oriented toward initial performance or early retrieval of equity are usually structured to meet the objectives of passive, relatively unsophisticated investors. Properties acquired by such syndications can usually be turned over to a nonassociated professional management team without sacrificing the long-run potential profit. Often, such long-term offerings are merchandised not by private entrepreneurs but by the major stockbrokerage firms.

The challenging aspect of a syndication lies in the creativity demanded of the sponsor. He or she is basically the person who conceives the syndication and structures it to everyone's benefit. Large, mass-marketed syndications usually fit into a preconceived mold, leaving little or often no room for structural creativity.

In setting your objectives for any given offering, you must keep your creative approaches, opportunities, and responsibilities firmly in perspective, where:

- You are the one exclusively determining the anticipated return on equity to your potential investors.
- You must unilaterally choose the appropriate level of financial leverage in accordance with the appropriate risk.
- You will ultimately be responsible to your investors if and when financial problems surface or investment objectives are not met.
- You will ultimately determine the syndication's success or failure through your ability to retain the appropriate people to manage, finance, and resell its assets.

Seeking competent advice in areas where one lacks the background or experience to handle the intricate affairs of a real estate syndication can be extremely helpful. In major tax-oriented offerings, I rely exclusively on projections provided by recognized and established certified public accountants. We are currently in the process of forming a syndication on a $13-million apartment complex where the credibility of the projections is supported by a "Big Eight" accounting firm in which our estimates are verified by computer printouts on their letterheads supported by the appropriate disclaimers. These official-looking presentations lend tremendous credibility to a real estate syndication, which in many cases can be sold to a majority of the clients of the certified public accountants.

## THE VARIOUS TYPES OF SYNDICATING ACTIVITIES

In analyzing the characteristics of the typical investor's profile earlier in this chapter, we touched upon types and varieties of syndications as well, emphasizing the recognizable appeal found only at the local or regional levels. One approach to classifying syndications is through the *tangibility of the asset*, which becomes increasingly abstract in the following order:

- specific property syndications;
- multiple-property syndications, with holdings known only to the managing partners; and
- blind-pool syndications.

The last category is by far the most sophisticated and least interesting to the investor who desires to follow the details of his or her investment's progress. *Blind pool syndications* are generally formed with the intent that the initial investment of the syndicated proceeds from the offering be placed in relatively safe, high-yielding securities. These funds are later reinvested in income-producing properties that meet the objectives of the offering prospectus as they are located, analyzed, and eventually acquired. The format of these syndications is almost always conservative in nature, as a substantial fiduciary responsibility always falls upon the individual or corporate entity acting as the syndicator. The mass-marketed offerings of the major brokerage houses are usually blind-pool syndications, typically presented with a broad and basic investment objective outlined on a tertiary basis to the investors through the offering circular.

The *specific-type syndications* are the most common and expedient in terms of marketing. They offer a specific goal attained through a recognizable asset that is attached and identifiable in the offering circular. Because the investment potential of the single, specific real estate asset is fairly obvious to both the syndicator and his or her potential partners, this type of offering elicits the least amount of developmental and managerial creativity.

*Multiple-property syndication* has considerable merit for the sophisticated individuals active and knowledgeable in this field, as it permits the syndicator to locate and group properties that have similar characteristics in terms of their long-term investment objectives. Assembling these similar holdings into one single offering creates and accomplishes the diversification necessary to balance the inherent risks found in syndications. This in no way guarantees that all such multiple offerings live up to their full expectations, irrespective of how well executed or conceived they may be. Still, the grouping of lucrative and what might turn out to be marginal holdings into one offering permits the safety of averaging the overall positive and negative cash returns plus the added interest or excitement of achieving a turnaround on one or more of the marginal holdings.

## WHY MULTIPLE SYNDICATIONS ARE SO PREVALENT

Aside from averaging the risk element, multiple syndications allow an extraordinary interplay between the cash-on-cash return and the tax-shelter benefits related to the various properties that can be uniquely combined into one syndication. Since most investors are desirous of obtaining diversified portfolios, they can be attracted to offerings with a blend of these important benefits substantially increasing the return on their invested funds.

Although we previously discussed multiple-property syndications and blind-pool offerings separately, both share in varying degrees the desirable characteristics of giving the sponsor a freer investment rein and a greater amount of flexibility in determining the syndicate's objectives and holdings. Blind-pool arrangements offer virtually unlimited opportunities for the syndicator to exercise creativity in locating and acquiring properties that offer the greatest long-term appreciation potential.

The tremendous fiduciary responsibility a syndicator bears in a multiple offering inherently inspires a natural degree of conservatism, especially in blind-pool syndications, where a single or multiple failure can simultaneously and systematically eliminate the sponsor's and his or her investors' equity, not to mention his or her credibility. One can afford neither inadequate experience nor excessive risk-taking in these types of offerings.

Under either type of multiple syndication, but more particularly the blind-pool arrangements, the sponsor's track record is equally as important as the actual properties acquired.

Over the last half dozen years, I have successfully packaged five for-sale condominium syndications developed from inception to completion and varying from 18 to 112 units per project. Many of these developments were offered within short intervals of each other, many utilizing the same passive investors in one or in some instances in a combination of the ventures. This hybrid form of multiple syndications works well where limited numbers of investors are desired and where sufficient investment funds can be committed for substantial periods of time.

I have observed that the degree of investor sophistication is more prevalent when it comes to analyzing specific properties or single-purpose syndications. But, even armed with the assistance of sophisticated investment counselors, many individuals lack the expertise necessary to understand all the ramifications of a complicated real estate investment. Under multiple-property syndications, investors must often rely completely on the ability of the sponsor to acquire, finance, manage, and dispose of the syndicated assets. This well-deserved reliance eventually pays off for the investors in the form of higher returns.

## HOW SINGLE-PROPERTY SYNDICATIONS DIFFER FROM MULTIPLE OFFERINGS

When a single, specific property is chosen for syndication, the degree of speculation inherent in the investment is known fairly precisely and the measurable risks and rewards can generally be outlined to investors. Once the parameters are disclosed, the syndicator then proceeds to acquire the appropriate holding in order to

- maximize the cash return on his or her investors' funds;
- maximize the tax benefits and financial leverage; or
- combine both to produce a substantial and respectable balanced yield.

When the major or stated purpose of an offering is to maximize the tax benefits, single-property syndication is particularly effective. Tax deductions, if properly structured and presented, are usually less complicated and more reliable to predict than the pro forma cash flow from operations. This concept alone assures many single-property syndications the ability to guarantee the full return of equity in the form of tax-shelter benefits during the initial years of investment. Investors are thereby persuaded that little is at risk, irrespective of the performance of the acquired holding, and that the tax benefits alone should fully guarantee the return of their equity investment.

A major pitfall found in single-property offerings lies in the negative ramifications of overleveraging. As mentioned previously, the blue-chip properties chosen for such syndications tend to be offered and acquired when valued at substantial premiums. When the market deteriorates and highly leveraged, nonrecourse financing has been used to acquire these properties, foreclosure often becomes a reality. In a deteriorating rental or sales market, limited partners generally lose their interest in advancing the substantial funds necessary to prevent properties from going into default or foreclosure. When these holdings do go south, the tax benefits as well as the investors' equity are generally lost in the process. For one's own protection, the sponsor of a highly leveraged, tax-oriented investment must out of necessity disclose all the potential risks and rewards fully and carefully prior to closing the syndication.

By contrast, a nonspecified or blind-pool offering provides the syndicator two distinct major advantages:

1. Funds are syndicated, isolated, and readily available when the appropriate properties surface.
2. The sponsor maintains a sufficient pool of funds drawing interest until the properties are acquired, providing immediate income to his or her investors.

The up-front funds generated in these syndications are obviously substantial. Under the blind-pool approach, investors are not generally required to be notified prior to a property being acquired. The syndicator alone unilaterally decides whether the acquired holding specifically meets the investment goals outlined in the offering circular. In this respect, blind pools can often find themselves on shaky footings in meeting the full-disclosure requirements under the securities provisions.

The requirement that blind-pool funds must either be reinvested or returned to investors within a prescribed period of time can also be detrimental to the syndicator. With the speed sometimes necessary to meet these predetermined reinvestment requirements, the syndicator could potentially lose sight of the initially described investment objectives and risk investor dissatisfaction by hastily investing in unsound or marginally profitable properties.

The syndicator of blind-pool investment funds also plays a curiously hit-or-miss game during periods of rapidly fluctuating economic cycles. All too frequently reinvestment deadlines coincide with periods of falling interest rates and widely available sources of mortgage funds, when property values correspondingly tend to be at their highest levels. The sponsor can often become the victim of these adverse economic conditions over which he or she has little or no control. Conversely, fate can sometimes be on the syndicator's side. Having an ample pool of investable funds readily available during periods of tight money and accelerated or fluctuating interest rates when property values tend to decelerate in value can put the alert syndicator in a position to acquire holdings at deep discounts, quickly justifying his or her investors' confidence in holding these real estate assets.

## HOW MULTICLASS SYNDICATIONS OPERATE

Within the framework of a real estate syndication, many sponsors prefer to differentiate between the various classes of investors, thereby stratifying the objectives and goals of each of the investing groups, emphasizing either a relatively predictable cash flow or, in the alternative, a longer-term capital gain accompanied by varying degrees of tax-deferred benefits. This tendency to stratify becomes more prevalent during periods when cash returns and tax advantages decline or when properties are generally not in great demand. By isolating the benefits, rewards, and risks, a syndication can, for example, offer a preferred cash return to one group and channel the tax benefits from the same property to another collection of investors. Isolating the investors' interests is a highly technical and complicated process usually requiring close coordination with one's legal and accounting advisors.

The marketing advantage of stratifying a syndication's mixture of benefits is obvious: Individuals that exclusively desire cash returns as well as investors who are tax oriented can be attracted to the same syndication. As with any other form of channeling investment funds, the balance of the syndication process becomes relatively simple if the sponsor can isolate the particular requirements of the investors. Dividing these investment benefits can, in some rare instances, increase the offering price of the syndication by as much as 50 percent. The additional syndicated funds raised through multiclass syndications generally have little or no relationship to the ultimate conventional value of the property. They merely reflect the syndicator's success in tailoring the offering's goals to meet his or her investors' needs, for which the syndicator is rewarded by the enhanced compensation.

In a multiclass syndication different entities within the partnership must be formed in order to reflect these diverse investment objectives. This is easily accomplished initially as the relationship between the cash-flow benefits and the amount of depreciation or other tax advantages taken is readily predictable and can likewise be allocated to the various interests prior to the syndication being formed. Since the managing general partner must represent all of the interests within the syndication, one can be placed in a somewhat schizophrenic position if and when investor conflicts of interest arise.

These conflicts of interest within a stratified offering usually revolve around the management, syndication, and brokerage fees. Since the majority of the cash flow is usually channeled to the conservative group of investors and a major portion of the tax benefits and appreciation is directed at the other, more aggressive individuals, the complications arise when, for some reason, either the tax benefits or the cash flow do not decline in tandem. Rarely are they in an equally declining position. This problem can be magnified when the sale of the asset is contemplated. The normal time for disposing of the syndicated investment is when the tax benefits materially decline, yet in many instances the cash flow increases substantially about the time these tax-shelter benefits dry up. When only one property is involved in a multiclass syndication, investor ill will can often run rampant.

There is no simple solution to the dilemma just described except through an additional multiclass syndication in which the syndicator can shift the investors' assets into other holdings to balance the objectives of all the concerned parties.

## HOW PUBLIC SYNDICATIONS ARE MERCHANDISED

The trend of the past decade has become evident: away from the smaller, private, tax-deductible-oriented syndications into the widely dispersed public offerings that specialize in income-oriented properties. There is a group of companies that accounts for at least three quarters of the total annual funds generated from public real estate syndications, as follows: Balcor Company; Consolidated Capital Corporation; Equitec Financial; First Capital Investors; Fox and Carskadon Corporaton; Hutton Realty Group; Integrated Resources, Inc.; J.M.B. Realty Corporation; Robert A. McNeil Corporation; Merrill-Lynch; National Partnership Investors; and Payne Webber Properties. These major firms have access to the large public markets and are always in a state of flux as to their ranking, adding to the dynamic nature of the industry. This trend can be best exemplified by the fact that Connecticut General Life Insurance Company has recently entered into the real estate syndication market, being the first insurance-related firm to offer its own $35-million limited partnership offering. These partnership interests are being marketed through Connecticut General's 1,500 licensed representatives, providing a tremendous built-in marketing advantage to this and similar organizations. It is anticipated that many of the other life insurance companies, as well as stockbroker firms like Dean Witter Reynolds, through its association with the diversified Sears marketing operation, will be the major dynamic forces to be reckoned with in the syndication industry of the 1980s. The majority of these newly formed syndication organizations, consisting of large institutional investors, prefer to acquire existing properties rather than develop their own.

We are currently constructing a 260-unit apartment complex that is being offered for syndication for $13 million. We have already received over two dozen inquiries from various syndicating groups offering to enter into a letter of intent to acquire this property. All of this activity has been generated without the benefit of an offering circular. There is a tremendous need for respectable product in this industry, with substantial amounts of funds chasing well-conceived ventures that often show a relatively minimal initial cash flow and substantial tax advantages, combined with a lucrative long-term potential-appreciation factor.

## GUIDELINES FOR PRICING THE SHARES OF A SYNDICATION

In most instances, the prior reputation of the syndicating entity will determine whether an offering commands a premium or a discount in price. Real estate syndications blossom when the need for investor funds is greatest, and these times of need usually correspond with periods in the economic cycles. At the opportune times, syndicators with the most enviable track records are generally competing with newcomers, the former commanding a premium and the latter, a discounted price. This new-kid-on-the-block situation can be compared or likened to the corporate bond market where companies with the highest credit ratings offer their long-term, fixed-rate securities at considerably lower yields than those corporations whose earnings tend to fluctuate and be more speculative in nature.

At best, pricing the shares of syndications requires an individualized and complex formula that almost always reflects

- the speculative nature of the venture;
- the predictability of the cash flow;
- the projected realizable tax benefits; and
- the potential appreciation of the property.

The nature and size of the syndication also have a direct bearing, as does the amount of financial leverage that accompanies the offering. In most markets, conservative offerings entailing long-term lease arrangements that produce relatively few tax benefits or minimal long-term appreciation will command a cash-on-cash yield or return considerably higher than those of a more speculative nature offering considerably greater tax advantages, financial leverage, and a greater potential for resale appreciation. The latter types of offerings tend to demonstrate their ultimate yield at the time of eventual sale.

In pricing real estate syndications, you as sponsor must comprehend that your offering will compete directly with a multitude of other avenues of investments such as the stock and bond markets, not to mention the variations within each of these categories. When syndicating real estate projects where the potential appreciation and the known tax benefits can be the major thrust of the marketing effort, we have always found that the potential yield to the investor, including the cumulative tax-sheltered aspects, must be set at a minimum of 10 percent and must often surpass 15 percent over the current inflationary rate to seriously attract syndicated investor funds. This overall yield also includes the potential appreciation factor. The offerings I price at this percentage premium over the rate of inflation are not necessarily conservative in nature. Rather, the risk factor can be considerable and must be communicated to our investors because of the amount of financial leverage required to sustain the important after-tax-shelter benefits. For a conservative project oriented strictly toward cash flow with somewhat of an inherently limited financial risk, I find that I can offer a return of 3 percent to 5 percent less than those promoted and still remain more than competitive.

The difference in return on equity reflects the various elements of risk in different ventures, and the premium over the inflationary rate is directly attributed to the nonliquidity aspect of syndicated real estate investments. In many respects, potential investors are attracted to real estate syndications as a long-term hedge against inflation. Individuals who purchase speculative corporate stocks can assess their downside risks and liquidate much more rapidly than those buying into speculative real estate syndications. The increased rate of return structured into real estate offerings must reflect this controlling market reality.

Another method for pricing or valuating a syndication is closely aligned to the amount of leverage utilized when acquiring the property. If the syndicate is highly leveraged, tax-deferred deductions often substantially augment the return, and the potential for appreciation also becomes greater due to the increased size of the holding. A syndication whose value is based upon acquiring a highly leveraged asset must also be structured in such a manner as to provide a realistic amount of financial reserves for contingencies. These reserves must be determined and maintained at a high point initially, because the investors are often hesitant to inject additional equity funds when projects develop problems, especially when tax-shelter benefits are decreasing rapidly. The necessary cash reserves built into the initial syndication price effectively lower the overall yield to the investors, yet they are a necessary cushion or hedge against a potential catastrophe. In a situation where these reserves are appropriately set, a cash-on-cash return of 8 percent to 10 percent after the debt service requirement on a highly leveraged appreciation-oriented syndication is adequate for marketing it, since the noncash benefits and resale potential will generally add substantially to the investors' return on their invested equity.

## WHY REALISTIC INVESTMENT PROJECTIONS ARE IMPERATIVE

I have emphasized the importance of reserves for replacement in order for any offering to be considered a success. Whether a syndicate projection is conservative or speculative in nature, it must above all be totally realistic. Realism is what establishes the track record of the syndicator and determines whether a project is marketable to the investing public.

Generally, syndications are marketed by independent agents on

- a best-efforts basis, or
- a guaranteed-sale arrangement.

A *best-efforts* offering is the less desirable of the two; however, it generally obtains a higher price for the property being marketed when successfully structured. In a *guaranteed-sale* syndication, the marketing entity has committed to acquire the remaining shares if the offering is not fully sold out during the prescribed period of time. The latter type is therefore thought to be more conservative in nature and reflects this in its pricing.

The more speculative offerings providing a minimal cash-on-cash return and oriented toward appreciation and tax-shelter benefits have a further condition of realism. They need to

- provide at least two and a half and often three dollars in cumulative after-tax benefits to the investors for every dollar of equity advanced, and
- offer the investors an unqualified potential for substantial appreciation through financial leverage techniques.

Successfully marketing these specialized syndications is often contingent upon the investors being in the highest personal tax brackets. Before the 1981 Tax Reform Act took effect, a higher tax-deductible ratio could have been achieved, since the maximum tax bracket prior to that legislation was 70 percent and has now been reduced substantially.

## HOW STAGING THE EQUITY IMPROVES THE OVERALL YIELD

We find that we can maximize the value of a syndication and the corresponding return on equity in tax-oriented offerings by staging the investors' capital contributions over a period of time. This device, when structured properly, always facilitates the marketing, as investors in tax-oriented offerings are not primarily concerned, at least initially, with the project's spendable cash flow. Rather, they are attracted to those highly leveraged ventures where initial tax benefits are substantial in relation to their equity contributions, and a downstream potential exists for a substantial capital gain once the tax benefits decline and the project is disposed of. We were recently involved in the syndication of a 188-unit garden apartment project in the midwestern part of the United States. The investment concept was to acquire and hold the asset for three to seven years, with plans eventually to sell it to an apartment converter for a substantial profit, taxed at the advantageous, long-term capital-gains rates. The immediate or near-term objective of the syndicate was accomplished through initially staging the investors' equity contributions to provide substantial tax-sheltered cash distributions, translating into tax losses in excess of the project's cash flow that were used to offset other income earned by the investors from unrelated sources.

The partnership acquired the apartment complex, including all syndication fees and reserves for operating losses, for $5,320,000. The syndicate assumed an existing first mortgage and additionally invested $2,450,000 in cash contributions payable in five annual installments as follows:

| | |
|---|---|
| At closing | $ 560,000 |
| 12 months after closing | 665,000 |
| 24 months after closing | 560,000 |
| 36 months after closing | 420,000 |
| 42 months after closing | 245,000 |
| | $2,450,000 |

The partnership issued 2,450 limited-partnership interests at $1,000 each. A maximum of 35 investors was structured into the partnership for regulatory purposes, with the average or median investment interest being 70 units or $70,000, purchased in five incremental installments as follows:

| *Date* | *Average Amount Advanced* | *Estimated Tax Writeoff* |
|---|---|---|
| Closing | $16,000.00 | 50% |
| 12 months after closing | 19,000.00 | 80% |
| 24 months after closing | 16,000.00 | 58% |
| 36 months after closing | 12,000.00 | 62% |
| 42 months after closing | 7,000.00 | 22% |
| | $70,000.00 | 272% |

The tax benefits were substantially *increased* by a minimum of 50 percent by staging the equity contributions over a 42-month period. This almost 3-to-1 ratio of tax deductions to invested equity is a relatively salable concept and one that probably would not currently be challenged by the Internal Revenue Service. A slight premium was paid for the complex, as the seller agreed to carry the unamortized equity on contribution over the 5-year installment sale. It is anticipated that the profit from the conversion will more than offset the slightly inflated purchase price and the inherent carrying costs. The tax deductions were not totally maximized in this case, as a conservative straight-line method of depreciation was used, since the partnership investment objective was eventually to merchandise the property to an apartment converter. By using the straight-line method, the recapture provisions of the Tax Code will not apply at the time of conversion. The limited partners received 99 percent of the operating losses and 70 percent of the net sales proceeds after the total return of their equity contributions, providing the appropriate frosting on this lucrative cake.

## TYPICAL RETURNS OFFERED TO CONSERVATIVE INVESTORS

Individuals looking for an assured return of principal and a respectable cash yield on their equity investment will usually anticipate a cash-on-cash return of at least half a dozen percentage points over the current or projected near-term rate of inflation. An exception occurs when a syndicate is organized to acquire a property of extremely high quality, in a prestigious neighborhood, having a substantial up-side rental and price-appreciation potential. In such a situation, we find that the necessary cash-on-cash return can be more closely related to the current yields found on quality corporate bonds. Investors will normally commit at this rate, as they fully understand that the potential appreciation and actual tax advantages found in such projects will add substantially to the overall yield and offset to some degree the financial risk and liquidity factors that are so prevalent and detrimental to real estate syndications.

In summarizing the salient aspects of pricing a syndication, we can realistically enumerate the six factors that generally govern the valuation:

1. the risks associated with projecting the income;
2. the unknowns associated with the resale potential;

3. the syndicator's proven track record;
4. the amount of leverage and tax-deductible benefits;
5. the size of the contingency reserves provided; and
6. the nature of the investment and its investors.

The last factor, and in many respects the most important, will be explored in the following chapter, where the various ramifications of structuring a syndication aimed at conservative types of individuals will be fully expounded upon.

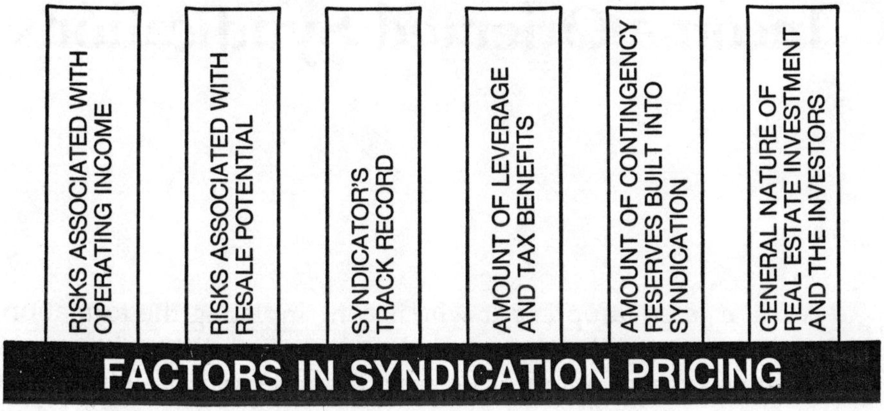


**Figure 1.3** Six factors generally governing the pricing of a syndication.

# 2

# The Unique Appeals of Income-Oriented Syndications

A real estate entrepreneur who is contemplating the formation of his or her first syndication should consider starting with an income-oriented type of offering. Relatively simple and straightforward, this provides an effective overview of the syndication process and an arena where the syndicator-to-be can effectively test his or her managerial ability. Income-producing syndications generally appeal to a mass market of small, unsophisticated investors clustered in the lower tax brackets whose total capital contributions fall in the $5,000-to-$10,000 range. These individuals look for safety of their invested principal combined with a predictable cash-on-cash return over a relatively long period of time.

Catering to the needs of these conservative investors interested primarily in generating spendable income requires relatively little in-depth background experience on the part of the syndicator. Basically, one must

- locate and analyze the appropriate property;
- option it for syndication purposes; and
- engage others to market syndication shares if one lacks the investor contacts.

Since the financing ramifications of these syndications are usually quite straightforward, the syndicator normally can structure them utilizing local lending institutions that he or she has dealt with in the past. These types of syndications generally require that the offering group must manage the property and be compensated through management fees that can be both substantial and predictable over lengthy periods of time. These management fees can, in fact, be substantial in the overall picture, since a project structured exclusively toward cash-on-cash returns will not generate the significant back-end profits that are customarily found in more leveraged, less conservative investments.

## COMPARATIVE DISADVANTAGES OF INCOME-ORIENTED SYNDICATIONS

Income-oriented syndications have relatively little appeal for the well-heeled, more sophisticated syndicator, since they often lack

- extreme financial leverage;
- predictable and valuable tax deductions; and
- the potential for significant appreciation.

The majority of the syndicator's compensation does not lie in the participation in the equity position upon dissolution but through the up-front syndication and ongoing management fees. Additionally, the extensive holding periods normally associated with income-oriented syndications leave a somewhat marginal potential for resale commissions if one relates them to the overall time and efforts involved. Since many sophisticated syndicators are Horatio Alger types themselves, they may also consider income-oriented investors to be about as compatible as the proverbial little old lady from Dubuque.

While one income-oriented syndication often competes with another of a similar type, less competition usually exists between syndications oriented toward income or cash flow when they are combined with tax-shelter and appreciation benefits. Investors participating in syndications generating cash flow from real estate investments probably also hold, or have held, common stocks and corporate bonds or have even participated in mutual fund investments. They expect comparable safety of their investment capital in real estate offerings and are not in tax brackets high enough to benefit from the tax-sheltering aspects of speculative, highly leveraged real estate investments. A total loss of their investment also becomes a more difficult pill to swallow due to the detrimental ramifications of a low tax-bracket deduction.

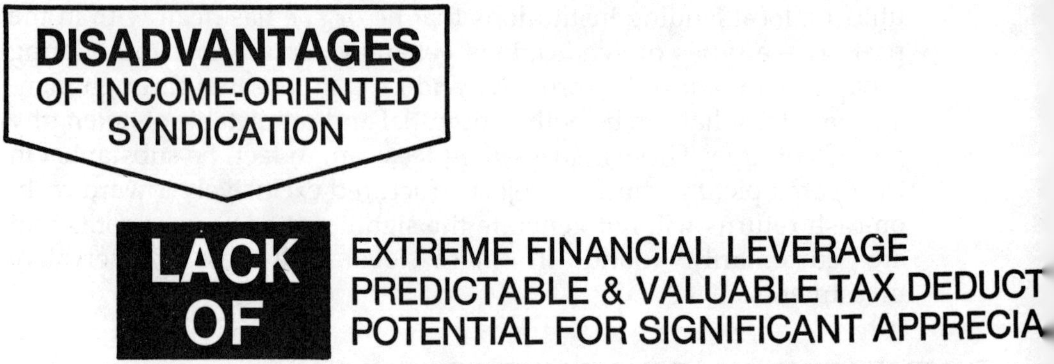


**Figure 2.1** Comparative disadvantages of income-oriented syndications.

Real estate syndications attract these conservative investors in part because they offer a higher return than normally found in the stock market and in part because they like to identify with the specific property that is generating the income for them. Disinclined to participate in the management of the property, they nonetheless enjoy the eye contact associated with ownership, knowing that they indirectly "own an interest in that building."

On the other hand, tax-oriented syndications require sophisticated backing and financially complicated structuring. They also command larger up-front syndication fees combined with other forms of lucrative syndicator compensation due to the ingenuity required in using leverage techniques and tax-sheltering gimmicks. Because of these predictable tax deductions, projects don't necessarily have to perform up to the level of their investors' expectations. Income oriented syndications, on the other hand, concentrate on only one type of benefit, a cash-on-cash return, which must be accurate and predictable and fulfill the investors' expectations regarding a return on their equity.

## THE SALABLE ECONOMICS OF INCOME-ORIENTED SYNDICATIONS

The successful marketability of an income-oriented syndication depends upon three interrelated factors:

1. acquiring the property at a favorable price, based upon its ability to produce a sustained, long-term, positive cash flow;

2. accurately predicting the current spendable cash flow after deductions for expenses for mortgage financing; and
3. determining the additional yield achieved through potential property appreciation based upon local market factors and conditions.

## PROFITABLE ACQUISITION

The price paid for a property should reflect a fair current market value at the time of acquisition, not a value reflecting the intermediate or long-run potential market price or the established worth that might be created by upgrading a substandard holding. Ideally, syndicated real estate should be acquired in a competitive buyer's market, not in the unfavorable conditions prevalent in typical sellers' markets. The extent to which a property meets the specific terms and objectives of the syndication can be almost as important as the acquisition price itself, as long as the syndicator is totally realistic with him- or herself and his or her investments. Many well-intentioned individuals contract at a premium for properties that appear to be under market value in terms of rental income, to realize later that their projections didn't fully materialize or that adjusting rents upward to market levels is offset by vacancy factors and costly upgrading expenditures. Several years ago we optioned a 200-plus-unit apartment project that was foreclosed and repurchased by the lender on the courthouse steps. We optioned the complex for cash at 60 cents on the dollar, with the assumption that it had possibilities for conversion into condominium units. Later, we realized that its reputation was so maligned, and rents and tenants were so substandard due to the lack of interim management, that a turnaround would have been prohibitively expensive. Additionally, as it turned out, Federal National Mortgage Association (FNMA) also had serious reservations and imposed presale requirements we could not live with.

The method by which a property is acquired and financed can sometimes be the most important make-or-break situation in a syndication. A realistically leveraged holding with a respectable cash-on-cash initial return adequately safeguarded against inflation can show considerable appreciation at the time of its eventual disposition. At the other extreme, the combination of paying a premium or meeting an excessive asking price for the benefits derived from advantageous owner financing may cancel out the majority of the profit potential to the syndicator and his or her investors at the time of resale. The mortgage-constant factor, a combination of interest rates and amortization, bears notice. It is affected by the duration of the financing, the interest rate, and whether that rate is fixed or variable. Since the investors in income-oriented syndications look to the potential yield in evaluating a price, a fixed, substandard market rate of interest over a long duration can enhance the value of an investment real estate syndication immeasurably.

Two additional devices by which the potential investors' yield can be increased, thereby creating a higher value for the syndication, are

1. creative timing of the acquisition; and
2. staged payment of the equity contributions by the investors.

Income-oriented syndicators should concentrate on acquiring first-rate properties in highly desirable areas, financing them at the most attractive rates whether they are owner financed or conventionally structured. This kind of acquisition provides the investor with liquidity and also permits an offering to be marketed competitively using relatively low investor yields.

## ANALYZING THE PROJECT'S CASH FLOW

Another consideration in determining the economics of an income-oriented syndication is to predict with consistency the positive cash flow that a property will generate after deducting operating expenses and taking into consideration realistic vacancy factors. Cash flow is always measured by two yardsticks:

1. the income generated in terms of a return on the overall value of the property after operating expenses and prior to normal mortgage encumbrances, or
2. the cash flow measured in terms of the cash-on-invested-cash return after all operating expenses and debt service obligations are met.

Income is not measured over the long run in fixed dollar amounts but rather in terms of purchasing power. Cash flow or return on equity in an inflationary period is measured in fluid dollars, reflecting their current deflated value.

Since income-oriented syndications are directly related to and priced consistently with current yields prevailing in stock and bond markets, it is imperative during periods of little or no inflation that the actual cash-on-cash return becomes real and can be predicted accurately.

Investors in corporate or government bonds take for granted the reliably steady income from these vehicles, and income-oriented syndications must compete at this same level. For any given property the syndicator, therefore, needs to analyze:

- the quality and variability of the actual or projected pro forma rents;
- the current or projected operating expenses and their potential aberrations; and
- the realistic vacancy factors given the uniqueness of the marketplace.

The two latter factors must be continually reviewed in light of the economic trends of the area combined with the age and condition of the property. Such line items as reserves for replacements, realistic maintenance budgets, expenditures subject to wide fluctuations, and realistic contingency factors become the future lifeblood of your project.

Should an inflationary period intervene during the projected holding period of the asset, a conservatively conceived income-producing real estate investment should adequately provide for the decrease in purchasing power of the dollar through the appropriately predetermined rental increases based upon or tied to the cost of living indices. This holds true to a lesser degree if expenses of operation can be passed through fully to the tenants. Even if an error in judgment was made initially in the cash flow analysis, proper leverage combined with fixed-rate mortgages will almost always ensure the eventually desired cash flow regardless of the inflationary process. In other instances, where financing was not properly conceived, increased costs inadequately passed on, and leverage not advantageously structured, a fairly conservative syndicated investment may provide at best only a hedge against the gradual erosion of the dollar.

## BALANCING LEVERAGE, INCOME, AND INVESTOR YIELD

A direct ratio exists between leverage and the investor's risk. If one is to make an error in analyzing and applying financial leverage in an income-oriented syndication, the error should be skewed toward the conservative side. One should always sacrifice income and yield at the expense of maintaining a sound financial position. What income-oriented investors expect and demand is stability, and any activities that deviate from this objective are questionable and are always subject to potential litigation. The appreciation factor in real estate holdings will more than compensate your investors for the 1 percent or 2 percent additional cash return on invested funds they might receive in more leveraged and riskier syndications.

Most projects develop severe and sometimes irreversible complications due to one or more of the following financial considerations:

- short-term, unreliable financing;
- financing with floating interest rates;
- negative amortization mortgages;
- financing that contains balloon payments;
- the inability to pass on increased operating expenses; and
- adverse legislation controlling rental adjustments.

These categories or conditions should not be structured into conservative, income-oriented syndications. If any one is unavoidable under the syndication plan, all your investors should be cognizant of the associated or inherent risk.

As you structure repeated offerings, your real estate experience and background combined with your ability to retain the appropriate individuals to structure and manage the affairs of the syndication will be the single most important ingredient of your success. Since the holding period of any income-oriented offering is lengthy, a major factor for meeting one's objectives lies in the proper management. Minor judgmental errors in financing often work themselves out eventually and can usually be glossed over, but intelligent and creative management is the key to keeping the cash flowing on a sustained, regular, and positive basis.

Earlier, we called attention to the concept that the novice syndicator might find the conservative offering an appropriate arena in which to test one's managerial ability. Diametrically, one may find rather quickly that one lacks the temperament to oversee the daily operations as diligently as one should. While hiring a professional management team may erode or evaporate a portion of one's profits substantially, this alternative may be the only realistic approach in

**COMPLICATIONS**

- SHORT-TERM FINANCING
- FINANCING WITH FLOATING LOAN INTERESTS
- NEGATIVE AMORTIZATION MORTGAGES
- FINANCING WITH BALLOON PAYMENTS
- INABILITY TO PASS ON INCREASED OPERATING EXPENSES
- ADVERSE LEGISLATION

**Figure 2.2** Frequent causes of complications in real estate projects.

establishing an immediately successful track record on one's first syndicated venture.

Professional management assures the smooth operation of a syndication's tedious affairs. When difficulties arise, third-party unassociated management can also act as a buffer between the syndicator and his or her limited partners. While investors may react negatively when a syndicator/manager requests additional equity funds to ensure or maintain financial soundness, they will normally be much more amenable to such a suggestion when it is advanced by an independent professional management group.

## THE RISK-REWARD BENEFITS OF INCOME-ORIENTED SYNDICATIONS

Three distinguishable categories of risk are associated with any income-oriented syndication:

1. associated financial exposure;
2. potential loss of purchasing power; and
3. lack of immediate liquidity.

All of these investment pitfalls are closely allied and each needs to be weighed and fully explained to the investors when a syndicator structures and markets an income-oriented offering.

We recently struck a balance among these three categories in a $4-million second-home resort project in the Southwest, where the

**CATEGORIES OF RISK**

1. ASSOCIATED FINANCIAL EXPOSURE
2. POTENTIAL LOSS OF PURCHASING POWER
3. LACK OF IMMEDIATE LIQUIDITY

**Figure 2.3** Categories of risk associated with income-oriented syndications.

land was leased and the corresponding payments were made as the units were sold. This advantageous structuring permitted us to utilize the syndicated investors' funds exclusively for the development expenditures, and not for the land acquisition. This safety-net approach provided a conservative investment vehicle in a situation where substantial leverage was utilized, providing the investors with a 50 percent annualized return on their equity contribution.

The associated financial exposure has the potential for loss of all (or in some instances, a majority) of the investors' equity. It can vary from a limited amount in ultraconservative real estate investments to the potential for complete equity annihilation attendant upon the syndicator's poor judgment at the acquisition stage coupled with poor management and utilization of improper leverage. Should these factors combine to lead to a foreclosure, all of the investors' equity as well as the syndicator's reputation could be eradicated. This happenstance is totally unacceptable in a syndication designed to appeal to small, unsophisticated, and unsuspecting investors. By comparison, individuals in high tax brackets who choose to invest in tax-oriented high-risk syndications can absorb comparable or substantially greater exposure, since they are usually fully compensated by tax deductions at the government's expense.

*Potential loss of purchasing power* is tied directly to the devastating effects of an inflationary economy. The potentially offsetting advantages that real estate offers as a counterinflation investment hedge can be quite advantageous. A positive cash flow is measured not in constant dollars but exclusively in sustained purchasing power when inflation prevails. Similarly, when adjusted for inflation, the dollar proceeds from the sale of a syndicated asset, if not adequately protected, can potentially purchase substantially less than an identical dollar amount would have commanded when the property was initially acquired. This risk becomes especially critical when the syndicated asset is involved in long-term fixed leases limiting income, disallowing the adequate compensation needed to protect against these inflationary factors.

*Lack of immediate liquidity* is common to all real estate transactions, syndicated or not, and involves the inability to resell an asset at any given time without having to sacrifice the resale price. For the protection of *all* partners, both general and limited, predetermined liquidity restrictions usually prevail in most syndications. The general partners must restrict the resalability of the limited partners' shares as a condition for not being subject to the corporate double taxation standard. In most offerings the ability to borrow against one's limited partnership interest is also restricted or at least subject to the general partner's approval. For these reasons, potential investors must be adequately warned about the illiquid nature of their holdings in syndication shares. Offsetting this disadvantage are the substantial after-tax yields obtained in well-structured and properly leveraged real estate offerings that are not commonly found in other comparable investments.

## APPRECIATION AS A MAJOR FACTOR IN SYNDICATIONS

Analyzing the potential for appreciation in an income-oriented syndication is probably the most speculative aspect of the projection process due to the lengthy nature of holding periods involved. Cash flows, equity build-up, and tax-deferred benefits are comparatively easy to predict within given tolerances for the initial and sometimes for the entire syndicated holding period, since they periodically adjust with changing conditions in the market place. Diametrically, appreciation must be measured in terms of real purchasing power, not constant dollars, and must be reflective of the local, regional, and national economic conditions. Nevertheless, appreciation can add substantially to the overall yield and even in the most conservative type of syndication should add between 8 percent and 10 percent annually to the investors' yield on a pretax basis. The potential for appreciation will often be a clinching factor in marketing a syndication's shares, and any misrepresentations in the offering prospectus can be grounds for extremely embarrassing, extensive, and potentially costly litigation.

In evolving a *formula* to calculate the potential appreciation, one must look to the positive and negative ramifications—rental income, vacancy factors, and operating expenses—and must also include in the equation such general considerations as:

- the specific nature or use of the investment;
- the up-side potential of the project's cash flow; and
- the reusable economics of the building after the optimum holding period.

Most syndicators substantiate their projections for potential appreciation by analyzing the specific nature of their investment based upon the actual historical market conditions for similar holdings, extending their conclusions over the projected holding period for the to-be-syndicated asset. For instance, if one is anticipating a five- or ten-year holding period for a property, one should document and analyze the appreciation history of comparable properties in the same geographic area for the preceding five or ten years. Logical inferences can then be drawn, and fairly accurate statements can be advanced to the effect that if the syndicated property continues to appreciate in accordance with historical trends, the effect of the appreciation factor on the overall yield to the investors can be realistically stipulated.

Appreciation is taxed at the favorable capital gains rate, placing a lesser burden on ordinary income, benefiting investors in high tax brackets more than it does the low-tax-bracket individual closely associated with income-oriented syndications. This aspect coupled with the general use of conservative financing makes appreciation a less distinct factor in income-oriented syndications. The exciting effects of leverage in creating tax shelter and additional yield will be explored in the following chapter.

Many syndicators prefer to structure in a conservative, unquestioned percentage appreciation factor that relates generally to the national market for real estate investments, to a large degree ignoring the complicated and time-consuming local conditions and calculations. If this figure is realistic and can be documented by national or regional indices, it can be and is used quite effectively in a syndication presentation.

Conservative offerings are viable alternatives to many investors for the purchase of common stocks and corporate bonds. It becomes important when these types of individuals are involved that the cash return on one's investment compares favorably with these alternatives. Generally, an income-oriented syndication's return will fall somewhere between the overall yield currently being offered for common stocks, on the conservative side, and the obtainable market yield for corporate bonds, reflecting the more liberal approach.

The lower equity yield on corporate securities reflects the potential stock appreciation, and the higher and more predictable yield on corporate bonds is an indication of the stability of income and the limited appreciation possibilities.

The overall yield on income-oriented syndications should be adjusted accordingly depending upon the amount of leverage used and the corresponding tax benefits directly derived from it. Obviously, an offering with relatively few tax-deductible benefits and low appreciation potential must be priced closer to the higher-yielding corporate bonds in order to be competitive. A syndication structured exclusively from tax-shelter benefits, offering substantial appreciation possibilities, will be priced at a lower yield, reflecting those found on more speculative risk-oriented common stocks. Investor returns can also be affected by the method of marketing. When a stockbrokerage firm syndicates the shares, investor yields will be substantially reduced in order to adequately cover the commissioned fees. Investor yields on income-oriented real estate syndications inevitably fluctuate with market aberrations and must be pegged or aligned to alternative investments if one's syndicated shares are to actively compete in the open marketplace.

## EQUITY BUILD-UP AND TAX-SHELTER BENEFITS

Mortgage amortization is a factor not normally available to individuals utilizing other forms of investments and deserves special attention when marketing income-oriented syndication shares. As we define it here, equity build-up is the regularly scheduled pay-off of principal as amortized through monthly or annual mortgage payment obligations. Equity build-up on a conventional mortgage is normally less than 1 percent of the total payment during the initial three to five years of a conventional 25- to 30-year mortgage; therefore, it is not a significant yield factor during the early years of a syndication's operation. With today's high interest rates and short-term balloon payments, mortgage amortization can be insignificant even over a long span of time. When owner financing is negotiated with short-term amortization and lower interest rates, however, equity build-up can be extremely important in increasing the investors' overall yield.

When one considers the possibility of refinancing syndicated real estate, the equity build-up portion becomes a significant factor. Higher rental income and property values prevalent when the offered property is refinanced often justify a substantial increase in the amount of financing without an additional burden on the net operating income projected in the initial offering circular. Here mortgage amortization combined with measurable appreciation is tangible, since the proceeds from refinancing an encumbrance against a syndicated real estate asset can be distributed to the investing partners tax-free, usually without a subsequent injection of funds needed to cover the additional debt-service payments.

The quality of most investments is generally measured by the return on the initial equity contribution. It is entirely possible that refinancing a well-conceived real estate syndication after, say, a five-year period would more often than not result in the total return of the investors' initial equity funds. Even the best performing bonds or common stocks would be strained to equal this extraordinary return, since most would have at least to double in value before comparable results could be achieved.

What totally distinguishes income-oriented real estate from other forms of investment are the tax-deferred benefits derived from the depreciation laws coupled with interest deductions, both often being quite substantial in nature. Quality properties that are carefully selected and maintained never actually experience any physical deterioration, yet the Internal Revenue Service allows for depreciation deductions whether or not the asset actually economically decreases in value. Depreciation occurs only on paper in these instances and constitutes an artificial loss that can be transformed into an investor benefit by offsetting these deductions against a taxpayer's ordinary income. Since return on equity is based on after-tax return to the syndicate, tax-deferred benefits will add substantially to the yield, subject, of course, to the alternative minimum tax requirements.

Tax-deferred benefits will be explored in greater detail in the following chapter when we consider syndications that are aggressively leveraged to totally maximize the investors' yield. The fact remains that some tax benefits accrue to the investors even in the most conservative of real estate syndications. Recently, we placed additional and secondary financing against a 20,000-square-foot office building, which we were able to absorb through rental increases associated with our annual cost-of-living escalation clauses. This was accomplished without requiring the partners to subsidize the increased debt service obligation. Each partner was distributed $50,000 tax-deferred until the property is eventually disposed of, at which time the partners will incur the taxable obligation.

## HOW INCREMENTAL EQUITY CONTRIBUTIONS INCREASE INVESTORS' YIELD

Many investment properties are being syndicated so that the investors advance their equity in installments over extended periods of time. Sometimes the seller's objectives dovetail with the syndicate's needs, since installment sales, if properly structured, can defer the seller's payments of capital gains taxes. Reducing the initial up-front investment not only increases the yield in the early years but also facilitates the merchandising of the syndication shares. When equity contributions can be financed partially out of the investors' annual earnings rather than exclusively from their savings, the market broadens to include substantially greater numbers of potential investors.

When the syndicator options an undervalued property with a strong potential for rental increases, an offering circular may be *cautiously worded* to the effect that the number of incremental payments may be reduced if certain income-generating events materialize prematurely. Nothing should be mentioned about the effective yield if these payments are not required in the long run, as this inference should be left to the imagination of the investor or his or her financial advisors.

The deferral of equity installment obligations can often be accomplished or supported through the use of letters of credit, where each of the investors guarantees his or her prorated portion as it is needed, should the seller of the property or the syndicator need adequate assurances. These letters then become bankable documents should the seller or the syndicator need to discount them for cash prior to their actual time schedule for funding.

Staged equity payments can be useful to syndicators in a variety of ways, beyond the advantages they offer in marketing. Utilization permits the syndicator to undertake a multitude of projects or in some instances larger and more complicated ventures with the same investors' equity funds. Staged payments as an alternative can be subsequently deposited in escrow accounts as potential reserves should one's financial projections not materialize immediately. Most investors react favorably to the concept of contingency accounts that might never be needed or used. Syndicators who advertise their intention of providing them gain credibility for what is considered evidence of their prudence and conservative intent. We have recently completed a syndication on a 46-unit condominium where 20 percent of the syndicated funds were unsolicited and earmarked for an interest contingency fund, as the interest on the construction mortgage was at a floating rate. To date, we have yet to call upon those funds; however, just their existence puts the partners in a more comfortable position.

## MARKETING LOWER-YIELDING PRESTIGE PROPERTIES TO INVESTORS

The most desirable type of holdings to acquire for income-oriented syndication are quality properties located in prestigious areas. Many unsophisticated individuals relate to the property's curb appeal and the prestige quality of the holding itself, often taking the time to regularly visualize it whenever circumstances permit. Top-of-the-line properties facilitate marketing for seven major reasons:

1. Appreciation is normally visualized as a more consistent objective by investors when quality properties in first-rate locations are involved.
2. Investors believe that initially low yields or rental levels will increase more rapidly when these types of holdings are involved.
3. Property identification and strength of location can in many instances substitute for a larger return on invested equity.
4. With quality properties, the syndicator can be more speculative in his or her estimates of income and value, especially when substantial appreciation can be a recognized quantity.
5. High visibility holdings usually appear to be safer investments, thereby eliminating the all-at-risk theory from real estate syndications. Many investors willingly forfeit sizable returns on their equity in exchange for this illusion of security.
6. Investors substantially believe that quality properties will generally command a premium regardless of the economic conditions. This mentality is highly prevalent among income-oriented investors.
7. Most investors rationalize that quality holdings are more liquid

than their less prestigious counterparts, overcoming their fears that syndications cannot be liquidated when problems surface.

By incorporating these concepts into your sales presentations and stressing them to your investors, you can normally reduce the overall return on an investment property by at least 1 percent or 2 percent. Without materially affecting your sales, this reduction in the investors' yield can add tens or even hundreds of thousands of dollars to your personal syndication income.

## TYPES OF PROPERTIES TAILORED FOR INCOME-ORIENTED SYNDICATIONS

*Apartments and residential properties* offer the syndicator a diversified range of possibilities. Most apartments are highly leveraged vehicles that cannot be purchased, at least initially, showing a respectable cash flow unless they are specifically structured with limited leverage or owner financing. Many apartment complexes are priced at a premium based upon the long-term potential they have for conversion into for-sale units. Apartments, therefore, are not normally lucrative vehicles for income-oriented syndications, due to the lack of initial, up-front cash flow. Over the long pull, they can be outstanding acquisitions, as rentals can normally be raised faster than operating expenses, at least in the absence of rent-control legislation. When leverage is not excessive, they often provide a well-balanced, relatively conservative investment.

Developing and syndicating residential "for-sale properties" is normally more lucrative for income-oriented syndicators than operating apartments, in spite of the high degree of risk associated with development-type ventures. The return on syndicated funds for many types of residential development—single-family homes, condominiums, resort properties, or sometimes even residential-land subdivisions—can run from 100 percent to as high as 500 percent, depending upon the degree of leverage and the sophistication of the developer. Syndicating a subdivision of raw acreage is a relatively risk-free way of entering the development business. In fairly typical instances, interim cash flow can be substantial, up-front development expenses are somewhat limited, and the long-run appreciation factor is predictable. This type of activity can be quite rewarding, especially where the equity investment is retrieved rather quickly. While development of subdivisions can generate large returns over an extended period of years, these rewards are not necessarily as predictable as one might find in other forms of syndicated investments, especially during the initial years of an offering, when the marketing momentum must be achieved. If such developments are excessively leveraged without the appropriate contingency reserves, the potential for loss can sometimes be catastrophic.

*Shopping centers and office complexes* are frequently acquired or developed by income-oriented syndications because of their predictability of income, their potential for offsetting the detrimental forces of inflation, and for their potential appreciation. The additional advantages for syndicating these types of developments are:

- their ability to support a reasonable amount of leverage, usually on a nonrecourse basis, when approaching a respectable occupancy rate;
- their curb appeal facilitates the marketing and attracts prestigious tenants;
- they provide an adequate hedge against inflation and under reasonable market conditions can be acquired showing a respectable return; and
- management is relatively easy to retain, even though balancing the tenant mix is complicated.

Shopping centers and office complexes are specialties unto themselves, and qualified experts are needed to market, maintain, and manage them efficiently.

*Management-intensive properties,* such as warehouses, motels, franchise operations, mobile-home and recreational vehicle parks, movie theaters, coin operated laundries, cemetaries, car dealerships, resort communities, video-game parlors, and industrial facilities, all carry relatively high cash returns and with proper management and location can be considered good candidates for income-oriented syndications. However, single-purpose structures can be difficult to lease if economic or demographic conditions change. Normally, these unconvertible, management-intensive structures will command at least a 5 percent premium in their yields because of their lack of reusability.

*Land leases,* if properly structured to protect against the detrimental effects of inflation and subordination, can also be lucrative and stable syndicated investments. Many times, though not readily available, they can provide the cornerstone for investment opportunities, though the holders of these specialized interests will not dispose of their treasured assets on a conventional for-sale basis.

## HISTORIC PROPERTIES

In older or mature communities, many historic or older buildings offer the income-oriented syndicator great potential as they

- can be acquired at prices far below their normal replacement value;
- are usually located in proven areas of moderate-to-high rental income; and
- provide unusual first-year renovation tax benefits taking the form of investment tax credits.

Whatever holdings one chooses to syndicate, the general partner must balance his or her abilities to manage a property within the general needs and demands of a specific community. This must be combined with properties that show sufficient residential value necessary to meet the minimum sustained projections for a return on the invested equity.

## A NEW BREED OF INVESTMENT SYNDICATION

Many older buildings that are self-sufficient in terms of cash flow have the potential for conversion that, when combined with the possible long-term capital gains on their appreciation, can provide an interesting and challenging situation for the syndicator. We recently became involved in a limited partnership that in many respects typifies the new breed of income-oriented syndications.

The partnership was formed to acquire and convert two old industrial loft buildings to residential condominiums in a once undesirable area of Chicago. The buildings generated such a low rental income from industrial use that they were purchased far below their replacement value. The two structures were acquired for $870,000 with approximately 180,000 square feet in the two eight-story buildings. The syndicate planned to spend an additional $4 per square foot for the demolition of the interior partitions.

*The Marketing Concept of the Loft-Conversion Project*

The goal was to convert the two industrial buildings into residential condominium structures, marketing them to individuals who wanted to be on the fringe of the downtown Chicago area but could not afford the excessive prices generated for prime residences on the near north side of Chicago. At a market value of $30 per square foot, the partnership intended to deliver the interior space bounded by perimeter walls and a front door, with basic plumbing and electric, to the potential purchasers. Owner-occupants could improve their own space using the "sweat-equity" concept at a fraction of the cost that one would expend to furnish a new, fully completed residential condominium in the downtown area.

The marketing plan was, in effect, to divide the two buildings into 60 residential units ranging in size from 1,485 to 2,707 square feet, giving the project a total salable area in both buildings of 130,000 square feet. The net loss of approximately 50,000 square feet was consumed by corridors and common areas. The partnership anticipated that approximately 14 months would be required to complete construction of the first phase of the project.

The syndication allocated a fee of 4 percent of the sales price for marketing, which was sufficient considering the location and pricing features of the project. Both the University of Chicago and the West Side Medical Center were nearby. The partnership visualized a market consisting of faculty and students of the university and professionals on the staff of the medical center. In addition, the space would be attractive to artists or middle management people of moderate income who worked in and commuted to the adjacent downtown area. As of the time of this writing, the project is more than half sold to buyers who were located within a mile of the existing structures, and all the initial projections appear to be on schedule. The marketing will not be hampered by parking, since an adjoining lot is entirely available during the evenings, which permits the potential purchasers to contract for this space.

*The Economics of the Project*

The capitalization structure of the limited partnership undertaking the loft conversion was conceived as follows:

1. The general partner contributed his contractual interest in the

buildings plus $15,000 cash and received 22.5 percent of the income from the partnership.

2. A second general partner contributed $150,000 in cash and similarly received 22.5 percent of the income.
3. The limited partners, 10 in all, provided $410,000 as a cash investment. The general and limited partners all agreed to personally guarantee a $480,000 first mortgage, which was obtained from a local bank for construction purposes. In addition to their cash contributions, the limited partners agreed to sustain losses limited to the first $300,000 of that loan amount if they ever materialized. For their combined loan guarantees and cash contributions, they received 55 percent of the equity in the limited partnership.

The offering was not circulated on a public basis, and the ten shares were sold to professionals who lived and worked within the same metropolitan area as the project. Some of the investors lived in condominiums within a short distance of the development that were selling for as much as five times the shell cost at which this project was being marketed. Needless to say, they fully understood the total upside potential of the syndicated offering.

The total cost of construction and development was projected to be $722,000 over and above the acquisition price. The syndication was structured so that the limited partners would receive the return of their equity and their share of the profits over a 15-year period, as the purchasers of the converted condominium units are offered 80 percent financing on their acquisition price with 13 percent interest payable over the 15-year period. The anticipated profit on the syndication is $2,300,000, which translates into a $3,900,000 total sales value less $722,000 in construction expenditures less the $870,000 acquisition price. Because of the interest that the partners are receiving on the deferred income received from the purchasers of the converted condominium units, their return has increased considerably.

*Advantages to the Syndicated Investors*

One of the up-front advantages of this offering is the fact that both buildings were acquired as ongoing rental properties used as industrial complexes. Each of the two buildings was converted at a separate point in time, meaning that the unconverted building provided income and limited tax-shelter benefits in the interim. The projected sellout value of $3,900,000 represents the appraised value of the residential buildings upon completion, which as it turned out appeared to be realistic.

Because a major portion of the sales to the purchasers of the converted condominiums will be financed over a long period of time, the advantages of the syndication are three-fold:

1. The industrial buildings themselves are self-sufficient in terms of cash flow, as it takes approximately $1.50 per square foot in rental income to show a reasonable return on the acquisition cost of the structures.
2. The $41,000-per-share investment by each limited partner will return approximately $2,500 to $3,000 per month on a 15-year basis, or potentially as much as $36,000 per year.
3. When the entire 130,000 square feet are converted and sold, the ongoing income will provide an almost 100 percent return per year to the investors during the 15-year payback of the consumer loans.

The local lending institutions in the Chicago area are financing the owners' improvement program, much of which is being accomplished with tax-free housing authority bond issues. Tax-free financing not only provides low interest rates that make these converted units extremely attractive for marketing purposes, but also places the permanent financing without any direct involvement of the syndicate. In effect, the entire payments from the purchasers after the second or third year were entirely on the profit side of the ledger, as the investors' equity was returned in a very short period of time. Many of the limited partners are using the continuing proceeds to establish educational trusts for their children, as this constant annual income can be channeled into tax rates that are substantially lower through these vehicles.

Among real estate syndications geared almost exclusively toward cash flow, the loft conversion project was both unique and typical. Few syndications approach its level of success in generating this type of cash-on-cash return and simultaneously reducing the tax obligations by deferring some of the tax implications over a 15-year period. This syndication, however, like many others was flawed in one way. Since the limited partners personally guaranteed part of the development loan, they were to be classified as "active" rather than "passive" investors, making it somewhat questionable whether the funds received from the 15-year payout can be subject to long-term capital-gains treatment. Offsetting this is the fact that many of the partnership shares are held in minors' trust funds where lower tax brackets prevail.

Nevertheless, the loft conversion project was well conceived and attempted to provide a secure financial return to the investors.

Being in the right market with the appropriate product is important to a syndicator's success. Not all luck comes, however, with experience, and not all experience is accompanied by luck. The syndicator who can inspire a sense of excitement in a venture and convey its potential for a lucrative return is the one who will attract a following.

Many sophisticated syndicators will not find income-oriented syndications lucrative enough for their talents, nor do they feel they are totally compatible with these conservative investors' basic philosophy. The types of ventures in which their interests are sufficiently stimulated are the subjects of our next chapter.

# 3

# How Tax-Oriented Real Estate Syndications Function

In the first chapter, we sketched a profile of the typical investor in a privately placed real estate syndication, stressing a characteristic mistrust of large, mass-marketed securities and a need for eye contact with one's syndicating associates and for a tactile awareness of the property one helps to finance. True as this portrait may be, it stresses the pessimistic aspect of any silent partner's personality. Those who invest in tax-oriented real estate ventures are even more prone to a pessimism that can frequently border on depression at least twice a year:

- prior to or at the end of each calendar year; and
- each April fifteenth, when income tax returns are due.

At the opposite personality extreme is the syndicator, whose optimism is so thinly subsurface that he or she must often force him- or herself to subdue it, much as one would forcibly attempt to cap a gusher in a newly drilled oil field. A syndicator's optimism usually peaks at about the time that the potential syndicated partners, especially those in the 50 percent tax bracket, plummet into the depths of despair. This accounts for the fact that so many new syndication offerings surface at these two critical times of the year.

Many of the current overloaded tax-oriented syndications purport to provide 3-to-1, and often up to 4-to-1, writeoffs over a 7-to-10-

year holding period. Loaded with accrued interest and characterized by negative cash flows, they tend to justify their excessive values through plumped-up appraisals, excessive syndication fees, and exorbitant real estate commissions. Many are structured for tax avoidance rather than for their real estate economic sense and, simply put, are not and never will be economically viable as investments.

This chapter will offer an important enlightenment to those tempted by syndications offering relief from federal and state taxes who often have no interest in or understanding of the actual properties or methods used in these syndicated offerings.

## THE CHARACTERISTICS OF TAX-ORIENTED SYNDICATIONS

The key to marketing a tax-oriented syndication successfully lies in maximizing the tax-deferred benefits and structuring them so they can be directly passed on to the investing partners during the early stages of the offering. Whatever property serves as the vehicle, the syndication must function as a giant conduit siphoning off the elixir of tax absolution to its investing partners. Utilizing a limited partnership entity is usually the most effective means by which these tax benefits can be passed through to the silent passive partners who generally incur no corresponding financial liabilities. To utilize this vehicle effectively, four ingredients are necessary:

1. A substantial amount of financial leverage must encumber the property.
2. The potential appreciation factor must be substantial in order to offset the relatively limited initial cash flow prevalent in most tax-oriented offerings.
3. The ratio of the value of the improvements should be high in relation to the cost of the land, or older buildings should be acquired where substantial investment tax credits are inherent.
4. Equity payments must be minimal or, in some cases, substantially deferred to achieve the appropriate balance of after-tax returns.

Financial leverage and appreciation normally produce after-tax benefits well in excess of 50 percent of the projected return on equity in most tax-oriented syndications. Calculation of these benefits must be simplistically presented to potential investors and their financial advisors to achieve the most effective marketing, to the point where other important and stabilizing aspects of real estate investments are deemed to be only second nature. Especially at year end, a combination of immediate tax shelter and staged or deferred contribution of equity can be overwhelmingly attractive, warming the hearts of those more resigned to the inevitability of death if they can somehow beat the inevitability of taxes.

Taxable losses attributable to depreciation deductions are figured on the total cost of the improvements in syndicated holdings, even when the investor's equity is a small portion of the total value of the asset. Passive investors taken in as limited partners normally can deduct losses only to the extent of their partnership interest or financial contribution. Under certain circumstances, as explained in detail later in this chapter, one can increase the tax deductions over and above one's basis of investment through financing techniques, where the limited partners are insulated from the liabilities or claims of the partnership creditors over and above their original stated investment.

## WHY THE SYNDICATE'S PARTS ARE WORTH MORE THAN THE WHOLE

The challenge of structuring a real estate offering is in stratifying the different investment interests in its holdings. At optimum success, a delicate juggling act balances similar and dissimilar interests for the eventual profit of all partners. For instance, many syndicators or managing general partners are substantially more interested in cash income than in tax deferred benefits. Many of the long-term capital-gains benefits are denied active syndicators due to the "dealer status" motive of their business operations. In relinquishing the tax-related aspects of the investment to one's limited partners, one can receive in return substantial up-front fees and an eventually lucrative equity interest in the project, generally without any capital contribution.

Similarly, lenders will also provide substantially higher ratios of loan to value on projects when they are given an equity interest, even if this interest does not surface until the asset is disposed of. Often in exchange for this equity participation the lender will provide a substandard rate of interest, thereby permitting the project to generate additional cash flow or alternatively providing additional funds for development due to the lesser degree or burden of the debt-service requirement.

A project in which we were recently involved provided an unusual combination of

- lender equity participation;
- an unusual amount of nonrecourse financing;
- major tax benefits to the limited partners;
- back-end profits of great magnitude to all parties;
- substantial fees to the managing partner; and
- a tremendous profit to the apartment converter.

This is a 576-unit apartment complex that went through bankruptcy in 1976. A group of 35 investors purchased it out of foreclosure from the real estate investment trust (REIT) lender for $8 million and sold it for the first time four years later to an apartment converter for $12 million. On the initial sale, the limited partners received only their equity contribution in return. The $4-million anticipated gain was to be spread out or phased and paid to them during the conversion or marketing of the units, allocated 50 percent to the limited partners and 25 percent each to the general partner and the mortgage lender as their partnership interests dictated. When the converter's financial situation and the near-term market conditions proved inadequate for the conversion effort to be commenced, an agreement was reached in which the converter received an extension for conversion by making up the substantial deficit in mortgage payments for a period of two years, at which time, in 1982, the market turned and the conversion was initiated. Upon the restructured sale to the converter, the profit to the initial partnership amounted to $2,100,000, substantially less than on the original sale, still, however, adequate for purposes of this syndication.

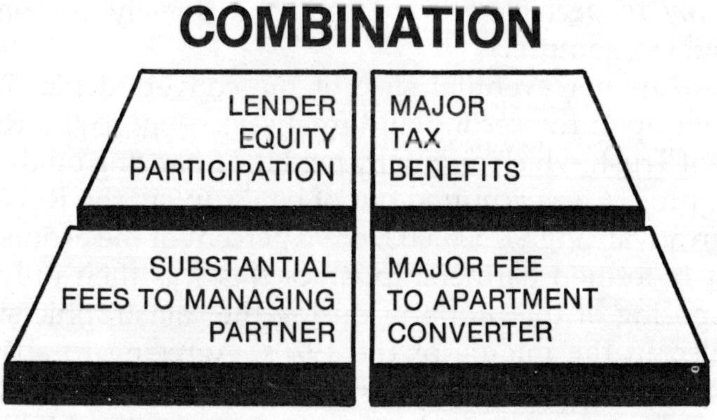


**Figure 3.1** Investment factors attractive to syndications.

Initially, each of the 35 partners (all of whom were in the 50 percent tax bracket) contributed $18,000 for a total investment of $630,000, which was obviously well leveraged considering the $8-million acquisition price. Subsequently, each investor received approximately $175,000 worth of cumulative tax deductions extended over the six-year holding period.

Upon restructuring the second sale, the original limited partners in the syndication received 50 percent of the net proceeds after deductions for conversion costs and for repayment of the existing mortgage encumbrances. This approximated $1,050,000, or $30,000 per limited partnership unit. The limited partners therefore received cumulative benefits, including the annual tax deductions, totaling $205,000 per partnership share. The after-tax ramifications generated profits equaling a 1000 percent return on equity in excess of 150 percent per year. Had the complex been better located—the project as it turned out was constructed in a declining midwestern suburb—this return would have been substantially greater. The apartments adjoined a major metropolitan city, and urban blight started to set in at about the time the converter defaulted and the restructuring ensued. Because of the changing demographic profile, the eventual profit from the conversion was somewhat less than the partnership had initially expected.

With no equity contribution, so to speak, the general partner also profited quite handsomely. In addition to the up-front syndication fee of $68,000, the general partner received an ongoing 5 percent management fee on the annual gross income, averaging $75,000 per year for a total of $518,000 over the 6-year life of the syndication, plus 25 percent of the profits after expenses on the second sale, which netted another $525,000. The combined general partners' earnings were $1,110,000, a highly respectable reward for an extremely complicated and often troubled venture.

Another eventual slice of the converted pie, 25 percent of the profit upon the second and final sale, went to the Real Estate Investment Trust, which originally held the financing on the property. When the project was acquired out of bankruptcy, the REIT restructured the loan advancing $7,500,000, or 95 percent of the acquisition price, to the newly formed partnership, since this was their only viable means of disposing of the property during the catastrophic situation that prevailed in the middle of the 1970s. Agreeing to absorb a substantial portion of the operating losses attributed to the debt service during a period following the sale, they underwrote this high level of financing that the project could not realistically support in return for 25 percent of the sales proceeds when the project was converted. Basically, they possessed a troubled loan interesting only to the appropriate investment group looking for tax-shelter benefits, high leverage, and complete or total lack of personal exposure. They had little choice but to mate with a syndication looking for these distinct and unique advantages. With receipts of $8,025,000 plus interest after the conversion, the Real Estate Investment Trust was probably not totally compensated for the initial loan amount when the deferred interest was considered, but they fared considerably better than they might have at a fire sale under foreclosure proceedings.

## THE ATTRACTION OF SYNDICATIONS TO INVESTORS IN HIGH TAX BRACKETS

For every dollar of equity invested, the best real estate syndications offer approximately $3 and in creative instances up to $4 worth of tax losses over the life of the investment. This concept is changing and can have retroactive ramifications, as outlined in Chapter 18, when Congress is attempting to eliminate abusive real estate tax shelter vehicles. Financing is almost always highly imaginative and leveraged, revolving around nonrecourse loans that leverage seven to eight times the limited partners' initial contribution. With correspondingly high levels of debt service, the first three or four years of the holding period provide enough tax writeoffs to permit investors to more than recover their equity contributions. Many of these strictly tax-sheltered syndications are being scrutinized by the IRS, and careful attention should be paid to the current guidelines as delineated in Chapter 18. Because the greatest advantages accrue to limited partners during the early years of the syndication, adequate reserves are essential to avoid financial problems surfacing at these critical times.

Even when a tax-oriented syndication is held for a relatively short period of time and accomplishes nothing more than breaking even from operations, it often serves its purpose well for any investor in the 50 percent tax bracket. When it demonstrates a return of equity plus a marginal profit, the investor's gain is not taxed as ordinary income but is calculated at the more favorable capital-gains rate. The Economic Recovery Act of 1981 enhanced the attraction of real estate investment syndications by shortening the economic lives of most buildings to 15 years, thereby eliminating the detrimental recapture provisions found in situations where the older accelerated methods of depreciation were utilized.

Another interesting aspect of this legislation enhances the potential deductions for renovation of older buildings and, particularly, historically significant edifices. Syndicators can now structure partnerships that will return, if creatively conceived, tax-shelter benefits equal to or exceeding the equity investment during the first year. Deductions for rehabilitation of older buildings are set up on a three-tiered deductible investment basis. For a *20-year-old building* that has not been substantially rehabilitated during its lifetime, 15 percent of the cost of contemplated improvements is allowed in the form of income-tax credits. The allowance for a *30-year-old building* similarly substantially unimproved during its lifetime is a 20 percent investment credit for the improvements. In either case, the credit is available only for nonresidential buildings. Improvements to any *certified historic structure*, residential or commercial, qualify for a 25 percent credit, though these improvements must be capital in nature and must have a useful economic life of at least 15 years.

We recently purchased an older office building, completely renovating the existing structure and constructing a newer addition, and in the process taking substantial investment tax credits. Although this building was not historically certified, it adjoined a building with historic certification and probably could have been plaqued with very little effort if we had so desired. We financed this development with a $1.5 million industrial revenue bond issue utilizing tax-exempt interest. We sold the bonds to a lending institution at 11 percent interest, approximately 250 basis points under the conventional market value at that time. We not only received submarket interest financing due to the tax-free status of the bonds, but in the process generated a substantial tax credit on the renovation improvements to the existing building, an almost unbeatable combination when one is attempting to syndicate tax-deductible investment-caliber real estate holdings.

## HOW LEVERAGE AND DEPRECIATION CREATE SIZABLE DEDUCTIONS

In the mere fact of acquiring real estate, an investor in a syndication has an asset generating substantial deductions for depreciation. Most often, if properly leveraged these paper losses can exceed the taxable cash flow, making them useful for offsetting other income. What makes them so valuable is that they are inherent to the property purchased, requiring no further outlay of investment funds for their continuance. Allowances for depreciation are based upon guidelines for determining the useful life of a building and its improvements and are divorced from or totally unrelated to the value of the land on which the structure is situated. A well-conceived real estate venture has a useful economic life far exceeding the depreciation schedules allowed by the Internal Revenue Service, and additionally the value of the land may well appreciate beyond that of any structure located on it.

Deductions taken for depreciation have in practical terms very little relationship to the true economic life of a real estate asset or its depreciated book value when it is disposed of. The basic purpose, in effect, is to generate a tax-free cash flow from the syndicated asset. The cumulative depreciation deductions taken on an unaccelerated level are deferred until time of sale when the difference between the depreciated book value and the appreciated sales price is taxed at the most favorable capital-gains rate. The heart of a tax-oriented syndication, however, is knowing how to structure and pass through the depreciation deductions early in the investment to accommodate the needs of the investors in high tax brackets. This often serves as a substitute for the syndicated property generating substantial amounts of cash flow on its own merits, at least during the initial years.

Utilization of financial leverage in acquiring a syndicated asset is an interrelated and interesting aspect of real estate offerings. Regardless of the syndicate's actual cash investment outlay, its investors can often be allocated 100 percent of the depreciation deductions up to the level of their invested funds and, in some instances, even substantially exceeding their cash outlays, though they may have contributed a small fraction of the overall purchase price. Furthermore, during the early years of a syndication, the principal payments on mortgages are relatively small in relation to the interest payments. As the mortgage amortization aspect is taxable and the interest payments are deductible and afford tax shelter, the combination of depreciation deductions and tax-deductible interest payments can and usually does afford an untaxed cash flow far exceeding the cash generated from operations during the initial four to five years of the investment. For this reason, most tax-oriented offerings are leveraged in the 60 percent to 80 percent range as a percentage of the acquisition price so that the interest and depreciation deductions can be channeled to the investing partners, substantially offsetting other sources of income not derived from the syndication itself.

## RATIOS OF LEVERAGE TO FUNDS SYNDICATED

With prudent leveraging of the property, six to eight times the unleveraged tax deductions can generally be provided to the syndicated investors. This was the situation with an apartment project in which we were recently involved. Located in the Midwest, this project consisted of a 166-unit garden-apartment complex comprised of 25 two-story buildings. The venture was syndicated with the long-run objective of converting the apartments to condominiums, although this concept has been temporarily postponed due to prevailing economic conditions in this particular industrialized city. The leverage and investor tax advantages structured into this offering provide extreme flexibility for the syndication in choosing the most appropriate time for disposing of the property to a converter.

This property was acquired in 1979 for $4,330,000 with the intent to hold it for three to seven years. Terms of the purchase contract were the assumption of a first mortgage in the amount of $2.5 million, with a second mortgage of $540,000 ballooned to the seller ten years after the property was acquired.

A total sum of $1,330,000 was syndicated and invested over four annual installments to create a rather typical leverage situation for tax-sheltered offerings. The annual estimated tax writeoffs as a percentage of equity contributed for the first four years were 53 percent, 121 percent, 96 percent, and 43 percent respectively, averaging out at about 78 percent per year. Leveraging this property with a combination of conventional and owner-provided financing produced tax deductions approximating three to four times those obtainable had the syndicate purchased this property strictly for cash, not utilizing the combined financial leverage.

The fact that this property was not converted on schedule remains somewhat irrelevant to the success of the syndication, since the tax deductions continue to generate substantial losses for the investors and the property's potential conversion value continues to accelerate. The reason for the optimism is that newly constructed dwelling units in the immediate area are being sold at increasingly higher prices. When the syndicated property is eventually marketed to a converter, the sales price will reflect the increase in the price of comparable dwelling units since 1979, and the investors will also be eligible to receive favorable capital-gains tax treatment at the time of the transfer.

## LIMITATIONS ON THE AMOUNT OF INVESTORS' TAX DEDUCTIONS

As evidenced in the project just described, the combination of leverage and depreciation can provide flexibility in terms of establishing staying power. The double-taxation aspects inherent in corporations is not prevalent in limited partnerships. Rather, real estate syndications permit the passing of profits and losses through directly to each partner without the presence of direct financial exposure. The losses and tax-shelter benefits that a partner may absorb in any real estate syndication are generally limited to his or her equity contribution in the partnership. For all practical purposes, this amounts to the invested funds or letters of credit one has contributed plus a prorated factor relating to the financial leverage placed against the syndicated property. This leverage multiplier must meet the at-risk limitations established by the Internal Revenue Service. If a property is substantially leveraged, for example at six to seven times the equity investment contribution, the deductions can be increased by a multiple of the amount of leverage divided by the percentage of the investors' equity interest subject to the at-risk provisions that basically pertain to the nonrecourse aspect of mortgage financing.

The at-risk rule *limits the amount of losses* that the syndicated investors can take, based upon three concepts:

1. the cash, other property, or other financial commitments the limited partners put up that can be construed as an eventual contribution to the partnership;
2. any amount of money that is borrowed by the partnership to the extent that the partners or the partnership are personally liable for the repayment of the debt; and
3. the fair-market value of any other assets that are pledged as additional collateral for securing the nonrecourse borrowing by the partnership.

The trick to turning a relatively routine syndication into an exciting and lucrative investment experience lies in the creative combination of:

- using the three variations of the at-risk factors just listed;

- using substantial tax deductions to achieve the desired rate of return;
- balancing the financial exposure the syndicator is willing to assume in light of the desired rate of return; and
- structuring the financing and attendant cash flow to parallel the appropriate holding period of the asset.

The aggregate amount of tax deductions to syndicated investors is limited only by the property itself and the imagination of the syndicator and his or her financial advisors. The Internal Revenue Service sets up guidelines for challenging partnerships that purposely take excessive deductions based upon overly aggressive positions supported by opinions of counsel that do not accurately reflect the commissioners' current thinking. These important and complicated guidelines are outlined in great detail in Chapter 18.

## THE IMPORTANCE OF REHABILITATION EXPENDITURES AS TAX CREDITS

Under the 1981 Tax Reform Act, tax credits are permitted for certain rehabilitation expenditures. These categories are defined as capital disbursements that improve the property permanently. Any improvement having a useful life of over five years is considered "permanent," and such items as the acquisition cost of a structure and mortgage interest payments are excluded. Interestingly enough, no limit is currently set on the number of projects that can be rejuvenated and thereby qualify for investment tax credits (I.T.C.).

Because of this lack of limitation, income-tax credit for rejuvenation can be substantially more beneficial under certain conditions than that found under the depreciation schedules. This credit can be applied directly against the income-tax obligations of individuals syndicated exclusively for rejuvenating a project and operates as a direct offset against the partners' tax liabilities. In most instances, it is available in addition to the normal depreciation allowances. These rehabilitation projects offer a 25 percent investment tax credit up front, substantially reducing the initial after-tax equity investment, providing an interesting, above-average return on investment. These credits can be carried backward and forward to apply to a variety of taxable years, constituting one of the most lucrative tax breaks found anywhere in the Internal Revenue Service Code. Rehabilitation investments are economically viable only where property appreciation is predictable over a period of at least five years, as this holding period is mandatory in order to avoid any recapture of the I.T.C.

Investment tax credits are also available for some types of equipment used in real estate syndications. The difference between improvements for rejuvenation and equipment is that the useful life of the latter is defined as three years rather than the five years needed to qualify for rejuvenation. Several years ago, we acquired and completely rejuvenated a 30-year-old commercial building and in the process constructed a new addition into the existing structure. We utilized much of the new mechanical equipment for both buildings, and by allocating the costs on a prorated basis to both structures, we were able to take substantial rejuvenation investment tax credit deductions on the older edifice.

## TAX BENEFITS FROM RESYNDICATION OF SUBSIDIZED HOUSING

Many of the older projects sponsored by the Department of Housing and Urban Development (HUD), more specifically the projects geared to assist the poor, handicapped, and elderly, such as the Section 8 Rent Subsidy Program, the Section 202 nonprofit Program for Elderly and Handicapped, and the Section 23 Leasing Program, combined with the low-income housing projects sold to and managed by nonprofit municipal housing authorities, offer interesting resyndication potential and in the process are creating tremendous opportunities for individuals who are desirous of participating in the ultimate in tax-sheltered syndications.

Many of these older residential housing projects were initially structured strictly for tax-shelter groups, utilizing thin equities and maximum nonrecourse financing guaranteed by the U.S. government. After the initial tax benefits have diminished, substantial numbers of these syndications show little economic benefit to the original investing groups. This, combined with the often burdensome management obligations placed on the individuals who syndicated them originally and retained the management contracts, is currently providing an attractive atmosphere to individuals capable of relieving these undesirable pressures through the resyndication process. In many instances, the original investors are not in a position to provide the additional resources to cure the deferred maintenance that has prevailed in many of these projects over the years. HUD traditionally has never made adequate provisions for the ongoing and unusual maintenance that is required in projects where a majority of the tenants basically have little if any pride of ownership. Within these situations lies a unique opportunity for the entrepreneur who can resyndicate the existing limited partnership, passing on a restructured set of tax advantages to a newly formed group of potential investors. By acquiring or restructuring an existing subsidized housing development, one can take advantage of the liberal tax-related deductions that are exclusively available for residential properties under the accelerated cost recovery system (ACRS), irrespective of whether the properties are newly constructed or currently in use. One can either offer the property itself or resyndicate the existing partnership shares to a new group of limited and/or general partners. In order for this to become a viable concept, HUD must approve the transaction, as a transfer of the property's physical assets requires their approval where 90 percent of the beneficial ownership of the assets is assigned to an unrelated entity.

Often the limited partners can be removed from an existing partnership, leaving the general partner in place with an equity interest and as the managing entity. Both HUD and the nonprofit city or county housing authorities are not only desirous of, but are actually promoting many of these resyndications, as a substantial number of the properties developed for the poor, handicapped, or elderly that have been in existence for extended periods of time are in extremely dilapidated physical condition. Both HUD and the local agencies are willing to approve the transfers of interest in these complexes, especially where substantial infusions of capital are advanced and earmarked for expenditures on deferred maintenance and replenishment of operating reserves. Conceivably, under the existing ownership, many of these loans are in default or are accruing interest payments that will never be brought current. One of the HUD requirements for transferring ownership is to bring these mortgage obligations up to date. These deferred-maintenance and interest payments are fully tax deductible to the new group in the initial year of resyndication, making these deductions extremely attractive to high-tax-bracket investors. Often, once the deferred maintenance is funded and the loans brought current, HUD will either defer some of the future interest and principal payments or advance additional mortgage funds in order to assure that the property will remain viable on a long-term basis. Very rarely in real estate investing can individuals acquire highly leveraged properties where the equity funds are applied exclusively to maintenance and accrued interest, the majority of which is deductible during the initial year of the investment.

Government agencies, including HUD, often prohibit secondary financing against these types of projects, and if deferred maintenance or operating expenses are underestimated, your investors should be prepared to contribute substantial funds at subsequent dates.

## STRUCTURING THE RESYNDICATION

Many of the older, existing partnerships are structured in such a fashion that the limited partners in the initial stages receive equity positions, cash-flow allocations and tax-loss partipations amounting to a 99 percent interest in the partnership, with the remaining 1 percent allocated as a token to the general partner. Upon sale many revert the proceeds to a 50–50 basis after the limited partners receive a return of their equity contribution combined with a predetermined amount of interest. Many of these ill-conceived subsidized projects will never show an eventual sales price in excess of the mortgage encumbrance, unless they are periodically rejuvenated. In many instances the partners' basis is substantially less than the outstanding mortgage encumbrance, potentially triggering a tremendous capital-gains liability in the event of a foreclosure. These events often leave the investors without any proceeds of sale to pay the incurred capital-gains taxes. For this reason, many limited partners in mature syndications can be convinced to dispose of their partnership shares for sums that are small in comparison to the overall value of the project. This pittance of a remuneration can be easily calculated based on the potential taxable obligation if the property were to be adversely liquidated. In a substantial number of instances a resyndication is the only way that the original investors will be made whole, unless they are in a position to inject substantial funds into a project in order to cure the deferred maintenance, which is so mandatory in keeping the rent structures competitive. One will find that many of these syndications were structured exclusively for tax purposes, and as the tax benefits expired, many investors were willing to settle for their past tax deductions, combined with enough consideration to pay their capital gains taxes upon the dissolution of the partnership.

Many of these partnerships can be restructured so that the initial managing general partner continues to control the project, and the syndicator receives a fee for finding the new source of investment funds. Sometimes under these conditions conflicts of interest can arise, as the newly resyndicated limited partners are desirous of having their cash contributions expended on tax-deductible deferred maintenance. When these circumstances prevail, the initial general partners, especially those who continue to retain ownership interests, are often at odds with the newly formed investment group. Treatment of resyndication expenses paid to the general partner for application into the project can often create uncomfortable situations, especially when these payments are expended for maintenance purposes, as they can be considered taxable as ordinary income to the general partner under certain circumstances. If the general partner treats these expenditures as capital gains, the new limited partners will have to capitalize and amortize them. A detailed analysis by professional accountants or advisors of any resyndication is important, as the tax ramifications both to the existing and newly formed investors are the basic reason for both groups' involvement. The accelerated depreciation, the high degree of nonrecourse leverage, and the lack of recapture provisions that pertain to low-income government-subsidized housing make this an extremely lucrative field for exercising one's entrepreneurial talent. Many general partners whose interests eventually revert to a 50–50 situation upon sale will immediately capitalize on resyndications, as they can provide one with an opportunity to profitably continue the operations of a project made viable only by insertions of others' risk capital, supporting their eventual equity interest and sustaining their ongoing management fees during the prolonged life of the resyndication effort.

## SYNDICATIONS THAT AVOID THE ALTERNATIVE MINIMUM TAX

Many high-tax-bracket investors who participate in syndicated real estate offerings can be the subject of the alternative minimum tax, as many of the deductions proposed or taken by these investors are fully allowable under the regular method of computing one's tax obligation, but may be prohibited as deductions when figuring in the alternative minimum tax (AMT). The AMT is structured or designed to require high-tax-bracket investors who are actively involved in tax-shelter activities to eventually be obligated to a minimum flat rate of 20 percent, irrespective of the amount, size, or number of their deductions. The *normal method* in which one figures one's income-tax obligation is to subtract the standard interest and depreciation deductions as well as other exemptions and exclusions, thus producing the bottom-line taxable obligation. Many investors in the 50 percent tax bracket have been able to convert ordinary income into long-term capital gains taxed at a maximum rate of 20 percent, or have taken accelerated depreciation, accrued interest, prepaid taxes, and other varieties of tax credits permitting them to reduce their taxable income to desirable levels and in many instances to a position where no tax obligation exists whatsoever.

The *alternative minimum tax* is designed to eliminate much of this activity. The AMT is designed to alternatively calculate one's taxable obligation by adding back into one's adjusted gross income certain deductible items of tax preference, eliminating certain tax exclusions, including the 60 percent exclusion for long-term capital gains, and disallowing deductions for payment of state income tax and other tax credits that are generally taken. The IRS requires that individuals with tax-sheltered income calculate their taxable obligation *using both methods,* requiring the taxpayer to choose the calculations that produce the higher taxable obligation. Under the AMT, a minimum exemption of $40,000 is available for a joint return, $20,000 for filing a separate return, and $30,000 when filing a single individual's return. To the extent that one's deductions do not exceed these exempted levels of income, one will not be subject to the alternative minimum tax. The appropriate approach is to reduce one's net taxable income, but not below the point where it triggers the alternative minimum tax situation. Depending on the individual and on certain circumstances, this means utilizing straight-line depreciation in lieu of accelerated, and amortizing the development costs, interest, architectural fees, and so forth, over a period of ten years. Long-term capital gains should be postponed or deferred if one falls into the category of incurring too many tax preference items. Many investors should be fully advised that in analyzing real estate tax-shelter syndications they should calculate their income both ways so that they are not presented with any surprises after committing to a project. Many sophisticated syndicators, when marketing offerings with high ratios of tax deductions to equity contributions, structure these various partnerships providing nonpreference types of tax deductions to their investors. The most commonly promoted nonpreference type of project is created through the syndication of low-income government-sponsored housing, either newly constructed or developed or through the vehicle of existing acquisitions or renovations. In these specialized types of ventures, items such as construction-period interest and taxes are not subject to the AMT, whereas in other real estate offerings, interest and taxes must generally be capitalized and amortized over a ten-year period.

## WHY RESERVES ARE IMPORTANT IN TAX-ORIENTED SYNDICATIONS

Especially in syndications where large equity positions are structured, the importance of financial reserves is often de-emphasized. This can usually be attributed to the general partner's optimism and to the limited partners' lack of experience with the potentially detrimental consequences that can surface in a highly leveraged project. After all, setting aside equity funds for contingency reserves automatically reduces the overall yield that a syndicated project can generate.

At risk, of course, is the potential profit upon sale essential to the intelligent structuring of real estate syndications and visibly absent through foreclosure. The protection of this critical element of investment must be judiciously analyzed against four specific categories of need.

1. *Financing:* Especially when mortgages are arranged at rates that float with prime, when balloon payments are incorporated, or when short-term owner financing is integral, a project can be at risk without these adequate financial reserves. Under such conditions of structuring, large sums of money could be required at

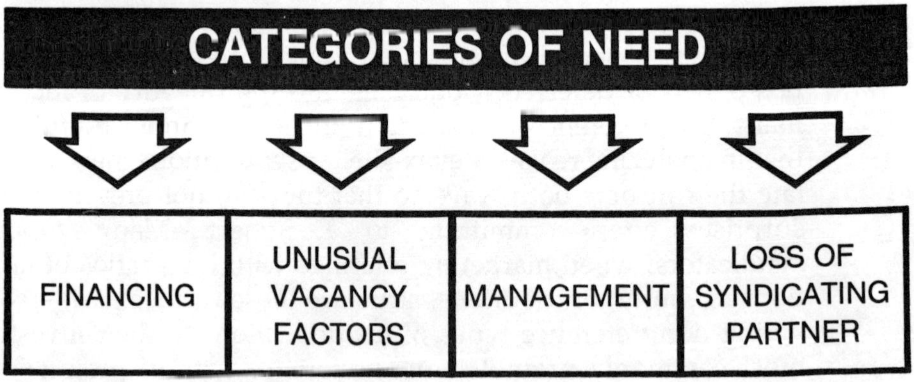


**Figure 3.2** Potential needs requiring the use of financial reserves.

times when it might be difficult or even impossible to raise funds.

2. *Unusual vacancy factors:* Should market conditions deteriorate, rental properties could be jeopardized in a variety of ways. Newer properties may not be fully absorbed, and older ones may develop substantial vacancy factors. Those rented on a percentage-of-gross-income basis will also produce less of a return. In any case, projections of cash flow can fall substantially under estimation, and the viability of the syndicating entity can be likewise threatened.
3. *Management:* Conventional management practices may have to be altered radically when an economic situation changes, and the quality of a professional organization can often deteriorate during the holding period of an asset. In either case, substantial funds may have to be generated in order to bring in new or enlightened management personnel or to reconstruct portions of a structure or add amenities to capitalize on new market demands.
4. *Loss of a syndicating partner:* When a general partner or an individual with a substantial holding in a syndicate dies or gets divorced, a sizable infusion of capital may be required to purchase that person's interest so that the partnership can continue to adequately function. Even more serious, a syndication may be threatened with litigation if it fails to buy out the interests of a potentially insolvent partner.

A final contingency deserves special attention. Clouds on titles can and often do arise, as do other adverse claims, where additional legal fees are required and can be, under certain circumstances, substantial. If a threatened property is foreclosed on, or legal judgments are assessed against, the accumulated tax benefits as well as the investors' equity are potentially wiped out. When the partnership has substantial holding power, losses from legal fees can be offset by a corresponding sale or through refinancing, thereby producing the appropriate income for meeting the partnership obligations.

## DETERMINING THE POINT OF DIMINISHING TAX BENEFITS

A tax-oriented investment in real estate is considered to reach maturity when the tax deductions begin to decline substantially in relation to the project's income. These benefits are derived from both depreciation allowances and interest deductions, which wane for one or more of the following reasons:

- In the initial years, mortgage obligations consist of large interest payments and correspondingly small amortization of principal. Interest is tax deductible; amortization is taxable. As time goes on, the interest portion decreases and the amortization aspect increases.
- The cash flow generated by any project generally increases during an inflationary period, though syndicators do not usually project the additional deflated dollars reflecting their true values. Under these circumstances, the cash flow during the later life of the project may offset the declining tax benefits.
- Depreciation deductions are correspondingly reduced each year in the life of a project when the asset is depreciated on an accelerated basis.

By anticipating the combined effects of reduced depreciation deductions, increased cash flow, and greater mortgage amortization, a syndicator can quickly determine the point at which a project's package of realizable benefits will be inadequate to meet his or her investors' needs. This normally occurs when the project's cash flow exceeds the deductions and itself becomes taxable to the syndicate as ordinary income. At this point, the tax ramifications of mortgage amortization usually take effect, requiring substantial funds to meet these obligations. This situation tends to negate the value of the return on investment, and at the earliest favorable time the syndication will usually divest itself of the property.

A far-sighted syndicator rarely will terminate a compatible partnership unless demands on his or her time and finances are inordinate. Most are actively plotting alternative investments shortly after the partnership is fully incorporated. Their optimism surfaces infectiously at critical moments, particularly when the pleasure of financial gain is reinforced by mutual respect and good fellowship among participating investors.

In the following chapter, we will analyze some of the qualities and acumen a syndicator must possess in order to feel comfortable in his or her position as general partner and to inspire the needed confidence among his or her associating silent partners.

# 4

# Acquiring and Negotiating Real Estate Properties

An established syndicator acquires investment real estate for one of two reasons:

- the intrinsic value of a property in the current or potential market place is obvious; and/or
- an established following of investors will be well served by the unique potential that a specific property offers.

For one of these reasons, or a combination of both, the syndication comes into being. Behind every offering lies the individual's unique philosophy of acquisition, as complex as the age-old speculation about whether the chicken or the egg came first. If our hypothetical syndicator were to take an inventory of present and past holdings and analyze them by one of these two categories of motivation, one would find the latter accounting for a larger percentage of his acquisitions. Yet percentages would vary greatly among individuals and reveal much about their working methods.

Since the purpose of this book is not to dictate working methods but rather to probe their soundness, the subject of acquisition will receive a lesser treatment in this chapter than that of negotiating, which is far less tactical than intuitive. Both demand that an entrepreneur have his or her finger on the pulse of the general economy, and specifically on the economic viability of the locality in which the real estate holding must compete. This combination is inseparable, as we shall see.

## DEVELOPING AN OVERALL ACQUISITION STRATEGY

Timing and location will determine the ultimate value of a real estate syndication. Management and financing are subordinate. One can improve on losers and winners, but realistically can't under normal conditions transform a total loser into an absolute winner. More often than not one can take a mediocre investment and through the use of mirror tricks make it appear to be a winner. Most syndicators choose and evaluate according to their temperaments and those of their potential investors. Winners always stay with quality holdings, even if premiums are involved in acquiring the appropriate property or location. Mediocre investments, on the other hand, can prove to be real long shots, which can potentially tarnish your image as a syndicator if they fail to materialize. Successful syndicators develop an investment acquisition strategy relying primarily on the following five factors:

1. Predetermine the types of investments you will consider for syndication.
2. Set the guidelines for the amount of leverage you will apply to any syndicated property.
3. Determine how much of a personal financial exposure you are willing to assume on any given syndication.
4. Predetermine how much of the ownership you will retain and the amount to be sold to your investors.
5. Establish guidelines for how long you and your investors plan to hold your investments.

Rarely should one invest in properties with negative cash flows, especially when one's investing partners are relatively unsophisticated. Seldom should one acquire risk-oriented properties, especially large holdings where additional and unforeseen capital requirements can force a sale under less than desirable circumstances. The potential risks and rewards of any syndicated investment are closely related, and you as the managing general partner must be the final judge of the appropriate balance, given your individual temperament and your investors' resources. We recently structured an offering on a 48-unit luxury condominium development, raising $250,000 in passive investor funds. Our philosophy in this instance and in most other situations is never to leverage more than the wholesale value of the developed units, using the investor funds as the risk element or equity cushion.

## ACQUIRING THE PARTICULAR INVESTMENT VEHICLE

In order to determine the appropriate investment strategy one must review and revise one's objectives frequently, as geographic areas, regional economics, tax laws, and leverage concepts are fluid. Four categories should be considered or weighed as they relate subjectively to one's various holdings.

1. *Newer versus older properties:* Seasoned properties should generally be avoided unless renovation and investment tax credits are sought. Most lenders also avoid commitments on older structures where physical as well as accounting depreciation can be a real factor. Maintenance, operating expenses, rental income, and vacancy factors are less predictable in older structures.
2. *Equities should always be ample, never thinly structured:* Mortgage financing should be conservative and debt-service payments realistic in the light of income generated after operating expenses and allowances for vacancy. Debt service coverage ratios of 1.2 to 1.3 should be a *minimum* when using investors' funds. This ratio means that rents can fall or expenses can increase, or a combination of both, by 20 percent to 30 percent before a negative cash flow surfaces.
3. *Large versus small holdings:* Equity contributions, management ability, and financial leverage will dictate to some degree the size of the property to be syndicated. As a general guideline, any single-purpose structure should be leased only to first-rate quality tenants on relatively long-term leases. Only relatively large structures should be considered for syndication, as they tend to have more appeal to investors than smaller, out-of-the-way holdings. The optimum size of these edifices can be categorized as follows:

- *apartment complexes*—100 units or more;
- *office buildings*—a minimum of 75,000 to 100,000 square feet;
- *shopping centers*—100,000 square feet or larger when a major supermarket is involved;

- *motels*—at least 125 units (full service) unless of the budget type without supporting facilities.

## AVOIDING SPECULATIVE AREAS AND PROPERTIES

Geographic areas that tend to have unstable or fluctuating long-term unemployment potential, whose economic base is dependent upon such industries as mineral extraction or heavy-polluting, resort communities, and defense or research-oriented areas should normally be avoided, since they lack the diversity of employment necessary or desirable for maintaining stabilized property values. Holdings with unpredictable cash flows, such as bowling alleys, funeral parlors, car dealerships, franchise operations, amusement or video parlors, restaurants and nightclubs, faddish retail outlets, golf courses, and bookstores or cinemas should be left to individuals who are not desirous of developing a consistently long-term successful track record with their investors.

I recently completed a syndication on a 36-unit second-home resort condominium project that initially had several speculative elements. A high degree of leverage and a subordinated land lease were the key ingredients, which when combined with the marketing effort materializing rather quickly, produced a return of the invested funds in less than a year.

## RELIABLE SOURCES OF ACQUISITION CONTACTS

The local economy is best understood through the network of professional contacts that the syndicator has established in the business community. Knowing the market intricately combined with your capabilities to effectively operate there can be your strongest promotional asset.

Although it may sound simplistic, the degree of a syndicator's success can often be measured by his or her willingness to listen. Among those offering the most rewarding conversations are:

- members of real estate brokerage firms;
- building contractors and architects;
- commercial lenders (officers of banks and savings and loans);
- pension funds; and
- personnel associated with professional real estate management firms.

**ADVANTAGEOUS CLOSE ASSOCIATION**

WITH:
- REAL ESTATE FIRM MEMBERS
- BUILDING CONTRACTORS
- ARCHITECTS
- COMMERCIAL LENDERS
- REAL ESTATE MANAGEMENT PERSONNEL

**Figure 4.1** Professional contacts useful to a syndicator acquiring property.

- personnel associated with professional real estate management firms.

Real estate brokers are often well informed on the intricacies of local market conditions and, even more important, can offer well-educated guesses about the potential gluts and shortages. Members of the building trades often have inside information relating to when a peer develops financial problems and is vulnerable to bargain-basement offers in order to keep afloat. While commercial lenders are ethically bound to discretion about their clients' affairs, they must often protect their own interests by inviting the participation of trusted developers or financiers into projects in danger of collapse. All of these sources are capable of adding to the depth of a syndicator's analysis of a market or of acquainting one with opportunities before they surface to the general public, yet none of the first three sources offer as much potential as that gained by close association with one or more professional real estate management firms.

Outside management teams lend professionality to any syndicate, both in minimizing areas of potential conflict of interest between the general partner and his or her investors and in providing an independent third-party view of a project's operating income and expenses. Qualified firms can be invaluable to the success of both major and minor syndicated real estate ventures. Fewer and fewer experienced syndicators working on any scale can comfortably forego this area of assistance, especially where long-term projects are combined with aggressive goals. Competent management quickly pays dividends in low-vacancy factors and potential appreciation, and the ancillary benefits to a syndicator with a long record of successful dealings with a trusted management firm are often the greater for being less tangible.

## THE ADVANTAGES OF CONSULTING PROFESSIONAL MANAGEMENT TEAMS

A well-seasoned working relationship with a qualified property management firm can be an invaluable tool in terms of developing an overall long-standing strategy for acquiring and syndicating commercial real estate investments. At the conceptual stage of a syndication when assets are under option for acquisition, management firms can be of great assistance in analyzing the seller's operating statements presented for potential syndications. Many semifabricated operating pro formas need local and professional interpretation in terms of

- operating expenses and income;
- unit composition and rentability;
- percentage of net leasable space;
- physical condition of the buildings;
- amenities that are needed or required;
- current area occupancy levels; and
- the number of management positions that are needed to staff a project.

Even active and sophisticated syndicators find it extremely difficult to analyze each specific market and property at any given period of time. A relatively simple apartment building might on the surface seem easy to compare with others, yet each structure has different room sizes and composition; desirable or undesirable amenities; different acoustical properties and/or views; varying accessibility to shopping areas, schools, public transportation, and places of employment; and different parking requirements. A single one or a combination of these factors can cause rental income to vary by as much as 10 percent in any given metropolitan area and can even more drastically affect occupancy rates in less-than-prime areas if the targeted market deteriorates.

Like commercial lenders, professional management teams have a vested interest in the properties they manage in terms of the ongoing fees they will continue to collect and the long-term continuity of their contracts. These individuals are the first to recognize undermaintenance, lower rents, or irregular vacancies that will eventually produce operating deficits.

To protect their future sources of revenues, professional management teams make periodic market assessments to determine whether rents should be maintained, reduced, or raised, and assess whether the property should be restructured, refinanced, or disposed of. These groups often act as intermediaries between owners ready to sell and buyers able to capitalize upon the deferred potential of a sound property in a changing and often lucrative market.

The inherent advantages of working with professional management teams is a topic to which we will return often in the following pages. Their role in providing consultation and advice is less visible at the acquisition stage than during the later periods of a syndication's existence, but is nevertheless important. Of all the sources a syndicator can draw or rely on in probing the local economy, real estate management firms are capable of providing the most comprehensive, objective, and specific advice.

## THE INTRICATE PROCESS OF NEGOTIATION

Negotiation is a complex psychological affair in which sizing up the strengths and weaknesses of the opposition is a major factor of success. Individuals negotiate for real property and for other purposes as well for one of two reasons:

- they feel that the other party can be of substantial benefit to them, or
- they fear the opposition can harm them unless they enter into negotiations.

The negotiation process, besides determining the value itself, can have important legal and tax ramifications and usually involves a considerable number of other interested parties, such as mortgage lenders, accountants, tax lawyers, and real estate brokers. While such individuals usually are not parties to the original contract, they must be considered when a purchase agreement is structured so that the appropriate time can be allowed to provide for an orderly review of the documents prior to the property being transferred to the new owners.

During the 1973–74 REIT fiasco, we acquired a project with an outstanding $2.5-million mortgage for slightly over three quarters of a million dollars based upon an assets-swap concept. The foreclosing bank had no direct collateral behind their loan except the REIT's stock, which was for all practical purposes worthless. They agreed to an out-of-court settlement in order to expedite the transfer. The number of attorneys, brokers, and mortgage lenders that attended the closing was astounding in relation to the value of this particular holding.

Because of the need to know the nature of the opposition and the involvement of a multitude of other parties, the same circle of professional acquaintances who serve the syndicator in acquisition can be valuable to him or her in the negotiating process.

## THE IMPORTANCE OF RISK FACTORS AND OPTIONS

Any serious negotiation involves taking a calculated risk, predetermining how the odds of a possible loss can be balanced against the potential for long-term, lucrative rewards. When a major syndicated development is involved, real estate entrepreneurs generally cannot afford to assume the entire risk unilaterally. This is why successful syndicators choose to associate with partners of substance and favorable reputation. Long before the negotiation commences, the syndicator must fully explore and understand the balancing of the calculated or manageable risks with the potential long-term rewards. By doing so, the syndicator will isolate and comprehend the factors that are essential to the eventual success of the negotiation as well as what can be waived as an unessential appeasement to the demands of the opposing party.

When negotiating for substantial real estate assets, one must develop an assortment of alternatives. The party more likely to emerge favorably from the negotiation is the one who arrives best equipped with extensive and imaginative options. This is analogous to the avenues a person of substantial means has when it comes to borrowing money. Lenders often conclude loan arrangements with a well-heeled individual in a matter of minutes, with few if any details being provided, while they will often negotiate extensively with someone of lesser means in dictating the terms and conditions under which they will enter into a loan agreement.

I recently negotiated a loan on an apartment structure for $9,500,000 with two other partners, both solid individuals with strong financial credentials. The mortgage was committed to in less than three weeks, as the lender, with whom we had never worked, knew and approved of the reputation of the three borrowers. This West Coast lender tentatively approved the documentation without actually visiting the 10-acre site.

## HOW EXPERTISE PLAYS AN IMPORTANT ROLE

The ability to display expertise at the negotiating table can be an important tool in presenting facts and conditions without having to be substantially questioned in turn. Intelligent negotiators will not only use their expertise to their full advantage, but will be prepared to demonstrate that they have consulted experts in areas where they may lack specific knowledge or where they know their opponent to be particularly well informed.

Regardless of the amount or kind of technical expertise a negotiator can bring to the bargaining table, no single asset can compensate for lack of patience and perseverance. Many otherwise colorless individuals have become enormously successful at negotiation solely because they realize that time is their ally when they become persistent in achieving their objectives by wearing down the opposition. Successful real estate entrepreneurs are normally tied to hectic schedules and tend to concentrate on other pressing matters as negotiations slow down. Many concepts do not surface in the initial stages of negotiations, primarily because negotiators do not like to play all their cards at once, and the persistent negotiator over a period of time can bring out these specific demands. Therefore, time is on his or her side if patience prevails.

## HOW DEADLINES AFFECT THE NEGOTIATING PROCESS

Without deadlines, many negotiations would never really settle down to the important conflicts that must eventually be aired and resolved. Deadlines can bring major issues to the forefront, especially if one of the negotiating parties puts a restrictive time frame on the other party's activities. Yet, most deadlines are contrived and many are arbitrary and capricious. Depending upon the legitimacy of the cutoff point, most concessions are made late in the negotiating process, as close as possible to the predetermined time schedules.

Patience is imperative when deadlines are involved, particularly since many are not as rigid as they might initially seem. The most important and critical concessions are often made long after established timetables have passed. While an inexperienced negotiator may regard deadlines as inflexible, sophisticated negotiators artificially use them to their advantage.

Unless a deadline is potentially critical, sophisticated individuals never reveal the true timing patterns set for any negotiation. Deadlines, like every other aspect of the negotiation process, are sensitive and should be a well-integrated product of the negotiating process. Those individuals who set arbitrary deadlines and then trap themselves by not observing them often show substantial weakness to the other side. As important as it may be to have a relatively fixed period of time in which one plans to conclude the negotiating process or move on to other activities, divulging such information is, more often than not, tactically detrimental.

Several years ago we acquired a defunct 50-unit condominium project from a real estate investment trust (REIT) that was in reorganization and in the throes of bankruptcy. We went past a scheduled closing to acquire the property at a negotiated price of $1,100,000. The REIT tipped its hand that the scheduled closing date was also a time that several bank loans had to be reduced in order for the REIT not to go into full bankruptcy proceedings. Upon learning of this, we subsequently offered the REIT $860,000 in cash with an immediate closing. The REIT and the strung-out lenders had no alternative but to accept our offer and close, which was accomplished in a matter of days.

## HOW TO DEAL WITH ENTREPRENEURIAL NEGOTIATORS

As we mentioned previously, negotiation is a complex psychological process. If the opposition was unknown at the beginning of the process, they will or should be more fully understood at the conclusion of the negotiations. *Few* syndicators of real estate holdings possess the amounts of patience and dogged perseverance required for optimum success at the negotiating table. There is, after all, a bit of the entrepreneurial spirit in all of us, and an overdose of patience might not serve as well in other areas of real estate developmental activity. If anything distinguishes the professional from the amateur or paraprofessional negotiator, it is not so much the quantity of money at stake as it is the individual's ability to control his or her impulsive actions. The unsophisticated tend to be impetuous, and the professionals use this tendency to their advantage. Short-term deadlines, even if they are contrived, often extract the best terms and conditions from the unsophisticated.

Other paraprofessionals tend to negotiate entirely through subordinates, usually to their ultimate disadvantage. Others find it more desirable to orchestrate the major aspects of any transaction, leaving the minor details to subordinates. When one is discussing the concepts in generalities, being there is of the utmost importance. When the negotiation process reaches the point of making concessions on details, subordinates can excel. Briefly stated, the authoritative negotiating party must determine what concessions can reasonably be made early in the bargaining process. By standing aloof from the horse-trading details, one can be in a position to see the full picture and determine which concessions might be substantive in nature.

Understanding the opposition can often take the form of analyzing the size of the incremental concessions the other side makes. Bureaucrats or individuals low on the corporate ladder tend to negotiate in small increments. The successful independent entrepreneur, on the other hand, eventually arrives at a realistic figure and presents it on a take-it-or-leave-it basis. By analyzing the increments in which an individual has the scope to bargain, one can determine rather quickly the true limits of his authorization and his ability to compromise in order to structure and complete a real estate transaction.

## NEGOTIATING THE PURCHASE PRICE, TERMS, AND CONDITIONS

The purchase price should be specifically stated, and the details or the method for determining it should be fully disclosed. The value of real property, whether improved or unimproved, is usually based on a known quantity of acres, number of units, or square footage. Building values rest on gross square footage or net rentable or occupiable space, with different values frequently assigned to these various portions of that space. In retail complexes, for example, ground floor, visible space is considerably more valuable. Even with raw acreage, some portions can be unusable, and adjoining parcels can differ in value due to access, topography, or zoning.

After values have been firmly established according to a predetermined formula, the terms and conditions for closing must be advanced with clarity to include such items as the

- nature of the conveyance, deed, or contract of sale;
- amount of financing and interest rate and the financing entity;

- amortization schedules or balloon payments if applicable;
- provisions for title insurance or abstracts;
- terms of the seller's financing and subordination, if applicable;
- specific contingencies to be removed prior to closing; and
- date established for closing and allocation of the closing costs.

Each of these important concepts should be an integral part of the negotiations, as the success of any arrived-at settlement depends upon all the pieces of the puzzle fitting tightly.

## IMPORTANT CONDITIONS PRECEDENT TO CLOSING

Most negotiated real estate offers to purchase are conditioned upon a predetermined series of events happening prior to the closing. A contract can be too cluttered with substantial numbers of unrealistic contingencies so closely spaced that it can readily be invalidated, since the failure to meet only one contingency is enough to void most proposals.

The following is a partial list of essential contingencies that a *selling entity* must conform to prior to finalizing a syndicated closing:

- provision of an unobstructed title insurance policy;
- assurance that the structure is in substantial conformance with existing building codes; or
- that the land is properly zoned for the intended purpose or, alternatively, conditioned upon obtaining the desired zoning;
- that the property has the necessary access and utilities;
- that there are no detrimental easements, encroachments, subsurface or drainage problems; and
- that there are no unfavorable leases, contractual obligations, mortgage encumbrances, or pending litigation.

Prior to the sale, the *purchasing entity* also has substantial items to address itself to, such as

- forming and completing the syndication;
- obtaining the apropriate financing and appraisals;
- obtaining a building permit or other developmental approvals;
- verifying income and expenses; and
- completing physical inspection of the property.

**SELLING ENTITY**

- UNOBSTRUCTED TITLE INSURANCE
- STRUCTURE IN CONFORMANCE WITH BUILDING CODES
- LAND PROPERLY ZONED
- NECESSARY ACCESS AND UTILITIES
- NO DETRIMENTAL EASEMENTS
- NO UNFAVORABLE LEASES

**Figure 4.2** Contingencies that a selling entity must conform to prior to a closing.

**PURCHASING ENTITY**

- SALE CONDITIONED ON COMPLETING SYNDICATION
- SALE CONTINGENT ON OBTAINING FINANCING
- SALE SUPPORTED BY APPRAISAL
- SALE DEPENDENT ON OBTAINING BUILDING PERMIT
- SALE CONTINGENT ON VERIFICATION OF INCOME
- SALE SUBJECT TO COMPLETE INSPECTION

**Figure 4.3** Contingencies of concern to a purchasing entity before a closing.

Removing any of these contingencies requires substantial amounts of time and money, especially where major developments are to be constructed that involve architectural or engineering services, financing costs, option payments, and other fees that must be advanced prior to closing. Yet most contingencies or conditions precedent are structured exclusively for the benefit of the purchaser, as assurances that the property can be put to the intended use. One must also have confidence that the seller's activities relating to the specific property are restricted. The negotiated contract must spell out the precise obligations of both parties and the remedies for failure to perform. Often overlooked is the need to specify who has the ability to waive the conditions precedent. If they are not to be unilaterally waived by one party or the other, the nonaffected group may be able to force rescission of the contract, even though this may be contrary to the intent of both parties at the time of the contractual agreement.

## INSPECTION CONTINGENCIES IN PURCHASE AGREEMENTS

Most contracts to purchase syndicated real estate specify confirmation of the representations that the seller is making concerning the condition of the property to be acquired. "As is" is usually the standard nomenclature used in describing the condition of the asset to be acquired, with a customary period of time specified in which the purchaser can review, accept, or reject the property in its current condition, whatever that may be. If an "as is" clause is inserted, such things as the roof, foundations, and structural soundness, heating, air conditioning, and mechanical, plumbing, electric, and other utilities are accepted by the buyer in their current condition, irrespective of the nature of the improvements that need to be made in order to bring them up to full warranty condition. Inspections should be under the guidance of independent third parties, such as engineers, architects, professional management or rental agents, or others qualified by their familiarity with similar properties.

Several years ago we entered into a purchase contract on an apartment complex of 150-plus units that appeared to be ideally suited for a condominium conversion. Located in a Sunbelt city, within a short distance of the major state university, and within close proximity to a rapidly revitalizing downtown area, the project appeared to have extremely interesting potential for moderately priced first time-buyer condominium units. The purchase contract had an "as is" clause that was very detailed, specific, and, in our case, completely binding. We reluctantly agreed to the language, based upon an MAI (Member Appraisal Institute) appraisal paid for and provided to us by the selling entity. The appraisal specifically stated that no deferred maintenance existed and that a high level of occupancy prevailed in the complex due to the excellent maintenance program in place. Prior to closing, a detailed inspection revealed that malfunctioning heating and air conditioning units existed in most apartments, that sound transmission levels were less than adequate, and that these factors, combined with substandard roofs, all contributed to a vacancy factor that was 10 percent higher than the area in general was experiencing. Since we were confronted by unsatisfied tenants, many of whom we planned to convert to purchasers, based upon the misrepresentations in the appraisal we were in a position to rescind the purchase contract. However, we had to forfeit part of our earnest-money deposit in the process, due to the gray area surrounding the "as is" clause in the contract.

## WHY TITLE INSURANCE PROTECTION IS NECESSARY

Title insurance is intended to guarantee that a syndicate acquiring property can enjoy the use of it peacefully without loss of ownership or possession, and without the threat or fear of litigation. Title insurance guarantees that the transfer is free from all legal defects, liens, and detrimental encumbrances. Areas in which real estate titles frequently can be clouded involve

- persons in adverse possession;
- improper or unrecorded conveyance documents;
- recorded leases or other binding contractual agreements;
- liens for construction, real estate taxes, or special assessments;
- dower or curtesy rights of the selling parties;
- detrimental easements, lack of access, and/or encroachments; and
- subsurface water or mineral rights.

Many if not all of these detrimental defects can be excluded from title insurance policies, and a careful review by one's legal counsel is a necessary precaution prior to accepting a title insurance binder.

Important areas *not covered* by standard title insurance policies are violations of zoning statutes and lack of building and/or occupancy permits. Title companies perform only the function of checking and insuring against the known documentation, as actually recorded concerning prior activities that affect a specific piece of property. The transfer of ownership through deeds and the recording and release of specific mortgage encumbrances are just two of many such activities. A seller's failure to inform the purchaser of a violation of municipal ordinances is liable through legal action, not title insurance coverage, as these types of losses must be recovered through the judicial process.

The specific nature of title insurance is not to inform the insured of potential defects in title, but rather to insure against losses that might arise from these defects. Many purchasers are willing to waive minor title defects as long as they do not materially affect the transfer.

All title insurance companies offer special endorsements providing additional coverage if so desired for such categories as

- specified zoning;
- rights of ingress and egress;
- restrictive covenants, easements, and rights of way.

Simply asking for this coverage sometimes has the effect of forcing these adverse conditions to surface without actually having to contract or pay for the coverage.

Several years ago we had under contract a multifamily site located near a state capital where, as part of the conditions for original rezoning (to which we were not a party), construction had to commence within 18 months. The restrictive ordinance was designed to prevent speculators from rezoning and reselling exclusively for a profit tracts of land on which they had no intention of building. The community was desirous of attracting developers who would construct much-needed apartments, which made the rezoning effortless on the surface. We discovered a reversionary clause in the minutes from the rezoning hearing when we requested insurance coverage, however, stating that the zoning would revert to single-family residences if the allotted time frame elapsed without substantial construction commencing. In our situation the time had elapsed, and the community had fulfilled or accomplished its rezoning goal, establishing for the time being a sufficient number of apartments. This reversionary clause enabled us to rescind the contract after relatively minor architectural expenditures.

## PROVISIONS FREQUENTLY OMITTED FROM PURCHASE CONTRACTS

One of the most important and often overlooked clauses in real estate contracts states that "time is of the essence." For the various contingency and closing dates a brief delay in the performance of any real estate contract, whether it be for the conditions precedent or for the timing of the closing date, is not considered a breach of contract unless a "time is of the essence" clause is included in the documentation. If this is expressly stated, then *any delay,* however insignificant, can be considered a material breach of the contract.

Another important consideration is the ability, or lack thereof, to assign the purchase contract to an additional noncontracting third party. When a property is under option it is often subsequently necessary to assign part or all of the interest to the syndicating entity or to other interim owners or lenders prior to forming and selling the syndication. This occurs so frequently and automatically that an assignment clause covering this situation should be inserted regardless of the original intent of the syndicating group.

Another concept that is often overlooked pertains to the restructuring of the specific nature and terms of the agreement. Most finalized purchase documents should include statements to the effect that the terms and conditions expressed in writing constitute the entire agreement and that any changes or conditions approved by both parties are valid only if they are in writing. This precludes the possibility that either party's rights can be waived by verbal agreements or tacit understandings subject to interpretation only through litigation.

Nothing in the purchase documents should be left to possible third-party interpretation, including such obvious, important concepts as

- a full and accurate description of the property and the contracting parties;
- the names and addresses of appropriate individuals to whom proper notices are to be given; and
- the complete time frame documentation for such things as removal of contingencies, providing title insurance, securing of financing, and date of closing.

Other considerations are the nature and terms of the escrow agreement categorically stating where the funds will be physically deposited. Many a contract has senselessly fallen apart due to the escrow not being established on a timely basis with an independent third party, as the contract documents specified.

## NEGOTIATING PREPAYMENT RIGHTS AND PENALTY CLAUSES

Syndicators often overlook the right or ability to make prepayment in whole or in part on any of the mortgage obligations when acquiring a property that carries seller/owner financing. Lack of such a provision can be extremely detrimental to the syndicate in that it can potentially prevent the selling or refinancing of a property at a later date if the new purchaser is not desirous of assuming the existing encumbrances. Most syndications are structured to take advantage of increasing property values where loan-to-value ratios widen as inflationary periods of time elapse. The lack of prepayment rights can cause serious hardships, especially in syndications oriented toward tax-shelter benefits where leverage adds substantially to the investors' after-tax yield. While the rules vary from one legal jurisdiction to another, it is a generally recognized concept that, if *no provision* in the documents specifically excludes prepayment of the mortgage, the purchaser/mortgagor of the property will have the right to prepay both interest and principal without penalty at any given point.

When a contract by its language specifically excludes prepayments, this provision is extremely difficult, and in many jurisdictions *impossible,* to walk away from. Straddled with a detrimental mortgage prepayment situation, it is conceivable that a syndicated holding can undergo significant devaluation, as it cannot be conveyed or re-encumbered at the sole discretion of the syndicator.

We recently purchased a site in the Southwest and constructed a 15,000-square-foot office complex that was financed through tax-free industrial revenue bonds. The seller had acquired the land with the majority of the financing being provided by the previous owner who had an extremely low tax base in the property. The mortgage encumbrance had a binding nonprepayment clause, which gave the prior owner's mortgage precedence over our lender's $1.5-million bond financing. This unacceptable situation required that substitute collateral be tendered and tied up for the duration of the owner's mortgage in order to assure that our bonds took prior position. The seller's motivation was obvious, as he had sold the property on an installment basis and would have incurred a substantial tax problem if the mortgage had been prepaid as it would have triggered a taxable gain on the outstanding mortgage balance. To make matters worse, the mortgage holder demanded and received a fee for consenting to the substitution of the collateral position.

## NEGOTIATING PROVISIONS OF OWNER FINANCING

Many real estate sellers find it convenient to provide the mortgage financing, as they have no immediate need for the majority of the sales proceeds, and if structured properly, this can generate substantial tax savings to the selling entity. Often, the use of owner financing coincides with the objectives of the syndicating entity if it is ample and not restrictive. Because the sellers or their advisors normally desire adequate protection for their first-mortgage encumbrance, many negotiations can result in severe limitations on additional financing that can be placed against a property. With the passage of time, additional funding may have to be injected into the syndicate's holdings, much of which might have to be raised through conventional debt financing. The syndicator needs to have realistic language negotiated and included in the seller-provided mortgage documents, permitting mortgage financing on the property either subordinate to or junior to the existing-owner financing. If the conventional leverage is to take lien priority over the owner financing, restrictions and limitations on the percentage of loan to value combining the conventional and owner encumbrances will obviously have to be negotiated with the seller in order to protect his or her security rights adequately.

When this situation prevails, documentation should be extensively detailed providing for a self-explanatory type of procedure in which the syndicator can automatically encumber the property without the seller's consent. Usually a mechanism is established whereby a fixed, predetermined upper limit of financing is structured, not to exceed a percentage of the appraised value or some similar independent yardstick. Unless the secondary or subsequent financing is specific and detailed as to the terms and conditions under which it may be used, many courts when litigating this provision will prevent the syndicator from obtaining the additional subordinated financing necessary to preserve the status or improve the developmental potential of the property. Again, close attention should be paid to prepayment penalties or privileges, especially if one can predict that substantial funds will be required at later dates. Normally, owner financing will produce mortgage constants considerably lower than those found in conventional mortgages. For this reason, syndications should make every effort to utilize this vehicle, if properly structured, whenever appropriate.

## NEGOTIATING IMPORTANT RELEASE PROVISIONS WITH OWNERS

Like the protections afforded in financing, any release documentation should be sufficiently detailed to be automatically effectuated, eliminating the need for the seller's approval each time a release is desired or contractually triggered. Favorable release provisions are imperative in land transactions and are equally important when apartments, office complexes, or other structures are purchased that might later be converted to condominiums or partially refinanced. The issue can become particularly sensitive when developments are phased or specific areas need to be released initially to test the market for conversion purposes.

Release provisions should be structured in such a way as to be equitable to all parties, providing the syndicator through the payment of predetermined sums a free and clear release of the portion of the property he or she desires to sell, convert, or otherwise encumber. These provisions should not jeopardize the seller's remaining position if portions of his or her land or improvements are released, and the remainder leaves the seller in an inequitable position.

Release provisions should also be structured so they become cumulative, especially where payments are made and releases are not exercised. The syndicator should protect him- or herself through documentation in order to convert his or her previous payments into tracts or holdings during subsequent periods, should the need arise.

When a transaction provides for seller-provided release provisions, the syndicator will want to be assured that all the documents are in escrow with a qualified title insurance company or another escrow agent where the appropriate instructions are well defined and automatic, needing no further interpretation by the various parties.

In addition to the release documentation, the parties must agree to execute any additional contractual agreements necessary for the orderly liquidation of the seller's encumbrances. For example, should a syndicate acquire an apartment building for eventual conversion to a condominium, the seller must initially acknowledge his or her awareness of this concept, since substantial portions of the designated common areas will have to be released prior to full payment of the seller's mortgage encumbrance. This can be complicated at the time of the sale of the first condominium unit, as the statutory requirements of the Homeowners Association will require an unencumbered asset in order to effectuate the conversion.

All release provisions should be predetermined by both parties in terms of minimum or maximum increments. Ground rules should be established for the size or the dollar amount of the releases, and a provision should also be included, if agreed upon, whereby collateral can be substituted for a cash payment in return for the unencumbered portions of the property. As cumbersome as substitution of collateral for cash can become, this provision can be extremely important under certain circumstances and provide tremendous flexibility to the syndicator.

## WRAPAROUND MORTGAGE FINANCING ADDS A NEW DIMENSION

Secondary financing is sometimes unavoidable in the syndicating process, since many properties need to have expedited closings or contain prepayment penalty clauses that do not permit a timely payoff of the mortgage or allow refinancing. Assumable mortgages generally have either high interest rates that make them noncallable from the lender's standpoint or submarket interest factors that make them attractive for assumption. If properly structured, wraparound financing can qualify as an installment sale, and many sellers are often willing to reduce the sale price substantially or to provide financing in excess of that found through conventional means because of the tax-deferred advantages.

To qualify as an installment sale, the amount by which the existing indebtedness, if assumed by the syndicate, exceeds the seller's depreciated basis is considered the taxable gain in the year of sale, when no recapture provisions are applicable. After adding this to the down payment the seller receives, one can then establish the taxable obligation for the first year. The remaining gain is declared and generally parallels the annual mortgage amortization schedules. From the syndicator's point of view, wraparound financing can provide extremely high loan-to-value ratios, especially if the conventional first mortgage is substantial in amount and the owner is not desirous of receiving the majority of his or her payments during the initial phases of the installment sale. Wraparound financing is often used on a short-term basis where the property has reached its near-term maximum potential cash flow or where the syndicator is ready to convert the holding to an alternative use. The syndicate then has the option to refinance the entire package and retrieve a majority of its equity contributions after a relatively short holding period.

Wraparounds can have pitfalls also, as we recently found out when we attempted to prepay a subordinated second mortgage on a commercial building. In the process we obligated ourselves for a substantial fee and had to cross-collateralize the second mortgage with a bank certificate of deposit (CD) in order to obtain a release, as the seller was not willing to accelerate his taxable obligation on this installment sale.

Many pitfalls can surface and must be avoided in structuring wraparound financing, particularly where restrictive covenants are found in the existing conventional first mortgages. Inclusions such as prepayment penalties, acceleration clauses, and detrimental release provisions must be taken into account so that they will dovetail with the terms and conditions of the second-position seller-provided wraparound financing. Obviously, the existing conventional mortgage cannot expire or balloon prior to the wraparound seller's mortgage, since this would create a situation in which the second mortgage would have to be expunged before any additional first-mortgage financing could be structured against the property, unless advance provisions were made otherwise. Proper escrow instructions also need to be in place, as they pertain to the wraparound seller's mortgage, insuring that the seller will make adequate payments on the existing first mortgage in a timely fashion.

As a general rule, all encumbrances in a wraparound mortgage situation should track or parallel each other in all respects pertaining to

- amortization;
- prepayment penalties;
- release provisions;
- required or stipulated loan-to-value ratios;
- acceleration clauses; and
- due-on-sale provisions.

Close coordination between all existing financial liens is necessary in order that a provision in one mortgage does not arbitrarily trigger a default in the other.

In spite of the multitude of potential problem areas we have discussed and the remedial contractual provisions that can prevent them, many syndicators commit the cardinal sin of acquiring complicated investment properties by utilizing "standard contracts" or "simplified forms" provided by real estate brokers. These documents provide only the minimum of conditions and essentials, and the syndicator who uses them without great care and discrimination is not earning his or her keep.

Negotiating is a complex process in which the various needs of the buying and selling entities are carefully balanced. Syndicators should remain ever cognizant of the fact that they are usually well compensated for the efforts they make in the negotiation process. The kinds of precautionary steps syndicators take in negotiating are similar to those they must follow in qualifying their investors. As we will discover in the next chapter, the impetuous entrepreneur can expect as little success in choosing the appropriate investing partners as he or she finds at the bargaining or negotiating table.

# 5

# Qualifying Investors for Syndications

Investment suitability standards protect the investors and syndicators alike. As critical as they are in ensuring the success of most real estate developments, they are consistently ignored, underexplained, and often misunderstood.

The governing regulatory bodies require that formal documents be presented and complied with prior to an investor being qualified to join a syndication. Satisfying these requirements consists of answering certain questions and meeting the minimum standards pertaining to one's financial net worth. This is mandatory for the purpose of establishing whether a given investor can adequately afford to shoulder the risk of a potential loss in a given syndication. Compliance is often as easy as it is important. In fact, a prudent syndicator attentive to protecting his or her reputation must sometimes refuse to qualify certain investors in order to meet the minimum suitability requirements. Should such an investor have to withdraw from the syndication for financial reasons, the promoter might have to face unnecessary ill will and potentially detrimental actions from his or her remaining partners.

Underexplanation of the potential risk factors and lack of diligence in meeting the investor-suitability standards are obviously a short-sighted, double-edged approach to getting a syndication off the ground. Many syndicators are overly cautious in their efforts at legal compliance, with the result that they scare off prospective investors by describing the potential risks in negative, legalistic terms without simultaneously conveying the underlying potential for a realistic return. Obviously, a balance is needed and striking that middle ground is the result of experience and market exposure to the investors' needs combined with compassion for the problems that passive investors encounter in comprehending relatively sophisticated offering documents.

The simplest way to realistically relate the risk element involved or associated with syndicated real estate is *not* through the complex financial projections contained in the syndication documents but rather by utilizing a simplified narrative approach basically outlining the

- general history of the project;
- anticipated return on equity;
- current market conditions for the investment; and
- prior track record and managerial ability of the syndicating entity.

Stressing the syndicator's past successes invariably leads to the explanation of experiences with similar properties developed in prior offerings involving comparable income and expense ratios. Introducing this element of comparison adequately demonstrates the most direct and effective means we have found to provide investors with a basis of judging whether or not they can relate to a given syndicated investment and if, in fact, it is suitable for them.

## ESTABLISHING THE SUITABILITY OF INVESTORS

The matter of suitability standards in most syndication documents is prefaced by negatively required explanation. The following language is somewhat typical in most offerings:

> An investment in the offering involves a high degree of risk, with no public resale market for the investment units, and investors could be subject to substantial and adverse tax consequences in the event that the IRS successfully challenges the partnership deductions. Further notice is given that the sale or disposition of shares requires prior written consent of all the managing partners and that the investment is suitable only for persons of adequate financial means who have no immediate need for liquidity of their invested capital.

The general partner must then prepare a questionnaire to determine whether the prospective investor meets the net worth and income requirements for the syndication. The items contained in this document are substantially as follows:

- name and social security number;
- business or residential address and telephone number;
- state of residence and registry of vote;
- state in which investor pays income taxes;
- present age and occupation of the investor;
- method for filing last year's personal income tax return;
- gross and net taxable income reported during the prior year;
- prior year tax bracket for the potential investor (combined federal and state); and
- estimated gross and taxable income for the current year.

In addition, a more formalized aspect of the questionnaire elicits the following information:

- estimated net worth exclusive of personal residence;
- estimated liquid assets;
- outline of the investor's educational background;
- description of occupational positions held over the last ten years;
- current tax-shelter investment holdings, year(s) purchased and the amount of investment;
- statement of securities purchased in reliance on nonpublic offering exemptions; and
- list of investments in real estate limited partnerships not covered in the foregoing items.

A supplementary catch-all portion asks the investor to provide whatever additional information the syndicator may need to determine whether the individual is suitable for the type of investment being offered. Its basic purpose is to delineate the abilities of the investor to absorb the substantial risks associated with a nonliquid speculative type of real estate investment.

We are currently involved in an income oriented condominium syndication where five investors each contributed $50,000. One of the limited partners borrowed the $50,000 from a lending institution on an unsecured basis, making representations that the bank loan would be fully repaid within a 12-month period. The bank required that the limited partner repay the loan prior to partnership funds being available for distribution to the limited partners, causing considerable friction within the partnership. Distribution of funds to limited partners in all but a few instances has to be uniform, and one investor cannot be singled out for repayment without an equal amount going to the remaining individuals.

The details pertaining to the mechanics of the documents relating to the investor-suitability standards are contained in Chapter 17, where a prototype private-placement circular is provided.

## MATCHING THE INVESTORS WITH THE OFFERING

Exclusive dependence on the required legal documentation and the full-disclosure provisions of the securities laws is not the easiest approach to dealing with your investing partners from a marketing viewpoint. The preferred method is to establish a match between the investment property and the potential contributor's objectives. This can be accomplished through a multitude of simplified vehicles.

The most logical approach to meeting your investors' objectives is to diversify the offering by mixing several properties, thereby reducing the overall exposure should any one of them fail to meet the syndication's performance expectations. With such a diversified offering, one can offer a true balance between the potential risk and return, thereby providing the safety and suitability needed or required for unsophisticated investors. The apparent disadvantage of this approach lies in the

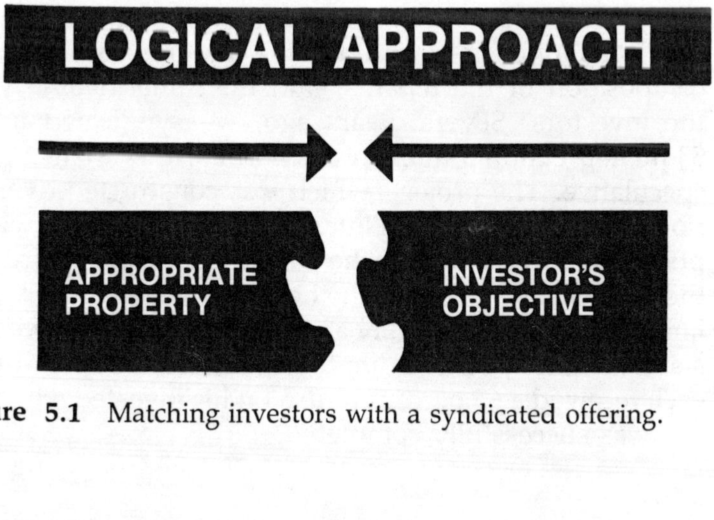


**Figure 5.1** Matching investors with a syndicated offering.

reality that a syndicator often cannot maximize the potential yield when he or she has the chance to capitalize on it.

Another means of balancing risk and return is to acquire properties in diversified geographic areas showing rapid or above-average appreciation. The cumulative effect of sustained growth leads to appreciation in real estate values, and such escalated values combined with adequate leverage leave ample margin for error. By acquiring properties in rapidly appreciating areas, the syndicator can afford to stub his or her toe occasionally if the syndicator and his or her investors were presented with a reasonable or logical alternative.

A diversified product mixture is also effective in conforming to the required investor-suitability standards. Here the syndicator can structure relatively conservative investments in one offering and alternatively provide a more speculative vehicle, thereby giving investors a well-defined choice. If the more speculative offering fails to materialize, the syndicator is somewhat insulated by the fact that his or her investors were presented with a reasonable or logical alternative.

Careful application of the appropriate amount of leverage is another way the syndicator can protect his or her flanks. Overencumbering a property frequently proves catastrophic to a syndicate caught up in uncontrollable adverse economic conditions, as do some of the more speculative techniques used in mortgage financing. In seeking leverage, the syndicator should restrict him- or herself to fixed-rate mortgages, avoiding short-term balloon payments. As a rule of thumb, leveraging in the amount of 70 percent to 80 percent of loan to value is considered fairly speculative. Most syndicates should usually be in the 50 percent to 60 percent range, depending upon the stability and predictability of the cash flow, the multiple uses of the structure, the composition of the tenants, and the initial overall yield desired by the investors. Several years ago, we syndicated and developed a $3-million condominium project where the financing was extremely speculative. The project, which was constructed over a two-year period, carried construction interest rates that floated two points over the prime rate. Even though the construction costs were relatively fixed, the market absorption for the houses was not entirely predictable. The limited partners were fully aware of the risks and were offered a substantial equity position due to the uncertainties. In the final analysis, each received a 65 percent return on his invested equity when the project was successfully completed.

## PROTECTING THE INVESTORS BY ACQUIRING QUALITY PROPERTIES

"In" properties are not faddish investments. To the contrary, they are projects appropriate to a given market place that are and will foreseeably remain in high demand. These investments often carry substantially lower yields than those in lesser favor and can be liquidated in relatively short periods of time if they fail to meet syndication requirements. For example, apartments and motels are usually worthwhile investments in broad-based, viable markets, since passive investors can readily understand that the rental rates in these ventures can be raised substantially and frequently over time due to the nature of the short-term occupancy arrangements. In general, special-purpose buildings can be risky investments in markets that are not substantially proven or where management is inadequate. Single-purpose buildings such as fast-food restaurants and other related structures can generate problems when retail sales do not materialize, as they can remain vacant for extended periods of time because of the limited number of potential tenants.

Investors are ill served when a syndicator attempts to out-leverage his or her competition or when he or she acquires a property with a higher cost factor or greater operating expenses than competing projects within the immediate marketing area. An offering acquired under these conditions will not have a break-even rental point similar to the competition's if the market becomes overcompetitive. Problems can be compounded when the property is locked into long-term leases without adequate protection against rising operating expenses.

Under such conditions, overleveraged projects and those structured with high break-even levels can pose special problems for the syndicator, as additional funds are frequently needed for operating capital, loan reductions, or for improvements to enhance the marketing potential. Most unsophisticated individuals establish investment objectives involving fixed rates of return, however unrealistic they may be in the market place. A project that requires additional investor funds reduces its attractiveness to the extent that it substantially modifies that expected rate of return.

In this connection, a cushion should always be structured into any real estate syndication, even if it requires retaining a portion of the investors' equity in a rainy-day account for potential emergencies. If the project is soundly conceived, well managed and located, this margin can normally, under conservative conditions, be accomplished with additional financial leverage, using part of the investors' contingency funds as a cushion against the additional debt-service requirement.

While "in" properties may vary from one market place to another, certain others have a tendency to rise and fall regularly with the economic cycles or the lack of attendant management expertise and are definitely not suitable as syndicated holdings. Any single-purpose structure or development is usually considered overspeculative, as are resorts, second-home projects, and specialized manufacturing plants, especially under these conditions. Such developments tend to fluctuate widely in value with local conditions or with the national economic picture.

We are currently in the process of completing a 160-unit motel in which 100 percent financing was obtained that sufficiently covers not only the acquisition and construction, but the potential start-up operating deficits. We have received a municipal inducement resolution to provide tax-free industrial revenue bonds. Due to the current climate in Congress, however, it is conceivable that these bonds will not be sold with a tax-free status. If, in fact, the $4 million in tax-free bonds are not funded, our partnership will form a syndication, bringing in and allocating to the various limited partners the tax and appreciation benefits, as this becomes an extremely leveraged investment where a majority if not all of the cash flow is absorbed by the debt-service requirement if the tax-free status is not achieved.

## CONVEYING THE RISK-AND-REWARD BENEFITS OF A SYNDICATION

Three major items that affect all real estate syndications should always be advanced forcefully and up front to the investors, as follows:

1. appreciation;
2. leverage; and
3. the potential tax benefits.

These three key factors or a combination of them will substantially determine the return on one's investment.

Although appreciation is not realized or fully calculable until the property is sold, it can account for a major portion of the overall return on investment, especially if properties are acquired in rapidly

**Figure 5.2** Risks and rewards of a syndication determining a return on investment.

appreciating areas and leverage supported by sophisticated techniques is used. This appreciation factor is closely aligned or related to leverage, a concept that passive investors often have difficulty comprehending.

The greater the degree to which a project is leveraged, the larger the real estate holding one can potentially acquire given the fixed amount of the investor's equity dollars. Passive or unsophisticated investors often fail to understand what leverage does for an investment and should be provided with a careful explanation that it not only increases the potential appreciation but also generates substantial tax-shelter benefits. Even more important, they must realize that additional mortgage financing or equity contributions at some point during the holding period of the asset might be needed. While exposing this possibility might result in the loss of some potential investors in a syndication, realistic presentations are best served when marginal investors are excluded.

Many syndications tend to emphasize the tax-shelter aspects of real estate investments, since this provides an immediate after-tax cash return to investors in high-tax-bracket situations. Tax shelter should not be considered a side benefit of real estate syndications closely tied only to the applied leverage techniques, as its effect on yield can be counted on and in most instances accurately predicted. We are currently constructing a $12.5-million apartment complex in the Southwest, which will be syndicated prior to completion. The $9.5-million first mortgage will consume the cash flow in its entirety during the initial years. The depreciation benefits alone amount to almost three quarters of a million dollars annually, and given the long-term appreciation potential, we are confident that the full $3-million equity position will be successfully syndicated without providing any initial cash flow to the investors.

Finally, it is important to establish that your investors know that a long-term view of investment in real estate is essential. Comparable to stock market prices, real estate values rise and fall depending upon the economy, current interest rates, or market conditions of supply and demand. When the syndicator has complete control over the day-to-day management of the asset and the unobstructed ability to sell it at what is deemed the appropriate time, many of the arguments for lack of liquidity associated with real estate syndications can be eliminated or diffused.

## HOW INVESTORS ACCEPT THE FINANCIAL AND EMOTIONAL RISKS

Convincing investors to fully disclose their income and net worth in order to qualify according to securities regulations need not necessarily be traumatic. Understanding the *realities* of potential loss of income or reduction of net worth is quite another matter and one that the syndicator cannot stress strongly enough when he or she unequivocally knows that a potential investor cannot afford to lose a third, a half, or even all of his or her invested funds. Individuals in the upper tax brackets literally suffer less, since any losses they incur will be offset by tax deductions, shifting a substantial portion of the pain to Uncle Sam.

When investors are informed or educated to the fact that much of the return on their investment in the early years of a real estate syndication is generated from tax-shelter benefits and corresponding use of leverage, they will be better equipped to accept the financial and emotional risks inherent in any real estate syndicated investments over which they have little control. The emotional factors related to passive investments often surface and are closely parallel or aligned to the welfare of the economy in general. During periods of tight money and high interest rates, many investors develop financial liquidity problems. Syndications are also likely to require additional funds at the same time and for exactly the same underlying reasons. This correlation must be explained simply and adequately early in the life of the proposed syndication to preclude the emotional reactions inherent to the risk factors associated with a downturn in economic conditions.

We normally relate to investors not so much in terms of what their current net worth or income is, but what it would be if they lost their entire investment in the syndicated real estate venture. Forcing investors to look at or analyze their personal financial conditions should the venture fail or falter is the surest method of conditioning their emotions when financial crises arise.

Most individuals have limited experiences with real estate investments, which they usually relate to only in terms of their personal residences. They generally cannot foresee the day when their homes and the equity established in these structures could completely evaporate. This naive complacency carries over into investment real estate where enormous sums are involved and the effects can be cumulative. Most syndications rely exclusively on the income generated from the venture to cover the leveraged portion of the debt. When income fails or is reduced substantially, a strong potential for foreclosure exists. This concept must always be conveyed realistically to your potential investors, especially to those whose experience is limited to home ownership or real estate holdings acquired through inheritance.

## HOW DIFFERENT INVESTOR OBJECTIVES CAN CREATE COMPLICATIONS

Unless all the investors in a syndication are equally matched as to tax brackets, net worth, and income generated, a strong possibility exists that they will establish varying investment objectives during the life of a real estate syndication. Normally, two forceful groups will tend to emerge:

1. those desiring stability and predictability of a cash return on investment; and
2. those seeking tax-shelter benefits combined with long-term appreciation potential.

Sometimes these two groups can be combined; however, it usually is not expedient to commence a syndication with investors having dissimilar objectives, since the initial disparity can ultimately evolve into serious and potentially irreconcilable conflicts of interest.

A syndication's goals should be an either/or proposition, and potential investors should be emphatically informed whether a cash-flow presentation or a tax-shelter and appreciation proposition is being emphasized. The underlying reasoning is that tax shelters tend to be exhausted early in the life of a syndication, whereas appreciation and equity build-up tend to materialize at later dates. Whatever timetable a general partner assigns for the eventual disposition of the asset will result in discontent among one group or the other when common goals are not shared equally.

Lack of compatibility among investors also often occurs, as some groups are more willing to take or absorb risks than others. The more venturesome are usually those seeking tax-shelter benefits and appreciation. Since they are better able to afford losses and are oriented toward utilizing the desirable tax-shelter benefits, they are similarly less reluctant to make infusions of additional cash at later dates if projects do not meet their initial financial goals or objectives.

Investors' gambling instincts also are reflected in the correlation that usually exists between their suitability for risk and the size of their investment. Some are inclined to put substantial funds into one or two large projects, while others, more conservative by nature, prefer to put smaller amounts into a variety of offerings as a potential hedge against a complete and unrecoverable disaster. This choice also reflects the investors' awareness of the implications of a financial disaster on their annual income and net-worth statements or of their realization that a return on their investment could be distributed on a basis that was not contemplated in the scheme of the original syndication.

An investor's willingness to assume risks and to indulge or provoke one's speculative instinct is not simply a factor reflecting an individual's financial security. One's conservatism generally increases with age, and this adds yet another dimension to the complications of choosing compatible investment partners. We have historically found that one needs to accumulate a group of investors who are approximately in the same age and income brackets.

As illustration of this truism about age, we have normally found that

- middle-aged professional people incline toward investments with equity build-up, long-term appreciation, and tax-shelter benefits; whereas
- older investors need or desire investments with a substantial, strong, and predictable cash flow.

The trick to avoiding a polarization of interests over the span of a syndication's life lies in the homogeneity of investing partners from the beginning. Chapter 14 provides a complete description of all the language that is applicable to investor suitability standards. Several areas are worth repeating due to the overall ramifications they have regarding syndicators and investors alike, and these are highlighted in the following pages.

## TYPICAL LANGUAGE PERTAINING TO ANALYZING AN INVESTMENT

All private-offering prospectuses should contain language similar to the following as a general explanation of investors' suitability standards. Typical language found in many private-placement circulars can be summarized as follows:

This Offering is intended to be made as a private placement, pursuant to Section 4(2) of the Securities Act of 1933 and Rule 146 promulgated thereunder (i.e., "a sale, not involving a public distribution"). Accordingly, the Units are offered only to persons who, prior to making such offer, the General Partner has reasonable grounds to believe, and believes, either have such knowledge and experience in financial and business matters that they are capable of evaluating the merits and risks of the investment, or are able to bear the economic risk of loss of the investment. Furthermore, prior to making any sales hereunder, the General Partner will determine, after making reasonable inquiry, that either:

(i) the offeree has such knowledge and experience in financial and business matters that he or she is capable of evaluating the merits and risks of the investment, and, in addition, that the offeree is able to bear the economic risk of loss of the investment; or

(ii) the offeree and his or her offeree representatives, together, have such knowledge and experience in financial and business matters that they are capable of evaluating the merits and risks of this investment and, in addition, that the offeree is able to bear the economic risk of loss.

## APPROPRIATE LANGUAGE FOR NET-WORTH AND TAXABLE-INCOME REQUIREMENTS

The following is typical of the language used in private-offering prospectuses to describe the financial status required of a potential investor:

An investment in the Partnership will involve a *high degree of risk* and will be illiquid. The financial benefit, if any, derived from an investment herein will depend to a large degree on the income tax bracket of the purchaser. The partnership will not sell a Unit(s) to any investor unless he represents, among other things, that he has: (i) adequate means of providing for his current needs and reasonably anticipated future needs and contingencies, (ii) no need for liquidity with respect to this investment, (iii) an investment net worth (net worth exclusive of homes, home furnishings and personal automobiles) of at least $______ and (iv) has in 19--, taxable income (exclusive of losses for tax purposes from "tax shelter investments") of $______, some portion of which was subject to *combined* federal, state and local income taxes at a rate of 50% or more.

Investment in the Partnership is not recommended for investors who are unable to hold their Unit(s) for an indefinite period of time and who cannot afford a complete loss of their investment or for investors who do not anticipate taxable income, some portion of which will be taxed at the rate of 50% or more for at least the next three years.

The suitability standards set forth above represent minimum suitability requirements for investors, and the satisfaction of such standards by a prospective investor does not necessarily mean that the Units are a suitable investment for him.

We are currently in the process of trying to rectify a legal settlement for a limited partner whose share in a 12-acre speculative land venture was consented to and pledged as collateral for a bank loan far in excess of the value of his partnership interest. The individual defaulted on his loan obligation, and the partnership agreement calls for the general partners to place a value on that limited partnership share within 12 months after notification and to compensate the affected party for his or her market interest over a ten-year period. This type of situation not only strains partnership finances, but also creates unneeded complications within syndications.

## RESALABILITY, TRANSFERABILITY, AND LIQUID ASSETS LANGUAGE

An investor's comprehension and responsibility are probed in the private-placement offering prospectuses stating that prior to the purchase of a Unit, each prospective investor represents that he or she meets each of the following requirements that:

- his or her commitment to all real estate investments is reasonable in relation to his or her net worth;

- he or she has the requisite knowledge or relies upon the advice of his or her own counsel, accountants, business advisors, or offeree representative with regard to the tax and other considerations involved in making such an investment;
- he or she is acquiring Unit(s) for his or her own account, for investment and not with a view to resale or distribution;
- he or she meets the suitability standards set forth on the preceding pages;
- he or she has no reason to anticipate any change in personal circumstances, financial or otherwise, that may cause or require any sale or distribution of his or her Unit(s);
- he or she anticipates recognition of income from other sources during the period when contributions are required under the Partnership Agreement, at a level that will enable him or her to utilize losses allocated to him or her during each year of such period in reduction of taxable income, of which some portion would otherwise be subject to combined federal, state, and local income taxes at a rate not less than 50 percent;
- he or she is familiar with the nature of and risk attending investments in real estate securities and has determined independently or on the basis of consultation with business and tax advisors or another appropriate offeree representative that the purchase of the Unit(s) is consistent with his or her investment objectives and income prospects;
- he or she is aware that no trading market for the Unit(s) will exist at any time and will at no time be freely transferable or transferable without potential adverse tax consequences; and
- he or she realizes that, since the Unit(s) cannot be readily transferred, he or she may not readily liquidate his or her investment for an indefinite period of time.

A prospective investor, therefore, must not purchase a Unit(s) unless he or she has sufficient liquid assets to assure him- or herself that such purchase will cause him or her no undue financial difficulties.

## INSERTABLE LANGUAGE FOR SUITABILITY OF INVESTOR STANDARDS

Further precautions about suitability are offered in the following terms in typical private-placement offering prospectuses:

Investment in Units involves a high degree of risk. There will not be any public market for Units, and sale or other disposition may result in substantial adverse tax consequences to the transferor and, in certain cases, to all partners. Also, sale or other disposition requires prior written consent of all partners, which consent may not be forthcoming. Accordingly, investment in Units is suitable only for persons of adequate financial means who have no need for liquidity with respect to their investment. Further, it is anticipated that the early years of the partnership's operations will produce operating loss deductions that may, under present law, be applied against other income of the investors. Only persons whose income is subject to the highest rates of income taxation will derive the full economic benefit of such deductions.

Units will be sold only to persons who represent in writing that they have a net worth (exclusive of homes, home furnishing and automobiles) in excess of $______ and a net income for the current year (before taking into account the effect of a proposed acquisition of Units) of $______, some portion of which is subject to taxation at a combined federal, state and local income tax rate of at least 50%.

Further, units will only be offered for sale to persons who the placement agents have reasonable grounds to believe, and believe, are suitable investors. The agents will request that prospective investors and/or their offeree representatives complete an offeree questionnaire and may request that such persons furnish other information. The General Partner retains the right to accept or reject subscriptions and to ascertain whether or not the persons subscribing are suitable.

## IN THE FINAL ANALYSIS

Few experienced syndicators will deny that conforming with securities laws takes much of the joy out of inventive real estate offerings, and most think of regulatory agencies as bureaucracies designed to make life miserable by squeezing the juice out of the entrepreneurial orange. None will deny that complaints about negative legalese and technicalities of enforcement establish a basis for camaraderie even among rival syndicators.

On balance, we have seen in this chapter that not all regulations are negative and detrimental. Those concerning investor qualifications are soundly based on common sense and mutual protection of both investor and syndicator. The intent of the law is best served when full confidence exists between the syndicator and his or her potential investor, and this same condition is essential to effective syndication management.

In the following chapter on merchandising, we will concern ourselves primarily with third-party marketing of syndications, in which the syndicator engages a broker or agent to act on his or her behalf in soliciting the investors. As we shall visualize, this has the effect of depersonalizing the relationship between the general and limited partners. Similarly, the lack of active involvement in merchandising can sometimes leave one less aware of the potential shortcomings in meeting the investor suitability standards.

# 6

# Merchandising Real Estate Syndicated Investments

Depending on the amount to be raised, the allocated time frame, and the number of potential investors to be attracted, the syndicator has to make a decision as to

- whether the offering can be accomplished on a private or a public basis;
- whether the syndication will be offered to investors on an intrastate or interstate basis; and
- who is best equipped to accomplish these goals.

These three factors make marketing a real estate syndication substantially different from the normal selling of investment properties. They also subject a transaction to more complex securities regulation, including the various exemptions and rules for interstate and intrastate offerings that will be detailed more fully in Chapter 14.

Furthermore, certain transactions must be handled with extreme caution if they are to unconditionally qualify as real estate investments, excluded from potentially disadvantageous securities regulations. Examples of these *borderline categories* include

- condominiums or cooperative housing;
- real estate investment trust shares;

- limited partnerships with totally inactive investors;
- sale-leaseback transactions; and
- in some instances, mortgage financing vehicles.

How these categories of investments are treated under securities laws depends upon the products and the methods of merchandising. Promoting these transactions means conveying the investment concepts in legal terms acceptable under the securities laws and yet explaining them in a simplified manner so that your potential investors can fully comprehend their ramifications.

**BORDERLINE CATEGORIES**

1. CONDOMINIUMS
2. REAL ESTATE INVESTMENT TRUST SHARES
3. LIMITED PARTNERSHIPS
4. SALE-LEASEBACK TRANSACTIONS
5. MORTGAGE FINANCING VEHICLES

**Figure 6.1** Real estate transactions subject to securities regulations.

## WHY THE REPUTATION OF THE SYNDICATOR IS IMPORTANT

The more complex a syndication becomes, the more negatively it must be described to comply with the regulations of full disclosure. Extremely detrimental connotations tend to dissuade potential investors. The one constant and positive factor that these offerings have is that the operating track record of the syndicator can usually be advanced on a fairly straightforward and positive basis.

Most minor syndications require little more than the efforts of an unsophisticated individual contracting for a specific property subject to obtaining financing and structuring a limited amount of equity prior to closing. These simplified syndications are not, however, in the majority. Most achieve their full potential only after a prolonged period of utilizing highly skilled financing and ongoing management techniques. Management is always complemented by such critical activities as

- timing the acquisition properly;
- disposing of it most advantageously; and
- maximizing net income and tax deductions during the holding period.

Little wonder that newcomers to the field must experience the frustrations and limitations of the learning curve, whereas experienced developers and syndicators can command substantial fees and equity positions solely attributed to their prior performances.

Successful syndicators merchandise real estate holdings in much the same manner as brokers sell corporate stocks, often without ever having to provide more than a well-documented pro forma income and operating statement combined with a brief description of the property and a broad outline of the partnership's investment objective. Many individuals can convincingly command syndicated compensation relating to the following four categories:

1. income derived form syndication fees;
2. substantial and ongoing management fees;
3. equity interests in the real estate asset; and
4. brokerage fees upon dissolution of the partnership.

Even when the terms and conditions of an offering are extremely favorable, many investors will decline to participate in a project where the syndicating entity is virtually unknown. This is not surprising when one considers that few investors who acquire common stocks ever visit the corporate headquarters, interview top management, or scrutinize profit-and loss figures. At the other end of the spectrum, many large, publicly held syndications are eagerly sought out by investors in spite of the substantial portions of the investor's equity they retain as

- syndication fees, sometimes as high as 15 percent of the funds generated;
- locked in, long-term, extremely lucrative management fees; and
- back-end real estate commissions.

We recently completed a syndication on a luxury hotel condominium venture with an existing and established operating entity. It was relatively easy to generate the investors for this project, as the hotel had an impressive and substantial guest list that enabled us to presell a majority of the newly developed units. This close association with a well-known viable entity enabled us to substantially prearrange the marketing of the $25,000 limited-partnership shares.

## WHY MERCHANDISING REAL ESTATE SYNDICATIONS IS UNIQUE

In real estate syndications, the marketing entity is basically offering its successful prior experiences. The property itself can oftentimes be secondary in importance to this image of success. A participant in a syndicate does not normally consider him- or herself as one who takes an active investment role in the specific real estate holding; these passive investors generally rely exclusively on the ability and track record of the syndicator, based upon the project's financial projections and the managerial capabilities of the syndicating entity.

A complete package is therefore being merchandised to the investors who are uninvolved and often uninformed of the decision-making process. Relatively few investors make the time available or have the ability to review in depth the figures that are presented to them by a prestigious syndicator. It is inherently redundant for an unsophisticated individual to attempt to analyze an investment package presented by a sophisticated syndicating entity. To describe the situation even more succinctly, a potential investor will probably decline a syndicated offering if it becomes imperative for this individual or his or her advisors to spend considerable time analyzing the economics of the offering. Doing so would demonstrate his or her lack of confidence in the syndicating entity. We recently completed a $250,000 offering consisting of five shares at $50,000 per share on a 146-acre tract of land, to be subdivided into a combination of single-family lots and condominium units. The investors required very little in-depth information and in fact substantially less than was presented to the interim lender, as their general awareness of the merits of the project, combined with our marketing expertise in prior ventures, was sufficient evidence for them to commit their investment funds.

In an earlier chapter, we described the eye contact aspect so prevalent at the simplest level of limited partnerships formed to develop a specific property. We are now concerned with the other side of the coin, the requisites of success that compel an investor to participate in a strictly "hands-off" syndication. In projecting such an image of success, a syndicator is well advised to remove him- or herself from the menial activity of orchestrating his or her own marketing efforts.

## WHEN TO USE AN OUTSIDE INDEPENDENT SALES FORCE

Among the licensed, limited or full securities dealers with independent sales organizations in which the syndicator could possibly engage in marketing his or her prospective offerings are

- diversified real estate brokerage firms with securities licenses; or
- independent professional investment securities marketing firms specializing in private or public placement offerings.

Either of these entities is capable of merchandising syndication packages on either a *best-efforts* basis or through *guaranteed-purchase* arrangements at a predetermined wholesale price that is then marked up to a retail level generating a commission to the organization's marketing staff. The obvious advantages of utilizing an outside sales force is that this vehicle takes a substantial amount of the marketing time and effort out of the offering, placing the fund-raising aspect under the control of full-time professional people with established sales teams who are constantly looking for more product to sell.

Utilizing independent marketing organizations also has several inherent *disadvantages:*

- An outside marketing program can often cost as much as 5 percent to 10 percent over the in-house efforts.
- The syndicator can lose a degree of control over the salespeople's representations and the corresponding pricing by using an independent wholesaler.
- Depending upon how it is structured, many wholesalers command a large percentage of the funds raised without proportionately sharing in the risk of a marketing failure.

Needless to say, a best-efforts transaction should be marketed and priced quite differently from a proposal where a guaranteed amount of the proceeds is contractually committed to.

The decision to develop an in-house sales force or to concentrate the marketing efforts in the hands of a wholesaler rests ultimately on the level of activity. If a significant number of projects are generated over a predetermined period of time, the syndicator will have a consistent inventory to maintain a cost-effective sales force. If, on the other hand, one anticipates a limited and inconsistent inventory, marketing by an independent wholesaler is usually the more attractive alternative.

## HOW TO CONVEY PROJECTIONS OF INCOME AND APPRECIATION

The full-disclosure provisions outlined in Chapter 16 can complicate a syndicator's efforts to convey to the average investor a proper sense of a respectable return on his or her investment. Complying with these legal technicalities often results in communications loaded with negative connotations. Many of the values created in real estate syndications relate to the creative tax benefits derived early in the investment, combined with the potential for increased future value generated through the inflation process. Both of these somewhat artificially calculated investment advantages are the direct offshoots of a high degree of financial leverage carefully determined or weighed by the syndicator and his or her advisors. Leverage can have a detrimental effect when

- the initial tax benefits are challenged by the IRS;
- challenged tax deductions are retroactively applied; and
- appreciation fails to materialize as a consequence.

For these underlying reasons, presentations made to one's passive investors must be conservative in nature or must be fully documented by well-respected accountants.

Certified public accountants can be of tremendous advantage to a syndicator, especially when one is building a reputation for success. Many accountants are delighted at the opportunity to provide supplemental exhibits in the documentation designed for potential investors. Equipped by training and experience to include appropriate disclaimers with their projections of income, appreciation, and anticipated tax deductions, they lend valuable credibility to an offering prospectus as independent third parties. Furthermore, their input tends to

- maximize the projections of tax and appreciation consequences; and
- substantiate one's pro forma figures relating to rates of return.

We recently structured a syndication on a large apartment project located in the Sunbelt in which the projections, if they were off by as much as 5 percent, could have meant a reduction of the syndicate's income well in excess of a quarter of a million dollars per annum. By utilizing one of the Big Eight accounting firms, we were able to present the investors with the projections that were accurately portrayed.

The effect of variations in projected rates of return is cumulative and can show enormous deviations over extended periods of time. If only to substantiate these projections independently, a certified public accountant performs a valuable function as the syndication plans and pro formas are formulated.

The more sophisticated investors have come to disregard many of the disclaimers found in these typical private-placement memoranda or public offerings relating to such areas as

- lack of a public resale market;
- stated investment risk factors;
- general partners' conflicts of interest;
- required investor suitability standards;
- fiduciary responsibilities of the syndicator; and
- lack of operating history for the project.

In the opinion of many, securities laws or regulations have a tendency to overemphasize the presentation with excess negation. Scrutinizing these memoranda for these individuals is analogous to reading and analyzing corporate annual reports of publicly held companies by ignoring the footnotes and standard disclaimer clauses. If the foregoing smacks of sour grapes, the bottom-line concept is that there is, without exception, no valid excuse for providing *unrealistic* projections of income, tax losses, and potential appreciation.

## THE IMPORTANCE OF TAX SHELTER OPINIONS

As real estate syndications increase in number and monetary volume, their promoters are finding it important, especially in sophisticated presentations, to include a tax-shelter opinion from a qualified independent tax practitioner. Armed with this supporting documentation, one's syndication generally takes on a more optimistic tone, especially in light of the current detrimental tax legislation expanded on in Chapter 18. These tax opinions take on a special importance in offerings that initially generate only tax-shelter benefits and are devoid of positive cash-flow features from operations. Practitioners who are asked to render these tax-shelter opinions must do so in accordance with the provisions found in the Treasury Department's Circular 230. This circular was originally issued in 1980, modified in 1982, and most likely will receive further structural changes in the not-too-distant future.

Treasury Department Circular 230 applies to opinions rendered exclusively on or about tax-sheltered investments, the recognized definition being that these syndicated offerings have significant advantages to the investors, offering either

- deductions in excess of income; or
- credits in excess of the tax liability.

In an offering where tax losses or credits do not exceed the taxable income of the syndication, real estate projects are excluded from Circular 230. A real estate tax-shelter opinion presents advice relating to the federal tax aspects of a tax-shelter vehicle, as it

- appears or is referred to in the public offering or the private placement memorandum; or
- is directed to individuals involved in a syndication other than the tax expert's exclusive clients.

In order to meet the minimum standards under Treasury Department Circular No. 230, the individual rendering the tax-shelter opinion *must provide* the following:

- an adequate statement that all material facts are complete and accurately presented;
- a statement that the appropriate tax laws relate to the actual conditions of the offering;
- a statement that all material federal tax issues, including those having an impact on the investors, must be disclosed as well as all potential penalties and interest charges that could or might be assessed against the investors;
- an overall evaluation stating that the material *tax benefits* of the offering *are* or are *are not* likely to be realized; and
- for each material tax issue at stake, an opinion as to whether the investor will or will not prevail, or in the alternative, will or will not give sufficient reasons for the practitioner's failure to provide an adequate opinion.

In addition, the individual advancing the tax-shelter advice must state that his or her opinion is accurately presented in the offering materials. In many instances several tax-shelter opinions are given, depending upon the nature and complication of the issues involved. If, in fact, more than one opinion is advanced, it is not imperative that the other individuals advancing tax-shelter advice pass judgment on their peers.

Tax-shelter opinions can be advanced even though a separate written document is not prepared or formally included. When this approach is utilized, a tax-shelter opinion can be inferred if the individual purported to have prepared the opinion is named as a professional advisor in the private-placement memorandum.

## MARKETING AREAS WHERE SECURITIES LAWS ARE OFTEN VIOLATED

Certain marginal area transactions barely qualify for unregistered real estate syndications. The pitfalls associated with these investments are discussed elsewhere in this volume; however, the underlying reasons for some require explanation here. Most of the violations can be directly attributed to a contract, implied or explicit, that relates to an ongoing business relationship established between the two parties, which is a strict departure from the traditional role of passively investing in real estate assets. These so-called *investment contracts* between the parties often border on securities laws violations, the three most common being:

### *1. Condominium Investments*

One of the most common or prevalent violations of securities laws occurs in the marketing of a condominium project when one of the following three conditions prevails:

- where the marketing emphasis is based to a large degree upon the financial or economic benefits, stressing either substantial rental income or potential long-term appreciation;
- where a rental pool, involuntary or not, conveys the impression that the condominium is not primarily a residential dwelling unit but is being marketed for its investment income potential; or
- where a project is promoted restricting the use of the individual condominium unit, especially where a rental agent is appointed to generate income during the nonowner occupancy portions of the year.

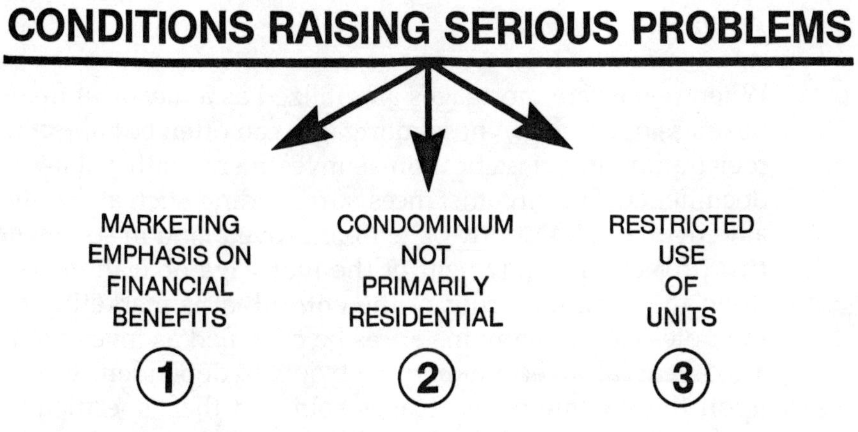


**Figure 6.2** Common reasons for violation of securities laws in marketing condominiums.

Any of these conditions can raise serious problems in terms of securities registration, since the image of an investment contract is conveyed. Time-shared projects also run the risk of required securities registration if representations are made that investment potential exists during the nonowner-occupied periods.

*2. Sale-Leaseback Transactions*

When the seller-lessee is involved in an ongoing business, a sale-leaseback transaction could be subject to a formal securities registration, as the securities laws tend to view such an arrangement as an investment contract. The buyer-lessor becomes a business partner of the seller-lessee as the potential return depends upon the success of the seller-lessee.

The risk or exposure is particularly significant when

- percentage-of-gross-income leases are utilized;
- options permit the seller-lessee to repurchase the property; or
- special-use management-intensive properties are syndicated and leased back.

In general, whenever an investor is passive in nature and completely dependent upon the success of the seller-lessee's business activities for a return on or of his or her investment, the securities laws can be invoked.

*3. Mortgage Financing*

When real estate mortgages are utilized as a means of financing one's business operations, those mortgages can often be subject to securities registration and classification as investments rather than as mortgage documents. The circumstances surrounding such a classification usually involve sales of raw or semi-improved land in somewhat speculative projects. If repayment of the mortgage obligations is dependent upon the eventual profit of the entity that is marketing the venture, the notes can in many instances be classified as investment contracts. The eventual determination is obviously dependent to a large extent upon the volume of mortgages sold and their speculative nature.

## ESTABLISHING A PROSPECTIVE LIST OF INVESTORS

The first step in establishing a workable list of prospective investors consists of categorizing your people's objectives. Your most consistent following is likely to be comprised of a conservative group of professional persons in relatively high tax brackets seeking large up-front deductions, combined with a desire for potential long-term property appreciation. On the other hand, others may look almost exclusively to the predictability of the rate of investment return. Still others may have uncompromising preferences relating to the specific types of property, such as apartment complexes, office buildings, shopping centers, or unimproved land ventures. If the list you compile is unsatisfactory for a given particular project, other avenues are always available.

The most obvious channel for locating and attracting investors is to concentrate on institutions dealing exclusively with passive investors' funds. Most advisory groups that specialize in these types of investment services generally have substantially more money to invest than they have worthwhile ideas to pursue. In prospecting these institutions, it is only sensible to come armed with the kinds of investment ideas that specifically appeal to their investors. Some of these specialized interests are readily predictable.

*Private pension funds* of corporations seek out solid, well-seasoned income-producing property. Because the investment income they generate is not subject to taxation, they tend to concentrate on income-oriented syndications. Their interests are generally consistent, regardless of the size of the offering, whether it is local, regional, or national in scope.

*Investment counselors* normally specialize in high-tax-bracket income groups, such as accountants, doctors, and lawyers. Their investors tend to be extremely passive and routinely delegate the majority of the decision making to the counselors with whom they invest their funds. Tax-oriented projects invariably appeal to these investment counselors with typical high-tax-bracket clientele.

*Bankers* and *trust departments* of lending institutions are also amenable to a syndicator's solicitation. Many a trust department can benefit from a conservative real estate offering. Typically appealing is a project where an underlying, unsubordinated land lease can be held by conservative investors, with the more speculative developmental aspects going to tax-oriented or appreciation-conscious individuals.

We recently completed a syndication on a $15-million second-home condominium project in which several of the investors were channeled to us through the interim lender, after it was satisfied that the project was economically viable. The lender had a substantial backlog of individuals who relied exclusively on its analysis of any project, making the syndication of this condominium venture effortless.

*Accountants* and *attorneys* usually have direct access to persons desirous of placing investment funds into real estate syndications. Introducing trusted syndicators to their clients is for them a matter of courtesy and evidence of professional interest, often costing the syndicator little more than the price of a luncheon. These individuals cannot generally request commissioned income, since doing so would involve a potential conflict of interest.

Many of the more sophisticated *stockbrokerage firms* have departments specializing in syndicated real estate ventures. Local and regional firms, not to mention the large operations such as Merrill Lynch, Dean Witter, and the like, have departments that are always receptive to attractive syndications if the timing is appropriate, the properties are in vogue, and the syndicating entity has a successful track record. Many of these organizations, especially those having subsidiary syndication divisions, are capable of completely underwriting a project. Fortunately, their sophistication leads to realistic investment objectives and fees when they deal with established syndicators of comparable talents.

Within the past few years, since the enabling of the Real Estate Broker-Dealer Licensing, another group has taken on added importance in marketing syndicated real estate. Many licensed real estate brokers and their salespeople have obtained a limited-securities license permitting them to market real estate limited-partnership syndications in conjunction with their normal real estate activities. The detailed requirements and procedural steps for obtaining these licenses are contained in Chapter 15. These individuals have the potential to earn both a syndication fee and a brokerage commission from the acquisition and syndication of the real estate asset. Additionally, they often prove to be the most convenient and compatible of marketing agents for syndicators. In the following pages this relationship between syndicator and the independent marketing entity will be examined in extensive detail.

## STRUCTURING SYNDICATIONS TO FIT RETIREMENT AND PENSION PLANS

IRA/Keogh plans are a tremendous source of new capital for the creative syndicator to work with. Many of these retirement or pension funds are relatively new and are managed by fairly unsophisticated individuals with more funds than ideas. Bank trust departments or other escrow deposit agents are the major source of these funds, which can be invested in worthwhile, leverage-free real estate investments. Since these IRA/Keogh plans or corporate pension and profit-sharing arrangements cannot use the depreciation or tax deductions that are normally generated by real estate offerings, the syndicator stands to profit handsomely by channeling much of his or her income into syndications using such funds.

The prime reason that these pension plans do not seek tax shelter is because the income generated by these funds is automatically exempt from federal income taxation. Consequently, the nonequity partner, in many cases either the syndicator or strictly tax-oriented investors, can be allocated the tax benefits generated from income-producing properties while the cash-flow portion of the investment is channeled to the pension or profit-sharing plan.

IRA/Keogh investors must avoid projects with mortgage financing, since they do not want to become vulnerable to the potential for federal income taxes relating to the so-called unrelated business taxable income (UBTI). Essentially UBTI is business-related income that a tax-exempt plan receives from its regular operations in the trade or business. Taxing unrelated business income in the hands of otherwise tax-exempt plans prevents unfair competition with other businesses forced to pay normal income tax. In other words, real estate holdings financed by mortgage proceeds have to treat a portion of the rental income as subject to taxation.

Were it not for this tax-liability aspect, submarket rentals could theoretically be charged for holdings funded by tax-exempt capital, making these properties more than competitive in the marketplace and providing an undue advantage to the investing entity. Because of tax exemption and the UBTI rule, syndicated offerings attracting pension and retirement funds are normally confined to real estate investments involving either cash purchase of land or first mortgage loans that do not generate tax benefits, or in some instances, a combination of both.

*Typical Participations by Tax-Exempt Organizations*

Many of the IRA/Keogh real estate funds are invested in a combination of "sale-leaseback" types of arrangements, often combined with first-mortgage financing on the improvements. The syndication normally acquires the land on which the improvements rest and leases the land back on a relatively short-term basis, with the improvements eventually reverting to the pension fund. In addition, the fund receives a constant fair-market return on the investment and participates in a percentage of the gross income or net operating cash flow from the property in excess of a predetermined amount required to meet the debt-service payments. The syndicator normally retains the option to repurchase the land at a predetermined point in time, usually adding a substantial appreciation factor to the pension fund's investment.

Many pension funds commit to first-mortgage loan obligations on projects whether or not they own the underlying land lease. Many others will offer a combination plan with a land lease and a loan commitment at a lesser interest rate on the mortgage financing, sometimes deferring the principal amortization during the initial period of a development. For these considerations, pension plans are often given the option to convert part of their mortgage debt to an equity position in the real estate partnership at a later date. Proper structuring gives them the best of both worlds, combining a conservative land lease with a first-mortgage position at a market rate interest and the potential for an equity participation, should they decide to exercise the option, converting part or all of their debt into the equity ledger. The conversion price can be

- set at the initial existing fair-market or appraised value of the project; or

- tied to a value that relates to the initial amount of mortgage funds as a percentage of the initial appraised value.

All of the foregoing concepts are negotiable and can vary substantially with each particular investment situation.

*How the Syndicators and Pension Funds Benefit Mutually*

Advantages to the syndicator are fairly obvious. He or she structures a situation where 100 percent financing of the land and the property is normally automatic. The high ratio of interest-only payments accrue tax benefits to him or her alone, at least initially producing an artificial cash flow that could not be obtained under conventional mortgage financing. Finally, he or she usually has the option to acquire the land at a predetermined point in time, giving him or her the important lead time to refinance adequately. Should inflation intervene, the syndicator pays off the mortgage indebtedness and the land-lease obligation in worthless dollars.

At the same time the IRA/Keogh investors accomplish many of the objectives they seek. The return they receive is substantially higher than would be found in the corporate-bond or government treasury-bill market and is not fixed by nature because of the participation in the increased net or gross operating revenues. Most important, they can benefit from a combination inflation/deflation hedge. Dividing the pension fund's investment into the two previously discussed categories—one relating to land lease and the other to a fixed mortgage position—provides an almost risk-free position.

If inflation continues, the pension fund receives a fixed and constant mortgage payment reflecting a fair-market value on the invested mortgage funds. When a land lease is involved, the institution receives a fixed rental income on the land plus participation in the equity appreciation through the increased rentals resulting from the inflationary process. Additionally, the fund participates in the appreciated value of the land through the purchase option granted by the syndicator. Should the pension plan convert part of its debt to equity, substantial appreciation can also be realized from that conversion option, while in some unique situations, part of the debt can still remain intact.

In the event of a period of deflation, the mortgage position is soundly protected with a constant yield being provided to the fund. The unsubordinated land lease continues to generate income in constant dollars unaffected by any erosion of property or currency values.

## ANALYZING THE COMPETITION'S OFFERINGS

You can rarely obtain too many offering prospectuses circulated by competing syndicators, due to the complex nature and variety of the properties offered through these diversified vehicles. If for no other reason, the more up-to-date and desirable formats should be reviewed and incorporated into your investor presentations. The advantages you will experience that are derived from the prior preparation when potential investors compare your documents with others being touted with similar properties delineating the comparable yields and tax-shelter benefits are invaluable. Investors can raise or generate difficult questions that might be unanswerable without the appropriate backup information supported by competing issues that are prevalent in the marketplace. Since *pricing*, *fees*, and *types of syndicated properties* are subject to market aberrations, one needs to keep an updated view of the competing projects in order to structure one's own offerings.

When constantly monitoring the competitive offerings, one can strengthen one's own syndication by

- visualizing the syndication process form a broader, totally different point of view;
- discovering mistakes or deletions by others that are not in conformance with regulatory requirements;
- concentrating on overlooked areas of compensation, tax aspects, and property-acquisition techniques;
- demonstrating the types of properties competing individuals are successfully purchasing for syndication; and
- comparing the pricing and terms that are being offered by the competition for similar syndicated ventures.

We recently reviewed an interesting offering prospectus relating to the renovation of a major old-line hotel in the Boston metropolitan area, where the investors' funds went exclusively into renovations, having great merit for tax-oriented investors. An almost three-for-one writeoff appeared to be obtainable, which most likely will go unchallenged even under the current Congressional legislation. This prospectus has triggered a lot of activity in our organization in terms of attempting to locate a similar hotel with similar renovation tax advantages.

Rarely should one openly attack or degrade a competitor's offering unless it is accomplished in terms of generalities, usually making reference only to the market conditions or the specific type of property, not the individual sponsoring the offering. Specific degradation will not be understood by unsophisticated individuals and will only serve to lower your own standing within the investment community.

## THE LICENSING REQUIREMENTS FOR MARKETING SYNDICATIONS

The major financial rewards found in a syndication infrequently get passed on to the marketing staff, who receive only as little as a tenth of the overall amount generated by the syndicating entity. Marketing syndications is completely different and often isolated from the normal real estate brokerage activities, as less productive time with one's clients is involved, usually translating into substantially lower commissions. A broker selling a property must out of necessity show it, many times perhaps, before entering into a contract, whereas syndication salespeople are rarely required to inspect a property physically. Generally, marketing personnel are presented with a well-defined document that they forward to their clients without understanding the investment specifics or the overall ramifications of the project described in that offering circular.

Marketing people must possess a securities license (to be described in Chapter 15) and a reputation for fair dealing combined with a large, fairly affluent and satisfied clientele. In the latter instance, they profit just as the syndicator does from an enviable and established track record.

Although the full and complete implications of the broker-dealer license will be dealt with later, it is important to stress that any *unlicensed* individual who becomes involved in marketing, even on the periphery, can often cause irreparable damage, since the syndicated investors have the legal remedies to claim and receive a refund of their investment if a violation of the securities regulations occurs. Exceptions to this requirement can occur when individuals are not compensated on a commissioned basis or where violations are frequently overlooked when the syndication proves to be successful.

Problems regarding unlicensed marketing personnel usually surface when syndications are not meeting their financial obligations or projections. Under such circumstances, the syndicator is least likely to have the readily available funds to repay his or her investors. Securities violations can extend past financial hardships, as unlicensed individuals and their principals are subject to a variety of punitive actions exercised at the discretion of the various securities regulatory bodies, which range from substantial monetary penalties to, in some rare instances, criminal sanctions.

The Direct Participation Program offered by the National Association of Securities Dealers features a Limited Representative's License for salespeople that substantially broadens the field for marketing small, private-placement-type syndications. These limited licenses are available to licensed members of any real estate brokerage firm and are not considered by most individuals as difficult to obtain. Many syndicators who own or are directly associated with real estate brokerage firms are requiring that their employees hold these Limited Representative Licenses. Detailed procedural steps are outlined in Chapter 15. Doing so entails the payment of substantial educational expenses and the investment of considerable time for extensive schooling. While the major thrust of the examination is geared toward the real estate syndication industry, a passing grade also entitles the successful candidate to receive commissions for marketing ventures involving oil and gas leases as well as motion picture investments.

## HOW TO MOTIVATE THE COMMISSION BROKERS

A number of curious anomalies surround the activities of brokers qualified to market real estate syndications. Not the least of them is the concept that the syndicator is generally more aware of the inherent advantages of the commissioned arrangement than the real estate personnel potentially qualified to merchandise one's offering. The syndicator therefore must often sell a trusted or reliable real estate firm on the advantages of this lucrative and ongoing brokerage activity.

A majority of real estate brokers are often convinced that they are competing with themselves by marketing syndication shares. Quite the opposite normally prevails. By engaging in these activities, many can potentially enlarge their market by including passive investors who would not usually be attracted to or have the necessary funds to consider investment-caliber real estate holdings.

The more passive the investor, the less likely he or she is to cross the threshold of a commercial real estate brokerage firm. The explanation for this is less likely to be related to the lack of investment funds than to having an interest in participating directly in the ownership and management of sophisticated real property. Truly ingrained passivity is always immune to higher returns and tax-shelter advantages.

Once real estate brokerage firms realize that marketing syndication shares enlarges their clientele, most are amenable to experimentation with a syndicator of impeccable reputation. Having made themselves aware of the repetitious mechanics of the offering circular and having marketed their first syndication, they come to realize that a sophisticated syndicator is not only a current but a continuous source of inventory appealing to an ever-expanding group of formerly disinterested investors. The fact that their commissions amount to a percentage of the equity funds raised, falling short of what they normally can generate on a leveraged real estate investment, no longer is of great concern when the other advantages are factored into the equation.

Particularly attractive is the potential for repetitious commissions, since successful syndications tend to develop substantial backlogs of potential investors, many of whom can be accumulated and counted on prior to the new offerings coming on stream. As a generality, for every individual who can afford or desires to be active in a major investment-type real estate holding, there are a least a hundred small, unsophisticated individuals who would like to share passively in the same investment—people without the means or the expertise to attempt such a venture on their own.

What makes the syndicator seek out the independent brokerage firms is sometimes explained by an ironic twist in the securities regulations that can best be comprehended by comparing two situations. When a syndicator seeks out limited partners for a complex real estate offering, such as those listed at the beginning of this chapter, he or she must remain in full compliance with the securities regulations regarding full disclosure. If the presentation is improper or is not well documented, the sale may be rescinded and the investors' funds returned.

By comparison, a commissioned real estate broker can sell an investment property to the same unsophisticated individual or to a group of investors without any obligation to reveal any of the intricate details if it does not require a syndication vehicle or use a limited-partnership format.

## MONITORING THE ACTIVITIES OF A SYNDICATION SALES FORCE

Irrespective of whether a syndicator sets up his or her own marketing team or contracts with an independent sales organization, one must take extraordinary precautions to assure that all representations pertaining to the syndicated offering advanced by the marketing agents relate exclusively or directly to the appropriate or required documentation and that no deviations are permitted. Additionally, it is imperative that the marketing team fully understand and be able to convey to their clients the investor net worth, income and risk requirements or standards that the potential buyers must meet. Human nature is not infallible, and salespeople often conveniently overlook these requirements because of their hesitancy to approach potential clients about sensitive questions pertaining to such things as estimated net worth and annual income.

Anyone who has attempted to develop an in-house sales organization knows the complications arising from fragilities of human nature. Top-notch real estate salespeople, especially those who are extremely successful, feel strongly obligated to convey the impression that they are knowledgeable about all the important facets of real estate syndications, including the complicated legal and tax ramifications. At best, these individuals probably relate to the local real estate market extremely well and have a fairly sketchy knowledge of the method in which syndicated investment properties are structured and function. Even those schooled or qualified to pass the National Association of Securities Dealers basically see only the tip of the iceberg when it comes to the legal aspects, accounting functions, or the intricate mechanics of a sophisticated real estate offering.

What makes a syndication attractive to its investors is the combined efforts and blending of talents of the specialized professionals, such as accountants, lawyers, appraisers, financiers, and sophisticated real estate entrepreneurs or developers. The typical real estate marketing agent is a necessary link in this chain, incapable in most instances of assembling an equally attractive investment package. Impressing this concept upon a high-producing real estate salesperson can sometimes be not only demeaning to one's self-esteem, but potentially detrimental to one's overall performance in other areas of real estate marketing. Similarly, a successful individual from other walks of life who passes the NASD (National Association of Securities Dealers) real estate licensing exam, deciding on a midcareer change in professions, must be persuaded that a long on-the-job learning curve lies ahead. In either situation, controlling a marketing staff's enthusiasm is essential if a little knowledge is not to result in a lot of litigation.

Merchandising a syndication effectively within the guidelines prescribed by regulatory agencies requires both skill and soundly based judgment. The syndicator or marketing agent responsible for finding financial backing for a syndication among solid, qualified investors desiring the type of return a given property offers should be amply compensated for his or her efforts. Appropriate fees for merchandising and compensation for a variety of other related activities throughout the life of a syndication will be the subject of the following chapter.

# 7

# Structuring the Appropriate Fees, Equity Interests, and Management Compensation

Syndications are complicated, time-consuming efforts requiring talented and dedicated individuals capable of acquiring the appropriate properties, selecting the participating investors, and merchandising these highly leveraged real estate investments. In the small- to medium-sized syndications that are the primary subject of this book, the syndicator generally performs most of these functions him- or herself, acting either alone or in conjunction with clearly subordinated support-type services.

A syndicator rightly expects compensation for his or her conceptual efforts and for the tender loving care with which he or she nurtures his or her offerings through infancy and adolescence. Real estate syndication is not necessarily the fastest or surest way to pave the streets with gold, as most of the proven and successful syndicators generally prefer the qualitative approach.

Often syndicators show signs of greed in structuring offerings with excessive forms of personal compensation, but even they must abide by minimal standards. According to the North American Securities Administrators Association (NASAA), all fees derived from real estate syndications must be *reasonable, customary, and competitive in the light of the size, type, and location of the property or syndication.* As guidelines go, this is sufficiently broad to leave considerable room for the imaginative syndicator and also to create problems of abuse, particularly prevalent when less than full disclosure is involved.

The matter of fair and adequate compensation is closely linked to that of management. If a syndicator is overcompensated up front, he or she may lack the motivation to perform fully as the project matures. Individuals generally work harder and more diligently as long as the carrot continues to dangle in front of them. In some instances much of the syndicator's compensation is reserved until the point of resale and described and distributed in percentages rather than set figures.

This chapter is concerned with two facets of a syndicator's compensation:

1. *what* is just; and
2. *when* compensation is most equitable.

The NASAA guidelines are precise about the details needed to substantiate the syndicator's financial disclosure. Because they are broadly stated, the industry has refined them into practices that are generally acceptable and in conformity with the various securities regulations that cover the majority of real estate syndications. The outlines and delineations of these reasonable or acceptable standards follow.

## THE MAJOR TYPES OF GENERAL PARTNER COMPENSATION

The financially rewarding aspects of a syndicate are continuous throughout a project's life expectancy. In general, five broad classifications of appropriate fees can be singled out:

1. real estate brokerage commissions, either up front or upon resale;
2. syndication or underwriting fees, directly derived from or related to the equity funds syndicated;
3. property or asset management fees, ongoing throughout the duration of the syndication;
4. fees relating to financing, leasing, or market feasibility studies; and
5. back-end compensation relating to the profit performance of the syndicate.

**APPROPRIATE FEES**

- REAL ESTATE BROKERAGE COMMISSIONS
- SYNDICATION OR UNDERWRITING FEES
- PROPERTY MANAGEMENT FEES
- FINANCING, LEASING OR MARKET FEASIBILITY STUDY FEES
- BACK-END COMPENSATION

**Figure 7.1** Major types of compensation to the general partner of a syndication.

While these categories of fees are largely listed in the chronological order in which they are generated, the first and third are obviously subject to variations in timing intrinsic to the identity of the syndication. Further variation relates to the degree to which any of these fees is subordinated to the repayment of the equity interest. The timing and structuring of these fees are the essential ingredients in distinguishing one syndication from another.

## WHY YOUR REPUTATION WILL DETERMINE YOUR COMPENSATION

Commanding compensation can vary in degrees, in stated or flexible amounts, and can be subject to variations in timing, all of which are directly attributed to three factors:

1. the reputation of the individual promoting the offering;
2. the syndicate's potential earnings and long-term appreciation; and
3. the noncash benefits that contributing investors will derive from the investment.

This section will address itself exclusively to the first concept.

The syndicator's track record of past performances is the key to his or her attracting investors. None but the most naive of individuals will back a syndicator who has left a trail of disappointed people or mediocre projects. The successful syndicator has the ability to balance an offering's results equitably with his or her investors' desire for a respectable return on equity. When, over the years, a syndicator's clientele have become comfortable with the fees earned in relation to or in exchange for the overall return they received, a syndicator has developed a following for which no formal advertising campaign can substitute. Not only does he or she have a viable, hard-core following, but he or she can also be permitted the luxury of structuring syndications for a higher percentage of personal gain or return during the time framework in which he or she works best.

Most syndicators operate best in a balanced situation with adequate compensation throughout the various stages of a project, including the acquisitional, operational, and sell-out phases. Unless he or she prefers to do so, the experienced syndicator need not make a substantial equity contribution, at least over an extended period of time. Neither should the syndicator expect his or her partners to contribute amounts of funds that are unrealistic in relation to the potential return. Just as one should not structure a syndication so that the majority of the compensation surfaces at the end, one should also not exclusively subordinate his or her compensation strictly to the ultimate profits in a venture. Doing so can often jeopardize the syndication by dampening one's efforts on behalf of the project if the initial projections do not materialize.

The overall fees to the syndicator, however, should ultimately be based upon his or her measurable performance. This is most conspicuous at the conceptual stage and when the partnership is dissolved, when the ultimate profits are counted. Yet compensation should not be denied during the operational aspects, when boredom centering around the daily activities is most apt to set in. Even if considered to be somewhat marginal, this compensation can be an important aspect of one's morale. The seasoned syndicator will structure and receive adequate compensation throughout the life of a project to ensure a continuing source of vitality of interest.

## FEES GENERATED FROM THE SUCCESSFUL ASPECTS OF SYNDICATIONS

One of the most lucrative (and least predictable) aspects of real estate offerings relates to the syndicator's participation in the excess cash flow or the eventual profits upon dissolution. Equity participation can be based in either the cash flow or the ultimate profits, and normally both are commonly involved. The distribution can be structured in two different ways:

1. direct participation in the syndicate's cash flow or eventual profits; or
2. an interest subordinated to a predetermined level of return on equity to the investing partners.

Whatever form the equity participation may take, it is uniquely dissimilar to the typical syndication or brokerage fees or compensation for specific services performed by the syndicator, which will be discussed in detail later in this chapter.

## DIRECT PARTICIPATION COMPENSATION

When a syndicator receives a percentage interest or equity ownership in the project regardless of its performance or eventual outcome, he or she is said to participate directly in the syndication. The direct allocation of profits is compensation for his or her efforts in locating the property and syndicating the investors. The syndicator usually expects and receives a fixed amount of the equity, a predetermined percentage of the cash flow over and above a stipulated break-even amount, or a combination of the two, based upon prearranged performance standards.

In prior years direct participation was the route generally chosen by the experienced syndicators supported by successful track records; however, the practice is less common now than it used to be, probably due to the increasingly competitive nature of the industry. Another major reason for switching to the subordinated participation approach relates to the tax laws that mandate that a syndicator can be subject to taxation relating to a percentage of the equity of guaranteed income he or she receives in a project. Many times this taxable income must be declared without receipt, especially in the initial phases of a syndication when the tax ramifications are usually substantial. Variations of the approach are now more prevalent, designed to minimize the tax implications.

## SUBORDINATED PARTICIPATION REMUNERATION

Because of the tax implications, most offerings are now being structured so that the syndicator's interest is clearly defined as subordinate to that of his or her equity partners. This normally translates into taking a predescribed percentage interest in the eventual profits or the cash flow, or both, *after* the investors have received their equity in return combined with a predetermined rate of interest on their contributions reflecting the risk factors of the investment. In a well-conceived project, such a subordinated interest can be just as lucrative to the general partner as a direct participation would have been without the attendant tax implications. It is potentially even more lucrative if the eventual sales price exceeds the initial projections. This offsetting factor can often augment the up-front fees that are limited in relation to the overall performance standards of the syndication.

We recently completed a syndicated offering, and as general partners retained two thirds of the eventual profits, on a high-end condominium venture after allocating to the limited partners a 30 percent annualized return prior to any distribution to our group. By not structuring large up-front fees and successfully raising the sales prices as the project matured, we were fortunate as general partners to generate a half million dollars in profits, as were the investors who received a 60 percent annualized return on their equity contributions.

The least speculative aspect to the syndicator in a subordinate participation is the tax liability. The Internal Revenue Service does not, under normal circumstances, tax the general partner holding a subordinated interest initially, since the exact nature of the compensation will not be known until the limited partners have received a return of their capital combined with a preferential percentage of eventual profits.

A syndication in which the general partner has a subordinated interest also takes on an important marketing advantage. The syndicator who declines participation in the profits until his or her investors have been amply compensated obtains the asset of credibility when he or she stakes his or her own fee income exclusively on his or her ability to succeed with a project. The investors will also draw the inference that he or she cannot afford to neglect the venture and will continually remain active, interested, and motivated in the group's affairs until the partnership is dissolved.

Subordinated participation works particularly well in tax-oriented syndications where the investors are desirous of receiving substantial tax benefits initially after the syndication is formed. When their compensation takes the form of significant tax shelter, many are content to receive their equity money in return combined with fairly minimal interest payments. The general partner then can find him- or herself with a substantial equity position, sharing appreciably in the residual value of the asset after his or her investors are satisfied with the combination of tax deductions and a minimal but satisfactory return on their invested equity. This subordinated interest also reassures the investors that excessive leverage will not be prevalent, as the general partner then has at least as much or more to lose than the investors in the event of foreclosure.

## FEES GENERATED DURING THE ORGANIZATIONAL ASPECTS

Most syndications provide for the general partner collecting a variety of fees upon the closing of the offering. This compensation can be quite substantial and is commonly referred to as "up-front" or "front-end" fees. These can be the least understood and often the most resented fees charged to the syndicated partners. Accordingly, they must be structured carefully and fully explained to each potential investor.

### *Real Estate Brokerage Fees*

A major source of income for many general partners is a standard real estate brokerage commission based upon a percentage of the value of the property being acquired by the partnership. This fee is often paid irrespective of the amount of the equity funds raised and can be equal to a full real estate commission normally set at a maximum of 6 percent. While the NASAA statement of policy guidelines recognizes real estate brokerage fees, a full commission is *not* always an acceptable situation in a syndicated offering.

Because the payment of a real estate brokerage fee can be a controversial matter with the NASAA, you as general partner should take extraordinary care to substantiate your contributional time and efforts toward justifying the collection of this fee. The full nature, extent, terms, and conditions of the acquisition must be fully disclosed to the potential investors when the syndicate is charged with a substantial brokerage commission. If the transaction or acquisition is conducted totally at arm's length by an independent third party, the full brokerage fee is normally acceptable by the NASAA. Complications also enter the picture when the general partner *owns* and plans to sell the property to be included in the syndication offering. Then the NASAA will closely scrutinize the pricing and fees related to these types of acquisitions. Severe repercussions are probable when a full disclosure of the acquisition terms, parties, and fees is not adequately made to equity partners. Complete and full documentation by the syndicating partner is a prerequisite to possible examination by a regulatory agency.

*Syndication Fees*

A more common method of up-front compensation is referred to as a syndication fee. It relates specifically to a percentage of the amount of equity funds that are generated and commonly has no relationship to or bearing on the real estate brokerage commission. This fee is compensation for the marketing efforts and costs involved in soliciting and closing the equity portion of the syndication. According to NASAA guidelines, up to 15 percent of the equity funds syndicated can legitimately be charged as a marketing cost to the partnership.

Usually regulatory bodies look somewhat unfavorably at a syndicator charging *both* a real estate brokerage commission and an equity syndication fee, but in justifiable situations both are allowable. Explaining and documenting the double-fee structure can be extremely difficult if called for the by various regulatory bodies. The safer route is to charge an up-front fee amounting to *either* 15 percent of the total capital raised by the syndicate *or* 6 percent of the purchase price of the property, especially where a syndicator's equity participation is involved.

To avoid complications, the general partner should compare and weigh the potential up-front fees carefully. If permissible brokerage commission and syndication fees are similar in amount, one should choose the latter of the two as the more conservative way to structure the up-front fee schedule, the underlying reasoning being that the seller (not the buyer or the syndicate) of a property normally pays the brokerage commission, even though the seller customarily builds the fee into his or her asking price. The commissioned broker is, therefore, accountable to the seller, not the purchasing syndicate, which automatically raises a conflict of interest. When a syndication fee based on a percentage of equity funds generated is charged, the syndicator is responsible directly to the equity investors and is compensated solely for the equity funds he or she solicits.

What tends to happen in reality is that the larger syndications charge up-front fees based exclusively upon a percentage of equity funds generated. Exceptions surface when securities underwriting houses have real estate brokerage subsidiaries with these firms acting in both capacities. In smaller offerings, real estate commissions are still an acceptable and appropriate way of dealing with up-front compensation. Conflicts of interest justifying both fees are often as legally indefensible as they may be real unless extraordinary efforts are taken to offer or provide full disclosure supported by complete documentation.

*Financing Fees*

In leveraged real estate offerings, many syndicators or their subsidiary companies generate fees for mortgage financing, usually calculated as a percentage of the funds raised. These fees obviously vary with the nature and size of the commitment and fluctuate widely depending upon whether the financing is interim or permanent in nature. In larger syndications, the standard acceptable to the NASAA is usually 1 percent of the amount of the loan and double that rate if interim and permanent financing are involved. Because of the potential conflicts of interest, full disclosure must surface, and often even with full documentation complications can still arise.

All too frequently, syndications are formed using leverage far in excess of that deemed to be prudent by the regulatory bodies. By charging a financing fee, the syndicator must reveal the amount of leverage and suffer the potential consequences of his or her imprudence should the project develop financial difficulty strictly attributable to the leveraged financing.

As a syndicator, you should weigh the up-front financing fees in relation to their potential exposure. The amount of debt or nonequity financing will obviously determine the eventual size of the property being acquired or developed. The size of the syndicated asset will in turn affect the amount of the real estate brokerage commissions and the syndication fees. Just as fractionalization of a holding normally increases its value, the ramifications of excessive leverage can compound your exposure disproportionately.

As a general policy we usually forgo the financing-related fees, as we recently did on a $9.5-million apartment project. This is attributed to the potential ramifications of highly leveraged and potentially catastrophic ventures. This particular offering had a $200,000 annualized negative cash flow after debt service, which was being accrued and negatively amortized by the lender on a seven-year balloon basis. Excessive or creatively structured financing, if not fully understood by all the partners including the passive investors, can have severe legal and ethical ramifications.

*Conflicting Syndication Fees*

When multiple fees are generated, the syndicator is always vulnerable to criticism. You should always interrelate the combination of up-front fees with extreme caution, in order not to jeopardize your credibility by appearing to lean on the side of imprudence.

Closely related problems of overleveraging and conflicting fees can be cured, for instance, by adequate financial reserves in a partnership. A sure formula for *financial ruin* can be attributed to:

- overleveraging in relation to equity, where financing fees are generated;
- overpaying for a syndicated property where brokerage commissions are charged;
- providing minimal financial reserves, where a syndicating fee is taken for raising the equity funds; and
- charging a fee for appraisals or market-feasibility studies where the results do not materialize.

A syndicator can reduce the criticism through complete documentation and by setting aside more than adequate financial reserves. This excess of caution can be expensive in terms of appropriating funds better used for acquisition or development; however, the "sleep factor" sometimes should enter into the successful equation of the active syndicator.

*Other Up-front Fees*

Formation of a syndication is an expensive, complicated, and time-consuming matter, and compensation can legitimately be required for a variety of miscellaneous services and expenses, as the following random and incomplete list will demonstrate:

- providing market feasibility studies;
- agreeing to restrictions or noncompletion clauses in similar projects;
- providing the insurance coverage for a property;

- guaranteeing the negative cash flow of a project;
- covering start-up costs and operating expenses during the formation stages; and
- absorbing corporate or partnership overhead.

All these fees will vary, and some are minor in nature. Of importance is their relationship to the type of organization required by the specific syndicated venture.

Fees are rightly suspect when they compensate a general partner for activities that are not carried out in the daily course of his or her business. Suppose, for example, a syndicator charges the partnership a fee for a market-feasibility study when he or she lacks the credentials of a recognized independent expert in this field. On the other hand, if a serious question arises pertaining to market existence, rates, or absorption and the syndicator retains an independent marketing expert to complete a feasibility study, little criticism will be leveled for the amount expended to cover the third-party fee for services rendered.

## FEES COLLECTED DURING THE MANAGEMENT PHASE

Of the four aspects of managing a syndication that we will elaborate on in this section, the managing of rental property is generally thought to be the least demanding of the syndicator's personal attention. For this reason, it can be delegated to a professional management team, as is frequently the situation in large, complex offerings. We will begin with this topic, assuming that the syndicator chooses to take on these types of activities himself.

### *Compensation for Managing the Syndicated Property*

This remuneration usually takes the form of a percentage of the gross and, in some rare instances, the net rental income. Depending upon the size and complexity of the property, this fee can be substantial and unlike many of the permissible up-front fees, can easily be determined, substantiated, and documented. The industry standard for property management is around 5 percent of gross revenues generated and can vary with the particular type of use. This figure or well-documented derivatives are normally accepted without question by the NASAA.

Special incentives can be built into a property management fee if excessively high rates of occupancy are desired by the syndicate and generated by the managing partner or his or her designate. When such incentives are offered, care must be taken to document the industry norm against the level of occupancy actually obtained. Offering this incentive can be well worth a substantial premium to the syndication through superlative standards of property management and maintenance.

*Compensation for Managing the Partnership*

Partnership or asset-management fees as differentiated from property-management compensation are structured in a variety of ways, the more complex of which are appropriate only to very large, sophisticated syndications. The details of such structuring are basically intrinsic to the operation of individual syndications and beyond the scope of this book. The simplest approach most frequently used in uncomplicated situations provides for the general reimbursement of the justifiable out-of-pocket costs incurred by the syndicator in the day-to-day operation of partnership affairs. These may be legal and accounting fees and the costs directly related to preparing the documentation necessary to report syndication affairs. Such out-of-pocket expenses should also be reimbursed *in addition* to the property management fee as previously described. In more complicated situations, additional expertise is often required, which is normally accompanied by justifiable expenditures for partnership management.

In more recent syndications we have been structuring in a few thousand dollars per month in order to cover our overhead in lieu of an itemization of our actual expenses or a substantial management fee. This seems to be a fair or adequate arrangement both to the investors and the managing general partners. Occasionally we are reimbursed for major unforeseen partnership expenditures, leaving the majority of our fees to be derived from the eventual profits of the venture.

*Cash Distribution Fees*

Expenditures are incurred by the syndicator at times when cash disbursements are not available to the partnership. In general, they should be minimized or eliminated, especially when substantial property-management fees are involved. When such fees are actually necessary for operation, the NASAA guidelines allow a maximum of

10 percent of the cash distributed for these categories of expenditures. The general partner who exceeds this percentage limitation invites trouble, particularly when his or her up-front cash contributions to the equity of the partnership are limited.

Often it is appropriate to take cash fees for marketing purposes on for-sale projects. We recently structured a 48–unit condominium venture, which we syndicated, where as general partners we received a $2,000-per-unit fee payable at the closing of each individual unit, which helped defray a portion of our marketing overhead.

*Compensation for Advances by the Syndicator*

Reimbursing the syndicator for the legitimate expenses incident to operating a property can be complex. Many syndicators find it necessary to assure a fixed rate of return to their investors, accomplishing this by guaranteeing operating income, covering excess expenses, or assuming personal financial obligations or commitments on partnership mortgages. Substantially, this translates into subsidizing the syndication until these obligations can be self-liquidating, met exclusively with partnership funds.

When this sort of underwriting is intrinsic to the successful structuring and maintenance of a syndication, the general partner must be prepared to keep careful records and seek competent legal advice whenever potential conflicts of interest show any sign of emerging. To a greater or lesser extent, these expenses can be subordinate to the interests of the investors unless specifically documented, and repayment to the syndicator for these unique advances should be incorporated in the offering prospectus. Specific guidelines should be established relating to the reimbursement or the cost of carrying these advances. The prudent syndicator wishing to make such guarantees should anticipate challenges from the outset and retain legal counsel delineating the method for repayment of these obligations.

## STRUCTURING THE BACK-END FEES AND COMPENSATION

Syndicated investors are least apt to challenge the fees or compensation their general partner receives upon dissolving the partnership, since the majority of this remuneration occurs only when a project is successful. What the general partner receives is usually dependent upon the conception and management of a venture. The more passive an investor is, the less concerned he or she is about the total compensation awarded to the general partner at the time of dissolution. This amount can be substantial if the syndicator structures the final phase correctly.

### *Real Estate Brokerage Commissions from Resale*

Early in this chapter, we mentioned that the syndicator may elect his or her remuneration through a real estate commission either up-front or upon resale of the asset or, in some instances, at both ends. Computed at a maximum of 6 percent of the value of the property, this commission is usually a substantial amount. When it is structured for payment upon resale, this fee should usually be subordinated to the total return of the equity partners' investment. This back-end structuring combined with the subordination to the partners' return of investment can often make this remuneration quite palatable to the syndicating investors even though it can extend into the hundreds of thousands of dollars in many instances. NASAA attaches some strings, specifying in its guidelines that the syndicating entity should collect only half of the amount of the normal real estate commission at the back end. The underlying reason for this is apparently to make the asset more marketable within the local brokerage community through the vehicle of split commissions. The ultimate decision, however, usually rests on the overall profitability of the syndicated investment.

### *Sharing Profits Derived from Resale*

Much of what the general partner receives at the time of resale depends substantially on a combination of fee income generated in the preceding two phases of the syndication combined with the percentage of profits to be distributed upon dissolution. NASAA recommends that the general partner receive 15 percent of the cash distributions from the proceeds of the sale or from the benefits of refinancing after the limited partners retrieve their contributed equity plus fair-market interest. For all practical purposes, there are no fixed guidelines, and the end result will be dependent upon six factors weighed by both the syndicator and the investors alike:

1. the nature and extent of the fees generated preceding the sale;
2. the cash contributions made by the general partner during the syndicated period;

3. the tax benefits passed on exclusively to the investors;
4. the amount of financial risk personally assumed by the general partner;
5. the length of time the investors' equity was utilized; and
6. the extent of the profits from resale to be distributed.

An imaginative approach to structuring a syndicator's compensation in the last phase of a syndication allows the general partner a percentage of the profit differential between the initial purchase price of the asset and the depreciated book value at the time of sale. Depending upon the size and ramifications of the passive investors' tax deductions, this approach can be considered equitable to the general partner and quite salable to the limited partners.

In a tax-oriented syndication, the general partner usually forgoes the tax benefits initially generated, allocating the majority to the limited partners. The advantages of these tax deductions are basically reflected in the depreciated book value of the asset at the time of sale. When the limited partners derive all or a substantial portion of the tax benefits, this lowers the partnership's basis, increasing the capital gains tax obligation. Compensating the syndicator for the lack of tax deductions by structuring a disproportionate percentage of the achievable profits in relationship to the contributed equity and realized tax deductions can be considered equitable under most circumstances.

Structuring an offering so that the syndicator receives the majority of his or her fees or compensation at the back end of the venture is particularly attractive to passive and unsophisticated investors. Most individuals subscribe to the carrot-on-a-string concept of protecting their interests by keeping the syndicator motivated until the termination of a project. This tendency is especially prevalent when the gen-

**FACTORS IN SHARING PROFITS**

$ $ $ $

1. NATURE & EXTENT OF FEES
2. CASH CONTRIBUTIONS
3. TAX BENEFITS
4. AMOUNT OF FINANCIAL RISK
5. TIME EQUITY WAS TIED UP
6. PROFITS FROM RESALE

**Figure 7.2** Major factors determining what the general partner will receive upon sale of a syndicated asset.

eral partner invests or advances little or in some instances no up-front funds of his or her own. The validity of the approach is substantiated by abuses. Some syndicators have been known to advance minute sums of seed money only to take substantial up-front fees amounting to a hundredfold or so on their initial investment. The most desirable arrangement for all partners is a balanced fee schedule for the syndicator structured and distributed throughout the various phases of the venture, with equitable risk, motivation, and compensation for all.

## THREE PROJECTS ILLUSTRATING UP-FRONT, ONGOING, AND BACK-END FEES

We have been involved in three major projects totaling over $50 million upon completion that illustrate the manner in which fees can be structured and funded to suit the nature and type of the investment and the objectives of the passive investors.

All three projects show minimal management fees generated during the operational phase. Even though the compensation in the aggregate is high due to the project's size and scope, fees are not disproportionate for managing and marketing assets of comparable magnitude. Project C is unique to the three as it shows substantial up-front syndication fees based upon a tax-oriented offering with no general partner personal financial exposure or invested funds of any substance involved. Projects A and B are diametrically different, involving:

- no up-front syndication fees;
- substantial equity investment, well in excess of $1 million by the general partners; and
- extensive personal liability to the general partners, exceeding $15 million in both instances.

Back-end fees on all three projects show substantial fees to the developers and/or general partners subject to profits materializing as follows:

- Project A, 60 percent of profits;
- Project B, 88 percent of profits; and
- Project C, 25 percent of profits.

Projects A and B are both cash-flow oriented, giving a preferential return to the investors. Project C is structured with substantial up-front fees and oriented toward tax deductions and leverage, showing a relatively conservative percentage return on equity upon dissolution. All three projects interweave investment concepts that can be *applied to any real estate syndication.*

### *Project A—112 Luxury Condominiums*

Located in the southwestern part of the United States, this condominium complex currently under development consists of 112 phased units with a total completion value of approximately $30 million. The equity contribution of the limited partners consisted of $1 million and was merchandised in five equal shares at $200,000 per share. One of the general partners signed for substantial revolving bank loans in excess of $7 million to complete this project. The general partners retained 60 percent of the overall equity. In return for acting as the local development and coordinating entity in this venture, I was granted 25 percent of the 60 percent share of the general partners' equity.

The limited partners in Project A are to receive a preferential 40 percent return on their equity before any distribution to the general partners and 40 percent of the net profits on the venture, with the understanding that their initial equity contribution must remain in the project until the venture is 50 percent completed. The general partners withdraw $25,000 per year to cover corporate overhead plus $4,500 per unit as the condominiums are sold. All other compensation to the general partners comes from the residual profits upon completion of the development. The anticipated profits to the partnership are judged to be between 12 percent and 15 percent on sales, netting the venture an anticipated $4 million to $4.5 million. The limited partners receive a 10 percent annual interest on their outstanding invested funds and, if all projections materialize, should receive approximately a 175 percent return on their invested funds over a projected three year period in which their investment will be tied up. The general partners, for conceiving the project and assuming the risks associated with the construction loan financing, stand to gain $25 million for their efforts if all projections are accurate. This offering is an example of extreme back-end compensation to the syndicating entity, where all rewards are almost totally contingent upon the eventual success of the venture.

*Project B—Second-Home Resort Development*

This project, also in the Southwest, is a luxury second-home condominium development with 47 townhouses and 11 single-family units to be constructed totaling approximately $15 million in sales upon completion. The investor equity of $250,000 was raised in increments of five limited-partnership units at $50,000 per share. The general partners advanced the funds for municipal approvals and architectural drawings and assumed substantial financial liabilities in the development aspect through personal guarantees of the construction loan. Our general-partner entity had full construction and architectural capabilities for the project and charged some up-front fees to the partnership for these services, not exceeding 10 percent of the phased value of the project. The management fee was somewhat similar to that of Project A, where $2,000 per unit was allocated to the marketing effort. Subordinated to the limited partners' return of capital plus a preferential return to the investors of 30 percent annually on the funds utilized, the general partners were able to retain 88 percent of the eventual profits generated from the venture. A 15 percent profit margin is anticipated, with the investors' funds being retained for two years, drawing 10 percent interest in the interim. If all projections materialize, the investors should visualize a return in the area of 100 percent, and the general partners should realize close to $2 million for their efforts.

*Project C—Apartments for Potential Conversion*

This existing complex consists of 188 apartment units located in a major midwestern city. The syndication undertaking the venture was structured primarily for the deferred tax shelter benefits afforded to its investors. When the deductions wane, the syndication plans to resell the buildings to an apartment converter, the proceeds being eligible for favorable capital gains taxes. $2,450,000 was syndicated into 35 shares at $70,000 per share, contributed over five annual installments. A total of $5.5 million was paid for the complex; $3,050,000 of the purchase price was consummated through the existing first mortgage.

The up-front fees to the general partner and marketing agent amounted to $196,000, or 8 percent of the funds raised. In addition, the general partner, through a wholly owned subsidiary, received from the seller $217,000 as a real estate brokerage commission.

A fairly standard management fee of 5 percent of the gross income was contracted for during the operational phase. Back-end fees to the general partner consisted primarily of a percentage of the profits when the units were to be sold to a condominium developer. After 100 percent return of the limited partners' original invested capital plus any deficiency of cash flow not received at an annual rate of 8 percent, the general partner received 30 percent of the net distribution of profits. During the operational period, the cash flow and tax losses were divided 99 percent to the limited partners and 1 percent to the general partner.

Assuming the property is disposed of at the end of the fifth year to a condominium converter at $50 per square foot as outlined in the prospectus, the partnership will receive $7,950,000 in net proceeds. After the repayment of the mortgage balance and a return of the limited partners' capital, it is anticipated that the *net proceeds* will be as follows:

- 70 percent to the limited partners—$1,999,000; and
- 30 percent to the general partner—$856,000.

Assuming the projections materialize, this would be a rather typical kind of proposal offering a fair return to both the general and limited partners.

*Summation*

The total fees for all three projects are tied directly to the projected profits of each development. Of particular importance is the structuring of the fees and demonstration of just how substantial the back-end compensation can be if an offering fulfills the syndicator's projections of profits. So far, projections have been fairly accurate, although Project A is now only partially through the development phase. Project C is completely syndicated; however, it has not yet been marketed to an apartment converter.

The following chapter will illustrate the distinctive role played by the syndicator when he or she teams up with traditional financiers such as banks, savings and loan institutions, life insurance companies, and corporate pension/profit-sharing funds. Many of these joint-venture arrangements require considerably less time and effort than partnerships of individuals in terms of syndication activity. Counterbalancing this advantage, they also require that substantially greater portions of cash flow and equity participation be allocated to these more powerful and sophisticated partners.

# 8

# Joint Venture Arrangements: An Alternative to Real Estate Syndications

One of the ego-warming experiences in store for a developer as he or she matures together with the successful projects is being approached by a substantial lending institution that is desirous of capitalizing on his or her expertise by backing him or her financially. The first such offer is a thrill for the developer or real estate entrepreneur regardless of the size of the project or the magnitude of the backing. When the overture is unsolicited in nature, objective proof is established that his or her efforts to maintain a viable track record have not gone unnoticed by those controlling the financial power. Yet, accepting such a proposal can often be an expensive, time-consuming, and frustrating mistake. The pros and cons of working or operating with powerful financial backers will be examined in greater detail in this section.

## HOW THE LENDER'S ROLE EVOLVED

The traditional role of lending institutions in the acquisition or development of real estate consisted primarily of their advancing substantial mortgage-related funds at higher than normal interest rates, often accompanied by equity kickers tied to a percentage of profits or an override on the rental income. For their part, lenders came to realize that they should be entitled to a share of the profits in a highly leveraged situation because they consistently shared a substantial amount of the risk. The concept-generating entrepreneur, on the other hand, often felt shortchanged in the development profit potential because these lenders demanded and were receiving a larger and sometimes preferential slice of the pie. Efforts at reconciling these conflicting interests led to the emergence of a blend in which the developer and the institutional investor combined objectives:

- the lender supplied the financing in its entirety; and
- the development entity provided the expertise and the development project.

As ventures grew in size and complexity, both groups began to assess their attendant risks and rewards in an attempt to establish guidelines for an equitable profit division, taking the following realities into account:

- Only the most substantial developers could afford the inherent financial exposure at risk in large ventures.
- If a project ran into irreversible financial trouble, the only realistic recourse was for the institution to take back a deed in lieu of foreclosure.
- Those institutions that scrutinized closely the projects they financed realized that they were not sharing in the substantial tax benefits accruing to the developers.
- Backers such as large life insurance companies and publicly held real estate investment trusts were denied the larger after-tax long-term earnings to which they might be entitled if they participated in the equity aspect of real estate developments.

These considerations, among others, led to the gradual and what now appears to be the permanent establishment of the joint-venture concept.

## THE VEHICLE FOR INSTITUTIONAL JOINT VENTURES

While the traditional role of lending institutions is providing development funds in the form of first mortgages, many are permitted to structure a certain percentage of their assets into wholly owned subsidiary companies that concentrate on equity participation in real estate ventures. Among the institutions *now permitted* to do so are

- life insurance companies;
- pension and profit sharing funds;
- real estate investment trusts; and
- savings and loans associations.

The parent mortgage company and the subsidiary equity partner are able to combine forces in providing the complete financing vehicle for any project in what is called a joint venture arrangement. The two entities normally relate to 100 percent or more financing for the project's promoter. If properly structured with a portion of the tax advantages allocated to the institutional investor, a combination of the equity and debt financing substantially increases the overall yield on the traditional debt portion of the financing with little additional exposure to the institutional investor. This pairing up also provides the developer with a relatively risk-free project if it is conceptually sound. Furthermore, an institutional investor can often salvage a troubled project by injecting additional equity funds, retaining the developer in his or her traditional position until the situation rectifies itself. These capabilities of an institutional investor are often critical in attracting the entrepreneurial talent. Relatively few developers or acquisition specialists have the substance to risk the exposure inherent in major developments without the assurance that their financial backers can inject additional equity funds as crises develop. Since large ventures are frequently equated with invigorating the local economy, almost every state in the union permits joint-venture arrangements between developers and lending institutions.

Obvious candidates for joint-venture arrangements are the institutions capable of committing substantial sums of mortgage money for extended periods of time. Lending institutions subject to demand deposits or those sensitive to interest rate fluctuations are less than ideal for long-term commitments to joint-venture projects. Yet, the importance of the joint ventures to current development is evidenced by the liberalization of regulations for participation. Among the latest to qualify as joint-venture partners under the relaxed regulations are the savings and loan institutions. The only major type of investment institutions now denied the privilege of participation is the chartered banks.

On many occasions we have joint ventured with various general contractors. A current venture of 261 apartments valued at $13 million is under development where the associate general contractor contributes his construction profit to the partnership, consisting of close to $1 million and, in effect, by accomplishing this, 100 percent financing is well assured.

## CONTRIBUTIONS TO THE JOINT VENTURE ARRANGEMENT

The lender's offer to participate usually means or translates into:

- the institution, most simply, having surplus capital to be lent on sound ventures; or
- having enough confidence in the developer to spare him or her the cost of marketing an investment syndication he or she would otherwise form; or, more interestingly,
- the lender being willing to speculate on his or her ability to succeed with a larger or more leveraged project than he or she has previously undertaken; or
- the entrepreneur being offered, best of all, all of the foregoing concepts, plus the lender's guarantee of additional equity funds in the event of trouble.

This arrangement can be a gift horse that should be looked squarely in the mouth.

Most lenders do not and probably never will have the in-house capability to locate, develop, or manage major real estate projects. The joint-venture concept keeps the entrepreneur interested in the project if, in fact, substantial problems surface. Many projects are so large and complicated that an entrepreneur who was unable to associate with a joint-venture partner might choose the more expeditious foreclosure route as a means to going on to more interesting opportunities. Left with a troubled or incomplete project, the foreclosing lender may sometimes be able to bring in consultant types or hired guns, but these individuals are invariably inferior in performing at the entrepreneurial level so necessary in complicated developments. Due to the costly and unproductive nature of extensive litigation proceedings, lending institutions generally stand to benefit from being joint-venture partners, especially if the agreement calls for either temporary or permanent restructuring of the equity position when additional injections of capital are required.

Developers can often incur serious communication problems with unsophisticated lenders who do not share an equity or risk position in a project. These complications are quite similar in nature to those encountered when syndicating with passive investors, especially those in high tax brackets attracted to tax-deferred offerings. Both can and often will throw up substantial roadblocks whenever additional funds are required to keep the project from running aground. By joint venturing with sophisticated lending institutions, one can eliminate the potential loss of control and gain a partner capable of keeping the venture viable by timely injections of funds whenever appropriate. Times of necessity do not always reflect upon an entrepreneur's competency, as the combination of inflation, fluctuating interest rates, and tight money have demonstrated so frequently in the past decade.

In opting to protect oneself by joint venturing, one may find oneself and the project subjected to far more unwanted control than one would find by syndicating with passive investors or by dealing with lenders only in mortgage capacities. More of these complications will surface later, yet even they can be minimized if precautions are taken to delineate in the joint-venture agreement the terms of control combined with the checks and balances necessary for a workable and manageable environment.

## THE DEVELOPER'S UNCHARACTERISTIC ROLE IN A JOINT VENTURE

Most successful developers have substantial egos and are mainly comfortable dealing with passive investors who advance funds asking relatively few questions until a project is completed. Failure is neither contemplated nor tolerated, since it is incompatible with the developer's self-image. How, then, do such self-styled champions of free enterprise accommodate to the bureaucracy typical of major lending institutions? At best, many real estate entrepreneurs find lending institutions strange bedfellows.

Joint venturing requires a substantial departure from the developer's traditional role. A typical arrangement opens the door or permits for the lending institutions to:

- deal with or partially control the architects and contractors;
- work with the key individuals within the developer's organization, thereby penetrating its strengths and weaknesses;

- impose limits on the amount of funds expended;
- monitor the day-to-day activities of the project;
- require that bonding capacity be available; and
- scrutinize any wholly owned subsidiary companies of the developer that are involved in the construction or management.

Someone is indeed looking over the developer's shoulder at every step in the development process, and the resulting resentment is always inevitable.

For many developers, resentment is only the tip of the iceberg. A true conflict of interest can frequently develop, as many entrepreneurs are concerned about revealing their trade secrets to their powerful financial partners. Once the institution knows the procedural steps and detailed mechanics of a successful project, they reason that they can develop their own in-house expertise. Armed with this recently acquired know-how and the financial clout to retain the personnel to implement it, the institution might eventually eliminate the need for the developer. And so the partnership becomes an armed camp.

Many developers fail to realize that lending institutions, due to their extreme regulations, require checks and balances not found in or necessary to most entrepreneurial organizations. They must, after all, report to and protect their shareholders. Depending upon the structure of the joint venture, these checks and balances may mean that the developing entity can be forced out of a project entirely if, in fact, the venture or its projections do not materialize. On the other hand, many are structured so that the lending institution receives an equity position after a predetermined period of time has elapsed and the nearly completed project is assured of success, with the amount of the equity distribution generally related to the extent of exposure incurred before completion.

At issue is the balance struck between control and the risk associated with the amount of up-front funds advanced. Sometimes friction can be avoided by giving the lending institution an option to enter the partnership at a later date at a time when the venture is relatively risk free. Under these circumstances, the developer is relieved of excessive controls when he or she needs elbow room and has only to deliver the finished product to the joint venture at or near completion.

Depending upon the degree of risk involved, many lending institutions will take less than the traditional 50 percent equity participation. By the same token, many developers can borrow the interim or equity funds on a project from other lending institutions based upon the strength of the joint venture institutional partner joining in as the project nears completion.

Several years ago we entertained a proposal to joint venture a five-star mobile-home park in the Southwest with a medium-sized life insurance company. The imposed controls, bureaucratic constraints, and arbitrary allocations of income for a relatively small project did not seem to warrant the effort, especially in this situation where the life insurance company was not providing the interim or permanent financing.

## WHAT THE INSTITUTIONAL INVESTOR SHOULD PROVIDE

From the foregoing, it becomes evident that no joint venture need fail because of personality clashes and conflicting interests. A wide range of structuring is available to assure an adequate agreement protecting both parties. A developer looks to an institutional partner for financing, and the institutional investor does not necessarily desire any more control than is necessary for its own protection. Whatever the structuring, the institutional lender should provide funds totally sufficient for:

- long-term, fixed-rate mortgage financing;
- acquisition financing to purchase the property;
- interim construction funds for developing the infrastructure;
- the basic construction loan covering the improvements and other interim financing costs; and
- monies required for the equity positions (funds over and above the development, construction, and acquisition loans needed to complete the project and to carry it).

The equity position, the last on the list, is normally the most difficult to structure since an arm's length situation must exist between the developing partner, the mortgage lender, and the joint venture equity partner, who is normally a subsidiary of the mortgage lender. If the relationship between the equity contribution and the mortgage loan is not well defined, the consequence may be a highly leveraged, thinly capitalized organization extremely susceptible to many troublesome negative ramifications. Such a joint-venture arrangement is particularly vulnerable to legal problems, since the corporate veil can be pierced and personal liability can flow to the joint-venture partners if any creditor is able to demonstrate that he or she was misled about the nature and extent of the capitalization. If it can be established that the corporation was substantially underfunded to accomplish only the development objectives, substantial liabilities to all parties can surface.

Some joint-venture agreements are being structured so that most, if not all, of the funds are provided strictly on a repayable mortgage basis, subject to restructuring at a later date, permitting the lending institution to convert part or all of its mortgage into an equity position in the development. A majority of the risk to the lending institution is thereby eliminated, since the burden of completing the project is shifted to the developing entity. This concept is being utilized more and more by pension funds, which desire a combination of high yields and low risks and are not in a position to utilize the tax-deferred benefits derived from a development.

In spite of the fact that many lenders are requiring developers to commit to a venture for prolonged periods of time, these types of arrangements are not without benefits to many developers. Among the advantages are

- they are freed from the oversupervision and conflict of interest aspects during the development process;
- they are allocated the majority of the tax benefits early in the development to offset other earned income;
- if a definitive arrangement can be structured providing the conversion of debt to equity relatively early in the development, the developer can normally borrow whatever funds are necessary to complete the project, which frequently include his or her profit.

## THE APPROPRIATE VEHICLE FOR STRUCTURING A JOINT VENTURE

A joint venture is most commonly structured through a series of corporate entities, providing the much-sought-after limited liability aspect. The proper balance must be struck between the acquisition or development entity, the lending institution, and the institution's subsidiary equity corporation so that appropriate funds can be passed through and double taxation avoided. While institutional investors have some restrictions in terms of the number of subsidiary companies they can structure, development entities can normally set up separate corporations for each particular joint venture they become involved in, often passing through the losses or gains under a Subchapter S vehicle. At a given point, the Subchapter S designation can be eliminated and the corporation structured as a regular entity if it then should fit the developer's long-term needs.

Most institutional investors, either through wholly owned subsidiaries or by filling a consolidated return with the subsidiary and parent companies, can pass on the benefits directly to the parent corporation without the double taxation aspect, since many institutional investors qualify for the 85 percent dividends-received deduction. Channeling the tax losses becomes more difficult for them. Potential conflicts can arise where the developer might favor the retention of profits and the institutional investor might want to distribute the profits upstream to the parent company in the calendar year in which they are generated. Again, the mortgage encumbrance should appropriately be structured through the parent company and the equity contributions through the subsidiary. Payment of interest on the debt is a deductible item to the joint venture, and profit distribution to either the institutional lender or the developer can have substantial tax ramifications.

## STRUCTURING THE INVESTMENT WITH THE INSTITUTIONAL INVESTOR

The relationship between the parent institution and its subsidiaries is the factor determining what laws will regulate their operation and, to some degree, your joint-venture arrangement. Governing legal regulations have significant overall ramifications on joint ventures and must be understood by the individuals interested in forming these types of relationships. For instance, many life insurance companies declare income from joint venture arrangements in one of two ways:

1. as *investment income* needed or escrowed to satisfy the direct obligations to their policy holders, which is nontaxable; or
2. as normal *company profits* subject to the usual rates of taxation.

Life insurance companies also have unique methods of stating their assets, normally accomplished in terms of either fair market or book value. Both the declaration of income assignment and the method of reporting assets directly affect the amount of taxable income a life insurance company will have to declare. The result is that the profits can be syphoned out of a joint venture with little or no tax ramifications to the institutional partner but often having substantial and embarrassing consequences to the developer.

When the joint-venture institutional partner insists on using a subsidiary company that has little direct tax consequences or obligations, a separate combination of debt and equity investments should be structured to avoid any discrepancies in reporting taxable income that might subject the joint venture to regulatory scrutiny. A substantial portion of the funds withdrawn by the institutional investor should be considered repayment of the mortgage obligation in order to eliminate unwanted or unnecessary tax implications to the developer. The relationship of debt to equity funding should also be measured or structured carefully since thin capitalization in a joint-venture arrangement can often be challenged.

Another method of alleviating the tax problems consequent upon income distribution is far simpler. The developer should insist that the institutional partner file a consolidated tax return in which the parent company reconciles allotment of income between itself and its subsidiary without any adverse implications to the developer. However, many institutional investors—including some life insurance companies, real estate investment trusts, and pension funds—cannot legally file consolidated tax returns. Knowing the details of the interrelationships between the parent and subsidiary companies is extremely important to an individual when contemplating a joint venture.

## LIABILITY CONSIDERATIONS IN STRUCTURING JOINT VENTURES

In partnership arrangements, either party can make commitments, financial and other, that are or can be binding on the other associates. The limits of exposure should be well defined in the agreements, particularly so when the lending institution is a well-known household name. Many litigation-oriented individuals challenge institutions of national stature in the courts with monotonous regularity creating problems no sensible developer would wish to share. Similarly, the activities of a prominent developer can open the door to a number of trumped-up lawsuits, less substantial perhaps in amount but equally as troublesome.

Legal complications also can arise around the distinctness of identity between the parent institution with its mortgage financing and that of its subsidiary holding an equity position. When projects develop financial complications reducing or eliminating the equity position either short-term or permanently, the lending institution must strongly maintain its exclusive role as holder of the first mortgage. Litigation can often confuse and complicate the identity of the seemingly separate parent and subsidiary companies, thereby placing a cloud on the potential first-mortgage obligation of the joint-venture arrangement. Courts have held that intermingling of equity and mortgage interests prove that subsidiary companies are nothing more than instruments for the parent organization. When this thinking prevails, parent companies have been held to be liable for the debts of their equity-oriented subsidiaries.

Much of this transpired in the 1973–1974 real estate market, which ended up in shambles for the REITs, which made these interrelationships a fairly common practice. As a result of one such incident we purchased a defunct 50-unit condominium project for $815,000, or for 30 cents on the dollar, when loans uncollateralized by specific real estate ventures were uncommon.

## ALLOCATIONS OF INCOME AND PARTNERSHIP CONTRIBUTIONS

Many developers inflate their contributions to joint-venture arrangements by exchanging properties or options to acquire real estate at values substantially above their acquisition price. This is normally considered strictly as an exchange for interest in the partnership and does not involve declarable gain or taxable implications to the developer. Definitive documents must be carefully drawn relating to these contributions, since taxable gain must be deferred on the appreciated aspect of the contributed property. The real estate should be placed on the partnership books at the developer's cost, not the acquisition price to the joint venture. This stepped-down basis normally causes no difficulties for the institutional partner except when the property is substantially developed.

The value placed on a property when contributed, whether or not it is developed, should relate directly to or have some bearing on the tax consequences to the individual partners. An improved property generates substantial tax benefits, and the true acquisition value means greater benefits to all parties. When the basis is stepped up to reflect the developer's contribution, one must understand fully the ramifications as they relate to one's tax liability. Sometimes the adverse effects of a stepped-up basis to the developer can be offset if an installment sale to be the partnership is structured. When this is accomplished, it is important that the developer receive some offsetting income to substantiate the taxable implications of the sale.

Normally the institution and the developer have equal equity positions in the development, making the income and tax losses deductible without need for further proration. This is usually achieved by structuring the first mortgage so that either the developer or the institution has full recourse, or alternatively that neither group has personal liability. For obvious reasons, most institutional lenders will not want their subsidiary companies to be liable for their interrelated mortgage encumbrances. The developer under such an arrangement has entry into the joint venture without personal exposure on the mortgage financing aspect of the project.

## MANAGEMENT OF THE JOINT VENTURE

Management is the issue on which joint venture arrangements differ markedly from syndicated real estate limited partnerships in which the syndicating entity statutorily has unchallenged control. Most institutional investors consider management the single most impelling reason to enter a joint-venture arrangement. Their inexperience in major real estate developments is the reason they seek out a partner with expertise. That same inexperience may lead to an overprotection of their interests to the point of threatening the successful management with an inordinate number of potentially inflexible constraints.

Joint-venture agreements generally detail specific areas of management about which the partners must advise and consent, such as

- the ability to mortgage and sell the asset;
- the approval of major expenditures for construction and marketing;
- the approval of the budgets and guidelines for operating expenses; and
- the contracting powers and corresponding constraints.

Beyond these major well-defined areas, the day-to-day operations necessary to implement the partnership's decisions should be left exclusively to the managing joint-venture partner.

This entity or his or her designated agents need enormous

**SPECIFIC AREAS**

1. ABILITY TO MORTGAGE AND SELL
2. APPROVAL OF MAJOR EXPENDITURES
3. APPROVAL OF BUDGETS
4. CONTRACTING POWERS AND CONSTRAINTS

**Figure 8.1** Areas about which joint venture partners must advise and consent.

amounts of discretion to vary procedures in order to accomplish the overall joint-venture objectives. To ensure the necessary control, many agreements are structured so that the managing joint venture partner has unquestioned control. When projections do not fully materialize in such arrangements, the management fees to the subsidiary companies controlled by the joint-venture partner are, as a matter of practice, either waived or deferred until the project again meets its stated fiscal objectives. With this check-and-balance system, the managing joint-venture partner cannot distribute funds to his or her subsidiary companies, thus systematically eliminating the profit potential for the other joint-venture partner.

Lenders have a tendency to put restrictive management policies in joint-venture agreements, similar to those that are sometimes not applicable and legally inserted in mortgages that attempt to govern activities at times of foreclosure. When these types of attitudes prevail, as we witnessed in a recent $6 million motel development, one is better off doing the project without the institution.

## REMEDIES FOR BREACH OF JOINT-VENTURE AGREEMENTS

Initially in the life of a joint venture much of the developer's expertise should be channeled into the effective management of the partnership and the project. How long this managerial function must continue depends upon the specific agreement and the surrounding circumstances, as a changing of the guard can be both costly and unproductive if the managing general partner does not completely fulfill his or her stated contractual responsibilities. Nothing short of an irreconcilable crisis with irreversible ramifications should dictate a change of management during the critical stages of acquisition or development.

Many joint-venture arrangements are structured so that the managing partner can be terminated only for "just cause." When this provision is incorporated, an arbitration agent should be designated so that this clause can be enforced in a judiciously short period of time. Even though this contractual arrangement can be quite arbitrary, it can potentially work to the advantage of all joint-venture parties. Some of the guesswork can be taken out of the eventual solution by a provision in the documentation that either of the joint-venture partners can choose a substitute managing agent, so long as the other partner has the right to approve, disapprove, or substitute his or her own candidate. Without this provision, the partner without the option to veto will generally not cooperate with the newly chosen managerial group, and the transition from the existing to the new management team will be rough and tumble at best.

The potential for conflicts of interest exists whenever companies subsidiary to either joint-venture partner are involved in any aspect of the development. It is normally a sound concept for the institutional investor to have the veto power over all contracts that directly involve the wholly owned subsidiaries of the joint-venture developer/managing agent. This works to the advantage of both groups. If an inappropriate contract is let with a company in which the developer has an interest and the institutional investor has no veto power, a potential violation of the joint-venture agreement could occur, causing a breach over a fairly insignificant incident or expenditure. When related or subsidiary companies are involved, contractual obligations should be scrutinized annually and reviewed for appropriateness of expenditures and contractual terms.

An unhealthy situation threatening the viability of any partnership exists whenever the institutional partner has unilateral veto power over the management of the project or where the agreement calls for the consent of both joint-venture partners when revamping contracts that relate to the project's management. Provisions this broad permit the money partner to withdraw his or her consent unilaterally and capriciously to the managing partner's activities, often destroying the project's real or potential achievements. Other means of more formalized withdrawal and replacement of management have been previously described and provide a far better protection for both partners.

## ALLOCATION OF PROFITS, LOSSES, AND LIABILITIES

As expert as they may be in analyzing the potential risks associated with first-mortgage lending, most institutional lenders are not fully prepared for the exposure they conceivably can encounter when they first begin to contemplate participating in joint-venture arrangements. Conventional mortgage loans are well documented with appraisals and supporting collateral, leaving a minor or sometimes nonexistent margin for error in projecting returns. Joint ventures are far more speculative, and agreements must be quite specific in terms of sharing in the losses or exposure as well as the profits. While initial equity contributions can be determined quite specifically, deficiencies and losses can exist in

- equity or capital accounts;
- mortgage financing payments; and
- operational expenditure funds.

The last item, as is the case with syndicated partnership shares, is a problem generator, since continuing operating deficits must be covered, sometimes with frequent and often substantial injections of capital.

The real estate entrepreneur who joint ventures with an institutional partner does so under the expectation that the optimum losses will be covered in some manner acceptable to both parties. Joint-venture agreements customarily state that the partners have the option not to advance or borrow additional funds and/or in the alternative have the option to sell the property in order to cut the losses. The experienced developer should carefully discuss this point with an institutional lender inexperienced in joint ventures, as one cannot afford to leave the matter of injection of additional capital open-ended.

The overall scope of the potential liabilities is also not always immediately obvious to the partners entering into a joint venture. The agreement should be detailed and specific about the far-reaching consequences of financial liability. Both parties should indemnify each other in the event that a major error or mistake occurs outside and/or contrary to the joint-venture documents.

Profit distributions are fairly standard in format in most joint-venture arrangements:

- First the developing entity receives compensation for the services provided during the development process.
- Then the allocation of income shifts to the institutional investor to satisfy the mortgage obligations.
- The next distribution of profits is normally applied to repayment of the equity funds advanced by the institutional partner or subsidiary.
- Then a predetermined split in the profits occurs among the joint-venture partners.

Normally, the equity-contributing partner is paid interest on his or her advances prior to the developer receiving any profit distributions, but exceptions to this occur when long periods of time precede the distribution of profits or where the developing entity must forego a portion of the normal up-front development fees.

## TERMINATION PROVISIONS OF JOINT-VENTURE AGREEMENTS

All contracting parties in a joint venture normally become quite dependent upon each other. The lending institution is involved in a series of financial commitments that cannot easily be untangled and that are often contingent upon the expertise of the developer for their ultimate repayment. For his or her part, under adverse or trying conditions, the developer must often look for a substitute lender with objectives that dovetail with his or her own goals or ambitions. Termination is complicated for both parties and, in varying degrees, can be extremely painful.

Joint-venture agreements are usually structured so that at some predetermined point in time one of the partners can sell or otherwise dispose of his interest. These termination clauses are usually effectuated at or near completion, depending upon the prescribed function of each party. If the agreement is structured to rely upon the developer's managerial expertise after completion, unwinding of the partnership is not feasible until all the contractual obligations are fulfilled. In the event that the lending institution opts for first withdrawal, the agreement should be structured to protect the developer from having to work with an incompatible substitute lender. In either case, the remaining joint-venture partner should have the right to veto the entry of any undesirable substitute associate.

Expediting the termination of the affairs of a joint venture can best be achieved through a typical buy-sell type of agreement. Anything short of this shotgun type of agreement in which one party has complete control compromises the value of the partnership interest. Because these relationships can be complicated, a respectable period of time should be allowed to wind up contractual obligations or arrange for a sale. Especially during periods of tight money or high interest rates or when substantial properties are involved, developers can find themselves at a disadvantage utilizing such terminations, since they normally cannot instantly raise the capital to acquire the interests of their institutional monied partners. If a developer cannot favorably structure a buyout or sale to his or her institutional partner, the next most equitable arrangement usually is a sale of the entire joint-venture interest to an independent third party. This option should be considered when the agreement is so structured and the time allotted between notification of intention and actual disposition is generously construed to assure equitable conditions for sharing the ultimate and substantial funds involved.

Death or disability clauses are normally quite detailed in joint-venture arrangements and generally apply exclusively to the developing entity. When a key person dies or is permanently disabled, it is not beneficial to either party to continue or prolong the relationship. In such a situation, the most equitable way to sever the relationship is through

- the use of independent appraisals supporting the buyout price; or
- key-man life or disability insurance with the proceeds allocated to the withdrawing party.

Arbitration clauses are also helpful in sensitive situations, permitting independent appraisers or disinterested parties knowledgeable about real estate values to determine the realistic fair-market value of an ongoing yet uncompleted project.

## ADDITIONAL CONCEPTS FOUND IN JOINT-VENTURE ARRANGEMENTS

A major contingency must be addressed in any joint-venture arrangement taking the form of restrictions placed upon the competing activities of the developer. Without the consent of one's institutional partner, many agreements prohibit one from participating in other similar ventures. Especially for those real estate entrepreneurs who are extremely active or operate on a regionalized basis, this limitation can often present substantial hardships.

We are currently involved in a $15 million residential joint venture where geographic restrictions are placed on our being involved in similar or competing ventures. The agreement is quite specific and requires the approval of all the joint-venture partners for additional activities in the immediate marketing area. As a matter of course, any competing venture would be counterproductive to all individuals.

Another requirement of many joint-venture agreements is that both the developer and the lending institution provide ongoing updated statements of income and net worth. If the language in these clauses is drawn too restrictively, many developers can sacrifice their equity in the event that their short-term financial affairs are temporarily insufficient to maintain an equitable balance within the partnership.

Many joint-venture arrangements are quite specific about the remedies relating to a breach of contract or potential partnership violation by either partner. Since the separation ramifications of a joint venture are widespread, this clause should be scrutinized carefully. Many agreements call for injunctive arrangements during periods of litigation, while other remedies can include actions pertaining to equitable relief of specific performance. If a specific performance clause is invoked, a developer may be unable either to compete in other projects or dispose of his or her unworkable and often unprofitable interest in the existing venture.

Finally, the partnership documents should reflect the laws applicable in the community where the project is being acquired or developed. When the joint-venture partners operate together in several states, legal problems are obviously compounded.

The potential for conflicts of interest in joint ventures makes many of them continual tugs-of-war. The hypothetical real estate developer or entrepreneur introduced at the beginning of this chapter, warmed to the cockles of his heart by an offer from a powerful financial backer, could well have been chilled to the marrow of his bones if he entered into a joint-venture agreement unprepared. The situation described is possible but not typical. More often than not, one seeks out the institutional backer for purposes of joint venturing and brings greater sophistication and expertise to the partnership. This situation need not and probably will not prevail indefinitely as institutions gain knowledge and experience in joint-venture arrangements. Structuring a partnership so that equality prevails is no small undertaking, and the advantage normally goes to the more sophisticated of the partners.

In the following chapter, additional pros and cons of joint venturing will be explored as we consider the complexities of choosing a partnership vehicle ideally suited for investment goals and syndicating activities.

# 9

# Choosing the Appropriate Partnership Vehicle

Most syndications have at their disposal a multitude of vehicles for forming a syndication. The joint-venture arrangement discussed in the last chapter obviously serves certain situations well but is less than versatile in terms of the happenstances that make partners seek each other out and in terms of their potential compatibility. In this chapter we will discuss a variety of other arrangements offering certain advantages and disadvantages to both syndicators and investors alike.

In terms of providing an overall versatility, two vehicles have historically been favored by real estate syndicators:

1. the limited partnership entity; and
2. the real estate investment trust (REIT).

Sophisticated syndicators have formed limited partnerships over the years because of the unique opportunities they offer for tax-shelter benefits. Taxable income and, more important, tax-deferred losses can be passed on directly to the limited partners without the corresponding financial exposure normally found in general-partnership arrangements. Without the double-taxation aspects of a corporation, this vehicle has many of the desirable limited-liability characteristics. To continue the comparison, a real estate investment trust has many of the same unique benefits as a limited partnership, with *one major disadvan-*

*tage:* The excessive losses that can be quite prevalent in leveraged holdings cannot in most instances be passed through directly to investors using a REIT structure.

Along with these more familiar vehicles, a variety of others will be discussed, including corporations with or without Subchapter S designations, so that you as syndicator can determine the overall needs and ramifications as they affect your offering and its investors. Each has its own unique advantages. Disadvantages, for the most part, pertain to the possibility that some can be classified as associations or corporations subjecting themselves to double taxation. Others develop complications that surface in the origination and operational phases. In order to offer a specific demonstration of the advantages and disadvantages, we will compare partnership and corporate entities in extensive detail in terms of such critical items as tax consequences, allocations of profit or loss, distribution of either losses or profits, property disbursements or distributions, and a host of other business-related considerations potentially affecting you and your syndicated investors.

## THE TRADITIONAL SYNDICATING ENTITIES

The major difference between a corporation and a partnership, whether it be limited or general, is the limited liability aspect combined with the ability of the partnership to pass through its taxable income and losses directly to the investors without the double-taxation aspects prevalent in the corporate entity and its shareholders. In order to qualify as attractive investment vehicles to potential investors, most syndications need to use financial leverage in order to pass on the derived or related tax losses directly to their investors. In the same vein, they must shelter those investors by providing or offering them liability limited to the extent of their capital investment. Except for this critical distinction, the functions of corporations and partnerships are quite similar in many respects. The fine line establishing the difference between a partnership and a corporation is concealed in the strict guidelines and rules promulgated by the Internal Revenue Service. Deviations from the prescribed conduct under these intricate rules can have major consequences for you and your investors.

Most syndications are not organized as straight corporations due to the lack of the ability to pass through the excess tax-shelter benefits. When a corporation is desirable, a Subchapter S designation is often used in order to provide all the advantages of corporate protection combined with the pass-through benefits that go untaxed at the upper level. A hybrid can also be structured using a Subchapter S corporation as a general partner in a limited partnership, so that limited liability is achieved for all parties and the double-taxation ramifications are also eliminated. Several years ago, we used a Subchapter S corporation as the general partner in a limited partnership in a $2.5 million residential development in the Southwest. The project was bought out of bankruptcy and had an extremely tarnished image. This potential turnaround exposure, combined with the extensive interest deductions passed directly through during the revival period, made the Subchapter S corporation an ideal vehicle to use under these circumstances.

The joint-venture arrangement often used is quite similar to the general-partnership vehicle except that the decision making is a matter of mutual agreement among *all* the joint-venture partners, rather than the sole prerogative of one of the general partners that prevails in a limited or general partnership. More of the intricacies will be provided in subsequent pages, where other alternatives will be explored.

## USE OF THE CORPORATE VEHICLE FOR SYNDICATIONS

The straight corporate entity has merit in real estate syndications where the following general conditions prevail:

- Projects are development oriented, where many deductions must be capitalized.
- They offer relatively few tax-shelter benefits.
- At completion, the corporation will be dissolved, providing long-term capital-gains tax benefits.

Corporations are used primarily to limit the exposure related to the financial-liability aspects that are so prevalent in many major real estate developments. They are geared toward sophisticated and reasonably actively involved shareholders where one either needs to pledge one's stock or is desirous of a relatively free transferability of one's interests.

In order to form this vehicle, the articles of incorporation and other appropriate documents are filed with the secretary of state in the jurisdiction in which the corporation is to conduct business. Most states require a minimum of three individuals to incorporate, and the entity can normally be dissolved by either:

- the action of the stockholders;
- through litigation; or
- the failure to file appropriate annual reports on a timely basis.

All corporations have the same divisions or designations of officers, directors, and stockholders. Overlapping among these three groups is often prevalent.

## ADVANTAGES OF THE CORPORATE ENTITY

The major benefits attributable to corporations are

- *centralized management* through officers duly appointed by the board of directors;
- *limited liability* for the investors and in many instances for the managerial personnel;
- *liability to transfer freely* one's shares or percentage ownership interest; and
- *continuity of existence,* even after the death of a major shareholder.

Of these four distinct benefits, the most desirable for real estate syndications (at least when nonpublic corporations are used) are the limited liability and the continuous corporate life. Centralized management and transferability of shares are obviously more important in major corporations whose names have become household words rather than in small, closely held corporations set up for specific one-time investment purposes.

## DISADVANTAGES OF THE CORPORATE ENTITY

Many syndications offer initial up-front tax-shelter benefits combined with deferred-equity installment obligations that in combination produce a respectable and salable return even before the success of a project can be judged. Under these conditions, a syndication should *not* be organized as a straight corporation since the following disadvantages will eventually surface:

- These entities are taxed at the corporate level, and dividends distributed to the stockholders are subject to double taxation.

- Corporations are more heavily regulated than partnerships and extensive reporting is always required.
- Many profitable corporations can achieve personal holding-company status that can be subject to a 70 percent confiscatory tax rate.
- In closely held corporations, many of the bonuses, perks, or other distributions to officers and directors are vulnerable to double taxation.

Several years ago we were involved in developing a residential subdivision with three other individuals as corporate stockholders. After we disposed of a substantial part of the project, the partners realized that they had different investment objectives, and due to the complicated nature of the remaining lot inventory, it was extremely difficult to dissolve the corporation and distribute the balance of the assets without major tax implications. The use of a partnership vehicle would have been a better choice in this situation.

## USE OF THE S CORPORATION

The Subchapter S designation provides the same limited liability, continuity, management, and ease of transferring benefits available in a normal corporation. In addition, it permits the shareholders, if they so elect, to bypass the corporate income tax by reporting their prorated share of the corporate obligation on their personal tax returns. Similarly, a Subchapter S designation permits each stockholder to receive his or her prorated share of any excessive tax losses that are attributable to him or her as a stockholder in that corporation. This is accomplished by filing what is in effect an informational tax return in which all income and losses are fully distributed so that each stockholder is subjected to taxation or lack thereof at his or her individual tax bracket.

The following considerations are *critical* in forming a Subchapter S corporation:

- the corporation can have no more than 35 stockholders;
- the stockholders cannot be other corporations;
- these vehicles can have only one class of common stock; and
- the consent of *all* stockholders is necessary in order to structure and maintain the Subchapter S status.

Subchapter S corporate status provides important *advantages* to a syndication in the form of:

- limited liability to the shareholders;
- direct pass-through of profits and losses;
- a centralized management function;
- shares that are easily transferable; and
- continuity of corporate life.

The *disadvantages* or limiting factors of Subchapter S corporations relate to:

- the limited number of shareholders;
- the fact that capital losses do not pass through;
- the impossibility of special allocations of income or losses;
- the disallowance or restriction in amounts of certain sources of income, generally passive; and
- the limitation of deductible losses only to the extent of the stockholder's adjusted basis and debt owed to the shareholders by the corporation.

**SUBCHAPTER S**

**ADVANTAGES**

- LIMITED LIABILITY.
- DIRECT PASS-THROUGH OF PROFITS AND LOSSES.
- CENTRALIZED MANAGEMENT.
- EASILY TRANSFERABLE SHARES.
- CONTINUITY OF CORPORATE LIFE.

**DISADVANTAGES**

- SHAREHOLDERS LIMITED.
- NO PASS-THROUGH OF CAPITAL LOSSES.
- NO SPECIAL ALLOCATIONS OF INCOME OR LOSSES.
- SOURCES OF INCOME RESTRICTED.
- DEDUCTIBLE LOSSED LIMITED.

**Figure 9.1** Advantages and disadvantages of S Corporation status to a syndication.

## S CORPORATIONS VERSUS PARTNERSHIP VEHICLES

Deciding whether a syndication should be structured under a Subchapter S corporation or a partnership depends, in many respects, upon the surrounding or supporting facts and circumstances. The most *important* consideration relates to how the tax losses are treated and passed through to the individual investors.

Under normal provisions, one's basis in a partnership interest can be increased by one's share of the partnership debt. When this situation occurs, a partner may then deduct losses in excess of the monies he or she has invested. On the other hand, when utilizing Subchapter S corporations, shareholders normally acquire a basis in the Subchapter S corporation's debt only to the extent that they actually lend funds to the corporation. Due to this differentiation, a lack of basis may cause a Subchapter S corporation shareholder to postpone or possibly not deduct his or her share of the losses until the shareholder's basis is increased substantially. Under these circumstances, a Subchapter S corporation may be less advantageous than using a partnership vehicle, especially when this relates to a leveraged tax-oriented type of investment. There are many ways to circumvent this particular situation, and the most obvious one is for the Subchapter S corporation shareholder to borrow the funds directly and then relend them to the corporation, thereby increasing his or her tax deductible basis in the Subchapter S vehicle.

We used this approach quite recently on a 103-lot subdivision where many of the deductions had been fully utilized and the interest capitalized. By transferring 14 of the lots to the individual partners from the Subchapter S corporation with recourse financing, we were able to increase the partners' basis in those specific lots, providing additional amounts of taxable deductions.

Another factor to consider when weighing the use of a Subchapter S or partnership entity pertains to the allocation of items of income, loss, deductions, and credits. While the pass-through of the corporate items of Subchapter S corporations generally follows that of partnerships, general and limited partners can *specifically* allocate items of income, loss, deductions, and credits if these allocations have substantial economic effect. This normally means that when a syndicated transaction requires flexibility in establishing and differentiating the interests of the various parties, which is quite prevalent in most real estate offerings, a partnership is normally the more ideally suited vehicle for accomplishing these highly desirable goals.

## REAL ESTATE INVESTMENT TRUSTS

A real estate investment trust is somewhat of a hybrid between a limited partnership and a corporation. Most are publicly registered, thereby creating a market for shares that, unlike limited partnership interest, are readily transferable. This is the primary advantage of REITs in comparison to limited partnership arrangements. REITs are complicated, require unique managerial abilities, and by statute need at least 100 investors. Since the documentation can be quite extensive and must be provided to large numbers of investors, the syndicator who is considering the formation of a REIT should investigate all the ramifications of this vehicle fully before making his or her decision.

## QUALIFYING AS A REAL ESTATE INVESTMENT TRUST

Several tests must be met in qualifying as a real estate investment trust:

- Real estate, government securities, or cash equivilants must constitute 75 percent of the total assets.
- The entity cannot hold a position exceeding 5 percent in other corporations or their securities.
- REITs must retain property for investment purposes only; a resale venture is strictly prohibited.
- Real estate projects must account for at least 75 percent of all income generated.
- Less than 30 percent of the trust's income can be derived from the proceeds of sale of property for the four years preceding its qualification as a REIT.
- And, there are limitations on the employment of closely held corporations, including strict rules stipulating that an independent contractor to the REIT can own no more than 35 percent of the beneficial interest.

In order to maintain the existing status of a real estate investment trust and avoid potential taxation at the corporate level, 90 percent of the ordinary income generated from a REIT must be *distributed annually* to its shareholders. This income is then passed on and taxed at the individual rates of the shareholders. Capital gains are similarly distributed annually and in almost all circumstances retain their capital-gains status to the investors.

Most REITs offset their artificial or accounting losses against ordinary income, thus passing the income on tax free directly to their investors. They are *prohibited from distributing* the excess tax losses to their shareholders, however, and herein lies one of their major investment disadvantages. This inability can be a major deterrent in marketing REIT shares or can reduce their value substantially, since many syndications are oriented toward tax-shelter benefits, especially in the initial years.

### *Organizational Criteria for REITs*

Strict guidelines must be met to *organize* and *maintain* the status of a real estate investment trust:

- 100 or more stockholders;
- an election in the first year to obtain REIT status; and
- a lack of the option to reverse this status after the first year's election.

Another drawback with the utilization of REITs is their extreme dependence upon regulatory bodies that routinely subject them to stringent tests of assets, income, and passive investment requirements. If the regulations are not followed to the strictest letter of the

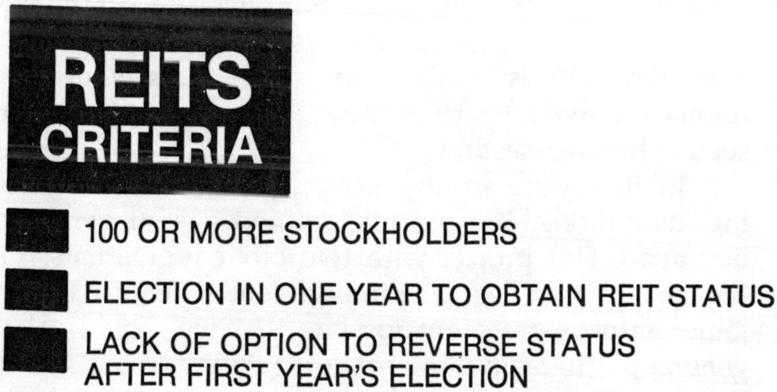


**Figure 9.2** Organizational criteria for real estate investment trusts.

law, violations can be punished with double taxation ramifications on a retroactive basis, resulting in enormous losses to the collective investors. REITs should be considered only for large, sophisticated public offerings backed by definitive initial and continuing advice from highly qualified lawyers and accountants.

## SYNDICATING THROUGH JOINT-VENTURE ARRANGEMENTS

Joint ventures are usually designed to acquire a specific real estate holding and to terminate upon its sale or disposition. Unsuitable for passive, unsophisticated investors, joint-venture arrangements involve sophisticated parties, each of whom undertakes a specific responsibility in a real estate project. The contractual obligations and duties are almost identical to those found in most general-partnership agreements, except that a complete consensus of all partners is required for a decision to be effectuated. In most partnership situations corporations are eligible as partners. However, many states exclude them as participants as joint-venture partners.

A joint venture can be formed by any two or more individuals without any written agreement, although real estate syndications that employ joint-venture techniques should be documented in writing. Areas of responsibility are normally assigned to partners contractually according to their expertise. Minor decisions are delegated to the most qualified member of the group so that the joint venture as a whole is not encumbered by the need to make these trivial and ongoing commitments. In other respects, joint-venture arrangements have the characteristics of general partnerships, except that greater management flexibility is available in partnerships where one or a limited number of general partners can guide or control the affairs, as we shall see in the next section.

Joint-venture arrangements are not necessarily favored by lending institutions. We recently formed a joint venture on a $13 million apartment project with two other individuals. Prior to funding the construction loan, the interim lender required that we amend the joint-venture agreement to state that we would act or operate as a general partnership in all matters relating to our real estate financing activities. The interim lender was uncomfortable with requiring all the joint venture's signatures on their documents, preferring to deal with one individual, whose activities would be binding on the other two partners.

## USE OF THE GENERAL OR LIMITED PARTNERSHIP FOR SYNDICATIONS

General and limited partnerships are both attractive syndicating entities because

- they both offer the advantage of single taxation to partners without tax consequences to the entity; and
- they permit losses to be passed completely through to the partners on a prorated or specifically allocated basis to the full extent of those losses.

The concept of partnership, individuals joining forces to achieve a common goal, is a natural one that long preceded the formulation of legal codes. Sharing of profits proportionate to the expenditure of resources and skills is basic to common law, and general partnerships are the natural creatures of these time-tested doctrines. Limited partnerships, in which one or more general partners manage the assets of passive individuals, are comparatively artificial. They come into existence by an agreement that must be set forth in documents recorded in the area of intended operation.

This intrinsic legal difference between a general and a limited partnership rests on the concept of operational authority inherent in the two entities. In general partnerships, all members have a voice in the decision-making process to whatever extent they are inclined to use it. By strong contrast, limited partnerships are governed autonomously by the managing general partners. Limited partners are given a voice usually only regarding the sale or disposition of the syndicated asset. Their interference in management at other times can potentially result in a legal denial of their limited-partnership status, with unpleasant tax and liability ramifications forthcoming to the passive investors.

Another significant variation between general and limited partners is that the liability of the passive individuals is normally limited to the amount of their initial equity investment. The general partner assumes responsibility for any losses in excess of the sum of his or her limited partners' equity investments. By contrast, the individuals in a general partnership prorate the recognized losses when a project fails according to the percentage of equity or some other predetermined formula. Because of the far-reaching liability provisions, the partnership document takes on an extremely important function in a limited partnership. In many other respects, general and limited partnerships are similar. Minimum membership for each is two persons, with no legal maximum set. For all practical purposes, both entities are workable only when the top limit of membership remains small. Disagreements or differing objectives potentially increase as membership grows and polarized voting groups can hamper the activities of either operation.

### *Legal Characteristics of Partnerships*

To be considered a partnership, general or limited, for legal purposes an organization must partake only partially in two of the features that characterize a corporation. These two may be chosen from four, which are

1. centralized management;
2. continuity of life;
3. limited liability; and
4. free transferability of shares.

A partnership can possess no more than two of these features. The first, centralized management, and the third, limited liability, are indispensable to an efficient and profitable real estate syndication. If the partnership is structured to partake of either of the *other* two features, continuity of life and free transferability of shares, the Internal Revenue Service will deem it to be an association taxable at both the corporate and shareholder levels. Many years ago, we structured a limited partnership on a mobile-home park in which our legal counsel invested as a limited partner to take advantage of a substantial amount of tax deductions. Although it was never questioned by the IRS, his involvement in the daily affairs of the partnership could have easily disqualified his limited-partner status.

Qualifying legally as a partnership means that a syndication can operate as a relaxed, closely held entity with minimum legal regulation, free from many of the bureaucratic factors affecting small corporations. In areas relating to tax matters alone, partnerships avoid the following problems commonly found at the corporate level:

- accumulated earnings tax;
- personal holdings tax;

- excessive executive compensation; and
- thin financial capitalization.

A wide range of other business-related problems indigenous to corporations are usually simplified when a real estate syndication is organized as a partnership.

Table 9–1 presents a graphic comparison of the relative advantages corporations and partnerships have in dealing with these problems. In some instances this table also expands upon possible variations in procedure between general and limited partnerships. While not all advantages necessarily accrue to partnerships, the requirements of real estate syndications generally are more efficiently served by a partnership rather than a corporate format.

### *The Limited Partnership Entity*

The limited partnership vehicle is ideally tailored for the vast majority of syndications engaged in the development or acquisition of small- to medium-sized real estate ventures and quite suitable for larger projects when exposure of the general partner is not an issue. The entrepreneur who desires complete control and has the wherewithal to manage the affairs of a real estate syndication in its entirety will invariably find him- or herself more comfortable in a limited partnership than in any other legally permissible investment vehicle.

In choosing this vehicle, because of the maximum autonomy it provides, a syndicator does not necessarily sacrifice the profit potential in dealings of greater magnitude. With something approaching a token equity contribution in a limited partnership, one can assume virtually complete control over substantial assets, provided to a large degree by his or her passive partners utilizing this capital with extraordinary flexibility in achieving the goals of the syndication. By devising a sound concept and executing it with the help of relatively risk-free mortgage financing, sometimes even on a nonrecourse basis, one can often ultimately receive and justify compensation in excess of the total profits collected by the contented passive partners. Doing so is not necessarily simplistic in nature, and success in meeting such a challenge enormously enhances the satisfaction derived from the monetary reward. One of the first syndications I successfully structured was on an 18-unit condominium project on leased land. In order to advance the venture to a point at which it was salable to the investors, I

*Table 9–1: Comparative Advantages of Partnerships and Corporations for Real Estate Syndications*

| *Function* | *Partnerships* | *Corporations* |
|---|---|---|
| Reporting income | Not taxpaying entities, but conduits for purposes of liability and payment of income taxes. | Income is taxed twice, at corporate level and after distribution at shareholder level. |
| Reporting losses | Deductible by a partner against other unrelated partnership income to the extent of his or her adjusted basis in partnership. Excess losses may be carried over and deducted to the extent of later or future increases in partnership basis. | Losses only deductible against corporate income of the prior three or subsequent five years. |
| Cash distributions | Tax free to partners to the extent of their basis in partnerhsip interest. Excess generally taxed as capital gains. | Taxable to shareholders as ordinary income to extent of earnings and profits. Excess considered a return of capital or capital gain. |
| Unusual allocations of profits and losses | Special allocations disproportionate to equity allowed if they have economic substance. | No special allocations allowed. |
| Property distributions | Generally untaxed to both partners and partnership. Some distributions subject to hot-asset rule. | Normally taxable to shareholders and may be taxable to corporation under certain circumstances. |
| Employee compensation | Not competitive for employee benefits. Fringe benefits for partners not deductible and may be taxable to partners. | Deductible fringe benefits and perks for employees. |
| Organizational flexibility | Accounting is extremely flexible taxwise. | A more rigid tax reporting system is mandatory. |
| Liability aspects | In *general partnerships*, all partners jointly and severally liable for obligations of partnership and activities of partners. In *limited partnerships*, passive partners liable only to extent of their equity contributions and general partners totally responsible for partnership liabilities. | Shareholders' liability is limited to their capital contributions. |
| Liquidity and transferability aspects | In *general partnerships*, no transfer of general partners without the consent of existing partners. Without the consent of other partners, assignee is entitled only to profits and appropriate accounting reporting. | No restrictions on transfer of corporate stock, but securities laws may restrict transferability of closely held entities. |

*Table 9–1: Comparative Advantages of Partnerships and Corporations for Real Estate Syndications (Continued)*

| *Function* | *Partnerships* | *Corporations* |
|---|---|---|
| | In *limited partnerships*, limited partners who assign interests without general partner's consent receive only prorated share of profits. General partners must consent to a substitute limited partner. | |
| Continuity of operations | In *general partnerships*, partnership dissolution occurs at end of a fixed term; by mutual agreement of partners; or upon death, bankruptcy, withdrawal, or expulsion of a partner unless provision is made for continuation. In *limited partnerships*, dissolution occurs upon retirement, death, or insanity of general partner unless continued by remaining general partners with consent of all members. Death, withdrawal, or bankruptcy of a limited partner does not normally cause dissolution. | Continuity not interrupted by death, insolvency, or withdrawal of a stockholder. |
| Management functions | In *general partnerships*, all partners equally involved, unless otherwise provided. In *limited partnerships*, general partners control management. | Management and equity interests separated through a board of directors elected by stockholders. Minority stockholders have little influence in management decisions. |
| Ease of operations | Need not issue shares, keep minutes, or hold annual elections. | Mandatory annual election of all officers and directors. |
| Registration requirements | *General partnerships* do not require filing fees. No minimum capital requirements for either *general* or *limited partnerships*. | Extensive filing requirements and minimum capital requirements sometimes with substantial fees varying from state to state. |
| Interstate operations | *General partnerships* are free to conduct business in other states. *Limited partnerships* should comply with applicable foreign limited partnership provisions and file certificates in states where they conduct business. | Must comply with statutory requirements that govern their charters. |
| Exclusion of information | *General partnerships* totally private; *limited partnerships* less so because of filing requirements. | Must file annual reports listing financial concepts not publicly disclosed by partnerships. |

had only to invest approximately $10,000 in architectural and engineering fees, combined with a letter of credit in the amount of $18,000 covering the first year's land-lease payment. After these two expenditures, the limited partners provided the balance of the risk funds with a local lending institution advancing the additional construction funds. In a period of less than 24 months, I made over $400,000 on this pittance of an initial investment.

In the following chapter we will discuss the many technicalities and complications inherent in forming, maintaining, and dissolving partnerships, with particular emphasis on the more highly regulated limited partnerships. As we shall see, securities legislation and the appropriate regulatory agencies demand their pound of flesh in allowing the general partner his or her enviable autonomy. Through documentation and reporting, one must be able to demonstrate a level of fair dealing with one's comparatively vulnerable passive partners and full and accurate disclosure to them of one's intentions in setting up the partnership goals and one's actions both prior and subsequent to achieving these objectives.

# 10

# Legal Aspects of Syndications and Partnership Law

The preceding chapter analyzed the various alternatives to conduct a real estate syndication. In most circumstances a limited partnership serves as the most appropriate vehicle. This chapter will examine in some detail concepts of partnership law under the Uniform Partnership Act (UPA), the Uniform Limited Partnership Act (ULPA), and to a lesser extent, the common law. Because individual state law provisions vary, they will not be explored in detail.

When considering the law of limited partnerships or when drafting a limited partnership agreement, the provisions of both the UPA and the ULPA must be kept firmly in mind, since certain of the UPA provisions will also apply to limited partnerships. In this connection, the UPA expressly states that it applies to limited partnerships except insofar as the relevant state statute relating to such partnerships is inconsistent with the UPA. What this means is that where the ULPA is silent, the UPA will control; conversely, where the ULPA contains a similar provision, it shall control.

In 1976 the National Conference of Commissioners on Uniform State Laws adopted a Revised Uniform Limited Partnership Act (RULPA) and recommended it for enactment by the states. A handful of states including California have adopted the RULPA (with modifications). Other states are currently considering its adoption. Since the RULPA is likely to be adopted by an increasing number of states in the future, its impact has also been considered throughout this chapter.

## UPA—GENERAL BACKGROUND

The UPA was first adopted in 1914 and today represents the principal element of partnership law in 49 states. We would hasten to add, however, that these laws are not completely uniform, since the provisions of the UPA, as adopted by the various state legislatures, can and do differ in many respects. Moreover, the courts of the various states can adopt, and indeed have adopted, different interpretations of the provisions.

## DEFINITION OF A PARTNERSHIP

The UPA defines a partnership as an association of two or more persons to carry on as co-owners a business for profit. Under the UPA, "person" expressly includes individuals, partnerships, corporations, and other associations. Co-ownership of a business, by itself, is not conclusive of partnership status. On the other hand, the profit-sharing element is a fundamental attribute of the partnership, and the evidence of this element is evidence of a partnership.

## SCOPE OF GENERAL PARTNER'S AUTHORITY

The authority of a general partner to bind the partnership is significant not only to the question of the capacity of one partner within a general partnership to bind another co-partner, but also is pertinent to a situation involving multiple partners in a limited partnership, among themselves as well as vis-a-vis third parties. The UPA expressly gives each partner the power to act as agent of the partnership for business purposes, but at the same time clearly permits variation of this mutual management power by agreement among the parties.

The law of agency is incorporated into the UPA, and accordingly, the fiduciary concept becomes relevant. The fiduciary duty of the general partner is often compared to the duty of a corporate director to his or her stockholders. Hence, most corporate fiduciary duties would apply with equal force, and a general partner should be fully aware of these duties.

It is generally recognized that in the exercise of one's fiduciary duties a partner cannot

- directly or indirectly use partnership assets for one's own benefit;
- take any profit clandestinely for oneself in conducting the business of a partnership;
- carry on another business in competition or rivalry with that of the firm, thereby depriving it of the benefit of one's time, skill, and fidelity without being accountable to one's co-partners for any profit that may accrue to one therefrom;
- be permitted to secure for oneself that which it is one's duty to obtain, if at all, for the firm of which one is a member; or
- avail oneself of knowledge or information that may be properly regarded as the property of the partnership, in the same way that it is available or useful to the firm for any purpose within the scope of the partnership business.

## THE PARTNERS AND THEIR VARIOUS RELATIONSHIPS

Unless the partnership agreement provides otherwise, all partners will be deemed to share profits equally, and this holds true even though they may not have contributed equally to the partnership capital. This same concept holds true with respect to partnership losses. If a partner's losses exceed his or her contributed capital, the deficit will be treated as an asset of the partnership, and upon the death of the partner or dissolution of the partnership, the partner (or his or her estate) would be required to contribute additional funds to the partnership to bring the balance of the capital account to zero.

The UPA further provides that a dissolution of the partnership does not discharge the existing liabilities of any partner. To effect such a discharge, an agreement must be executed between the partner, the creditor, and the continuing partnership.

The UPA also provides that new partners are liable on old partnership debts, but not beyond the new partner's share of partnership property. New partners may, however, become personally liable for old debts if they so agree. A retiring or resigning general partner will always remain liable for existing partnership debts, unless the new partner assumes such obligations.

Dissolution should not be confused with termination of a partnership. When a partnership ceases to exist, it will

1. dissolve—an act that terminates all authority of the partners to act on behalf of the partnership, except for those actions that are necessary to wind up the partnership;
2. wind up; and finally
3. terminate.

During the process of winding up, partners will have the following power:

- Generally speaking the remaining partner(s) who will carry on the business can contract on behalf of and bind the partnership by any act necessary and appropriate for winding up partnership affairs. Unless a creditor has actual notice of the process of dissolution, a partner can bind the partnership and hence create partnership liability, even though the partner had no authority. For this later reason, it is desirable to publish notice of dissolution in a newspaper of general circulation if there is any possibility that an unauthorized partner might attempt to conduct business.

## CREATION OF THE LIMITED PARTNERSHIP UNDER ULPA

ULPA defines a limited partnership as a partnership formed by two or more persons having as members one or more general partners and one or more limited partners. ULPA goes on to state that formation of the partnership is contingent upon "substantial compliance" in good faith with certain requirements, as follows.

At least two persons must execute a certificate containing the items discussed in the following paragraphs. It is interesting to note that ULPA does not even mention a "partnership agreement" or "articles of partnership." RULPA, on the other hand, clearly recognizes the partnership agreement as the cornerstone document and relegates the certificate to serve only two functions, to

1. notify third parties concerning the partnership capital and contributions to and withdrawals from the partnership; and
2. identify when persons become partners.

Under ULPA the certificate is filed in an office where the partnership records are maintained. RULPA, on the other hand, requires filing of the certificate in the office of the secretary of state. This filing requirement is similar to the practice and procedure of most states concerning the formation of a corporation and has the effect of transforming the certificate from a "local" to a "statewide" document.

Among the items required by ULPA to be a part of the certificate are the following:

- *Partnership name.* ULPA is silent on the use and reservation of names, except that generally speaking a limited partner's name may not appear in the partnership name. RULPA, on the other hand, contains the requirement that the name of a limited partnership contain (without abbreviation) the words "limited partnership."
- *Character of the business.* Unless the particular state prohibits an activity, a limited partnership can carry on any business that is permitted under general partnership law, that is, any lawful business. RULPA adopts a similar approach.
- *Principal place of business.* Most states require that a place of business be maintained within the state to satisfy the recording requirement. RULPA also requires a limited partnership to have an agent for service of process in the state.
- *Name and residence of each general and limited partner.* Both ULPA and RULPA require the certificate to state the names and residences of each partner separately.
- *Description of cash and other property contributed by each limited partner.* ULPA limits contributions by limited partners to either cash or other property; services are not permitted. RULPA makes a dramatic change and allows limited, as well as general, partners to contribute "cash, property, or services rendered or a promissory note or other obligation to contribute cash or property or to perform services."
- *Term of the partnership.* Typically the term will be fixed so that it expires after all mortgage financing is retired.
- *Additional capital contributions.* Future contributions agreed to be made by each limited partner and the times at which or events on the happening of which they shall be made must be described. Typical real estate syndications call for deferred capital payments.
- *The share of profits* or other compensation by way of income that each limited partner is to receive by reason of his or her capital contribution.
- *The right,* if any, of a limited partner to substitute an assignee as

contributor in his or her place and the terms and conditions of the substitution.

- *The right,* if any, of the partners to admit additional limited partners.
- *The right,* if any, of one or more of the limited partners to priority over other limited partners, as to contributions or as to compensation by way of income and the nature of such priority. Absent such priority, all limited partners stand on equal footing.
- *The right,* if any, of the remaining general partner or partners to continue the business on the death, retirement, or insanity of a general partner. ULPA provides that so long as the certificate permits, the remaining general partner(s) may continue a limited partnership.
- *The right,* if any, of a limited partner to demand and receive property other than cash in return for his or her contribution. ULPA provides that, unless otherwise agreed to, limited partners may demand and receive only cash in return for their contributions.

The act of filing the certificate creates the limited liability. The certificate is a statutory prerequisite to creation of a limited partnership, and until it is filed, the partnership is technically not formed.

Where compliance with filing requirements is made before third parties have had any dealings with the partnership, no problems should exist. As between themselves, however, limited partners will be estopped from asserting that a limited partnership had never been formed because the certificate was not recorded, where the partners held themselves out to the public as limited partners.

ULPA establishes various requirements for amending the certificate. ULPA generally requires the certificate to be amended upon the happening of any of ten contingencies listed therein, most of which relate to the items required to be set forth in the original certificate as just described.

Failure to file an amendment to the certificate where there is an extension or renewal of the term of the partnership may lead to general liability of all partners if the partnership's term has ended and a limited partner has not renounced his or her interest. However, failure to file an amendment to the certificate as to any of the other nine matters need not make the entity a general partnership, nor does it render the limited partners liable as general partners. RULPA adopts a 30-day "safe harbor" against claims of creditors or others who assert they have been misled by the failure to amend the certificate.

## RIGHTS OF LIMITED PARTNERS

ULPA describes a limited partner's interest in the partnership as "personal property." This is significant in that it allows for a Uniform Commercial Code (UCC) financing statement to be filed as a way to obtain a security interest in a partner's partnership interest. Moreover, upon the death of a partner, the partnership interest passes to his or her estate as personal property and, assuming record title to the real property is held by the partnership (and not the partners), not to his or her heirs or legatees as real property.

A limited partner has no interest in the individual partnership assets; hence, such assets cannot be reached by a creditor of the limited partner. The only indirect way for a limited partners's creditor to reach assets of the partnership is through foreclosure of the partnership interest of the indebted limited partner.

ULPA specifically deals with transfers of limited partnership interests and provides generally that a limited partnership interest is assignable. However, all of the limited partners must approve admission of a substituted limited partner unless, as is often the case, the general partner is granted the right to do so in the certificate. A properly substituted limited partner has all the rights and powers and is subject to all the restrictions and liabilities of his or her assignor, except those liabilities of which he or she was ignorant at the time he or she became a limited partner and which could not be ascertained from the certificate.

Substitution of an assignee as a limited partner does not release the assignor from certain liabilities, including the liability for false statements in the certificate and the liability of the assignor to the partnership for certain unpaid capital contributions.

## LIABILITIES OF LIMITED PARTNERS

Perhaps the most significant issue to a limited partner is his or her potential liability arising out of participation in partnership business. This is known as the "control" problem. A limited partner generally will not be held liable for the obligations of the partnership on the basis that he or she merely possessed a potential ability to control the business; it is actual participation, not an unexercised power to control, that violates the ULPA. The question is whether a limited partner's conduct is factually and legally sufficient to lead another person to believe he or she is a general partner.

Limited partners may be employed by the partnership so long as their employment does not infringe upon the general partner's powers. Stated another way, a limited partner ordinarily may serve as an employee or consultant to the partnership unless, by virtue of his or her expertise or responsibilities, he or she usurps the power of the general partner to make decisions regarding the regular business operations of the partnership.

Some states have modified the provisions of ULPA in an attempt to define specifically the "control" issue or at least define certain types of activities that can be safely engaged in by limited partners. These provisions vary considerably and are beyond the scope of this text. Since this is an important issue, however, it is prudent to focus in on the language of the state law that will govern the partnership.

RULPA recognizes the common practice of granting limited partners voting rights and identifies certain matters in which limited partners may participate without fear of liability as general partners. These include

- dissolution and winding up of the partnership;
- sale, exchange, lease, mortgage, pledge, or other transfer of all or substantially all of the assets of the limited partnership other than in the ordinary course of its business;
- incurrence of indebtedness by the limited partnership other than in the ordinary course of its business;
- change in the nature of the business; and
- the removal of the general partner.

RULPA also identifies four matters as being activities in which a limited partner may engage without becoming liable as a general partner. These include

1. being an agent or employee of the partnership;
2. consulting with the general partner regarding partnership business;
3. acting as a surety for the partnership; and

4. approving or disapproving amendments to the partnership certificate.

Finally, RULPA provides that a limited partner whose participation in the control of the business is "substantially the same as" that of a general partner would apparently be generally liable to anyone, whereas a limited partner whose participation falls short of this standard will be liable only to persons who transact business with the limited partnership with actual knowledge of his or her participation and control.

*General Partners*

The general conduct and management of the business of a limited partnership are vested in the general partner(s) under ULPA. The rights, powers, and duties of the general partner are made analogous to those of a partner of an ordinary general partnership discussed earlier with certain additional restrictions. However, the principal-agent relationship that exists between partners of an ordinary partnership is not present between general and limited partners in a limited partnership. What does remain generally the same under either type of partnership is the fiduciary obligation of a general partner.

As is true with a limited partner's interest in the partnership, in the absence of agreement to the contrary, a general partner's interest is assignable. Withdrawal of the general partner, however, dissolves the partnership, unless there is a provision in the certificate for continuation by the remaining general partners or unless there is consent of all members. Assignment by the general partner of his or her interest in the limited partnership, without making adequate provision in the limited partnership certificate, will cause a dissolution of the limited partnership.

## THE TYPICAL LIMITED PARTNERSHIP AGREEMENT—CHECKLIST OF SIGNIFICANT PROVISIONS

Thus far we have discussed some of the basic legal principles of partnership law as embodied in the UPA and the ULPA (and, to a lesser degree, the RULPA). The remainder of this chapter focuses on the more practical aspect of a typical limited partnership agreement and, specifically, discusses the more common provisions found in such agreements. The provisions of any agreement must necessarily be tailored to the specific transaction involved; the following discussion is included only as a guide to identify the principal areas of concern.

A typical limited partnership agreement may begin with a narrative summary of the general purposes of the limited partnership and the overall transaction, including identification of the parties, the properties, the financing arrangements, and so forth. It is also common to include a separate definitional section.

1. *Name of the partnership.* Care must be taken in assigning a name to a limited partnership. To preserve limited liability, the name of a limited partner should never be included in the name of a limited partnership. It should also be noted that various states have different requirements in terms of the use of the term "Ltd." or "Limited." Curiously, RULPA also requires that the name of each limited partnership "contain without abbreviation the words 'limited partnership.' "

2. *Purposes of limited partnership.* This section will set forth the specific purposes of the partnership (that is, to acquire or build a particular building or buildings, and the like) and should include all reasonably foreseeable activities of the partnership.

3. *Place of business of limited partnership.* This section will describe the principal place of business of the partnership that is required under ULPA. If a place of business in another jurisdiction is contemplated, it should also be set forth to make certain that filings in such other locations are made to preserve limited liability for the limited partners.

4. *Term of limited partnership.* Generally, a limited partnership should have a definite term that will extend beyond the expiration of any mortgage financing. The typical agreement will also provide for earlier dissolution upon the occurrence of certain stated events and, equally important, for the continuation of the business of the partnership after the occurrence of certain events.

5. *Capital contributions.* This section will describe the capital contributions to be made by both the general and limited partners. A limited partner is not permitted to contribute services as part of capital contributions, except that RULPA will allow for contributions of services rendered and to be rendered. In recent years it has become typical for capital to be paid in installments over the early years of a project, and hence this section should provide for contingencies if installments are not paid when due and establish a mechanism for other partners to acquire the interest of a defaulting limited partner.

6. *Profits and losses and cash flow.* This section will establish provisions for sharing of profits and losses, cash flow, and allocation of

credits and deductions for tax purposes. Generally speaking, the profits and losses would normally follow cash flow, though losses may instead be allocated in proportion to the partners' capital contributions. Certain specific allocations are permitted but must be carefully considered to determine whether they will be successful from a tax point of view (see Chapter 12).

7. *Maintenance of books and reports.* This section will identify whether a cash or accrual method of accounting is selected. In real estate projects, accrual is more common. This section will also provide for the requirements of maintaining financial statements, books and records, reports, and tax information and returns (that is, Federal Forms 1065 and K-1).

8. *Fiscal year.* This section will define the fiscal year of the partnership, which may or may not be the calendar year.

9. *Sale/refinancing proceeds and related distributions.* Because a sale of all the partnership's assets will be a significant (and normally taxable) event to the partners, it is conventional for the limited partners to have the right to vote upon any such sale. Such right of approval should not result in the limited partner's becoming a general partner. Similar considerations should be true for refinancing, although the tax consequences of refinancing are not likely to be as serious to the limited partners as would be a sale. Proceeds of any sale or refinancing would normally be distributed in the same manner as income and losses or cash flow, but it is not uncommon to have variations on this theme, with the general partner taking a substantially larger share.

10. *Management of the partnership: the "control" question.* As previously discussed, ULPA provides that a limited partner shall not have personal liability unless "in addition to the exercise of his rights and powers as a limited partner, he takes part in the control of the business." Thus, it is critical that the limited partner not take part in such control of partnership. Accordingly, this section should provide that the partnership is to be managed by the general partner, and if there are multiple general partners, there can be one or more designated managing partners. Limitations or restrictions, if any, on the power of the general partner to operate within the general purpose of the partnership should be enumerated.

11. *Other activities of general partners.* Since the general partner is a fiduciary to all partners, to the extent that he or she may engage in other competing ventures, such activities should be clearly disclosed. It is common for such a statement to authorize limited partners as well to engage in any competing ventures.

12. *Fees.* This section will identify all fees that will be paid to the general partner (or any affiliate). These would typically include property management fees, real estate brokerage fees upon acquisition, partnership management fees, real estate commissions on resale of the property, loan guarantee fees, and sales commission for the sale of partnership units. This, of course, is a very sensitive area and should disclose in considerable detail the total as well as component remuneration to the general partner.

13. *Transfer of a general partner's interest.* Since a limited partnership must always have a general partner, it is highly desirable to require the general partner to remain with the partnership until an acceptable substitute general partner has taken his or her place. Provisions for substituting a general partner should be set forth in detail.

14. *Right of partners to continue business of partnership.* The retirement, death, or insanity of a general partner normally dissolves the partnership unless the business is continued by the remaining general partners under a right to do so stated in the certificate.

15. *Transfer of a limited partner's interest.* This section will provide for transfer of a limited partner's interest. It will be remembered that an assignee of such an interest does not necessarily have the rights accorded to a substituted limited partner. An assignee shall have the right to become a substituted limited partner if all the members (except the assignor) consent, or if the assignor, being so empowered by the certificate of limited partnership, gives the assignee that right. Any transfer that might result in adverse tax consequences to the remaining partners and/or violate applicable federal or state securities laws should be prohibited.

16. *Termination.* Upon termination (that is, dissolution) without a continuation of the business, provisions should be made for liquidation of the partnership assets in accordance with a clearly defined mechanism.

17. *Amendments.* This section will set forth provisions for amendments to the partnership agreement, including the requisite vote for amending the agreement. It is highly desirable to provide that the limited partners agree to do whatever has, in fact, been agreed to by a stated required percentage of limited partners. Moreover, it is not uncommon to have different percentage requirements, depending on the nature of the amendment.

Having established the legal guidelines for the formation and operation of general and limited partnerships, we will go on in the following chapter to consideration of the problems inherent in managing a syndication for real estate development. In a variety of different contexts, the vital issue of control frequently touched upon in the preceding pages will surface again and again, justifying the attention this continues to receive in judicial procedures relating to syndicated real estate development.

# 11

# Managing the Affairs of a Real Estate Syndication

In the earlier chapters we explained and illustrated how real estate syndications functioned between groups of passive investors and an entrepreneur who conceptualized and actively managed a development to its successful conclusion. Chapter 7 outlined the fees the syndicator could legitimately charge for his or her continued active involvement. This two-party active-and-passive approach to a syndication's affairs is far from uncommon, and often the beginning syndicator profits enormously from the experience of running the entire effort him- or herself. Only by understanding and enduring the day-to-day demands of the total responsibility can one appreciate one's own capabilities and potentialities.

As you gain in experience and confidence, establish a track record to command a following, and analyze the range of successes you have achieved, you will realize that two distinct and very different types of management exist in any real estate offering. The more ambitious and long range your projects become the more explicit the separation. These two managerial categories revolve around

1. the actual physical holding itself or property management functions pertaining to the income, expenses, maintenance, and resale; and
2. the intractably complicated affairs of the syndicating partners,

both active and passive, more commonly known as asset management.

The first category demands knowledge of the local market conditions, including ratios of operating expenses to rental income, reasonable levels of occupancy within the locality, and acceptable and tolerable standards of maintenance. The emphasis here is on experience within the specific community in which a property is located.

The second category, asset management, can be less standardized and is generally thought to be more sophisticated. Managing the syndication's affairs involves unique and specialized knowledge in the areas of

- applying proper and prudent use of financial leverage;
- assessing economic trends and acknowledging market strengths and weaknesses;
- comprehending current real estate tax laws and potential changes that can affect your investing partners; and
- understanding which types of properties will syndicate best or be the most desirable to market.

These two categories of managerial expertise are by no means mutually exclusive. Overlapping areas of responsibility do and should exist. Yet, rather different facets of talent are called upon for each. As a matter of everyday human psychology, those whose talents lie in the creative aspects of formulating or structuring syndications may lack the temperament to be fully attentive to the daily, detailed housekeeping aspects so necessary to a successful offering.

## ISOLATING THE MANAGEMENT FUNCTIONS INTO THREE PHASES

Formulas for managing syndications effectively are as numerous and complex as the offerings themselves and the capabilities of the general partners. The successful syndicator recognizes those areas where he or she needs the advice and assistance of other professionals and accepts the necessity of delegating responsibilities for his or her own benefit and for that of the investors in the partnership. When one becomes overburdened or complacent, the entire partnership will be detrimentally affected.

Like any well-written or well-conceived story, syndicated real estate offerings have a beginning, a middle, and an end, more familiarly known to those in the profession as

- the origination phase;
- the operating phase; and
- the final wrap-up or closing phase.

Of the three, the operating phase is usually both the longest and the best suited for delegation to outside individuals. Many entrepreneurial types retain full-time professional property managers to conduct the bulk of the routine syndication affairs during this extended period.

While the details of rentals, operating expenses, maintenance, and fiscal accounting can be appropriately delegated to professional management teams, a substantial number of other responsibilities falls directly on the shoulders of the syndication manager. As a brief overview, the following activities are usually designated as the *sole* and *separate* responsibility of the managing general partner:

1. establishing the financial prospectus for the investors;
2. determining the criteria for investor suitability in the proposed partnership;
3. drafting and developing the syndicated offering;
4. monitoring the important financial aspects of the syndication;
5. overseeing the management of the partnership's assets;
6. maintaining an updated and accurate status on the properties and informing the investors;
7. preparing the appropriate financial reports, tax returns, and accounting statements upon dissolution;
8. transferring interests of both the general and limited partners; and

**Figure 11.1** The three phases of syndicated real estate offerings.

9. effectuating a sale of the syndicated property at the appropriate time.

## PHASE ONE: THE ORIGINATION PHASE

### *Keeping the Investors Fully Informed*

Of the foregoing responsibilities or activities, the first three categories relate to or are tied directly into the origination phase. During this time frame, the syndicator's prime function is keeping the equity investors fully informed. From the initial conception and presentation until the time it is finally marketed and closed, an offering can change drastically. Many of the revolving or revised concepts take form sometime between the preparation of the original prospectus and the actual acquisition of the property. Several years ago I was involved in the acquisition of a defunct and foreclosed 126-unit condominium project where we had commitments from ten investors with $25,000 each. At the eleventh hour our $2.5-million financing commitment fell through, at which time we felt obligated to return the investors' funds. Several months passed, and during that period we were successful in negotiating a new and in some respects, an improved financing commitment, and through constant communication we were able to bring back into the fold nine of the ten investors within 48 hours, which resulted in a successful closing.

### *Dealing with the Technical Language*

Special problems exist in regard to the documents offered to investors being solicited for participation in a syndicated offering. Not only is the required language extremely technical and difficult for unsophisticated investors to comprehend, it is also of necessity so full of legal jargon and disclaimers that the total initial impact can often be quite negative. Investors who have received numerous offering packages over the years become accustomed to the legalese inherent in these documents, which must out of necessity meet the standards of full disclosure required by the appropriate securities regulations. With these ever-present overhanging legal obligations the syndicator needs to stress

- the lack of liquidity in real estate investments;

- the potential exposure accompanied by financial leverage; and
- the lack of resalability of the partnership shares.

The unsophisticated investor can hardly be faulted for the negative feelings he or she retains after reviewing these countless and colorless documents.

During this phase of the offering the syndicate's managing general partner plays an extremely important role in marketing the shares that cannot for all practical purposes be effectively delegated. In addition to filtering out and deciphering what is required by statute and how this legal terminology translates into practical investment determinations, only the syndicator, through his or her own efforts, can verbally communicate a positive sense of the excitement of the venture and its potential for lucrative and long-lasting investment rewards. This need becomes particularly prevalent when a project is conceived almost exclusively to capitalize on the long-term potential that a real estate asset has for future appreciation. When the regulations regarding disclosure of financial risk are fully met, this element of reward is all too often lost on prospective investors without the proper verbal communication.

*Projecting Budgets and Providing Accurate Records*

Prior to an offering being formed, the syndicator must establish detailed and realistic budget projections showing

- rental income;
- operating expenses;
- vacancy factors;
- tax benefits; and
- potential appreciation.

These accurate prognostications are essential to the preparation of an offering circular and its subsequent effective marketing.

The syndicator must formulate the appropriate accounts to keep accurate track of the investors' financial commitments to the project. For purposes of marketing and full compliance with securities regulations, potential investors *must* have access to such fundamental information as

- the committed investors and their financial ability to acquire and hold the investment;

- statements of income and expenses, including accurate and complete advice on the tax ramifications;
- the plan for distributing dividends, return of investment funds, and sharing in the cash flow;
- how and in what manner available funds will be received and disbursed within the partnership;
- details of the method of accounting, specifically as it relates to the cash or accrual basis;
- the fiscal year of the partnership; and
- preparation of the tax returns and the investor's K-1 forms.

Budgeting and maintaining accurate records are ongoing processes. As the origination phase progresses and the operating phase nears, pro forma figures or concepts must be substantiated or replaced by actual costs incurred, and future projections should be constantly reviewed in the light of actualities. Commencing when the first share is offered, the committed and potential investors must be advised as to

- what shares have been sold and to whom;
- what funds have been received and disbursed;
- what interests are remaining to be syndicated; and
- when the syndicate will be formulated and closed out.

However scant the facts or estimates, the syndicator must continually share them with his or her passive partners if he or she is to have their trust, confidence, and cooperation through the three phases of the syndicated offering.

### *Estimating Operating Expenses*

Particularly during inflationary periods, accurately budgeting many of the pro forma operating expenses is difficult at best. In all probability you can, under certain circumstances, be poorly equipped to project accurately for the proposed life of your syndication such *variable costs* as:

- utilities;
- maintenance;
- real estate taxes;
- insurance; and

- reserves for replacement.

When syndicating rental properties, you will also need assistance in projecting potential income in relation to future markets and competing ventures. Difficulties are compounded when for-sale properties are involved where catastrophes can result from wide swings in value estimates or short-term market aberrations. Such a situation presented itself when we recently syndicated a 50-unit, moderately priced condominium project. The for-sale units were appraised several months prior to their being offered for sale. During the traditional delays associated with closing and construction, the market shifted upward by approximately 10 percent. When the units were finally marketed, the entire project sold out in less than 48 hours as word of the undervalued units quickly permeated the brokerage community. By not adequately adjusting our prices to reflect the current market conditions, we left $4,000 per unit or $200,000 on someone else's table.

When marketing complications arise, a syndicator's best source of assistance is usually an impartial and complementary management or marketing group that specializes in similar types of properties bringing vast experience and often covering extended periods of time. A qualified management team has sufficient backlogs of statistics on comparable projects from which it can draw for a wide range of market vagaries. The syndicator's association with a marketing entity may well extend beyond this initial advisory relationship, since accurate and detailed records become even more of a necessity in the operational phase of the syndication's existence, as we will dwell upon extensively in the latter part of this chapter.

*Establishing the Holding Period for the Property*

The nature of the acquisition of a property can often drastically affect the overall plan of a syndication, as without some operating experience a syndicator cannot accurately predict how long a property must be held in order to maximize the investors' return on equity. For this reason you must keep the investors fully informed on the details pertaining to the ultimate timing of the sale, even though the eventual disposition may be years away, and the anticipated terms of sale are only speculative at best.

This element of flexibility at the acquisition stage is difficult to convey to the limited partners, especially in the offering circular. Definitive statements are awkward because of the market vagaries and potential variations in the tax-shelter benefits directly related to a specific property. Convincing investors of the need for this resale flexibility is best communicated verbally, and establishing the confidence necessary to optimize the investors' yield is at the ultimate extremely difficult.

In syndicated offerings the only major decision that the limited partners can participate in pertains to the sale and disposition of the acquired holding. This right is guaranteed them in all but the fewest number of documents. If your investors are prepared and informed of the basic guidelines for the eventual disposition of the property prior to its acquisition, they will be less inclined to question the ramifications of the sale, which often helps expedite the termination process.

Many syndicators overlook or downplay the fact that limited partnership shares are not easily transferable. Careful and precise disclosure of the parameters governing the eventual sale can pay off handsomely in harmony and investor satisfaction due to this lack of liquidity. Before presenting the offering memorandum to your investors, you must avoid boiler-plate, inappropriate language, feeling totally comfortable with the provisions that relate to the percentage of partner's votes needed to ratify the sale of the syndicated asset.

## PHASE TWO: MANAGEMENT DURING THE OPERATIONAL PHASE OF A SYNDICATION

During the middle or operational aspect of an offering, the following activities are considered *key elements* to its success:

- collecting the rents and operating the structure;
- physically maintaining the property;
- reporting of the cash flow and taxable income; and
- monitoring the problematic areas directly related to the day-to-day operations.

Many syndicators use independent property management firms for the first two listed activities. When they do so, they forgo substantial fees to which they would be entitled if they handled the management exclusively. Obversely, there are many solid reasons for not performing these functions in house.

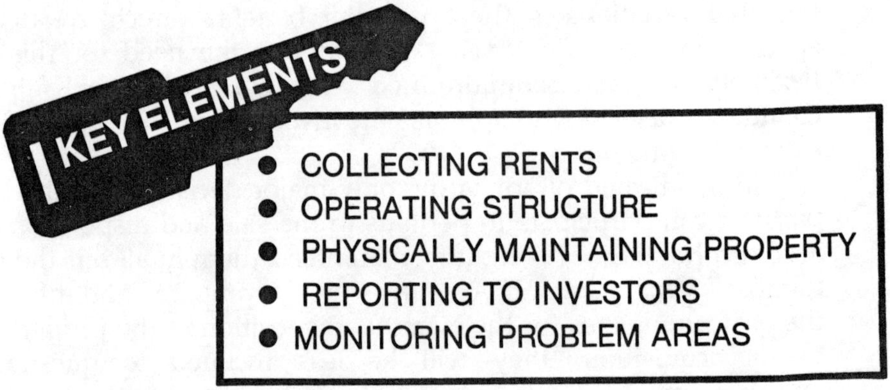


**Figure 11.2** Critical activities during the operating phase of a syndication.

*The Advantages of Retaining Independent Property Managers*

When the syndicated holding unpredictably develops a negative cash flow, the investors are often justifiably reluctant to inject additional funds into its resurrection. Their resentment is compounded when the syndicator him- or herself takes substantial fees for acting in his or her capacity as the property manager. Often under these conditions one must reluctantly agree to defer management fees for a prearranged period of time until a positive cash flow once again prevails. In such a situation ill will can run rampant, to the point where adequate operating funds are not advanced in time, management services disintegrate, substantially altering the value of the property, and the overall mood of both the limited and general partners is affected.

When an independent property manager is retained, comparable clashes of interest between the syndicator and his or her partners can in most instances be avoided. For this reason alone, many syndicators will never involve themselves in the daily activities of property management. They consider payment of a realistic fee to a professional real estate management team the best possible allocation of partnership funds, particularly when times are troubled, and especially when they can safeguard the partnership interests with a 30-day cancellation clause if the contracted firm fails to live up to expectations. Investors rarely complain about realistic property management fees when they are negotiated at arm's length and are paid to an independent third party not associated with the managing general partner. The majority of active syndicators feel they can utilize their time more productively when confining themselves to the critical up-front and back-end complicated real estate activities.

Other bones of contention or criticism can also surface. Syndicators who choose to personally direct the management of properties have a tendency to become disenchanted or complacent, especially over extended periods of time. Because of their close involvement in the tedious daily operations, some tend to wash their hands, dispose of the assets, and close partnerships long before the profits are fully realized. For obvious reasons they can be justifiably criticized by their investors. The opposite scenario also frequently prevails. Syndicators are often accused of perpetuating projects long past their economic viability strictly for the management fees they generate, thereby tying up their investors' capital for unnecessarily lengthy or unwanted periods of time.

### *Reporting and Documenting the Syndicate's Activities*

Whether the sponsor serves as a property manager or retains an independent team for this purpose, a variety of records extending the original syndicate projections and budgets must be maintained. Detailed entries are not only invaluable in keeping investing partners informed, but are a prerequisite required for offerings that are publicly registered and subject to periodic scrutiny by the Securities and Exchange Commission (SEC).

Proper reporting and documentation of a syndication that will stand the test of time and regulatory scrutiny involves five basic documents. Many must be completed on a monthly or quarterly basis. In all instances a running total should be maintained in the reporting period combined with a year-to-date compilation to reflect to your investors the appropriate period of time covered in the financial documents.

1. The first document relates to a summation of the current partnership operations. Comparable to a profit-and-loss statement for a typical business, it provides an itemization of income and expenses relating to the specific property.
2. The second report is a detailed and complete accounting of the income generated from the project, including a summation of the rent roll and all miscellaneous income-generating receipts.
3. The third document is an itemized and detailed statement of the cash disbursements, amounting to a recapitulation of the total operating expenses incurred for the reporting period.

4. The fourth report is a typical balance sheet in which receivables and payables are listed together with the depreciated value of the assets and the corresponding mortgage obligations.
5. The fifth document is a narrative analysis for the reported period. While it is not always necessary, it can generate deeper understanding of the figures provided in the other documents. It can also serve to flag potential problem areas without causing undue alarm. As an alternative, the other four documents can be footnoted where necessary, informing investors on a narrative basis of potential problem areas.

Without periodic updating, many of these basic reporting documents could not be prepared properly. The substance of most is adequately contained in the normal reports provided by a professional independent management team.

The foregoing generalizations about reporting and record keeping will be supplemented in Chapters 14 and 15 where details of compliance with the requirements of the Securities and Exchange Commission are analyzed. Chapters 12 and 13, which are concerned with the federal tax aspects of syndications, presuppose detailed and accurate record keeping following sound accounting practices as critical weapons in supporting the appropriate or desired tax position of a syndication in the event of IRS audit. The form of records kept for a syndicated development are not substantially different from those adequately maintained for any other real estate holding. Developers and qualified management teams exclusively rely on professionally devised accounting and reporting forms available from industry sources. Standard forms can be modified to accommodate specific in-house or special-project needs. While the importance of formal reporting cannot be overemphasized, the discussion of details in executing these forms would probably belabor the obvious for most readers of this book.

### *Unique Services Offered by Management Firms*

Previous arguments for retaining qualified firms revolve about fees, but equally convincing arguments for retention can be raised in terms of professional specialization. The computerized data processing equipment now in common use requires a high degree of sophistication when it is used to its fullest potential. In an area where competitive management firms are capable of providing sophisticated analysis and reporting services, most syndicators do not have, nor will they be able to economically develop, the expertise to provide comparable managerial service at a competitive price. We recently turned over the management on a five-year-old 46,000-square-foot office complex that we own to a full-time property management firm at a total cost, including on-site supervision, of less than what we would be spending for the in-house paperwork alone.

Property management becomes increasingly complicated when real estate holdings are syndicated to generate tax benefits as well as an income stream, as these types of investment properties no longer compete on a strictly local or regional basis. They are marketed nationwide. The syndicated management team continues to rely on regional orientation, and must be versed and knowledgeable in such specialized areas as

- changing federal tax laws;
- properties in vogue for syndication;
- options in accounting methods;
- mortgage-lending patterns;
- rental and maintenance guidelines; and
- current data on property values.

*Ancillary Benefits Found in Professional Management Teams*

A sophisticated and trustworthy firm can be a syndicator's valuable ally in matters affecting the syndicate as well as the property management. More finely tuned to appropriate rental values, operating expenses, and maintenance policies, these organizations can directly influence the cash flow from real estate holdings and have a significant bearing on the resale value of an asset. They upper managerial staff of such firms are often in a position to inform the syndicator of potentially detrimental economic problems arising from market oversaturation or to alert one to strengthening market positions based upon a greater exposure to the rental market. In either event, one can develop an edge on the competition by anticipating potential vacancies and/or raising rental rates.

Professional management firms do not exclusively patronize with syndicators. Many of their clients are passive property owners whose economic benefits and tax brackets are well known to the groups serving them. When these individuals exhaust their tax-shelter benefits on a property, the asset to be disposed of often never surfaces in the active market place. These property management teams sound out their established clients, precluding the necessity for public advertising of their well-maintained holdings.

Syndicators are often apprised of desirable holdings because property management firms are motivated to continue working with a property with which they are acquainted, but which is no longer viable to the current owner. At the opposite extreme, they can also pair up syndicators with potential buyers, many of whom are qualified, established, and well known, when the property no longer serves the needs of the syndicator. Since they tend to work with clientele who specialize in various types of properties, management organizations can make quick and realistic decisions about who is appropriate for a given property in terms of similarity of operation, investment objectives, and financial capability. We recently acquired a small office building from the trust department of a major bank at a reasonable price. I am convinced that if the property had been adequately exposed to the entire brokerage community, we would have had to contract at a 10 percent to 15 percent premium.

Syndicators are not the only group of business people who search out management firms for the ancillary benefits they generate. Many lenders periodically monitor the most prestigious property management firms to determine if any of their clients need financial assistance. This behind-the-scenes maneuvering can be important to a syndicator in a number of ways:

- Both the management companies and the financial institutions with which they are associated can substantiate the credibility of a project and its sponsors.
- Through their professional contacts, management firms can take entire portfolios and refinance them with little if any owner involvement once the current financial statements are provided.
- A professionally managed property will command a higher loan-to-value ratio, since the hypothetical vacancy factor that most mortgage lenders structure into properties is an established commodity.

Professional management teams are also important in substantiating, or sometimes even initiating, changes in the use of real estate assets that are held for extended periods of time. Such shifting or reutilization may be positive, to capitalize on an innovative concept or lucrative market. It conceivably can have negative connotations, a defensive measure to retain or salvage the value of property affected by adverse market conditions, increased maintenance requirements, or a host of other adversities. Particularly in a deteriorating market, the syndicator can better convey the revised concept of use to his or her partners if his or her judgment and recommendations are substantiated by an independent management firm. When additional leverage is required to accomplish the appropriate change in use, it can be facilitated by the financial contacts generated by these management firms.

*Leasing and Maintenance Requirements*

Successful rental achievement in real estate developments depends to a large extent on two factors:

1. to what extent the location is convenient to the potential renters and (in commercial buildings) to their clients; and
2. the sheer visibility of the structure, often a factor of its massiveness and the gilt-edged image of stability this projects.

Even the soundest properties eventually age, and the passage of time brings changes affecting their rentability:

- With demographic changes in areas and neighborhoods, what was once a prime location could become second rate in a few short years.
- What was a massive structure when constructed years or decades ago can be dwarfed by the development dimensions of the 1980s.

Time itself also takes its toll on rentability, regardless of the standards of construction and maintenance. The older and less visible a property, the greater the advertising and promotional efforts that will be required to maintain full or near-full occupancy. The larger the vacancy rate and promotional costs, the lower the bottom-line income will be.

Especially when an aged property is involved, an independent professional management team can do much to ensure its ongoing success. Because of their association with well-established local clients, professional management firms can provide large and otherwise unavailable categories of potential tenants or purchasers for properties, sources that far exceed those of the professional real estate syndicator or of the brokerage community. Not only do they draw from a broader spectrum of clients in terms of potential leasing or sales, but they are positioned to structure and negotiate professional lease obligations, fine-tuned to fit the local economy and the syndication's specific and overall needs.

With careful timing made possible through the experience they have acquired, property management firms can stage leases to fit the particular occupancy pattern of a building and plan for lease expiration when major maintenance is required. This is extremely important in terms of maintaining older buildings. Lengths of leases should be pegged to appropriate times for renovation, thereby keeping a positive and constant cash flow. Should the need for renovation outstrip the accumulation of capital, the management team's working relationship with potential lenders is added assurance to both the syndicating partners and the tenants that necessary expenditures need not be postponed.

A qualified property manager is in many respects the ultimate authority in determining the need and timing of a successful maintenance program for a building. Only independent professionals can provide the necessary balance between

1. preventive maintenance, on which the physical life of a building depends;
2. corrective maintenance, necessary to the physical attractiveness of the structure; and
3. custodial maintenance, the day-to-day janitorial work that keeps the tenants content.

Knowing what can be deferred in an older structure is often as important as determining what must be funded. Ultimately, the correct balance between these three areas will maximize the value of the structure upon resale.

Newer edifices can generate unique problems involving sophisticated equipment used in heating, ventilating, and air-conditioning systems, or complicated electrical or cooling systems geared toward computers. Improper maintenance of a newer building can, in fact, be much more serious than undermaintenance of an older, less complicated structure. Professional understanding of and attendance to maintenance requirements for a technologically complex structure is the only assurance its owners have that the building will be in operative order at the time of its disposition.

## PHASE THREE: THE COMPLETION OR CLOSING PHASE

### *Reviewing the Function of Management*

Once the majority of the syndicating functions are complete and the wrap up or closing phase nears, one should review the syndication process in its entirety with special emphasis on the

- reporting procedures;
- relationships with investors;
- overall management of the property; and
- general management of the partnership assets

to determine its overall effectiveness. While the origination phase is usually overregulated by securities laws, large gaps exist in the regulations regarding management functions, duties, and responsibilities during the latter aspects.

First-time syndicators frequently get caught up in the excitement of initially structuring the transaction and raising the investment funds to the point where they are made aware of their shortcomings only in hindsight. The conclusion of the operational phase is an ideal time to review the appropriate management functions as they transcend all phases of the syndication process. At that point it becomes possible to view the operation objectively, where one can accurately determine how the project fared under the existing management arrangement.

Many syndicators become isolated from their partnership's activities when they delegate a majority of the management functions. Some find that they lack the ability to react quickly enough to negative events and then to capitalize fully on favorable occurrences in the syndication's affairs. Feelings can run strong both among syndicators and investors that setbacks can be handled properly *only* when the syndicator is close at hand to deal with them promptly and efficiently.

Many other syndicators with extensive experience and more hectic schedules feel that their direct involvement in daily management clouds the overall objectives of the syndicate, which can be more accurately reflected in the asset management function. This view usually prevails after a syndicator has conceived a multitude of offerings, only to realize how truly repetitious the management problems can be during the operational phase. The argument continues that the syndicator serves his or her investors best by viewing operations objectively from a distance, having the flexibility to bring in specialists whenever complicated problems surface.

### *Structuring the Sale of the Syndicated Asset*

The real test of proper management surfaces at the end when the syndicator attempts to dispose of the partnership's assets. Most offerings provide for the limited partners having a voice at the time of sale, this provision being their only major area of input into the management of the syndication's affairs. It therefore becomes imperative that the investors be kept fully apprised from the project's inception concerning

- at what point it is likely that the property will be sold;
- the terms under which the sale might be transacted;
- the financial arrangements and the tax investor's ramifications; and
- the approximate amount of up-front and deferred proceeds that investors might receive at the time of sale.

Providing this information early and updating it periodically is a necessary preventive measure in avoiding the dissent that often occurs when the syndicator decides that the time is appropriate or when an attractive offer is received, as any delay from the optimum time of sale can substantially affect the overall return on the investment.

If the investment is not properly managed during the operational phase, the syndicator's flexibility may be extremely limited in the end. Properties that are undermaintained, poorly managed, or lacking adequate cash flow will be sold at a discount or must often be merchandised with secondary owner financing. Both discounting and financing provided by the syndicate will lower the overall yield and can reduce or delay the return of the investor's equity.

### *Transferring and Valuing Partnership Interests*

During both the second and third phases of an offering, the managing partner must be prepared for the possibility of a request for a transfer of a partnership interest. Limited partners often get divorced, die, or for a variety of reasons need to dispose of their shares. Pressures will be mounted by accountants and lawyers for a current valuation of the investment. Many will request the syndicator to provide unrealistically high or low values, depending upon the individual's particular needs. For example, deflated values are requested for divorce or estate purposes. If such a value is tendered, legal recourse is often waiting in the wings, especially in divorce situations, where the other party feels short-changed.

Issuing statements of value should, if at all possible, be avoided. If they are provided, they should contain qualifying remarks, providing a range of high and low values to accommodate all the interested parties. It is also imperative that all transferability requirements set out in the partnership documents be complied with to the letter. Syndicators should look at these provisions closely upon forming the partnership to be sure that boiler-plate language will not act as a deterrent resulting in a forced sale of the asset.

A standard clause in some partnership documents permits any limited partner the privilege of withdrawing by giving 12 months' notice. Over a predetermined period of time they are then repaid their capital contributions or the fair-market value of the partnership interest from the remaining partnership assets. When this provision applies, the general partner must retain a fair amount of liquidity should any of the limited partners change their investment strategies. We recently syndicated a 12-acre tract of commercial land in which the sole limited partner pledged his interest as collateral for a loan on which he subsequently defaulted. We reluctantly consented to the assignment, and the lender demanded that we either liquidate the asset or compensate him for the assigned prorated share of the fair-market value. This can be an extremely uncomfortable position to be put into if the funds involved are substantial, or the asset has not yet reached its full potential.

The status of the partnership holdings must be kept fairly liquid so that the general partner can, if necessary, freely move other passive investment funds into the syndication to substitute for a withdrawing limited partner. An amended Certificate of Limited Partnership must be completed and recorded to replace each original certificate whenever there is a change of ownership among either the limited or general partners. Each remaining investor must also receive a copy of the amended certificate to be fully apprised of the partnership affairs.

### *Liquidating the Partnership's Assets*

As most syndicators come to realize, many offers to purchase are neither straightforward nor uncomplicated. These technical features must be worked out to everyone's satisfaction by the general partner prior to closing. In the event that one has not communicated fully with one's investors, they often become confused or defensive and demand to know the specific terms and conditions under which the asset is being disposed of. Explaining all of the intricate details of an offer to purchase not only consumes a great deal of time, but can also provoke prolonged discussions to the point where a consensus among the selling partners is virtually impossible. Each situation will vary, as the end result is always measured in after-tax return on equity. The syndicator should establish the mean or average tax brackets of his or her investors, partially governing the sale on that basis, weighing a combination of the project's cash flow and residual value with the investors' stated objectives.

On the other hand, if the syndicator has done a proper job of managing the partnership affairs and has fully communicated all the important and ongoing management decisions, his or her recommendation for sale will be almost unchallenged when the day of reckoning comes. Armed with the total confidence of one's investors, one normally is in a position to structure the contingencies and potentially negative aspects of the eventual sale without interference from the passive investors.

Upon the sale of the syndicate's assets the partnership must be formally dissolved to avoid any future liability to the individual investors. Some partnership documents call for an audited financial statement upon dissolution. Such a procedure is costly, time-consuming, and can often unnecessarily hold up the partnership liquidation. The investors should have the option to approve the additional expense of an audited statement if they so desire, but only upon a majority vote.

### *Communicating the Sale Conditions to Investors*

Surprises always surface at or just prior to the closing of a syndicate's affairs. One of our recent projects, an apartment syndication, will help to illustrate the difficulties in structuring and communicating the details of a sale and effectuating a closing.

Structured strictly for tax-shelter and long-term appreciation, this venture was acquired from a troubled real estate investment trust for

$8 million with less than 5 percent down payment. The lender in default agreed to fully cover the operating losses, which were in excess of a quarter of a million dollars annually, in exchange for a percentage of the eventual profits derived from the resale.

The project was sold for a multimillion-dollar profit to an apartment converter who defaulted after his initial down payment on the majority of the scheduled installments when a tight money situation, combined with high interest rates, prevented him from selling the converted apartments. Several years elapsed before the converter made good on his obligations to our partnership. During this period of time he was contractually permitted to continue to manage the venture for a sum stipulated later.

At the time of sale to the converter the operating losses were no longer contractually covered by the lending institution as part of the stipulated agreement. Nonpayment and foreclosure of the $8-million mortgage could have been disastrous to the limited partners, as they had taken almost $200,000 worth of tax deductions for each $20,000 investment share. The communications with the investors, the converter, and the original lender were extensive, complicated, and not often pleasant over the two-year period that was needed to restructure, close, and eventually receive payment from the apartment converter.

The legal ramifications of attempting to force the converter to close on schedule would have been time consuming, extremely expensive, and potentially unproductive, since no resale market existed at the time for the converted apartments due to tight money conditions and high interest rates. The converter agreed to cover the operating losses that the lender had previously been obligated for, as consideration for a two-year option payment for keeping his purchase contract intact. Under this arrangement the limited partners continued to receive the tax benefits, and the lending institution's mortgage remained current as a result. After prolonged and diligent efforts to communicate the details of these negotiations, this relatively simple compromise placated all parties.

### *Installment Financing and Sponsor Compensation*

When the syndication, as part of the sales price, must carry a portion of the purchase mortgage financing, the managing partner will have to determine if the basis for the loan is well secured and calculate whether the investors will receive sufficient initial disbursements to meet their taxable obligations. When an installment sale is involved, the partnership under normal circumstances need not be liquidated or dissolved unless the notes payable can be distributed directly to the partners and a trustee is appointed for their administration. As most sponsors usually have an alternative source for reinvestment of the limited partners' funds when a syndication is dissolved, the method in which the syndicator's compensation is presented to the limited partners can be extremely delicate, especially where substantial brokerage fees or profit sharing exist.

A good prerequisite for informing the investors of your claim to back-end compensation is the timely filing of reports and disbursement of dividends, which builds a level of confidence that cannot be shattered easily when back-end compensation or fees are high. Especially in tax-oriented ventures, the back-end fees the syndicator receives in the form of brokerage commissions and profit-sharing bonuses can equal or sometimes exceed the net cash distributions to the investors. This discrepancy can be particularly alarming when the limited partners' funds are disbursed on a deferred basis due to an installment sale where the managing partner receives his or her commissions up front. In such circumstances the syndicator should inform his or her partners fully of the circumstances surrounding the sale and also exercise utmost tact and diplomacy in convincing his or her investors that an equitable and fair partnership arrangement was struck and that his or her profits from the sale of the asset were distributed in time and were not excessive in nature.

In summation, the general partner's back-end fees are sometimes subject to investor resentment and challenge. A strong probability exists that the back-end fees the general partner derives from the sale of the syndicated asset will depend upon

- the way the property is managed; and
- the communication the syndicator established with his or her investors through *all* the management phases of the offering.

The quality of the management and the extent of the communication between general and limited partners is most tangibly expressed in the nature and frequency of reports documenting the syndication's affairs, whether they are generated in compliance with securities regulations, for timely reporting to passive partners, or as routine spot checks on subordinates of the managing general partner. If the inherent paperwork sounds formidable, it is nonetheless necessary and accounts for the strong preference many syndicators have for working with professional management teams whose computers can generate required statistics almost instantaneously.

Bureaucracy inevitably begets more bureaucracy, too often stuffing files and trash containers, generating the necessity for paper shredders. Syndications and their promoters have no choice but to join in the paper chase if they are to justify their existence and activities under the critical scrutiny of the Internal Revenue Service, the Securities and Exchange Commission, and the various state regulatory agencies. The best defense against a threatened retroactive penalty or lawsuit is often found in a seemingly unimportant but required document.

# 12

# Federal Tax Aspects of Limited Partnership Syndications

The first chapter defined syndication as the ultimate refinement of the art of using other people's money. Chapter 9 described the various legal entities found to be most appropriate, as they relate to the complex and varied advantages of real estate investments. We concluded that of the many legal entities available, limited partnership is generally found to be the most flexible in terms of catering to the investor's needs, the underlying reason being that such partnerships are disregarded as entities for federal income tax purposes.

If a limited partnership does not qualify for partnership-tax treatment, it will be taxed as an association (that is, a corporation), and the intended tax benefits will in all probability be lost. This results because a corporation is taxed at the entity (that is, corporate) level on all items of income, gain, and loss. The losses so common in the early years of acquisition and development cannot be isolated and passed through to individual partners. Two exceptions to this principle exist:

- subchapter S corporations; and
- Real Estate Investment Trusts.

Both were described in more detail in Chapter 9. As indicated there, these two entities will not usually offer the structural and operational flexibility that a limited partnership can.

Because of differences in legal definition, what qualifies as a limited partnership under state law may not meet federal requirements. For federal income-tax purposes, a partnership "includes a syndicate, group, pool, joint venture, or other unincorporated organization through or by means of which any business, financial operation or venture is carried on, and which is not . . . a corporation or a trust or estate." Neither clarity of intention of associated partners nor characterization under state law guarantees that a limited partnership will qualify for federal income-tax benefits, though state law may be relevant in determining whether the entity has certain characteristics and relationships that affect the determination of tax status.

The confusion surrounding the classification of an organization for tax purposes has provoked considerable controversy. In an attempt at clarification, the Internal Revenue Service first issued detailed regulations in 1960 (which have been amended from time to time), which set forth certain factors to be weighed in characterizing an organization. Under a literal application of these regulations, most organizations qualifying as limited partnerships under a state statute corresponding to the Uniform Limited Partnership Act would be characterized as partnerships for tax purposes. The IRS nevertheless has at times, and with inconsistent application, interpreted and applied the regulations in a very restrictive manner. Several important court decisions, however, have recently rejected IRS positions and have applied these regulations in a more liberal fashion consistent with the language of the text.

The following section of this chapter will discuss the tax principles governing the question of whether a limited partnership will in fact be classified as a partnership.

## REGULATORY FRAMEWORK

Under the relevant Treasury regulations, a partnership may be taxed as a partnership or as an association (that is, a corporation). The treasury regulations set forth six characteristics that are ordinarily found in a pure corporation (although as noted below, two will be disregarded). To achieve partnership status, the entity generally must have *no more than two* of four designated corporate characteristics. The six relevant "corporate" characteristics are as follows:

1. associates;

2. an objective to carry on business and divide the gains therefrom;
3. continuity of life;
4. centralization of management;
5. liability for corporate debts limited to corporate property; and
6. free transferability of interests.

The determination as to classification of an organization is made by taking into account the presence or absence of these six characteristics. Since corporations and partnerships both have associates (1) as well as an objective to carry on business and divide the gains therefrom (2), however, these two characteristics are normally disregarded, and the determination is based upon the presence or absence of the remaining four corporate characteristics.

As indicated, an unincorporated organization will be taxed as an association (corporation) only if it has more corporate characteristics than noncorporate characteristics; that is, if it has at least three of the enumerated characteristics. Stated conversely, if an unincorporated entity (that is, a limited partnership) can establish the *absence* of *at least two* of the four characteristics, it generally will not be classified as an association taxable as a corporation.

### *Continuity of Life*

Of the four corporate characteristics, continuity of life is the easiest for an entity seeking to be characterized as a partnership to "flunk." To avoid this corporate characteristic the partnership agreement should provide that the entity's life does not continue indefinitely (which is typical of a corporation), but ends upon the occurrence of certain definite events.

For this purpose, the Treasury regulations rely upon the technical concept of dissolution of the organization under local law. Thus, continuity of life does not exist if any of the following events causes dissolution of any partner of a limited partnership:

- death;
- insanity;
- bankruptcy;
- retirement;
- resignation; or
- expulsion.

Equally so, continuity of life will not exist if retirement, death, or insanity of a general partner causes a dissolution, even if the remaining general partners (or all remaining members) agree to continue the partnership.

The regulations also provide that if, as a matter of local law, *any member* of the organization has the power to dissolve, continuity of life will not exist. Accordingly, a limited partnership that is subject to a statute corresponding to the Uniform Limited Partnership Act would lack continuity of life.

Careful drafting of the limited partnership agreement will enable the limited partnership to avoid having the corporate characteristic of continuity of life. The documents need only state that the limited partnership is dissolved by the death, retirement, insanity, bankruptcy, resignation, or expulsion of a general partner (but not of a limited partner) and that it will be reconstituted and its business continued only upon the consent of all remaining members of the partnership.

It is common practice for most partnerships to have a fixed date when the partnership will dissolve. It should be pointed out, however, that a fixed date of termination alone will not be sufficient to avoid the continuity of life characteristic.

### *Centralization of Management*

"Flunking" the corporate characteristic of centralization of management is not quite as simple. The regulations state that an organization has centralized management "if any person (or group of persons which does *not* include *all* members) has continuing exclusive authority to make the management decisions necessary to the conduct of the business for which the organization was formed." The regulations further state that such persons would resemble, in powers as well as functions, the board of directors of a conventional corporation. However, the courts have interpreted the regulations to mean that, even though there may be centralized administration by a general partner, the centralization of management will not be met if the general partner has a *meaningful proprietary interest*.

The regulations contain two examples in which centralization of management is found to exist in situations where limited partners contributed approximately 94 percent and 97 percent of total partnership capital. How much below this threshold level must one go to fail the test is an unanswered question; most practitioners use 80 percent as a "safe harbor" rule of thumb.

It should be pointed out that in the typical real estate limited partnership syndication, limited partners will generally own, at least in the early years, in excess of 90 percent of partnership capital and profits. Therefore, it should be assumed that the IRS will often assert that the organization has the corporate characteristic of centralization of management.

Moreover, in many limited partnerships, the general partner may neither make a capital contribution nor have an interest in partnership capital. Instead, the general partner's interest may be limited to partnership profits. In such a situation, the argument can be made that the limited partners do not own "substantially all" the interests in the partnership. A substantial profits interest of a general partner, therefore, might cause the limited partnership to lack centralized management. Again, however, this question is not free from doubt and, absent a significant capital interest by the general partner, the prudent route is to *clearly establish* the absence of two other corporate characteristics.

*Limited Liability*

We have thus far observed that the typical real estate limited partnership can probably avoid continuity of life but may find it difficult to avoid centralized management. That takes us to the corporate characteristic of limited liability. Although most real estate limited partnerships are structured to avoid limited liability as a matter of local law, the ultimate question in this area for tax purposes is the identity *and* substance of the general partner.

The regulations conclude that "a[n] organization has the corporate characteristic of limited liability if under local law there is no member who is personally liable for the debts of or claims against the organization." Personal liability exists, therefore, if a creditor may seek personal satisfaction against any member to the extent that the organization's assets are insufficient to satisfy the claim. Generally speaking, personal liability will exist with respect to each general partner of a limited partnership formed under a statute corresponding to the Uniform Limited Partnership Act. A real estate limited partnership formed under a Uniform Limited Partnership Act statute, therefore, often can avoid the corporate characteristic of limited liability.

The regulations contain several exceptions to this broad principle and are concerned primarily with the financial substance of the general partner (because this is the person who may have personal liability for the partnership's debts). These exceptions differ, depending upon whether the general partner is a corporation or an individual.

Generally speaking, under the regulations personal liability will not exist if the general partner has no substantial assets that could be reached by a creditor *and* is merely a dummy acting as agent of the limited partners. The regulations further state affirmatively that if a corporation is a general partner, personal liability will exist if the corporation has substantial assets that can be reached by a creditor of the limited partnership.

The regulations thus suggest different tests for individuals and corporations. To enable the limited partnership to avoid the corporate characteristic of limited liability, therefore, a literal reading of the regulations leads to the conclusion that an individual general partner need not have substantial assets if he or she is not a dummy acting as agent for the limited partners. (Under current ruling policy, however, the IRS consistently includes the premise that an individual as well as a corporate general partner has substantial assets, which ruling policy is discussed in detail hereafter.) On the other hand, a corporate general partner must have substantial assets.

The regulations do not adequately define "substantial assets." It is clear, however, that substantial assets do not include the general partner's interest in the limited partnership in question. Moreover, the regulations do imply that the assets of the general partner may be considered substantial even if the assets are not sufficient to satisfy a substantial portion of the limited partnership's obligation.

The IRS has attempted to articulate standards for determining when a sole corporate general partner will be deemed to have substantial assets and to that end has promulgated rules defining when it will grant advance rulings in this area. These so-called "safe harbor" rules, setting forth net-worth guidelines for a sole corporate general partner, will be discussed.

While there are no corresponding net-worth guidelines for individual general partners, most practitioners believe that an individual general partner, acting alone or with a corporate general partner who is not a dummy acting as agent for the limited partners and who has *some assets* subject to partnership liabilities (that is, is not insolvent), qualifies the partnership for the absence of the limited-liability characteristic. Again, however, the area is murky and the greater the general partner's net worth, the stronger the case.

### *Free Transferability of Interests*

The scorecard thus far tips slightly in favor of partnership status (lack of continuity of life with two potentially uncertain characteristics). Thus, if the limited partnership is to avoid at least two of the four tests, the remaining corporate characteristic of free transferability of interests becomes critical.

The regulations provide that an organization will have free transferability of interests "if each of its members or those members owning substantially all of the interests in the organization have the power, without the consent of other members, to substitute for themselves in the same organization a person who is not a member of the organization." The regulations further state that a member must be able, without consent of other members, to confer *all* attributes of his or her interest upon a substitute partner.

Free transferability of interests will not exist under the Treasury view, where a limited partner cannot, without consent of other members, designate a transferee as a substitute limited partner, even though he or she can assign at will his or her rights to share in partnership profits. The IRS, however, has ruled that, although the general partners of a limited partnership had not consented to a transferee becoming a substituted limited partner as required by the partnership agreement, the transferee was a substituted limited partner for the purpose of reporting a distributable share of partnership

- income;
- gain;
- loss;
- deduction; and
- credit.

What is not clear is whether this revenue ruling applies to the question of tax classification. The prudent approach is to draft the relevant documents to prohibit an assignment of any interest in a limited partnership without the unanimous written consent of the general partners.

### *Judicial Attitudes*

Having reviewed the IRS and Treasury positions, let us offer a brief analysis of the judicial attitudes. Two court decisions illustrate the difficulty often involved in classifying an entity either as a limited partnership or as an association taxable as a corporation for federal income-tax purposes. In Larson v. Commissioner, 66 T.C. 159 (1976) the United States Tax Court first held that a limited partnership was an association for tax purposes and then reversed its position in a later opinion, over vigorous dissent. The Justice Department subsequently withdrew its appeal to the Ninth Circuit in Larson, and the IRS has acquiesced in the Tax Court decision. A similar decision was rendered by the United States Court of Claims in Zuckman v. United States, 524 F. 2d 729 (Ct. Cl. 1975), which the IRS did not appeal. Although Larson and Zuckman involved limited partnerships with sole corporate general partners, a substantial part of the courts' rationale would apply as well to limited partnerships with individuals as general partners. Both opinions involved partnerships investing in real estate.

In Larson, the Tax Court held that under the current regulations the corporate characteristic of limited liability will be found to exist in a limited partnership only where the general partner has no substantial assets *and* when he or she is merely a "dummy" acting as agent or nominee for the limited partners. The court further held that the general partner is not a "dummy" if the partner has an active involvement in the business and is independent of, and unrelated to, the limited partners.

The Tax Court in Larson also concluded that the interests in the partnership were freely transferable because an assignee could acquire all the rights of a limited partner without discretionary consent of any other member, since the general partner could not unreasonably withhold consent to the substitution.

The foregoing discussion, of course, is based upon the validity of existing Teasury regulations. In Larson and Zuckman, the courts specifically found the regulations valid. In Larson, however, three judges of the Tax Court expressed the view that the regulation was invalid. Equally important, the majority of the court indicated that, had they not been bound by the existing regulation, they would have concluded that "the practical continuity and limited liability of [the limited partnerships under review] would decisively tip the balance" in favor of taxation of such partnerships as associations.

Moreover, in Larson, the Tax Court specifically indicated that the Treasury Department had authority to amend the regulations in a manner that would result in the classification of the limited partnerships then under review as associations. The Treasury Department published notice on January 5, 1977, that it proposed to amend the regulations. The proposal was withdrawn on the same day by order of the

Secretary of the Treasury to permit further consideration. On January 14, 1977, the Treasury announced that the proposed amendments "should not be reproposed" and that the "existing regulations on the subject will remain in force."

## ADVANCE IRS RULINGS

The Internal Revenue Service has issued two important revenue procedures that limit the circumstances when the IRS will issue advance rulings that an organization will not be taxed as an association. While the refusal by the IRS to rule favorably is not necessarily critical to ultimate favorable treatment, such refusal might be applied informally by IRS agents during a tax audit.

In 1972, the IRS published Revenue Procedure 72–13, 1972–1 C.B. 735. This procedure contains guidelines that must be met by a limited partnership having a sole corporate general partner, to obtain an advance ruling that it is taxable as a partnership and not as an association taxable as a corporation. If a limited partnership cannot satisfy these guidelines, it cannot obtain a ruling even if it otherwise does not have any of the four corporate characteristics. Alternatively, it must satisfy the test for the absence of two corporate characteristics in addition to the revenue procedures to obtain a favorable ruling.

Revenue Procedure 72–13 provides that the IRS will not issue an advance ruling with respect to limited-partnership tax status if the limited partners own, individually or in the aggregate, directly or indirectly, more than 20 percent of the outstanding stock of a sole corporate general partner or any of its affiliates. Furthermore, the sole corporation general partner must have a minimum net worth at all times during the life of the partnership equal to 10 percent of total contributions to the partnership or, if total contributions are less than $2.5 million, the lesser of 15 percent of total contributions or $250,000.

A real estate development concern frequently requires a general partner for a limited partnership but does not wish to subject its assets to general liability. To accomplish this, the developer may form a wholly owned subsidiary corporation to serve as the sole general partner. To provide the subsidiary with sufficient assets to satisfy the net-worth requirements, the developer will have to transfer adequate assets to the subsidiary.

The most important unanswered question left open by Rev. Proc. 72–13 is whether the revenue procedure has any bearing on limited partnerships that have a noncorporate general partner either alone or together with a corporate general partner. For ruling purposes, the IRS is applying the same substantial assets test to individual general partners.

As indicated previously, it is common to allocate most or all of the limited-partnership tax benefits to the limited partners. In Revenue Procedure 74 –17 1974 –1 C.B. 438, which applies to the issuance of advance rulings concerning classification of organizations as partnerships, the IRS addressed the issue of the viability of the general partner. If the rules of this revenue procedure, as well as all other provisions of the Code, regulations revenue rulings, and other revenue procedure (including Revenue Procedure 72–13) are satisfied, a favorable ruling generally will be issued; if the rules of the revenue procedure are not met, the IRS will decline to rule. Although the revenue procedure is not intended to be applied on audit of taxpayers' returns, agents may use the guidelines on an informal basis during audits.

The revenue procedure provides that the interests of all general partners, in the aggregate, in each material item of partnership income, gain, loss, deduction, or credit must be equal to at least 1 percent of each such item throughout the term of the partnership, without regard to limited-partnership interests the general partners may own. The 1 percent test refers to tax items; to satisfy the test, a general partner presumably need not have a corresponding interest in partnership capital and distributions or make a capital contribution to the partnership. An allocation of tax items without a corresponding interest in partnership capital and distributions, could conceivably generate other problems.

In addition to the 1 percent test, which is not difficult to satisfy, the revenue procedure sets out additional requirements. The aggregate deductions to be claimed by the partners as their distributive share of partnership losses for the first two years of the partnership operations must not exceed the amount of equity capital invested in the limited partnership. Since many real estate limited partnerships provide a higher ratio of tax deductions to invested capital than one to one (indeed, that is the tax-shelter objective), this requirement has caused many real estate limited partnerships to discard the idea of obtaining an advance tax ruling.

Finally, the revenue procedure requires that a creditor who makes a nonrecourse loan to the limited partnership must not have or acquire as a result of making the loan any direct or indirect interest in the profits, capital, or property of the limited partnership other than as a secured investor.

Few private real estate limited partnerships will seek advance IRS rulings with respect to federal income-tax status. Instead, an opinion of tax counsel usually will be obtained. The reasons are several:

- Avoiding a ruling application saves time, prevents expense, and maintains some confidentiality (since private rulings are now a matter of public record).
- To obtain a ruling under current guidelines, the business aspects of the transaction may have to be structured rather unfavorably, and this is especially true with respect to the requirement that deductions for the first two years of the limited partnership's existence cannot exceed equity capital.

It must be emphasized, however, that an opinion of tax counsel will by no means guarantee that the partnership will be treated as such for federal income-tax purposes and by no means is binding on the IRS. Like an IRS ruling, it is just another opinion of a tax advisor.

## FEDERAL INCOME TAXATION OF A PARTNERSHIP AND ITS PARTNERS

The partnership itself, for federal income-tax purposes, is not subject to any federal income taxes. It is, nevertheless, required to file an Annual Federal Information Return of Income. Each partner is required to take into account in computing his or her federal income-tax liability the distributive share of all partnership income, gain, loss, deduction, credit, and items of tax preference for the tax year of the partnership ending within or with the tax year of the partner, whether or not he or she has received or will receive any cash distributions from the partnership. The amount of any loss or deduction that each partner may utilize in computing his or her federal income-tax liability is generally limited to his or her adjusted tax basis for his or her partnership interest.

Each partner's distributive share of the partnership's income, gain, loss, deduction, credit, and items of tax preference is determined in accordance with the allocations made in the partnership agreement, provided such allocations are recognized for federal income-tax purposes. The character of any item of income, gain, loss, deduction, or credit included in a partner's distributive share is determined as if such items were realized directly from the source from which it was derived. A partnership will normally furnish each limited partner the necessary information with respect to the partnership to enable each limited partner to prepare and file his or her own federal, state, and local income-tax returns.

### *Special Allocations in Partnerships*

For federal income-tax purposes, the allocation of overall taxable income or loss, as well as any item of income, gain, loss, deduction, or credit among partners of the partnership for federal income-tax purposes will be controlled by the partnership agreement, unless the allocation is found not to have "substantial economic effect." An allocation will generally be found to have "substantial economic effect" if it can actually affect the dollar amount of the partner's share of the total partnership income or loss independent of tax consequences. These rules are extremely complicated, and any detailed analysis is beyond the scope of this book. However, a brief discussion follows.

In a typical syndication, the partnership agreement allocates 99 percent of the partnership's yearly profits and losses (and cash flow, if any) to the limited partners until the limited partners have received cash distributions totaling their initial cash contributions plus a percent simple cumulative (noncompounded) return thereon. Profits and losses and cash flow allocations are often altered after the limited partners have received their investment back from the cash flow (75 percent to the limited partners and 25 percent to the general partners would be conventional).

Furthermore, the typical syndication may provide that gain to be recognized by the partnership in connection with the sale, exchange, or other disposition of all or substantially all of the assets will be first allocated to those partners who have deficit balances in their capital accounts at the time of the disposition, up to an aggregate amount not to exceed the sum of such deficit balances; then to those limited partners who have not yet recovered their capital contributions at such time, including the percentage cumulative return preference; then to all partners on the basis of their liquidation partnership interest (again 75 percent to the limited partners and 25 percent to the general partners).

This type of special allocation (switch from 99 percent/1 percent, to 75 percent/25 percent upon repayment to limited partners of initial capital contributions) should be respected for federal income-tax purposes, since it should possess "substantial economic effect" provided such allocation corresponds with cash distributions and is reflected by appropriate entries in the partners' capital account.

The guidelines concerning those types of special allocations that will be respected by the IRS are somewhat uncertain at this time, especially since Section 704(b) of the Code was substantially amended first by the Tax Reform Act of 1976 and recently by the Tax Reform Act of 1984. The IRS, as a matter of policy, will not rule when requested on this issue (see Revenue Procedure 74–22, 1974–2CB 476), so that advance assurance cannot be obtained. In the event that an allocation is disallowed by the IRS as not having "substantial economic effect," then the partner's share of the item or items will be determined in accordance with his or her interest in the partnership, after taking into account such factors as his or her interest in partnership profits and losses, cash flow, and rights to distribution of capital upon liquidation. In the event that the IRS successfully challenges some allocations as being without "substantial economic effect," the result may be that some expenditures allocated would be nondeductible additions to the basis of the limited partner's interest in the partnership, deductions allowable in later taxable years or offset in whole or in part by a reallocation of partnership income.

The Code also permits items of income, gain, deduction, or loss of a partnership to be allocated to a partner only if they are received, paid, or incurred by the partnership during the portion of the year in which the partner is a member of the partnership for tax purposes. In determining whether items of income or loss have been paid or incurred prior to a partner's entry into a partnership, a partnership may

- either prorate items according to the portion of the year for which a partner was a partner;
- or, in effect, separate the partnership year into two or more segments and allocate income, loss, or special items in each segment among the persons who were partners during that segment.

Again, the application of these so-called "retroactive" allocation rules is beyond the scope of this book, but suffice it to say that this is a fertile area for tax audits by the IRS. Moreover, these rules were significantly tightened by Congress first as a part of the Tax Reform Act of 1976 and recently as a part of the Tax Reform Act of 1984 (which Act is considered in detail in Chapter 18).

*Basis in Partnership Interest*

A partner is entitled to deduct on his or her personal tax return the allocable share of partnership losses only to the extent of his or her basis in the partnership at the end of the taxable year in which the loss occurs (and subject to the "at-risk" limitations hereafter described). Generally, the tax basis of any partner's interest in a partnership is equal to his or her cost (capital), reduced (but not below zero) by the partner's share of partnership distributions and losses and increased by his or her share of partnership income. In addition, the tax basis of an interest in a partnership generally is increased by a partner's proportionate share of liabilities to which partnership assets are subject (to the extent that such liabilities do not exceed the fair-market value of the properties subject to such liabilities), but for which neither the partnership nor any partner has any personal liability (such as real estate acquired subject to a mortgage that is not assumed by the partnership or any of its partners). Each partner's proportionate share of such nonrecourse liabilities for this purpose is determined by the proportion in which such partner shares profits of the partnership.

Section 465 of the Code provides that noncorporate taxpayers and certain closely held corportions (whether held directly or through investment in a partnership) will not be permitted in any year to deduct or offset against other income a loss from an activity to the extent that such loss exceeds the aggregate dollar amount that such taxpayers have at risk in such activity at the close of the taxable year. These limitations do not apply to a loss arising from any activity that constitutes "the holding of real property." To the extent that such loss is not permitted to be used in any year (or is recaptured under Section 465 [e] of the Code), it may be carried over by such taxpayer to subsequent years and allowed to the extent of the amount that such taxpayer has at risk.

Although "the holding of real property" has not been defined, it seems clear that Congress did not intend the limitations in Section 465 to affect partnerships engaged in real estate activities or partnership investments in real estate joint ventures. Hence, the typical real estate syndication addressed in this book should not be subject to the so-called "at-risk" limitations of the Code.

# 13

# Federal Tax Treatment of Syndication Partnership Dissolution

In the previous chapter we explained the conditions under which a syndication qualifies for favorable tax treatment by current Internal Revenue Service standards. As complex as this subject may be, involving many gray areas and seemingly contradictory rulings, it pales by comparison to the federal regulations governing taxes payable upon the sale of a syndicated asset. It is not only conceivable but probable that no two investors in a limited partnership will be taxed in exactly the same way when the syndicated asset is sold or the partnership is terminated. The managing general partner must bear this in mind as he or she finalizes the negotiations for sale and/or dissolution and may be well advised to seek appropriate tax advice prior to concluding the sale. His or her function is to serve all the syndicating partners as equitably as possible in winding up a syndication's affairs and doing so without taking into account the tax ramifications of the sale to all participants in the partnership is difficult at best.

The technicality of the subject matter in this chapter precludes any serious attempt at simplification of the language of the relevant documents. The overall ramifications of this material should be digested with great care and applied diligently to any real estate syndication.

## SALE OR OTHER DISPOSITION OF PARTNERSHIP ASSETS

Upon the sale of any partnership asset, taxable income will normally be recognized to the extent that the amount received from such sale (which may include the then unpaid balance of the mortgage on the property to the extent that the acquiring party assumes, or takes subject to, such mortgage even though no cash would actually be received) exceeds the adjusted tax basis of the property. Any profit or loss that may be realized by a partnership on the sale of any partnership investments (except to the extent that such profit represents depreciation recapture taxable as ordinary income, as hereafter described) will be treated as long- or short-term capital gain or loss, depending on the length of time the property is held, unless it is determined that

- the assets sold constitute stock in trade, inventory, or property held primarily for sale to customers in the ordinary course of the partnership's trade or business; or
- the assets sold constitute Section 1231 assets (that is, real property and depreciable assets used in a trade or business).

In the event that the assets are of the first type described, any gain or loss on the sale or other disposition of such property would be treated as ordinary income or loss. If the assets sold constitute Section 1231 assets, the gains or losses recognized by a limited partner in that year and his or her net Section 1231 gain or loss would be taxed as capital gain or constitute ordinary loss, as the case may be. It should be noted that the Tax Reform Bill of 1984 reduced from one year to six months the holding period necessary to qualify for preferential capital-gains treatment. The new provision is effective for assets acquired after June 22, 1984, and before January 1, 1988.

Moreover, a limited partner will be deemed to have received a cash distribution for tax purposes to the extent that the proceeds of the sale of a partnership property are used to pay off any liability to which such property is subject. As a result, the amount of income upon which the limited partner can be taxed, and the amount of federal income tax actually payable on such income, may be greater than the sale proceeds distributable to a limited partner as a result of such sale. In general, involuntary transfer of partnership property (such as a mortgage foreclosure) would have the same effect as a sale. Unless the amount realized from the sale of a property (whether voluntary or involuntary) substantially exceeds the then unpaid balance of the mortgage on such property, it is quite possible that a limited partner would have a tax liability in excess of the amount of the cash distributed to him or her from such a sale.

No gain or loss would be recognized on the simple refinancing of any mortgage loan by the partnership so long as the new mortgage equals or exceeds the unpaid balance of the old mortgage. Any sale or refinancing proceeds distributed to the partners from a new mortgage that equals or exceeds the unpaid balance of the old mortgage would not be taxable income to the partners if at the time of distribution the distributee's tax basis in his or her partnership interest equals or exceeds the amount distributed. To the extent that the amount of any new mortgage exceeds the existing mortgage, each partner will increase his or her basis by his or her pro rata share of such excess, but the total basis of the partners attributable to the debt to which a property is subject may not exceed the fair-market value of the property. Such basis would be decreased by the amount of any cash proceeds of such mortgage distributed to such partner.

## SALE OR OTHER DISPOSITION BY A PARTNER OF A PARTNERSHIP INTEREST

In the typical syndication, the partnership interests will be transferable subject to certain restrictive limitations. However, there is typically no public market for these interests. Consequently, limited partners may not be able to sell or otherwise liquidate their investment in the event of an emergency or for any other reason.

Upon a sale of a partnership interest, a limited partner will recognize gain or loss equal to the difference between

- the proceeds of such sale plus the proportionate share of the partnership's nonrecourse liabilities; and
- the tax basis.

Such gain or loss from a sale of an interest by a limited partner who is not a "dealer" in securities and who has held such interest for more than one year will be long-term capital gain or loss, as the case may be. As already noted, Congress recently reduced the applicable holding period from 12 to 6 months.

There is an exception to this principle: that portion of the selling limited partner's gain allocable to "substantially appreciated inventory items" and "unrealized receivables" as defined in Section 751 of the code will be treated as ordinary income. Included in "unrealized receivables" is depreciation recapture (discussed hereafter) determined as if the selling limited partner's proportionate share of all the partnership's properties had been sold at that time for fair-market value. If a limited partner's tax basis, before taking into account his or her share of the partnership's liabilities, has been decreased below the price he or she paid for his or her interest by tax deductions and cash distributions, his or her tax liability will normally exceed the actual cash proceeds of such sale.

The Tax Reform Act of 1984 added a provision to the Code relating to disposition of partnership interests. The new law requires a partnership to inform the IRS, the seller, and the buyer of the fair-market value of the allocable share of unrealized receivables and appreciated inventory when partnership interests are sold or exchanged.

In general, upon the death of a limited partner, neither the decedent nor his or her estate will recognize any gain or loss. It is unclear what the tax consequences are, however, if the decedent's proportionate share of the partnership liabilities exceeds the adjusted basis of his or her interest at death. In this event, some gain may be recognized to the decedent or his or her estate upon the distribution of the interest to the extent of such excess. Generally speaking, the basis of an interest acquired from a decedent will be "stepped up" to the fair-market value of the interest at the date of death.

## DISSOLUTION OR TERMINATION OF PARTNERSHIP

In the event of a dissolution of a partnership prior to the expiration of its term, the partnership might be required to sell its property during a limited period of time. This might cause the partnership to sustain losses (measured in terms of the original cost of the property). Nevertheless, the partnership might realize taxable income on such sale as a result of the reduction of its tax basis in the property by depreciation of deductions previously taken.

If at any time no part of the business of the partnership continues to be carried on by any of the partners in a partnership, or if within a 12-month period there is a sale or exchange of 50 percent or more of the total interests in partnership capital and profits, a termination of the partnership would occur, and the taxable year of the partnership would close. In this case, the properties of the partnership would be treated as having been distributed to the partners, and capital gain or loss (and recapture taxed as ordinary income) would result from such termination. Following the deemed distribution, contribution of the same properties, in the form of undivided interests, would be deemed to be made to a new partnership.

## TAX DEDUCTIBILITY AND ACCOUNTING TREATMENT OF CERTAIN ITEMS OF DEPRECIATION (ACCELERATED COST RECOVERY SYSTEM)

The Economic Recovery Tax Act of 1981 has greatly changed the calculation of depreciation for assets placed in service after December 31, 1980, by adopting the Accelerated Cost Recovery System (ACRS). Generally, ACRS allows the cost of an asset to be depreciated over a period that is predetermined and generally shorter than the useful lives previously used to compute depreciation on real property. Under ACRS the actual useful lives and salvage values of the assets used by a partnership are no longer taken into consideration in determining the depreciation deduction. Therefore, the Internal Revenue Service will not be allowed to redetermine these factors or the rates of depreciation utilized. Of course, the IRS may redetermine the allocation of costs between personal property, real property, and land that could result in a reduction of allowable depreciation. It is normally prudent for the developer to obtain an appraisal of the property, including the allocation between land and depreciable assets, in an attempt to minimize a subsequent IRS challenge. Because this is a factual issue, counsel cannot opine as to the ability of the IRS to reallocate such costs.

Under ACRS, residential real property (other than land) can utilize a 15-year recovery period, and the property can be depreciated using either the straight-line method or a table that is based on the 175 percent declining balance accelerated method. Real-property depreciation for the first taxable year of the partnership is determined by the number of months in such year in which the property is in service. Most partnerships will adopt the accelerated method with respect to the partnership property. Once again, however, it should be noted that the Tax Reform Act of 1984 changed the period of depreciation from 15 to 18 years, effective for property placed into service after March 15, 1984 (subject to certain transitional rules).

In certain situations, the IRS has successfully contended that the depreciable basis of property acquired by a partnership cannot include any nonrecourse indebtedness incurred by the partnership in acquiring the property because the indebtedness exceeds the property's fair-market value at the time of purchase. In such a situation, the depreciable basis of the property subject to the nonrecourse indebtedness would be reduced and the purchase money note would not constitute a bona fide indebtedness of the partnership. If the IRS successfully contended that the amount of the partnership's note exceeded the fair-market value of the property securing it, the partnership could be denied the use of all of the note in calculating the adjusted tax basis of the property, and depreciation and interest deductions would be practically eliminated.

This problem is normally overcome where the general partner and the seller of the property negotiated the purchase price in an arm's-length transaction. Again, the general partner should consider obtaining an independent appraisal of the property indicating that its fair-market value is not less than the purchase price paid by the partnership.

*Recapture of Depreciation as Ordinary Income*

Under the IRS Code, all accelerated ACRS depreciation deductions allowable with respect to nonresidential real property must be fully recaptured (that is, taxed at ordinary income rates rather than at capital-gain rates) to the extent of any gain upon disposition through sale, mortgage foreclosure, or otherwise of such property. Under prior law, where an accelerated depreciation method was applied to nonresidential real property, only the excess of accelerated ACRS depreciation deductions over depreciation computed under the straight-line method had to be recaptured, to the extent of gain upon the sale or other disposition thereof. Gain on the disposition of either type of real property generally will not be subject to depreciation recapture where the taxpayer elects to depreciate such property under the straight-line method. However, all depreciation on real property that is disposed of within twelve months after its acquisition is subject to full recapture to the extent of any gain applicable thereto. All depreciation deductions allowable with respect to personal property must be fully recaptured as ordinary income when such property is sold or otherwise disposed of, to the extent of any gain allocable thereto.

*Deductibility of Acquisition Fees*

Partnerships will often incur acquisiton fees paid for negotiation and evaluation of possible investments in properties that are ultimately *not* acquired by the partnership. Prior to the Tax Reform Act of 1984, there were, in general, *two* alternate grounds, either of which if held applicable would permit the deduction of such acquisition fees without regard to the validity of the other ground.

1. Such expenditures are deductible if they are related to a trade or business that is carried on by the taxpayer at the time such expenditures are incurred. It is not entirely clear at what point the partnership will be treated as engaged in a trade or business related to acquisition fees deducted by it.
2. Even if the partnership were not deemed to be engaged in a related trade or business at the time such expenditures were incurred, such expenditures should be deductible if they were deemed to have been incurred in a transaction entered into for profit.

The IRS may, of course, challenge the deductibility of all or part of such expenditures on the ground that neither of the aforementioned tests was met. Even if either or both tests were satisfied, it is possible that the IRS may contest the deductibility of such expenditures on the ground that they are attributable to the negotiation and evaluation of investments in properties acquired by a partnership. In such a case, such expenditures would, to the extent they constitute qualified start-up expenditures as discussed hereafter, be eligible for amortization over 60 months. In the event such expenditures were not eligible for 60-month amortization, they would be required to be capitalized.

The Tax Reform Act of 1984 contains a new provision to the effect that pre-opening or start-up expenditures (other than interest, taxes, and research and experimental expenses) must be amortized over a five year period. This provision is effective for taxable years beginning after June 30, 1984.

### *Deductibility of Interest and Other Similar Amounts*

The availability, timing, and amount of deductions taken by a partnership will generally depend not only on the general legal principles but also on various determinations relating to the partnership and particular real-property investments. Such determinations include, among other things,

- the allocations of basis among buildings, the underlying land,

and personal property that qualifies for ACRS and property that does not qualify for ACRS;

- the characterization of various expenses and payments made to sellers or their affiliates (such as between interest, management fees, "points," guarantee fees, commitment fees, or other similar items on the one hand, and purchase price on the other);
- the characterization of the relationship between a partnership and its affiliates and the seller or manager of a property (or their affiliates);
- the characterization of a partnership's interest in a property;
- the characterization and purpose of acquisition fees paid by the partnership;
- the nonrecourse character of partnership debt;
- the reasonableness and timing of fees;
- the date on which the partnership commences to do business; and
- the date on which the partnership is treated as acquiring an ownership interest in a property, as well as various other matters.

It is conventional for significant portions of net tax losses of partnerships to be attributable to interest and other payments made to sellers (or affiliates) and expected to be deducted under a recent IRS ruling either over the term of the loan or, if such commitment is not exercised, at the time it expires. In the event the deduction of interest, commitment fees, guarantee fees, or other items paid by a partnership to sellers of properties (or affiliates) is denied on the ground that such payments constitute purchase price down payments or are otherwise required to be capitalized, no current deductions for such payments would be allowed, but the partnership might be able to amortize such payments. In this connection, the IRS has been upheld, in Kenneth v. LaCroix, 61 T.C. 471 (1972), in denying a deduction to a limited partnership for an item characterized as interest where it was concluded that the item was, in fact, a down payment on principal due.

### *Prepaid Interest, "Points," and Certain Other Items*

Section 461(g) of the IRS Code requires a taxpayer using the cash method of accounting to capitalize prepaid interest and deduct the interest only in the taxable years for which the interest represents a charge for the use or forbearance of money. Furthermore, "points" paid as compensation for the use of borrowed money, in general, must be deducted ratably over the period of the loan to which they relate. Certain other items, such as higher-than-normal loan-commitment fees are, in effect, treated as prepaid interest.

The Tax Reform Act of 1984 extended this principle to the prepayment of expenses other than interest. Under the new law, cash basis tax shelter organizations will not be allowed to deduct any amount of expense prior to the time it would be properly deductible under an accrual method of accounting. For this purpose, a tax-shelter organization includes certain partnerships having the principal purpose of tax avoidance. An exception to this new rule is provided for prepaid expenses if economic performance with respect to the item occurs during the taxable year.

### *Capitalization and Amortization of Construction-Period Interest and Taxes*

Under Section 189 of the Code, as amended by the Tax Reform Act of 1984, construction-period interest and taxes (that is, interest and taxes paid or accrued during the construction period of the real-property improvement to which they relate) must be capitalized in the year in which they are paid or accrued and amortized over a specified number of years within the allowable amortization period depending on the type of real property involved and the year in which the interest and taxes are paid or accrued. With respect to all real property, the construction period begins on the date on which construction begins, and ends on the date on which the property is ready to be placed in service or ready to be held for sale. In the case of nonresidential real property, one tenth of the construction-period interest and taxes paid or accrued in a taxable year beginning after 1981 may be deducted in the taxable year in which such interest and taxes are paid or accrued, and the balance must be amortized over nine years beginning with the later of the succeeding taxable year or the taxable year in which the property is ready to be placed in service or ready to be held for sale.

It is conventional that a significant portion of interest payments made by syndicated partnerships during early years constitutes construction-period interest, and the effect of the foregoing provisions is to limit the deductibility of such interest and thereby decrease the net losses that would otherwise have been available to the limited partners during the early years of the partnership's operations.

### *Interest Related to Tax-Exempt Obligations*

Section 265(2) of the Code provides that interest on indebtedness incurred or continued to "purchase or carry" tax-exempt obligations is not deductible. It has been held that, if indebtedness is incurred to avoid liquidating tax-exempt obligations, Section 265(2) will operate to preclude the deduction of interest on such indebtedness. In the case of an investor who holds tax-exempt securities, the IRS might seek to disallow deductions by such investor of

- his or her share of interest on indebtedness with respect to partnership properties; or
- interest on any borrowings by such investor to finance his or her investment in the partnership.

However, if a taxpayer's holding of tax-exempt obligations is not substantial, indebtedness of the taxpayer will not be deemed to have been incurred or continued to purchase or carry out such obligations, absent direct evidence to the contrary. Whether the indebtedness is incurred to purchase and carry tax-exempt obligations must be decided on the basis of the individual circumstances of any particular case.

### *Deduction of Management and Other Fees*

The partnership will normally claim deductions for fees that it will pay to a general partner and his or her affiliates for various acquisition and management services. Some of these fees are payable out of the proceeds of the offering and in the aggregate may be substantial. The IRS may examine closely any deductions for fees payable to a general partner and his or her affiliates, or any other party, and may challenge such deductions based upon

- the payment being excessive;
- a recharacterization of the payment; or
- the payment being to a partner in his or her capacity as a partner rather than in some other capacity.

Because such recharacterization depends on various facts and circumstances that may be viewed subjectively, it is difficult to generalize on this topic. If the IRS is successful, the disallowance of the deductibility of such fees would result in a proportionate increase in the taxable income or decrease in tax loss of the partnership, with no associated increase in cash flow with which to pay any resulting increase in tax liabilities.

*Minimum Taxes, Capital Gains, and Interest-Limitation Provisions*

Among the more significant provisions of the IRS Code that may affect limited partners and that are currently in effect are the following:

1. Sixty percent of all long-term capital gains (capital assets held for more than six months) may be deducted from gross income in computing a noncorporate taxpayer's regular tax liability.
2. For individuals, the maximum rate on the excess of long-term capital gains over short-term capital losses is 20 percent. Only one-half of the net long-term capital losses may now be used for the $3,000 annual deduction from ordinary income available to individuals.
3. A limitation is placed upon the deductibility of interest on funds borrowed to acquire or carry investment assets ("investment interest"). In general, investment interest is deductible by noncorporate taxpayers only to the extent that it does not exceed the sum of the following items:

- $10,000 per year (but only $5,000 for a married taxpayer filing a separate return and $0 for a trust); and
- net investment income (that is, the excess of "nontrade or business" income from interest, dividends, rents, royalties, depreciation recapture, and net short-term capital gain from investment property, excluding any long-term gains, over expenses, including straight-line depreciation, incurred in earning such income).

Investment interest that is disallowed as a deduction may be carried over to subsequent years within certain limits. Interest incurred in real estate ventures, if the property involved is rented under what is deemed to be a net lease, is regarded as investment interest, subject to disallowance, rather than business interest that remains fully deductible.

4. Section 265(2) of the Code disallows any deduction for interest paid by a taxpayer or indebtedness incurred or continued for the purpose of purchasing or carrying tax-exempt obligations. The IRS announced in Revenue Procedure 72–18 that the proscribed purpose will be deemed to exist with respect to indebtedness incurred to finance a

"portfolio investment." The Revenue Procedure further states that, while a partnership's purpose in incurring indebtedness will be attributed to its general partners, a limited partnership interest will be regarded as a "portfolio investment," unless rebutted by other evidence. Therefore, in the case of limited partners owning tax-exempt obligations, the IRS might take the position that a partner's allocable portion of any partnership interest expense, or any interest expense incurred by him or her to purchase or carry a limited partnership unit, should be viewed as incurred by him or her to continue carrying tax-exempt obligations and that such holder should not be allowed to deduct all or a portion of such interest.

5. Non-corporate taxpayers are subject to the alternative minimum tax to the extent that it exceeds their regular tax. All "alternative minimum taxable income" in excess of the first $30,000 of "alternative minimum taxable income" ($40,000 for joint returns; $20,000 for married taxpayers filing separately) will be taxed at a 20 percent rate. The alternative minimum taxable income is generally computed by adding tax preference amounts to adjusted gross income and then subtracting specified itemized deductions. Items of tax preference include "excess depreciation" on real property and the deductions for long-term capital gains.

The allowable itemized deductions are:

- charitable contributions,
- medical expenses that exceed 10 percent of adjusted gross income,
- casualty losses,
- wagering losses,
- estate tax,
- qualified housing interest;

and other interest to the extent that such does not exceed the taxpayer's qualified net investment income for the taxable year. "Qualified net-investment income" includes income from a limited partnership interest. Thus, income from a real estate investment may in some cases effectively increase the deduction for interest. However, it is unclear whether, conversely, losses from a partnership interest may reduce a partner's net investment income and thereby effectively reduce the amount of the deduction for interest. Furthermore, a partner's limited partnership interest will be subject to the above-mentioned limitation on the interest deduction. Thus, if a partner borrows to acquire or carry his or her investment in a partnership, he or she may thereby effectively increase the amount of his or her alternative minimum taxable income.

*Implications of Section 183*

Section 183 of the Code limits deductions attributable to "activities not engaged in for profit." The term "activities not engaged in for profit" means any activity other than one that

- constitutes a trade or business; or
- is engaged in for the production or collection of income or for the management, conservation, or maintenance of property held for the production of income.

The determination of whether an activity is engaged in for profit is based on all facts and circumstances.

If the income derived from an activity for two or more of five consecutive taxable years exceeds the deductions attributable to such activities, the activity is presumed to be engaged in for profit for the second profit year and all subsequent years within the five-year period, unless the IRS establishes the contrary. Under certain conditions, a taxpayer may elect to defer the determination of whether the foregoing presumption applies in each of the five taxable years involved. However, the regulations under Section 183 indicate that an organization can satisfy the requirement of a profit motive even if the five-year test is not met. Because a test of whether an activity is deemed to be "engaged in for profit" is based on facts and circumstances that exist from time to time, there is always a risk that Section 183 may be applied to disallow deductions to investors. The IRS is paying increased attention to the application of Section 183 to partnerships and has ruled that Section 183 applies to the activities of a partnership (rather than its partners) and that the provisions of Section 183 are applied at the partnership level.

*Penalty for Substantial Understatement of Liability*

The IRS may impose a penalty of 10 percent on any substantial understatement of income tax, which is defined as the amount of a taxpayer's actual income-tax liability in excess of the amount of income tax shown on his or her return for a given year. A substantial understatement of income tax would exist if the understatement for the taxable year exceeded the greater of 10 percent of the tax required to be shown on the return for that year, or $5,000.

With respect to "tax-shelter items," the penalty may be avoided if the taxpayer establishes that, in addition to having substantial authority for his or her position, he or she reasonably believed that the treatment claimed was more likely than not the proper treatment of the item. For this purpose, a "tax-shelter item" is one that arises from a partnership or other entity, plan, or arrangement, the principal purpose of which is the avoidance or evasion of federal income tax. The IRS may waive the penalty with respect to any item if the taxpayer establishes reasonable cause for his or her treatment of the item and that he or she acted in good faith.

## STATE AND LOCAL TAXES

In addition to the federal income-tax consequences just described, investors must consider potential state and local tax consequences of an investment. An investor's distributive share of the taxable income or loss of a partnership may be required to be included in determining his or her reportable income for state or local tax purposes in the state or locality in which he or she is a resident. In addition, other states or localities in which a partnership may own and operate properties may require the filing of tax returns by nonresidential partners and impose a tax on nonresidential partners determined with reference to their pro rata share of partnership income derived from such state or locality. The investor may be taxable on income derived from sources within a particular state or locality, regardless of whether the partnership sustains losses from properties located outside that particular state or locality and regardless of the amount of such losses, even though such losses equal or exceed the income derived from sources within that particular state or locality or even though the total operations of the partnership result in a net loss.

On the other hand, tax losses derived through the partnership from properties in such states or localities may be available to offset income from other sources within the same state or locality. To the extent that a nonresident limited partner pays tax to a state or locality by virtue of partnership operations within that state or locality, he or she may be entitled to a deduction or credit against taxes owed to his or her state or locality of residence with respect to the same income.

In this chapter and the one preceding, we have been concerned with the tax aspects of syndicating and how syndications can pass or fail tests administered by the Internal Revenue Service. In the following chapter we will view syndication holdings as securities subject to legislative regulation enforced by the Securities and Exchange Commission. Compliance with SEC registration requirements is scarcely less complex than following IRS guidelines.

# 14

# Federal Securities Law and SEC Registration Requirements

The purpose of the Securities Act of 1933 is to assure full disclosure of material facts so as to permit purchasers to make informed investment decisions. It is not a regulatory, but a disclosure statute. This act has been frequently amended in the half century since its inception. In addition, sellers and purchasers of securities must conform to state regulations, a few of which are specific or stringent to the point of requiring special attention. In this chapter we will consider those provisions of the Securities Act of 1933 applying specifically to real estate syndications as well as the laws of several important states with unusual ramifications, as they relate to real estate transactions.

## THE SECURITIES ACT OF 1933 AND THE RECOGNIZED DEFINITION OF A SECURITY TRANSACTION

To assure the availability of adequate and reliable information about securities that are to be offered to the public, the Securities Act of 1933 was enacted. This act is essentially a disclosure statute making it illegal to market securities unless they are registered with the SEC (Securities and Exchange Commission). The required registration statement consists of two parts:

1. a prospectus, which must be furnished to every purchaser of the security before sale; and
2. information and exhibits that need not be furnished to prospective purchasers but that must be available with the SEC for public inspection.

Section 10 of the Act, referring to Schedule A, sets forth the information required in a prospectus. Schedule A delineates the information required in a registration statement. The SEC has published different registration forms for different types of offerings. Form S-1 is the basic document prescribed for use in all offerings for which no other form is authorized; Form S-11 is often used for real estate syndications.

A Form S-11 prospectus should contain the following information, pursuant to the detailed specifications found in Regulation S-K:

- risk factors and ratio of earnings to fixed charges;
- use of proceeds from the offering;
- determination of offering price;
- dilution;
- investment policies;
- description of real estate;
- plan of distribution;
- description of securities to be registered;
- interests of named experts and counsel;
- various financial information with respect to the registrant; and
- tax treatment.

The information contained in Part II of Form S-11, which is not required to be included in the prospectus, includes:

- the expenses of issuance and distribution;
- indemnification of directors and officers;
- recent sales of unregistered securities;
- exhibits and financial statement schedules; and
- undertakings.

In the context of the typical real estate syndication, the sale of a limited partnership interest will inevitably involve the sale of a "security," as broadly defined in Section 2(1) of the Act. Since a registration of the security with the SEC is time consuming and expensive, most promoters will attempt to avoid the laborious registration process through utilization of one of the several exemptions available under the Act. Generally speaking, the principal exemptions that can be relied upon are the private-placement exemption under Rule 4(2) of the Act, the intrastate-offering exemption under Section 3(a)(ii) of the Act and the new Regulation D exemptions. Because the later exemptions tend to be invoked by most promoters, they are considered in depth in the ensuing pages.

## REGISTRATION EXEMPTIONS UNDER REGULATION D (EFFECTIVE APRIL 15, 1982)

Regulation D was enacted to coordinate previous private and small-offering exemptions. It is the product of the SEC's evaluation of both the impact of its rules and regulations on the ability of small businesses to raise capital and Congress's enactment of the Small Business Investment Incentive Act of 1980. Regulation D contains six new Rules, 501 to 506. Rules 501, 502, and 503 are definitional in nature, and Rules 504, 505, and 506 contain the specific exemption provisions. An offering under Regulation D, however, must still meet applicable registration requirements under state law. Furthermore, such a transaction is not exempt from the antifraud or civil liability provisions of the federal securities laws.

*Rule 501* contains definitions, the most important being that of "accredited investor." This is significant in that an accredited investor is not counted toward the limitations on the number of purchasers. There are eight categories of accredited investors:

1. institutional investors such as banks, insurance companies, investment companies, or employee benefit plans;
2. any private business development company as defined in Section 202(a) (2) of the Investment Advisers Act of 1940;
3. any charitable or educational institution, as defined in Section 501(c) (3) of the Internal Revenue Code, with assets over $5 million;
4. any director, executive officer, or general partner of the issuer of the securities;
5. any person who buys at least $150,000 of securities offered, pro-

vided the purchase does not exceed 20 percent of his or her net worth (or joint net worth with spouse) and who pays solely or in any combination of cash, marketable securities, an unconditional obligation to pay in cash or marketable securities within five years of sale, or the cancellation of a debt owed by the issuer to the purchaser;

6. any natural person with a net worth (or joint net worth with spouse) over $1 million;
7. any natural person with an annual income of over $200,000; and
8. entities comprised of accredited investors under any of the above categories (except 5).

Any purchaser who falls into one of these categories, or who the issuer is led to believe after reasonable investigation falls into a category at the time of sale, is an accredited investor for purposes of Regulation D.

*Rule 502* sets forth a series of general conditions that must be met in a Regulation D offering. One problem that an active promoter must be aware of is the "possible integration" of a series of separate offerings. The "safe harbor" integration provision is set forth in 502(a) and provides that offers and sales made more than six months before the start of a Regulation D offering will not be part of that Regulation D offering, as long as no such offers or sales by or for the issuer are of the same or similar class as those sold under Regulation D.

Whether offers within six months of each other are part of a single offering for Regulation D purposes depends on the following factors traditionally employed by the SEC. If the offerings are

- part of a single financing plan,
- involve the same class of security,
- are made at or about the same time,
- involve the same type of consideration, and
- are made for the same general purpose,

they *will* probably be considered integrated. These are subjective factors, but the more that are present, the more likely that the offer will be integrated. If the offerings are part of a single plan of financing, however, the offering will most likely be considered integrated.

The SEC has in the past issued advice with regard to real estate limited partnerships. The SEC has used several factors in finding nonintegration, which include:

- for specified property offerings, the fact that the properties are on different, nonadjacent sites;
- offering proceeds will not be used for any of the other projects;
- assets will not be commingled;
- financing is separately negotiated and secured; and
- the partnerships will be separate legal entities with separate accounts.

*Rule 502(c)* prohibits issuers from offering securities by any form of general solicitation or advertising. This includes, but is not limited to, advertisements in newspapers or magazines or on television or radio and also any meeting whose attendees are invited by general advertising or solicitation.

*Rule 502(d)* sets limits on the resale of Regulation D securities. Such securities cannot be resold without registration under the Act, unless such resale would be exempt. The issuer has a duty to exercise reasonable care to make sure that the purchasers of Regulation D securities are not underwriters under Section 2(11) of the Act. The issuer must issue a written disclosure to each purchaser prior to sale that the securities cannot be resold without registration unless an exemption is available. The issuer must also place a legend on the certificate evidencing the securities that refers to the restrictions on resale.

*Rule 504* is an exemption for offerings not exceeding $500,000, in small offerings by small issuers, such offerings to be regulated by state blue-sky laws and federal antifraud and civil liability provisions. Under Rule 504, no specific information need be furnished to any prospective offerees or purchasers; there is no limit on the number of purchasers, but the aggregate offering price, as defined by Rule 501(c), cannot exceed $500,000. In practice, however, it is normally prudent to provide some form of disclosure document to the prospective investor.

If an issuer makes an offering under Rule 504 exclusively in one or more states, each of which provides for registration of the securities and requires the delivery of a disclosure document before sale, such issuer need not comply with two Regulation D rules. Rule 502(c) prohibiting general advertising and Rule 502(d), which limits the resale of such securities, do not apply to such an issuer provided that such offering is in fact made in accordance with the applicable state provisions.

If, however, a Rule 504 offering is made in two states, the offering being registered in one state and the disclosure document delivered, but the second state offering is made pursuant to an exemption, then the offering is not entitled to a waiver of Rules 502(c) and (d). Regardless if such offering is made in states requiring disclosure, the general rule that no specific information need be furnished to prospective purchasers always applies to a Rule 504 offering.

*Rule 505* is an exemption for offerings not exceeding $5 million and under this Rule an offering cannot have an aggregate offering price in excess of $5 million and can involve no more than 35 purchasers. Several categories of purchasers, however, are excluded from this limitation of number of purchasers:

- accredited investors under Rule 501(c) discussed earlier in this chapter;
- non-United States citizens and residents;
- any relative, spouse, or relative of the spouse of the purchaser with the same residence as the purchaser;
- any trust or estate in which a purchaser or spouse or relative with the same residence collectively has more than 50 percent of the beneficial interest; and
- any corporation of which a purchaser, spouse, or relative with the same residence is beneficial owner of more than 50 percent of equity securities or interests.

Form S-18 also requires information on the plan of distribution, use of proceeds, organization of the issuer if such organization occurred within the past five years, description of business and property, legal proceedings to which the issuer is a party, directors and executive officers, options to purchase securities, and interest of management in certain transactions must be furnished.

If an issuer uses Form S-18 , only the financial statements for the issuer's most recent fiscal year must be certified by an accountant. If Form S-18 is not available and another document is used, only the financial statements for the two most recent years need be furnished and only the statement for the most recent year need be certified. If an issuer, other than a limited partnership, cannot obtain audited financial statements without unreasonable effort or expense, then only the issuer's balance sheet dated within 120 days of the start of the offering must be audited. A limited partnership in the same situation may furnish tax basis financial statements prepared in accordance with generally accepted accounting standards by an independent or certified accountant.

Rule 505's offering must also meet certain other requirements specified in Rule 502. Exhibits normally required to be filed with the SEC in a registration statement need not be furnished if the exhibits are made available to the purchaser on his or her written request prior to purchase. At a reasonable time prior to purchase by a nonaccredited investor, the issuer shall furnish any written information given to any accredited investor, if the nonaccredited investor requests such information in writing.

The issuer must also make available to each prospective buyer prior to purchase the opportunity to ask questions and receive answers about the offering and to obtain any additional information the issuer possesses, or can acquire without unreasonable effort, that is necessary to verify the accuracy of information the issuer was already obligated to disclose. In addition, a Rule 505 offering is subject to Rule 502(c) prohibiting general advertising, and Rule 502(d) limiting the resale of Regulation D securities.

*Rule 506* is an exemption for offerings without regard to dollar amount. Under this exemption, an issuer must reasonably believe that there are no more than 35 purchasers of the securities being offered. As with Rule 505, however, several categories of purchasers are excluded from this limitation:

- any relative, spouse, or relative of spouse of the purchaser with the same residence as the purchaser;
- any trust or estate in which a purchaser or spouse or relative with the same residence collectively has over 50 percent of the beneficial interest;
- any corporation of which a purchaser or spouse or relative with the same residence is a beneficial owner of more than 50 percent of equity securities or interests;
- non-United States citizens and residents; and
- accredited investors under Rule 501(c).

In addition to these requirements, nonaccredited buyers must also be "qualified" purchasers. The issuer shall reasonably believe, immediately before sale, that each purchaser who is not an accredited investor, either alone or with his or her purchaser representative, as defined in Rule 501(h), has such knowledge and experience in financial and business matters that he or she is capable of evaluating the merits and risks of the prospective offering.

The disclosure requirements under Rule 506 are the same as those under Rule 505. As under Rule 505, if there are any nonaccredited investors, the information required under Rule 502 must be furnished to all purchasers.

## STATE BLUE-SKY LAWS

State laws specifically regulating securities transactions are commonly known as blue-sky laws. Such laws vary from state to state, but *three* typical provisions are usually found in each state's laws. Most states have prohibitions against fraud in the sale of securities, which contain a general prohibition against fraud and authorize government officials to obtain injunctive relief or prosecute offenders. Most states also have requirements for registration of brokers and dealers. Finally, almost all states require some affirmative action to be taken by an issuer to register securities before they can be sold in the state. The general requirements of three principal states, California, Illinois, and New York, are here discussed.

### *California*

California blue-sky laws provide for registration of securities by an issuer through either coordination or notification. Registration by coordination is permitted when any security in connection with the offering has been filed in a registration statement under the act. The information to be filed with the state commissioner includes:

- the federal registration statement;
- future amendments to that statement;
- a form specifying the name and address of the applicant;
- a description of the total number of shares being qualified in California;
- the proposed maximum offering price per unit; and
- the proposed maximum aggregate offering price for securities being qualified in the state.

Such registration is generally effective when the federal statement becomes effective.

Registration by notification is permitted for any security issued by an issuer of any security registered under Section 12 of the 1934 Exchange Act or issued by an investment company registered under the

Investment Company Act of 1940 and that is not eligible under registration by coordination. The same information required under the state form for coordination is required under the notification method. If no stop order is issued, such registration becomes effective after ten business days of filing.

California has several exemptions to its blue-sky laws. Any security consisting of any interest in all or portions of parcels of real property in subdivided lands, a subdivision, or in a real estate development is exempt, except that the exemption is not available to an investment contract sold or offered for sale with, or as part of, any such interest. California also has an exemption similar to Regulation D. An offer or sale to no more than 35 persons is exempt. Each purchaser must either have a pre-existing relationship with the offerer, or his or her experience or the experience of his or her professional advisors leads the offerer to reasonably assume a capacity to protect his or her own interests. The purchaser must be buying for resale purposes.

*Illinois*

Illinois provides for registration by notification, description, or qualification. Registration by notification is permitted for any security registered under the Act where the effective date of such registration is no more than ten days prior to the filing with the Illinois Secretary of State. The issuer must file two copies of a prospectus and amendments thereto, a consent to service of process, and a statement describing the title of securities and amount to be offered in Illinois.

Registration by description is allowed for any security registered under the act if the effective date of the federal registration is not more than 30 days before the state filing. The state application must set forth:

- the name and address of the issuer;
- title and total amount of securities being offered;
- amount of securities being offered in Illinois;
- price of securities;
- the aggregate underwriting commissions and discounts;
- one copy of the federal registration statement;
- an opinion of counsel regarding the validity of the securities; and
- a consent to service of process.

This method cannot be used, however, if underwriters will receive an aggregate remuneration or discounts exceeding 20 percent of the initial offering price.

Registration by qualification is identical to registration by description except that the issuer need not file the registration statement under the Act and any amendments or exhibits relating to that statement. In addition, a prospectus must be filed containing such information as:

- the date of and organization of the issuer;
- a description of its business;
- its capitalization and authorized securities;
- proposed method of sale and price of this offering;
- the use of the offering's proceeds;
- names of officers, directors, and those owning 10 percent of any class of the issuer's securities;
- any legal proceedings in which the issuer is involved; and
- certain financial statements.

Illinois has an exemption similar to Regulation D, which became effective on January 1, 1984, and which applies to any offer, sale, or issue. All the sale of securities in the offering to Illinois residents within 12 months shall not be to more than 35 people. No general advertising or solicitation is allowed, except that a prospectus in the registration statement filed under the Act does not constitute general advertising if it is not sent to more than 150 residents. In computing the 35-purchaser limit, any security sold under an exemption or registered at the time of sale is excluded.

*New York*

The New York blue-sky laws contain a special provision dealing with real estate syndication offerings. Such offerings are defined as securities constituting participation interests in real estate, mortgages, or leases, including stocks, bonds, debentures, evidences of interest or indebtedness, limited partnership interests, or other securities when such securities are participation interests or investments in one or more real estate ventures.

Prior to such an offering, an issuer must file a written statement known as an "offering statement" or "prospectus," unless there is an exemption by rule or action of the attorney general. Such offering statement must include:

- detailed terms of the transaction;
- a description of the property involved;
- the nature of interest and title to be held;
- the basis, rate, and method of depreciation;
- current leases and terms of mortgages on the property;
- the principals involved;
- interests of the promoters;
- any restrictions on transfer of interest;
- a statement of securities involved; and
- the use of the proceeds from the offering.

No such offering is allowed unless such a statement is filed. All advertisements with regard to the offering must state no offer is made except by the "offering statement."

A prospectus as well as the "offering statement" must be furnished to all prospective purchasers before sale. The prospectus must contain a full and fair summary of all material aspects of the offering. A Regulation D type of exemption exists in New York with regard to such offerings. The attorney general may exempt such offerings made to no more than 40 persons, if the securities are fully registered with the SEC or if the issue comes under a federal exemption.

## THE UNIFORM LIMITED OFFERING EXEMPTION RESOLUTION

In October of 1981, the North American Securities Administrators Association adopted the Uniform Limited Offering Exemption (ULOE) as an official policy guideline. The objective of ULOE was to create a basic framework of limited offering exemptions to apply uniformly at state and federal levels. Rules 501, 502, 503, and 505 of Regulation D were the principal elements of the exemption. (The ULOE was amended in 1983 to make the rule 506 exception available on an optional basis.) ULOE was designed to respond to the needs of small-business financing and create uniformity among states and compatibility with an appropriate federal limited-offering exemption.

ULOE provides that any offer or sale under Rule 505 (and in conformance with Rules 501 to 503) is exempt if it satisfies additional limitations. An exemption is not available to the issuer if any party described in Rule 230.252 (Sections (c)-(f) of the act)

- has also filed a registration statement subject to a stop order pursuant to any state law within five years of the offering;
- was convicted within five years of the offering of a crime involving the sale or purchase of a security or a felony involving fraud or deceit;
- is subject to any state administrative order or judgment entered by that state's securities administrator;
- is subject to any state's order prohibiting the use of any exemption; or
- is subject to any court order entered within five years of the offering restraining conduct in connection with the sale or purchase of securities.

In all sales to nonaccredited investors, the issuer shall have reasonable grounds to believe and, after making a reasonable inquiry, shall believe that the investment is suitable for the purchaser and that the purchaser alone or with his or her purchaser representative has such knowledge and experience in business and financial matters that he or she is capable of evaluating the risks and merits of the prospective investment.

Finally, nothing in ULOE is intended to relieve issuers from their obligation of providing disclosure to prospective investors to satisfy antifraud provisions of state securities law.

The Securities Act of 1933 was followed by another significant statute regulating, among other things, broker-dealer registration requirements, the Securities Exchange Act of 1934. The following chapter will consider the implications of this statute in real estate transactions.

# 15

# Registration Requirements for Securities Brokers and Dealers

The Securities Exchange Act of 1934 was enacted to assure the availability to the public of adequate information on companies with publicly traded stock, to regulate their trading markets, and to control the activities of those dealing in these securities. The 1934 Act established the Securities and Exchange Commission (SEC) to enforce the provisions of the federal securities laws. Among its terms, the 1934 Act contains antifraud provisions to ensure the integrity of the securities markets and to promote public confidence for investing in the various issues.

These antifraud provisions, or rules of fair practice, are varied, and several specifically relate to brokers and dealers. The broker or dealer is essentially acting as a fiduciary of his or her client and cannot convert this agency role into that of a principal without express, informed authorization from the client prior to each transaction. A broker or dealer *cannot*

- recommend securities not suitable for the customer;
- make uninformed representations or predictions; or
- execute unauthorized purchases or engage in fraudulent or deceitful practices.

The National Association of Securities Dealers (NASD), the only national securities association registered with the SEC, has its own

Rules of Fair Practice. These rules apply to all brokers and dealers registered with the SEC. In general, every member of the NASD must observe high standards of commercial honor and just and equitable principles of trade. If an issuer is distributing an offering without an underwriter, each participant engaged in the sale is responsible for determining that the terms of the issue are fair and reasonable. In determining fairness and reasonableness of offering terms, the following factors are considered:

- the size of the offering;
- the type of underwriting commitment if an underwriter is involved;
- the securities being offered;
- restrictions on the offering;
- overall compensation to the underwriter; and
- any lack of arm's-length bargaining positions or
- conflicts of interest connected with the offering.

An NASD member cannot make an offer to buy or sell securities at a stated price unless he or she is prepared to buy or sell at such price and under the conditions stated in such an offer. A member acting as an agent, trustee, or in a similar capacity who has received information as to the ownership of securities cannot use such information to solicit purchases or sales except at the request and on behalf of an issuer.

An NASD member cannot make any transaction by means of a manipulative, deceptive, or other fraudulent device. A member is also prohibited from making improper use of a customer's securities or funds. One cannot lend a customer's securities without the customer's written authorization, and then one cannot lend more than is fair in light of the customer's indebtedness. In addition, there are rules governing limitations on offering expenses and suitability of recommendations to customers. All the guidelines were designed to ensure that the securities business would be conducted in a just, reasonable, and nondiscriminatory manner.

## STATUTORY FRAMEWORK—BROKER AND DEALER REGISTRATION PROVISIONS OF SECTION 15(a) (1) OF THE 1934 ACT

The 1934 Act requires registration of all brokers and dealers except those engaging exclusively in intrastate business or dealing only in exempted securities, as it is unlawful for any broker or dealer to use the means of interstate commerce to effect transactions in securities unless registered. A broker is defined as a "person engaged in the business of effecting transactions in securities for the account of others." A dealer is a person who is actively engaged in the business of buying and selling securities. He or she is different from a person who is strictly a passive investor, and is not actively engaged in the business of buying or selling securities. Although he or she might own securities, he or she is not actively engaged in the business.

Registration as a broker or a dealer is separate from securities registration and is not waived even if the securities are sold under an exemption. An issuer is not considered to be a dealer as he or she sells only securities. Whether a real estate syndicator offering securities, however, is considered to be a broker is a factual determination. Registration as a broker is the prudent course for any syndicator engaged in more than one offering.

To register with the SEC, an applicant must file Form BD and additional financial information. The applicant must indicate on Form BD in which states it will be making the offering. Various questions regarding previous false statements, felonies, and injunctions regarding the applicant must be answered. Schedule A for corporate applicants requires a list of officers, directors, and each other beneficial owner of over 5 percent of the corporation's securities. Schedule B for partnerships requires a list of all general, limited, and special partners and their respective percentages of capital contributions to the partnership.

In addition to Form BD, a statement of the applicant's financial condition as of a date within 30 days of the date the statement is filed is required, as well as revisions to indicate material changes. The statement must disclose the nature and amount of assets, liabilities, and net worth of the applicant. The applicant must also provide

- the nature and source of capital contributed by the applicant;
- arrangements for establishing and maintaining facilities and financing for business as a broker or dealer; and
- a statement of arrangements for funds for the first operating year, uses to which the funds will be put, expenses to be incurred, and arrangements (if any) for additional funds.

There are capital requirements for brokers and dealers, which vary depending on the type of business in which the applicant engages. In general, no broker or dealer shall permit its aggregate indebtedness to exceed 1500 percent of its net capital. For those in the general securities business, the aggregate indebtedness cannot exceed 800 percent for 12 months after commencing business, and at all times such a party must have and maintain not less than $25,000 as a minimum capital requirement.

Once a broker or dealer has registered with the SEC, he or she must file audited annual statements of financial condition. The annual report should contain the following information:

- financial condition;
- income or loss;
- changes in financial position;
- changes in stockholders' equity or partners' or sole proprietor's capital;
- changes in liabilities;
- computation of net capital;
- computation of reserve requirements;
- information on control requirements;
- a reconciliation; and
- a supplemental report.

The statements must be audited and certified by an independent accountant. The report must be filed within 60 days of a fixed date each year.

The SEC has authority to censure, limit the activities of, suspend up to 12 months, or revoke the registration of a broker or dealer if such broker or dealer has engaged in certain prohibited activity. Such action by the SEC is warranted if the applicant has:

- made false or misleading statements on its application;
- been convicted within ten years of registration of any crime involving the purchase or sale of securities, a false oath, a false report, bribery, perjury, burglary, or conspiracy to commit these crimes, or a crime arising from its business as a broker or dealer;
- been enjoined by court order from acting as a broker or dealer; or
- has willfully violated the provisions of the federal securities laws.

## EXEMPTIONS FROM REGISTRATION—THE "EXCLUSIVE INTRASTATE BUSINESS" EXEMPTION

The 1934 Act exempts from broker or dealer registration the sale of "any security which is part of an issue offered and sold only to persons resident within a single state or territory, where the issuer of such security is a person resident and doing business within, or if a corporation, incorporated by and doing business within, such state or territory." This exemption is available to all issuers except investment companies and does not depend on the lack of use of the means of interstate commerce. Furthermore, availability of this exemption is not dependent on state "blue-sky" registration.

The SEC and the courts have issued interpretations on this exemption. All securities must be offered and sold only to bona fide domiciliaries, defined as permanent voting residents, of a single state. A sale to a domiciliary temporarily living in another state would probably be acceptable. The issuer, if a corporation, must be incorporated in the offering state; if a partnership, must have its principal office in the state; or if an individual, must maintain his or her principal residence in the state.

The "doing business" requirement is met if the issuer derives 80 percent of its gross revenues during its most recent fiscal year (if the offer is made during the first six months of such fiscal year) or 80 percent of its gross revenues for the first six months of the current fiscal year or during 12 months of the fiscal period ending with such six-month period (if the offer is in the last six months of the current fiscal year) from activities within the state and if the issuer has at least 80 percent of its assets within such state (at the end of the most recent six-month fiscal period). The issuer must intend to use, and must use, at least 80 percent of the proceeds from the offering in connection with business activity within the state of offering. The proceeds cannot go to activities or subsidiaries outside the state. The securities can be resold to out-of-state residents only after nine months from the date of the last interstate sale. A legend must be placed on each certificate stating such restrictions, and the issuer must disclose such restriction to each buyer in writing. A written representation of the state of the buyer's residency is required.

If the offer or sale of any part of the issue violates any part of the exemption, the exemption is lost for the entire issue. An issue is not necessarily limited to securities sold at one time because of integration. Sales separated in time may be integrated if, in substance, they are part of the same issue.

## REGISTRATION REQUIREMENTS FOR THE SYNDICATOR AND ITS PRINCIPALS AND EMPLOYEES

A registered broker or dealer must meet operating capability standards established by the SEC. The broker or dealer and all natural persons associated with these individuals must meet certain standards of training, experience, and competence. The personnel of brokers and dealers engaged in sales must be licensed as salespeople or agents under appropriate state law and, if the broker or dealer is a member of the National Association of Securities Dealers (NASD) or a national exchange, the salespeople must be registered with the NASD or take the appropriate examination given by the national exchange.

## REGISTRATION WITH THE SEC

The 1934 Act provides that a broker or dealer required to register under the 1934 Act must also either be a member of a securities association registered with the SEC or effect transactions solely on a national exchange of which the broker or dealer is a member. The NASD is the only national securities association registered with the SEC. As of December 6, 1983, all brokers and dealers must belong to NASD and follow its rules and guidelines.

Any broker or dealer authorized to transact and whose regular course of business consists of the securities business in the United States is eligible under state or federal law for membership in the NASD. A broker is defined by the NASD as "any individual, corporation, partnership, association, joint stock company, business trust, unincorporated organization, or other legal entity engaged in the business of effecting transactions in securities for the account of others, but does not include a bank." A dealer, like a broker, is engaged in "the business of buying and selling securities for his own account, through a broker or otherwise, but does not include a bank, or any person insofar as he buys or sells securities for his own account, either individually or in some fiduciary capacity, but not as part of a regular business."

No broker or dealer can become a member of the NASD if he or she

- has been and is suspended or expelled from a registered national securities association or exchange;
- has been denied, suspended, or revoked registration by the SEC;
- has made a false or misleading statement in an application or report filed with the NASD;
- has been convicted within ten years of various fraudulent crimes;
- is enjoined by court order from acting as a broker or dealer; or
- does not meet the NASD qualifications.

Both the principal(s) and representatives, if any, of the broker or dealer must register with the NASD.

Before a principal can become a member of the NASD, he or she must pass an examination prepared by the NASD. Principals are defined as sole proprietors, and if the broker or dealer is an organization, provisions apply to officers, partners, managers of offices of supervisory jurisdiction, and directors of corporations. An applicant for membership, except a sole proprietor, must have at least two officers or partners who qualify as principals. There are various classes of principals for registration, depending on the type of business in which the principal engages.

Representatives must also pass an examination before becoming NASD members. Representatives are assistant officers other than principals who supervise, solicit, or train those associated with the broker or dealer. As with principals, there are different classes of representatives.

## REGULATION OF CREDIT ARRANGEMENTS—REGULATION T

In the typical real estate syndication, installment contributions by limited partners are often staged over a period of years. Regulation T, which prohibits a broker or dealer from extending or maintaining credit or arranging for the extension of credit to a customer for the purpose of purchasing a security, is potentially applicable. It is clear that in a public real estate syndication, Regulation T would be applicable, and the margin rules promulgated by the Federal Reserve System would be applied. In the case of private real estate syndications (that is, those exempt from registration under Regulation D discussed in Chapter 14), however, it seems reasonably clear that the margin rules would not be applicable. This is the view of the staff of both the SEC and the Board of Governors of the Federal Reserve.

## THE PROCEDURAL STEPS FOR OBTAINING BROKER AND DEALER REGISTRATION

The NASD requires that certain examinations be taken and passed not only by broker and dealer principals, but also by sales individuals or reps who plan to merchandise under the umbrella of the NASD broker/dealer license. Simply passing the Direct Participation Program (DPP) examination does not in itself qualify an individual to market real estate securities. To sell interests in direct participation programs or limited partnerships, one must become a member of a licensed broker or dealer firm that operates with a minimum net capital requirement of $25,000. The NASD requires this to establish that the organization has financial staying power sufficient to its operation. Several states, in addition to the NASD, require minimum capitalization and these requirements should be cleared in the states in which one plans to merchandise one's offerings.

## ACTIVITIES THAT REQUIRE NASD REGISTRATION

Initially, one needs to determine whether the marketing efforts or those contemplated actually require a formal registration with the NASD. In many areas, exemptions from NASD registration, as outlined in several of the preceding chapters, could apply exclusively, preempting one's registration requirements. Because of their limited activities, many individuals need not form their own firms and are better served by joining an existing organization complementary to their syndicating activities.

In the event that forming a DPP firm becomes imperative, one should definitely partake in a sophisticated course of instruction to comprehend the securities process in its entirety and to pass the examinations. These technical and complicated examinations cannot generally be glossed over by individuals unused to specialized short-term crash courses. The most professional instruction offered for the DPP exam is given by the Real Estate Securities and Syndication Institute (RESSI), a division of the National Association of Realtors, located at

430 North Michigan Avenue, Chicago, Illinois 60611 (312-670-6760). Their courses are offered several times a year at convenient geographic locations throughout the United States.

Upon successfully completing this or a comparable accredited course, one should then complete the appropriate NASD application form and submit it with a $40 application fee. The NASD exam should be taken as expeditiously as possible after the instructional course is completed, as the material covered is quite complicated, and many details can be forgotten with time.

The next step is to establish the type of entity in which the broker or dealer license is to be housed, which depends to a large degree on the detrimental liability aspects of the operation. Where several broker or dealer associates are contemplated, the corporate entity appears to have the most validity. This vehicle downplays the liability aspect significantly and also eliminates the tedious filing that is required by the Securities and Exchange Commission, notably their requirement for filing a certified annual financial statement.

When an individual and not a corporation is the registered entity, *all the assets* of the individual must be certified annually to the SEC under Rule 17A-5. By structuring or maintaining one's individual assets outside the DPP corporation, exposure, as well as the expenses for accounting and certification, are a known commodity. Many DPP firms wisely contract for errors-and-omissions insurance covering their employees, since the overall ramifications relating to potential liability are based upon *the actual funds* that are solicited and passed through the DPP firm's various trust accounts.

## CAPITALIZATION AND APPLICATION REQUIREMENTS

After selecting the type of entity and clearing the operational name with the NASD and the appropriate state in which the DPP is to operate, the concept of capitalization must be addressed. A newly formed organization cannot hold a broker or dealer registration on either a state or a local level without the prescribed minimum amount of financial capitalization. The $25,000 usually required by the NASD sometimes can be reduced to $5,000, and in those states with separate capitalization requirements these amounts are usually in the $5,000 range. In lieu of a cash equity contribution, many firms furnish a surety bond comparable in amount acceptable to the NASD. The value of this bond varies with required minimum capitalization requirements at the state level and should be verified prior to the surety document being issued.

Application for membership as a DPP firm involves contact with several agencies:

- Membership Department, Member Firm Section, National Association of Securities Dealers, Inc., 1735 K Street, Washington, D.C. 20006 (202-728-8106);
- the various securities departments in the state or states of intended operation should be contacted; and
- both the SEC and the NASD have separate filing requirements, which can be obtained from the Securities and Exchange Commission, Division of Market Regulation, 500 North Capital Street, Washington, D.C. 20459 (202-523-5566).

## THE NASD AND SEC PROCEDURAL STEPS

When an application is filed with the SEC and all appropriate forms and documentation are complete and in order, that agency requires up to 45 days to process or clear the application or show cause for denial. In most instances the SEC application is filed in conjunction with the appropriate state documentation, thereby expediting the process. The exception to this practice occurs in California, which requires the full SEC approval prior to state registration. Applications are rarely denied, except when the individual has had prior dealings with the SEC entailing serious legal, ethical, or technical complications. Clearing the application usually requires far less than the required 45 days, especially when one has a pending offering and the SEC sets up a mandatory hearing with the applicant upon clearance.

Procedures require that the NASD cannot act on a registration application until it has first cleared the SEC. Once NASD clearance is obtained, the applicant must obtain and provide the NASD with approvals from the regulatory bodies of the various states in which securities are anticipated to be marketed. At that point, the NASD schedules a "premembership interview" at the most convenient local or district office. The purpose of this interview is to determine whether the firm and its principal members are basically qualified and capable of meeting *all* the appropriate NASD rules and regulations.

By statute the SEC is authorized, however not required, to have what is known as a "posteffective registration" conference, which is automatically waived in most instances. If it is scheduled, the applicant meets with qualified staff members of the SEC in one of their regional offices, or the interview is appropriately conducted by telephone.

## PERTINENT QUESTIONS RAISED AT THE NASD PREMEMBERSHIP INTERVIEW

These interrogatories revolve around the facts that most broker and dealer firms are relatively small in nature and normally intend to confine their activities exclusively to the marketing of limited partnership interests in real estate syndications without participating in equity positions. Their activities are generally confined to depositing investor funds in escrow accounts and disbursing them to the syndicating entity when the offering is formed, closed, and functional. Typical regulatory questions, therefore, concern themselves with

- the firm's ability to meet the NASD's capitalization and reserve requirements;
- evidence of the firm's actual in-place fidelity bond;
- proof of registration in the intended state(s) of operation;
- documentation of SEC registration approval or clearance; and
- the promulgated rules or regulations that will guide the firm procedurally.

The NASD premembership interviews *rarely* focus on the relative *types of investments* that are to be syndicated, nor do they require the details of the in-depth knowledge the syndicator possesses in terms of the economics or the viability of any proposed syndicated offering. Rather, their purpose is to establish that the applicant knows the NASD rules and regulations appropriate to his or her firm and is able to set up and maintain adequate financial records supporting his or her firm's activities. Concrete evidence must also be presented as to where the DPP firm will house its escrow account, a fairly straightforward procedure governed by NASD rules. When the interview is completed, it is summarized in report form and copies sent to the NASD headquarters in Washington, where it becomes a part of the applicant's permanent file.

If the SEC posteffective registration conference is required, its format is similar to that of the NASD premembership interview. The applicant is judged for capability of following the various SEC rules and regulations, particularly Rules 15C-3–1 and 17A-5 pertaining to the capitalization requirements and record-keeping documentation.

The entire process of making or structuring applications and receiving approval from the NASD and the SEC, including the premembership interview, usually takes no more than *60 to 90 days* from the time the initial applications are fully completed and submitted.

## PITFALLS TO BE AVOIDED IN THE DPP REGISTRATION PROCESS

The single document most *critical* to one's application is the NASD's *Form BD.* Completing it inadequately will most assuredly result in a significant delay. If the applicant cannot provide appropriate or adequate answers, he or she should indicate this clearly rather than leave questions unanswered or incomplete. Extensive documentation of the entity itself, whether it be a corporation or a partnership, should include the appropriate officers, directors, or partners.

The most technical section of Form BD is that headed "Statements and Representations Pursuant to SEC Rule 15B-1–2." This section is the most exhausting to complete and also the most closely monitored. Its principal components relate to:

- *Rule 15BL-2(c) (1),* in which the applicant represents that the capital indicated in the statement of financial condition has been contributed and that the designated amount will be continuously devoted to the business of the applicant as a broker/dealer. The initial capital of the applicant represents a contribution in cash or equivalent to the newly formed entity.
- *Rule 15BL-2(c) (2),* where the applicant represents that arrangements have been made for the establishment or maintenance of adequate business facilities and where ample capitalization is available for continuing the broker/dealer business.
- *Rule 15BL-2(c) (3),* where the applicant must represent that the revenue obtained from his or her business will consist strictly of compensation derived from sales as generated. One must also state that the projected revenues are an unknown commodity and cannot reasonably be predicted and must estimate the cost of sales and general overhead, certifying that if additional funds are

needed the applicant or attendant investors can contribute whatever is necessary for continuance of operations.

## ADDITIONAL PERTINENT REGISTRATION INFORMATION

The Securities Investor Protection Corporation (SIPC), whose sole purpose is to protect innocent investors through the reimbursement process if they lose their deposits when a broker or dealer firm declares insolvency, is supported and backed by the U.S. government. To minimize the net capital requirements of the NASD, most DPP broker or dealer firms will not concern themselves with unescrowed customer funds. Regardless of this, all DPP broker or dealer firms must register with the SIPC, 900 Seventeenth Street NW, Suite 800, Washington, D.C. 20006 (202-223-8400) and contribute the current membership fee of $25.

The Uniform Securities Agents State Law Examination (USASLE) is administered by the NASD for the benefit of some 26 states who require that this test be passed in lieu of another state-supported examination. The results are forwarded to any state in which the applicant is desirous of operating. To take or qualify for this examination, a candidate must obtain NASD Form U-63 by separate request, since this document is not included in the DPP membership kit. With the completed form, the candidate must submit a $40 nonrefundable filing fee.

## HOW STATE OR BLUE-SKY LAWS INTERACT WITH THE BROKER AND DEALER PROVISIONS OF THE 1934 ACT

A broker or dealer registered with the SEC must still register under the appropriate state blue-sky laws. All states have requirements for broker and dealer registration. The laws of California, Illinois, and New York will be noted.

Under California law, a broker or dealer is any person engaged in the business of effecting transactions in securities for the account of others or him- or herself. A broker or dealer registered under the 1934 Act with no place of business in California who sells only to other brokers, dealers, banks, or institutional investors is exempt from registration in California. Real estate brokers licensed by the California Department of Real Estate are exempt from broker or dealer registration, provided that limited partnership interests sold in certain real-estate-related entities are owned by no more than 100 persons and were formed for the sole purpose of and engaged solely in investment and/or gain from interest in real property, including but not limited to a sale, exchange, trade, or development.

In Illinois, a dealer is defined as "any person other than a salesperson . . . who engages in this state . . . in the business of offering, selling, buying and selling, or otherwise dealing or trading in securities issued by another person." Therefore, an issuer selling its own securities is not required to register.

On the application for registration as a dealer, the applicant must give its name and address, other licenses, and, if more than 60 days before application, any lawsuit pending against the applicant involving fraud and the applicant's articles of incorporation (if a corporation). To register a salesperson, the applicant must furnish the salesperson's name and address, employers for the past ten years, and any lawsuit pending against the salesperson involving fraud. The salesperson is also required to take an examination.

No dealer can permit its aggregate indebtedness to exceed 1500 percent of its net capital. The dealer must file certain financial reports each year. Among the antifraud provisions governing dealers is that they are not permitted to "churn" customers' accounts. A dealer is also required, before the completion of any sale, to send a written confirmation of such sale to the customer.

Under New York law, an issuer selling its own securities must register as a dealer. A salesperson employed by a firm that is a member of the NASD and is engaged in selling securities outside New York must also register as a salesperson. A dealer is required to maintain net capital of at least $5,000.

Having reviewed the provisions of the 1934 Securities and Exchange Act in this chapter and those of the Securities Act of 1933 in the preceding chapter, we will continue to consider these two closely interrelated pieces of legislation insofar as they affect the key document of any real estate syndication, the private-placement memorandum. As we will see in the following chapter, the syndicator must go beyond the letter of the law in drafting this memorandum if he or she is to inform the potential investors fully and protect him- or herself from the consequences of not doing so.

# 16

# Requirements of Full and Accurate Disclosure

The private-placement memorandum is the single most important document in a real estate syndication application. A properly drafted private-placement memorandum will definitely describe the nature of the transaction, the parties involved, the property to be invested in, and the economics of the transaction. The document is designed, in addition to meeting the technical requirements of the exemptions relied upon under the securities laws that are discussed elsewhere in this book, to disclose all material information to the prospective investor that will enable him or her to make an informed, reasonable judgment on the merits of the prospective investment. This document will inevitably involve not only the general partners, but their outside advisors, attorneys, and accountants as well.

In rare circumstances a formal private-placement memorandum will not accompany a real estate transaction. An extensive private-placement memorandum may be dispensable when

- the investor group is relatively small;
- each investor knows the other investors and is thoroughly familiar with the proposed project and its potential risks; and
- each investor is financially sophisticated and capable of bearing the risk of losing the entire investment.

Even under these circumstances the general partners may choose to prepare an elaborate private-placement memorandum to avoid any exposure to liability if the project is not successful and if the investors might otherwise take the position that they were not fully apprised of the details of the transaction.

## OUTLINE OF PRIVATE-PLACEMENT MEMORANDUM

Most private-placement memoranda tend to be similar in form and, to a lesser extent, common in content. The SEC has issued guidelines that provide a format for the disclosure of information in connection with public real estate limited-partnership offerings. These guidelines identify the following 21 specific disclosure items, the more important of which will be described briefly as follows:

1. *Cover page.* The cover page of a private-placement memorandum will describe, in summary fashion, the economics of the transaction and specifically the amount of equity being raised and the amount of each particular investor unit. The cover page may also identify the general partner or partners, the location (if it is a particular real estate project), and will introduce the reader to the fact that the transaction will certainly involve the taking of certain risks that are described later in the private-placement memorandum.

2. *Suitability standards.* This portion of the private-placement memorandum has been touched upon in Chapter 14 in connection with the various exemptions available under the securities laws. The suitability section will set forth the requisite net-worth requirements of the individuals who are qualified to invest in the project and will again identify in general terms the potential risks involved in the transaction.

3. *Summary of the real estate partnership and use of proceeds.* As the title suggests, this section will briefly describe the transaction, including the economics, the cast of characters, the property, the financing, the investment objectives of the partnership, how the partnership intends to use the proceeds from the offering, the allocation and distributions of profits and losses, and cash flow to the general and limited partners.

4. *Compensation and fees to the general partner and affiliates.* This is perhaps one of the most critical sections of a private-placement memorandum in that it is likely to attract considerable scrutiny from the investors and their advisors reviewing the document. Because of its im-

portance, details of content will be discussed later in this chapter.

5. *Conflicts of interest.* Once again this section can be of critical importance and will be the subject of elaboration later in this chapter.

6. *Statement of fiduciary responsibility owed by the general partner to the limited partners.* This topic was considered in some detail in other chapters relating to general-partnership law principles. A typical private-placement memorandum will set forth the various fiduciary obligations that the general partner must observe in organizing and operating the limited partnership.

7. *Principal risk factors including tax risks.* Anyone who has reviewed a private-placement memorandum may ask the question: "Why am I even considering this investment, given the apparent tax risks involved?" This section of the private-placement memorandum is replete with caveats and disclosures that can have a chilling effect. Nevertheless, this section of the document is essential, given the inherent tax considerations and motivations underlying most real estate syndications. Once again, because of its importance, it will be treated later in this chapter in some detail, including an identification and description of a number of more conventional risk disclosures.

8. *Track record disclosure.* The prior performance of the general partner in other real estate transactions is certainly relevant information to a prospective investor and accordingly will normally be described in a memorandum. Moreover, failure to include this information could jeopardize the availability of certain exemptions, since this is material information that would be included in a registration statement filed with the SEC. This section would contain a narrative summary providing potential investors with a comprehensive description of the general partner's overall operations and his or her experience over a period of years. The information will normally include at least the following:

- number of programs sponsored;
- total amount of money raised from investors;
- total number of investors;
- number of properties purchased and location of such properties;
- total dollar amount of property purchased;
- breakout of properties that are commercial versus residential; and
- percentage of new, used, or construction properties and the number of properties sold.

The SEC guidelines also provide for certain tabular information that should be included in a disclosure document as a part of the general partner's track record. These tables include

- experience in raising and investing funds;
- compensation to the general partner in past programs;
- operating results in prior programs;
- results of completed programs;
- sales or disposals of properties; and
- acquisitions of properties by other programs.

9. *Management Identity*. This section of the disclosure document will describe the sponsors of the project, including their educational and employment history. Moreover, the financial status of the general partner would normally be included in the disclosure document. In the case of a corporation, a recent balance sheet and income statement would be appropriate; and in the case of an individual, a net-worth statement would be included. Finally, any prior securities law violations, prior bankruptcies, or other material litigation involving the general partner or any of his or her affiliates should be disclosed.

10. *Investment objectives and policies*. This section of the disclosure document will identify for the investor what the general partner intends to do with the project, both in the short term and in the long term.

11. *Description of specific real estate to be acquired from the proceeds of the offering as well as risks associated with such property*. This section of the document should be quite extensive and will normally include a description of the property, location, terms of acquisition and mortgages, nature of interest in title, type of construction and use, zoning, regulatory problems, age, details of surrounding areas, competition, maintenance and repair experience, construction estimates, and availability of transportation, educational facilities, hospitals, and other facilities, such as shopping centers, restaurants, and places of entertainment. Moreover, the risks associated should be identified in detail and will be considered later in this chapter.

12. *Federal income tax aspects*. This is an essential element of any real estate syndication and we will set forth in detail those federal income-tax principles applicable to the partnership as well as to the partners. Many of these principles have been identified in other chapters of this book and are not reiterated here. The risks associated with

the tax principles will be highlighted in this section of the document. These risks are again identified later in this chapter. Finally, it is typical for outside tax counsel to render an opinion in connection with a real estate syndication, and such opinion will normally be appended to the document.

13. *Glossary of technical terms used in the private-placement memorandum.* This section is simply designed to assist the reader in working his or her way through the document.

14. *Summary of partnership agreement.* This section of the private-placement memorandum will highlight the major elements of the agreement, many of which are considered in Chapter 17.

## RISK FACTORS AND SAMPLE DISCLOSURE THEREOF

It is essential that a private-placement memorandum contain a detailed description of the risks involved in the investment to minimize exposure to the general partner from future litigation by the investors. Some of the principal risks that can be found in a disclosure document include

- the lack of liquidity of the particular interest, as it normally will not be salable or transferable;
- the fact that the projected tax benefits (and tax losses) may be challenged by the IRS and, on audit, may result in disallowance of such losses; and
- the possibility that the economics of the transaction may make it a poor investment.

Less important risks, but nevertheless items to be disclosed, would involve potential competition, experience or lack thereof of the general partner and the management and environmental and governmental regulations that could affect the viability of the project.

The specific language often used to describe risks in a private-placement memorandum tends to fall into two general categories: that pertaining to tax risks and that describing other risks.

### *Tax-Risk Disclosures*

Some of the more conventional tax-risk disclosures are as follows:

1. *General disclosure.* There are a number of tax risks associated

with this investment. Each investor is urged to consult with his or her tax advisor with respect to the federal, state, and local tax consequences arising from this investment in the partnership.

2. *Partnership tax status.* The partnership will not apply for a ruling from the Internal Revenue Service that it will be classified as a partnership rather than an association for tax purposes. Tax counsel to the partnership has issued an opinion that the partnership will be classified as a partnership, not an association taxable as a corporation. Such an opinion is not binding on the Internal Revenue Service, however, and consequently there can be no assurance that the partnership will not be taxed as an association. In the event that the partnership is treated as an association for tax purpose, certain tax benefits will not be available and projected losses of the partnership could be substantially reduced.

3. *Deductible expenses.* The partnership as well as its partners will claim a variety of tax deductions. There can be no assurance that the IRS will not attempt to disallow these claimed deductions in whole or in part.

4. *Changes in the tax law.* It is possible that legislative, judicial, and administrative changes in the provisions in the federal income laws applicable to partnerships in real estate investments will be initiated subsequent to the offering. There can be no assurance that such changes, if enacted, would not adversely affect the taxation of the partnership as well as the limited partners.

5. *Risk of audit.* Returns filed by the partnership are subject to audit by the Internal Revenue Service, which in recent years has been giving very close scrutiny to limited partnerships such as the type we are discussing. An audit of the partnership could lead to disallowance of certain deductions and other adjustments that could, in turn, lead to an audit of the limited partners' individual tax returns and a corresponding adjustment. The partnership will not pay or reimburse a limited partner for any expenses incurred with the audit of his or her individual return or a determination of his or her individual tax liability, even though such determination is based on an audit and adjustment of the partnership tax return.

6. *Taxable income and tax liability in excess of available cash.* Deductions that the partnership will claim in earlier years will normally be larger than in later years. Hence, at some future date, the partnership and the partners may begin generating taxable income, and each limited partner will be taxed on his or her share of that income, which

share may exceed cash, if any, distributed to the limited partner by the partnership. Moreover, if the partnership disposes of mortgaged property or if a limited partner disposes of his or her units, the disposition may generate taxable income or a tax liability in excess of the cash, if any, that the limited partner receives.

*Nontax Risk Disclosures*

Nontax risk disclosures often found in private-placement memorandums include the following:

1. *Limited transferability.* Units offered will have limited transferability, since there is no public trading market for these units and it is not anticipated that one will develop. Accordingly, a limited partner may not be able to liquidate his or her investment in the event of an emergency, and there are substantial restrictions on the transferability of units, including restrictions imposed by the partnership agreement. Accordingly, any investor considering the purchase of a unit should do so only as a long-term investment.

2. *Reliance and dependence on general partners.* All decisions with respect to the management of the partnership will be made exclusively by the general partners. A limited partner will have no right or power to take part in the management of the partnership, and accordingly no investor should purchase the unit unless he or she is willing to trust all management to the general partner. Moreover, the death or other incapacity of the general partner could significantly and adversely affect the operations of the partnership.

3. *Unspecified property offering.* In many situations the specific properties with which the proceeds of the offering are to be used will not be identified in the private-placement memorandum. Accordingly, it is conventional under these circumstances to indicate that a prospective investor will have no information as to identification and location of the properties, financing or other relevant economic terms relating to such property that would normally assist him or her in evaluating the merits of the investment.

4. *Competition.* The partnership is competing for property with many other persons or entities engaged in real estate activities, many of which have substantially greater resources than the partnership.

5. *Risk of ownership of property.* The partnership will be subject to the risks inherent in the ownership of real estate that include, but are not limited to, changes in general economic and local conditions.

6. *Availability of cost and financing.* Recent money-market fluctuations have generally increased mortgage rates and have reduced the amount of money available for mortgage financing. Accordingly, the partnership may find it difficult to obtain adequate financing, for the cost of such financing may be substantially greater than anticipated. Moreover, changes in the interest rates may adversely affect the economics of the investment as well as the ability of the partnership to sell properties at a later date.

## CONFLICTS OF INTEREST

In most real estate syndications, the general partner and his or her affiliated entities and companies will be faced with a number of conflicts of interest, all of which must be thoroughly disclosed in the private-placement memorandum. The following disclosures pertaining to conflict of interest are typically found in a private-placement memorandum:

1. *Compensation of general partner.* The agreements and arrangement, including fees between the partnership and the general partners, were determined exclusively by the general partners and, as a result, are not necessarily arm's length.

2. *Competition.* The partnership will be managed by the general partner and hence will not be independent. The general partner will devote only so much of his or her time to the business as, in his or her judgment, is deemed reasonably necessary. The general partner is actively engaged as a general partner in many other limited partnerships and can expect to continue to do so during the life of this investment. As a result, the general partner will inevitably have conflicts of interests in allocating management time, services, and functions between this partnership and other partnerships.

3. *Competition by the partnership for the purchase and sale of real property.* The general partner may form other limited partnerships in the future that have similar investment objectives to this partnership. Furthermore, the partnership may purchase property in geographic areas that are closely located to the present partnership. In this event there may be competition between this partnership and other partnerships.

4. *Lack of separate representation.* The partnership on the one hand and the general partner on the other hand are not represented by separate counsel. Moreover, counsel for the general partner does not represent the interests of the limited partners.

5. *Affiliated property-management company.* The general partner has organized an affiliated management company that will receive property-management fees from the partnership. The services rendered by such company may result in certain conflicts of interest with the partnership.

## PERFORMANCE PROJECTIONS

The SEC guidelines make no reference to projections included in the private-placement memorandum. Anyone who has reviewed a typical private-placement memorandum, however, will note that such projections regarding the project will inevitably be included in the disclosure document. The general partner and his or her outside advisors, particularly the accountants, must carefully prepare such projections to ensure the accuracy thereof, including the underlying factual and economic assumptions that give rise to the projections. Again, the projections should carefully disclaim certain items that would include the following:

- that they are premised on availability of certain provisions of the federal income-tax laws that may not continue in the future;
- that they are based on estimated expenses, costs, and income from the property that may or may not be realized; and
- that projected appreciation and the fair-market value of the property may be affected by a number of factors.

The guidelines promulgated by the North American Securities Administrators Association provide that all forecasts included in a disclosure document should include the following information:

- annual predicted revenue by source, including the occupancy rate used in predicting rental revenues;
- annual predicted expense;
- mortgage obligations—annual payments for principal and interest, points, and financing fees;
- the required occupancy rate in order to meet debt service and all expenses;
- predicted annual cash flow, stated assumed occupancy rates;
- predicted annual depreciation and amortization with full description of methods to be used;

- predicted annual taxable income or loss and a simplified explanation of the tax treatment of such results (assumed tax brackets are not to be used);
- predicted construction costs, including disclosure regarding contracts; and
- accounting policies.

These guidelines further contemplate that forecasts should be for a period at least equal to the lesser of the projected period the property will be owned or ten years and should also project a probable resale of the property, including depreciation recaptured, if applicable.

In the following chapter we will present the three key documents typically used in merchandising a syndication to prospective limited partners. The Private-Placement Memorandum, Subscription Agreement, and Limited-Partnership Agreement reproduced are representative of what an investor potentially interested in a privately placed syndication might receive in an offering meeting full regulatory requirements. They are intended as models against which a prospective general partner might check his or her draft syndication documents and against which a prospective limited partner might check the completeness of offering documents he or she might receive.

# 17

# Case Example of a Syndication Project: The Private-Placement Memorandum and Limited Partnership Documents

The preceding chapters leave little doubt as to our preference for a limited partnership as the appropriate vehicle for the majority of private real estate syndications. This is not an eccentric preference, but one shared nationwide by the industry. Limited partnerships offer passive investors a combination of limited liability, participation in the profits, and the potential for a disproportionate tax writeoff in relation to their equity investment. To syndicators they offer amazing autonomy, flexibility, and unusual profit potentials.

Many of the factors we have emphasized in previous chapters such as investor qualification and full disclosure are most effectively illustrated through a series of documents pertaining to an actual syndicated project, more than coincidentally in limited partnership format. We have chosen to present the offering documents for one specific, privately placed syndication as a frame of reference against which other sets of limited partnership documents can be compared or tested.

In most respects the following syndication documents are typical of private offerings. Deviations from the norm lie in their relative simplicity. The syndicator was a prominent individual with a strong following among a selected group of prospective investors. The offering consisted of a single, extant asset that was privately promoted, not under public scrutiny. Under this combination of circumstances, complete disclosure and the explanation of investment risks were minimized. What is remarkable is that somewhere between two thirds and three fourths of the texts of these key documents were prepared not in explanation of the project or the syndicator, but in fulfillment of the legal requirements set forth by the Securities and Exchange Commission and in conformity with the appropriate state regulations.

In choosing this particular set of documents for its typicality and simplicity, we are also coincidentally touching upon another significant advantage of syndication implicit but possibly understated in the preceding chapter. In common with all other investors, developers or syndicators of real property experience changes in their investment goals. Personal financial circumstances materialize and opportunity knocks, consistently offering exciting challenges that must sometimes be foregone due to the lack of liquid assets. Equally as important, developers and syndicators must also closely watch their financial exposure as they take on new developments of greater magnitude. Syndication of an existing holding can be an integral factor in retaining control and freeing equity for other developments. In this instance the developer of a newly constructed office building chose to free himself of the total burden of mortgage financing and liquefy some of his equity by aligning passive investors to participate in both the cash flow and tax advantages in what promised to be a sound investment vehicle.

The developer's continued interest in the property being syndicated is reflected in several provisions of the private-placement memorandum. Offering a total of 35 limited partnership units, the general partner reserved the option to acquire ten of these units in the event of an incomplete sellout, intending to take them only in this contingency. If all shares were successfully marketed, the profits and tax benefits were to accrue to the limited partners, with the general partner being compensated solely by a management fee. As mentioned in Chapter 2, management and syndication fees frequently constitute the greatest area of profit for the general partner of a conservative syndication. Receipt of these fees plus greatly reduced exposure can combine to constitute a significant advantage absolving the syndicator from possible charges of excessive altruism in structuring an offering.

The somewhat generalized documents presented are in part tailored to the blue-sky laws of the state of registration. These laws are typical of most states in reflecting the requirements of the Securities and Exchange Commission without such unusual provisions as those we previously discussed, applicable to the states of California, Illinois, and New York. The three documents presented in the following pages are only a part of the total package presented to potential investors. Some of the exhibits listed in the private-placement memorandum are omitted for purposes of brevity. We will discuss those exhibits and their ramifications following this first sample document.

PRIVATE-
PLACEMENT MEMORANDUM

CONFIDENTIAL Number ______

ABC LIMITED PARTNERSHIP
Anytown U.S.A.

January 31, 19____

35 Limited Partnership Units
(Minimum Purchase 1 Unit)

$50,000.00 Per Unit—Payable at Time of Subscription

ABC Limited Partnership (the "Partnership") will be formed upon subscription for the Units offered hereby as a (any state) limited partnership to acquire from Developer the land and office building located at __________ Street, Anytown, U.S.A. and lease the land and the office building to __________ Lessee, which uses the building as its headquarters. Developer is the General Partner of the Partnership.

| | Price | Selling Commission | Proceeds to Partnership |
|---|---|---|---|
| Per Unit | $50,000.00 | -0- | $50,000.00 |
| Total | $1,750,000.00 | -0- | $1,750,000.00 |

The Partnership will pay all organizational expenses, which are estimated at $180,000. The General Partner will receive a management fee payable only out of proceeds of sale of the property.

THIS OFFERING INVOLVES A HIGH DEGREE OF RISK (SEE "RISK FACTORS"); IS SUBJECT TO VARIOUS CONFLICTS OF INTEREST ARISING OUT OF THE RELATIONSHIPS BETWEEN THE PARTNERSHIP AND ITS GENERAL PARTNER (SEE "FICUCIARY RESPONSIBILITY" AND "CONFLICTS OF INTEREST"); MATERIAL INCOME-TAX RISKS ARE ASSOCIATED WITH THIS OFFERING (SEE "RISK FACTORS" AND "FEDERAL INCOME TAX CONSEQUENCES"); NO PUBLIC MARKET FOR THE UNITS IS LIKELY TO DEVELOP; AND THIS OFFERING IS SUITABLE ONLY FOR PERSONS OF ADEQUATE MEANS WHO HAVE NO NEED FOR LIQUIDITY IN THEIR INVESTMENT, SINCE THE UNITS MAY NOT BE SOLD UNLESS, AMONG OTHER THINGS, THEY ARE SUBSEQUENTLY REGISTERED UNDER THE SECURITIES ACT OF 1933 ("THE ACT") OR AN EXEMPTION FROM SUCH REGISTRATION IS AVAILABLE.

THE OFFERING IS MADE ONLY TO PERSONS THE GENERAL PARTNER BELIEVES ARE "ACCREDITED INVESTORS" AS DEFINED IN REGULATION D UNDER THE ACT.

DURING THE COURSE OF THE OFFERING AND PRIOR TO SALE, EACH OFFEREE AND HIS OFFEREE REPRESENTATIVES, IF ANY, ARE INVITED TO ASK QUESTIONS OF AND OBTAIN ADDITIONAL INFORMATION FROM THE GENERAL PARTNER CONCERNING THE TERMS AND CONDITIONS OF THE OFFERING, THE PARTNERSHIP, OR ANY MATTER REFERRED TO HEREIN. THIS MEMORANDUM CONTAINS SUMMARIES, BELIEVED TO BE ACCURATE, OF CERTAIN DOCUMENTS, COPIES OF WHICH ARE ATTACHED HERETO OR ARE AVAILABLE. PROSPECTIVE INVESTORS ARE REFERRED TO SUCH DOCUMENTS FOR COMPLETE INFORMATION CONCERNING THE RIGHTS AND OBLIGATIONS OF THE PARTIES THERETO, AND ALL SUCH SUMMARIES ARE QUALIFIED IN THEIR ENTIRETY BY THIS REFERENCE. ALL DOCUMENTS RELATING TO THIS INVESTMENT WILL BE MADE AVAILABLE TO THE OFFEREE NAMED BELOW OR HIS REPRESENTATIVES UPON REQUEST.

THIS MEMORANDUM CONSTITUTES AN OFFER ONLY IF AN OFFEREE IS NAMED BELOW, AND ONLY TO SUCH NAMED OFFEREE.

THE UNITS OFFERED HEREBY HAVE NOT BEEN REGISTERED FOR SALE TO THE PUBLIC UNDER THE ACT OR THE SECURITIES LAWS OF ANY STATE. THIS MEMORANDUM HAS NOT BEEN FILED WITH OR REVIEWED BY THE SECRETARY OF STATE OR OTHER OFFICER, DEPARTMENT, OR AGENCY OF ANY STATE OR GOVERNMENTAL UNIT.

THIS MEMORANDUM HAS BEEN PREPARED SOLELY FOR THE BENEFIT OF PERSONS INTERESTED IN THE PROPOSED PRIVATE PLACEMENT OF THE UNITS AND ANY REPRODUCTION OR DISTRIBUTION OF THIS MEMORANDUM IN WHOLE OR IN PART, OR THE DIVULGENCE OF ANY OF ITS CONTENTS, WITHOUT THE PRIOR WRITTEN CONSENT OF THE PARTNERSHIP, IS PROHIBITED. THE OFFEREE, BY

ACCEPTING DELIVERY OF THIS MEMORANDUM, AGREES TO RETURN IT AND ALL ENCLOSED DOCUMENTS TO THE PARTNERSHIP IF THE OFFEREE DOES NOT SUBSCRIBE FOR ANY OF THE UNITS OFFERED HEREBY.

THE OFFERING WILL TERMINATE NO LATER THAN DECEMBER 31, 19____ UNLESS EXTENDED BY THE GENERAL PARTNER. IN CONNECTION WITH THE OFFERING AND SALE OF THE UNITS, THE PARTNERSHIP RESERVES THE RIGHT, IN ITS DISCRETION, TO REJECT ANY SUBSCRIPTION IN WHOLE OR IN PART OR TO ALLOT TO ANY PROSPECTIVE INVESTOR LESS THAN THE NUMBER OF UNITS APPLIED FOR BY SUCH INVESTOR. THE PARTNERSHIP FURTHER RESERVES THE RIGHT TO RESCIND ITS ACCEPTANCE OF ANY SUBSCRIPTION AT ANY TIME UNTIL THE PROCEEDS OF THIS OFFERING HAVE BEEN FULLY INVESTED IN ACCORDANCE WITH THIS PRIVATE PLACEMENT MEMORANDUM.

PENDING THE RECEIPT AND ACCEPTANCE OF SUBSCRIPTIONS FOR 35 UNITS AND CERTAIN APPROVALS OF THE SALE OF THE REAL ESTATE TO THE PARTNERSHIP, ALL SUBSCRIPTION PROCEEDS WILL BE KEPT BY THE PARTNERSHIP SEPARATE AND APART FROM ALL OTHER FUNDS AND WILL BE DEPOSITED AND HELD IN TRUST IN ONE OR MORE INTEREST-BEARING BANK ACCCOUNTS. THE GENERAL PARTNER MAY ELECT TO SUBSCRIBE FOR UP TO 10 UNITS.

THIS MEMORANDUM SUPERSEDES ANY PREVIOUS MATERIALS RELATING TO THIS OFFERING. SUCH MATERIALS MUST BE DISREGARDED IN THEIR ENTIRETY. THE USE OF OR RELIANCE UPON ANY SUCH MATERIALS OR OF ANY REPRESENTATIONS OR PROJECTIONS, WRITTEN OR ORAL, WHICH DO NOT CONFORM WITH THIS MEMORANDUM, IS ABSOLUTELY PROHIBITED.

Name of Offeree

______________________________________________

The date of this Memorandum is ____________, 19____.

Suitability Requirements

The Units are being offered only to persons who the Partnership has reason to believe at the time of making a sale are "Accredited Investors," as that term is defined in Regulation D under the Securities Act of 1933 and explained in part hereafter.

There is no public market for the Units and it is highly unlikely that any such market will develop. The Units have not been registered under the Securities Act of 1933, as amended or qualified or registered under the laws of any state or other jurisdiction. Therefore, the Units cannot be sold or assigned unless either subsequently registered or qualified under applicable law or unless an opinion of counsel for the Partnership is provided to the effect that such compliance is not necessary. Accordingly, purchasers must bear the economic risk of this investment for an indefinite period of time.

Investment in the Units is not recommended unless a noncorporate purchaser is in at least the 49 percent marginal tax bracket for federal income-tax purposes in 19____. Only persons whose income is subject to high rates of income taxation will derive the full benefit of the tax benefits expected to be available to purchasers. Any such purchaser's ability to derive full benefit will also depend on other factors, including tax preferences, investment interest, and the like. For a purchaser to take full advantage of the potential net investment interest deductions, he will need to have substantial investment income. A purchaser may incur significant adverse tax consequences in the event of resale of the Units.

Each prospective purchaser will be required to make certain representations to establish his qualification as an Accredited Investor under Regulation D. Ordinarily, in order for a purchaser to qualify as an Accredited Investor, he will have to represent either that he has a net worth (including both liquid and illiquid assets) of in excess of $1 million or had annual income of at least $200,000 in the two years prior to the subscription and income of at least $200,000 in 19____.

Any such purchaser will be required to make certain further representations, including that (a) he is able to bear the economic risk of the investment; (b) his overall commitment to investments that are not readily marketable is not disproportionate to his net worth, and his investment in the Units will not cause such overall commitment to become excessive; (c) he has adequate means of providing for his current needs and possible future contingencies and has no need for liquidity in his investment; (d) he has evaluated the risks of investment in the Units; and (e) he is purchasing for his own account, for investment, and not with a view to resale.

The Partnership may require prospective purchasers to provide reasonable documentation of their accredited investor status and may make or cause to be made such further inquiry as it deems appropriate.

## SUMMARY OF THE PARTNERSHIP AND USE OF PROCEEDS

The following summary is intended only as a quick overview and is qualified in its entirety by the more detailed information in this memorandum and the exhibits.

## The Partnership

### Business

The Partnership will be formed to undertake the acquisition of land and a three-story office building located at __________ Street, Anytown, U.S.A., from Developer, and to lease the land and the office building to Lessee. The real estate including the land and building is referred to as the "Project."

### General Partner

Developer is the general partner. (Here follows a description of the operations and activities of Developer.)

### Termination Date

The Partnership will terminate on December 31, 1999, or earlier upon (1) retirement, expulsion, or cessation to exist of the General Partner if the Limited Partners do not designate a new General Partner, which elects to continue the business of the Partnership; (2) majority vote of the Limited Partners; or (3) disposition of all of the Partnership assets.

### Compensation to General Partner

The General Partner will receive substantial profits from the sale of the Project to the Partnership. In addition, the General Partner may receive substantial compensation but payable only out of proceeds of any subsequent sale of the Project by the Partnership. See "Compensation and Fees."

### Allocation of Income, Loss, and Distributions

Net losses, net income, and cash from operations of the Partnership shall be allocated 100 percent to the Limited Partners and none to the General Partner.

Cash from disposition of Partnership assets will be distributed first to the General Partner in an amount equal to the management fee, see "Compensation and Fees," and the remainder to the Limited Partners.

### The Project

(Here follows a detailed description of the Project.)

### Depreciation

The Partnership currently intends to use straight-line accelerated cost recovery system depreciation deductions over a 15-year period. This method, however, is subject to proposed changes in federal legislation. See "FEDERAL IN-

COME TAX CONSEQUENCES—Accelerated Cost Recovery System Deductions."

First-Mortgage Financing

(Here follows a summary description of the mortgage financing on the Project.)

Sale of the Project to the Partnership by Developer

Developer will sell the Project to the Partnership for approximately $1 million in cash. The sale will be effected by general warranty deed.

The Lease to Lessee

The lease of the Project by the Partnership to Lessee is for a term of 15 years and will commence on or before December 31, 19_____. The lease is a net lease pursuant to which Lessee pays substantially all operating expenses. The monthly rent is intended to cover debt service under the first mortgage. Beginning after the tenth year of the lease term, Lessee will have an option to purchase the Project for the fair-market value at the time of exercise. (Here follows a detailed description of Lessee.)

Subscriptions

The subscription price for the limited partnership units (the "Units") is $50,000 payable in cash. The Anytown Bank has informed the General Partner that it may consider lending the amount of the subscription price to investors. The Bank's decision to make any such loan would be based on the credit worthiness of the individual investor, and the terms and conditions would be dependent upon and would vary with the particular investor. The General Partner would have no involvement with any loan. There is no assurance that any loans will be made.

Use of Proceeds

The following table summarizes the intended use of the proceeds of the offering by the Partnership. The table reflects current estimates. See Exhibit G for further details.

| | Amount | Percent |
|---|---|---|
| Organizational Expenses.......... | $ 180,000 | 10.3% |
| Cash Portion of Project Purchase Price.................. | 1,000,000 | 57.1% |
| Prepayment of Mortgage Note...... | 365,000 | 20.9% |
| Working Capital Reserve.......... | 205,000 | 11.7% |
| Gross Offering Proceeds | $1,750,000 | 110.0% |

## COMPENSATION AND FEES

Sale of the Project to the Partnership

The General Partner will realize a profit of approximately $200,000 upon sale of the Project to the Partnership. The purchase price to be paid by the Partnership was calculated as follows:

| | |
|---|---|
| Cash paid by Developer for Project including upgrades . | $ 600,000 |
| Expenses of acquisition of Project by Developer ........ | 150,000 |
| Expenses of transfer of Project to the Partnership....... | 50,000 |
| Profit to Developer .................................. | 200,000 |
| Total | $1,000,000 |

Developer's profit consists of approximately (1) $100,000 of appreciation during a nine-month construction period calculated at 6 percent per annum, although this rate may not be reflective of actual market appreciation; and (2) $100,000 of construction discount, the benefit of which will accrue to Developer.

Reimbursement of Organizational Expense

Upon closing of the sale of the Units, the General Partner will be reimbursed by the Partnership for all expenses incurred by the General Partner in the organization of the Partnership and offering of the Units. Such expenses are estimated to be $180,000.

Interest in Sale of the Project

Upon sale of the Project, the General Partner shall receive a fee for management of the Project and the Partnership and for services rendered as General Partner equal to 15 percent of the net proceeds of sale of the Project.

## CONFLICTS OF INTEREST

Purchase and Sale of the Project

The General Partner owns the Project and is offering to sell it to the Partnership. The General Partner believes that the sale price to the Partnership will approximate its fairmarket value, but the General Partner will receive a substantial profit on the sale. The Lessee has the option of repurchasing the Project from the Partnership upon and after the tenth anniversary of the commencement of the lease, based on the appraised value of the Project at the time of exercise of the option. The Lessee is not obligated to exercise the option, and there is no assurance that he will do so. Appraisals are only estimates of value and should not be relied on as a measure of realizable value.

No Arm's Length Negotiations

In connection with the operations of the Partnership and the purchase of the Project, any conflict between the General Partner and the Limited Partners will not be resolved through arm's length negotiation but through the exercise of good faith judgment by the General Partner. In addition to the obvious conflicts that may arise in connection with the transactions relating to the Project, it is also possible that other transactions, including the liquidation of the Partnership, may not have the same impact on the General Partner and the Limited Partners.

No Separate Legal Representation

The same law firms represent both the General Partner and the Partnership.

Voting by Limited Partners

Current officers, directors, and employees of the General Partner may subscribe for Units and will be entitled to vote as Limited Partners, and if he or she subscribes for any Units, the General Partner will be entitled to vote.

## FIDUCIARY RESPONSIBILITY

Any General Partner is accountable to a Limited Partnership and to the Limited Partners thereof as a fiduciary and consequently must exercise good faith and integrity in handling Partnership affairs. This is a rapidly developing and changing area of the law, and Limited Partners who have questions concerning the duties of the General Partner should consult with their own counsel.

The General Partner may not be liable, responsible, or accountable for damages or otherwise to the Partnership or to the Limited Partners for any act performed within the scope of the authority conferred by the Partnership Agreement, or for any failure to act, except for acts or failures to act by the General Partner involving fraud, bad faith, willful neglect, or negligence, since provision has been made in the Limited Partnership Agreement for exculpation of the General Partner. Therefore, purchasers of Units may have a more limited right of action than they would have absent the aforesaid limitation in the Limited Partnership Agreement.

The Partnership Agreement also provides for indemnification of the General Partner by the Partnership for liabilities arising out of or incidental to the Partnership business of the General Partner's performance of his duties thereunder, except in the case of fraud, gross negligence, or breach of fiduciary duty by the General Partner. To the extent that the indemnification provisions purport to include indemnification for liabilities arising under the

Securities Act of 1933, as amended, in the opinion of the Securities and Exchange Commission, such indemnification is contrary to public policy and is, therefore, unenforceable.

## RISK FACTORS

Investment in the Units involves a high degree of risk and is suitable only for persons of substantial financial means who have no need for liquidity in such investment and who can effectively utilize the anticipated tax benefits and that accrue to the Limited Partners. Investors should carefuly consider the following risk factors:

### Federal Income-Tax Risks

#### Complexity and Uncertainty of Tax Treatment

Federal income taxation of partners and partnerships owning real estate is highly complex. The Partnership will receive an opinion from its counsel regarding the major tax risks associated with ownership of the Units. However, there is uncertainty regarding some of the federal income-tax consequences relating to the operations of the Partnership and ownership of the Units. Such counsel's opinion is expressed as being not free from doubt and the opinion is not binding on the Internal Revenue Service. Moreover, there can be no assurance that the present income-tax treatment of an investment in the Partnership may not be modified by legislative, judicial, or administrative action at any time to the detriment of the Partners, and changes or developments in the tax law could have retroactive effects. Prospective Limited Partners are urged to consult their personal tax advisors and to familiarize themselves with the discussion herein under the heading "FEDERAL INCOME TAX CONSEQUENCES," which sets forth additional tax risks.

#### No Internal Revenue Service Ruling

No Internal Revenue Service ruling has been applied for as to partnership tax status or any other matter relating to the tax consequences to investors. The Internal Revenue Service, therefore, may on audit make a determination depriving investors of all or part of the tax benefits associated with the offering.

#### Extent of Tax Liability

It is likely that Partnership taxable income eventually will exceed the cash, if any, available for distribution to the Partners. In such event, the taxes payable by the Limited Partners with respect to such income could also exceed, by an amount that could be substantial, the cash, if any, available for distribution in such year. A Partner's share of profits will be subject to tax at ordinary federal income-tax rates with a current maximum marginal rate of 50 percent. See the subheadings "Taxation of Limited Partners" and "Sale or Disposition of the Project or Partnership Interest" under the heading "FEDERAL INCOME TAX CONSEQUENCES" herein.

Disposition of Units or Project

Gain recognized upon the sale or other taxable disposition of Units or of the Project may result in a tax liability to a Limited Partner substantially greater than the cash proceeds, if any, realized by such Partner from such sale. Furthermore, any such sale may result in a recapture of accelerated cost recovery deductions and any allowable investment tax credits. See the subheading "Sale or Disposition of the Project or Partnership Interest" under the heading "FEDERAL INCOME TAX CONSEQUENCES" herein.

## State and Local Taxation

Depending upon applicable state and local laws, deductions that are available to the Limited Partners for federal income-tax purposes may not be available to a Limited Partner for state or local income-tax purposes. Prospective Limited Partners are urged to consult with their own tax advisors with respect to state and local taxation.

## Business Risks

General Partner's Lack of Experience

The General Partner has not previously had any substantial experience in similar partnerships or real estate investments or management.

Default by General Partner

The ability of the Partnership to make the required payments on the Mortgage Note will depend on timely payments by Lessee to the Partnership of the rent under the lease. In particular, the Mortgage Note is subject to mandatory prepayment in the discretion of the holder upon certain dates. If Lessee defaults in payment of the rent under the lease or in any of its covenants made in connection with the Mortgage Note financing, it is probable that the Partnership would default under the Mortgage Note, and the Deed of Trust securing the Mortgage Note would be foreclosed. The Limited Partners, therefore, could lose their entire investment and suffer severe adverse tax consequences. See "FEDERAL INCOME TAX CONSEQUENCES."

Failure of Rent to Cover Debt Service

The rent payable to the Partnership under the lease would cover debt service under the Mortgage Note at current prevailing interest rates. The lease provides for a fixed rental, however, whereas the debt service on the Mortgage Note is subject to increase upon increases in the prime rate of Anytown Bank and certain other events. The lease further provides, however, that the Partnership, in its discretion, may increase the annual rent by an amount not to exceed 6 percent of the then current rent. If the debt service should exceed the rent and the Partnership has not accumulated a sufficient reserve to cover the excess or does not cover such excess by an increase in rent, it could default under the Mortgage Note.

Limited Control by Limited Partners

The General Partner will have exclusive authority over management of the Partnership. To assure that the Limited Partners will not become personally liable as General Partners, none of the Limited Partners will have any right to participate in management. The vote of the Limited Partners, however, is required under certain circumstances under the Limited Partnership Agreement.

Liability of Limited Partners

The Partnership has been structured to provide reasonable assurance that the liability of a Limited Partner will be limited to the amount of his payment to the Partnership plus his share of any undistributed profits of the Partnership. There can be no assurance, however, that the limitation on liability will not be challenged or that such a challenge would not be successful. In particular, there is uncertainty under present law as to whether the exercise of the voting rights by the Limited Partners as previously discussed or the allocation to the Limited Partners of 100 percent of current net income, net losses, and distributions from operations would affect adversely their status as Limited Partners with a resulting loss of their limited liability.

Additional payments by the Limited Partners to the Partnership may be required under the Limited Partnership Agreement in the event the Partnership is unable to meet its obligations. The aggregate of such additional payments may not exceed 10 percent of the original investment by all of the Limited Partners. To the extent any Limited Partner defaults in making any required additional payment, the other Limited Partners will be obligated collectively to contribute the unpaid amount. The interest of the defaulting Limited Partner in the Partnership will be reduced proportionally.

Illiquidity

An investment in the Units will be highly illiquid because no public market exists or is likely to develop. The Limited Partnership Agreement provides that no transfers of Units may be made without the prior approval of the General Partner, who may withhold approval in his discretion, and no Units may be assigned if the assignment, in the opinion of counsel to the Partnership, would result in termination of the Partnership under Section 708 of the Internal Revenue Code. In addition, federal and state securities laws restrict transferability of the Units.

Risks of Real Estate Ownership

The Partnership will be subject to the risks associated with the ownership of real estate, including adverse conditions in the local real estate market, which could reduce the value of the Project or render resale difficult, with the risk of uninsured losses and the risk of changes in local real estate, environmental, or zoning laws.

## THE PROJECT

General Description

The Project consists of . . . (here follows a detailed description of the Project).

The City of Anytown

Anytown in located . . . (here follows a detailed description of the location of the Project).

## THE MORTGAGE NOTE FINANCING

General

The Project is being financed primarily by the Mortgage Note. The purchaser and holder of the Mortgage Note is Anytown Bank. Pursuant to the Deed of Assumption between Developer and Anytown Bank, Developer agreed to make all payments under the Mortgage Note. The Limited Partnership will acquire the Project subject to the Note, the Deed of Assumption, the Note Purchase Agreement, and the Deed of Trust that secures the Mortgage Note. Developer will be released from liability for payments under the Note upon satisfaction of certain conditions.

Amortization

The $1.6-million principal of the Note is payable in 240 monthly installments beginning October 1, 19____ with the final payment on September 1, 20____in accordance with a payment schedule based on a 20-year amortization schedule prepared on the assumption of a 9 ⅞ percent per-annum interest rate, which would require combined monthly payments of principal and interest of approximately $11,816, if the interest rate remained constant. The interest rate, however, is a fluctuating rate equal to 110 percent of the prime rate of interest of Anytown Bank as declared by the Bank from time to time. Any payment not made within 20 days from its due date bears interest at 18 percent per annum plus a 5 percent late charge.

Optional and Mandatory Prepayments

The Mortgage Note may be prepaid either in whole or in part at the option of Developer upon certain conditions. Any partial optional prepayment must be in multiples of $20,000.

The Mortgage Note is subject to mandatory prepayment in full in the sole discretion of the holder on September 1 of 1990, 1995, or 2000. In addition, the Note is subject to mandatory prepayment at the option of the holder in the event of any default.

Deed of Trust and Other Security

The Mortgage Note is secured primarily by a first lien Deed of Trust on the Project. The lien covers the land, building, fixtures, certain machinery and equipment, insurance proceeds, and other personal property. In addition, the Mortgage Note is secured by an assignment of all leases of the Project including the lease to Lessee by the Partnership.

Events of Default

In addition to failure to make the payments on the Mortgage Note, there are numerous events of default upon which the holder of the Mortgage Note could foreclose on the Project and other security, among its other remedies. These events of default include the placing of encumbrances on the Project or related property without consent of the holder, failure to construct and equip the building, failure to comply with requirements of any government authority, failure to make any payment on other indebtedness of Lessee, insolvency of Lessee, failure of Lessee to occupy more than 50 percent of the Project, and the making of any false or misleading statement to the holder in connection with its purchase of the Mortgage Note.

In addition, failure to comply with any covenant by Lessee in the Note Purchase Agreement, Deed of Trust, or Deed of Assumption constitutes an event of default. Such covenants include the obligation of Lessee to maintain its principal banking relationship with the holder, Anytown Bank, to maintain demand deposit balances with the holder of not less than 15 percent of the outstanding principal balance of the Mortgage Note, and to limit the combined liabilities of its general and restricted funds to less than or equal to two and one half times the combined-funds balance.

Damage, Destruction, and Condemnation

In the event of damage, destruction, or condemnation of all or part of the Project, the holder of the Mortgage Note will have the option of applying the insurance proceeds or condemnation award toward the prepayment of the Mortgage Note or replacement or restoration of the Project. If the holder elected to require replacement or restoration and the insurance proceeds or condemnation award were not sufficient, then Lessee would be required to pay the difference. Failure to make such payment would be a default under the Mortgage Note.

## THE LEASE OF THE PROJECT TO LESSEE

### Term

The term of the lease is 15 years, unless sooner terminated pursuant to provisions described hereafter. The lease will commence on or before December 31, 19____.

### Rent

The initial basic annual rent is $150,000 payable in equal monthly installments on the first day of the month. The rent is adjustable in the event of refinancing or acceleration of the Mortgage Note. All real estate taxes and condominium fees or assessments are payable by Lessee as rent. The Partnership in its discretion may increase the annual rent by an amount not to exceed 6 percent of the then current rate. Rent is not abated as a result of damage to the Project.

### Operating Expenses and Repairs

Lessee is responsible for all expenses of using the Project including utilities, insurance, maintenance, and repairs.

### Assignment and Subletting

Lessee may assign the lease or sublet all or a portion of the Project, but is not released from liability under the lease. Any assignee or sublessee must be bound by the terms of the lease. Lessee currently does not expect to assign the lease or sublet any significant portion of the Project.

## OPTION TO PURCHASE AND RIGHT OF FIRST REFUSAL

Lessee will have an option, but not an obligation, to purchase the Project from the Partnership under a provision of the lease. The option is exercisable during the period beginning after the tenth anniversary of the commencement date of the lease and ending upon termination of the lease. The purchase price will be the appraised value of the Project at the time of exercise. The purchase price will be payable by taking the Project subject to the Mortgage

Note and paying the balance in cash. At the closing of the purchase, the Partnership must transfer clear title, except for the Deed of Trust securing the Mortgage Note, and must correct any defects at its expense. There is no assurance that Lessee will exercise the option.

In addition to the purchase option, Lessee has the right of first refusal to purchase the Project in the event the Partnership receives a bona fide offer. Lessee could purchase the Project on terms at least as favorable as such offer within 60 days of notice that the offer has been made.

## FEDERAL INCOME TAX CONSEQUENCES

### Introduction

The Federal tax treatment currently available with respect to the ownership of real estate has a material effect upon the advisability of investing in real estate generally and in the Partnership in particular. Each potential Limited Partner should be aware that the Internal Revenue Service may attempt to disallow some or all of the deductions claimed with respect to this investment and that the courts may sustain the position of the Service in this regard. Nothing in this Memorandum or in the accompanying tax opinion can be viewed as a guarantee of the tax treatment set forth in the tax opinion, and each Limited Partner must be prepared to bear the economic consequences of either administrative or judicial disallowance of some or all of the claimed tax deductions associated with this investment.

Tax-shelter investments, including real estate, have for some time been subjected to wide-ranging criticism by Congress, the Administration, the press, and the public. In the Tax Reform Acts of 1976 and 1978, the Economic Recovery Tax Act of 1981, and the Tax Equity and Fiscal Responsibility Act of 1982, Congress enacted new provisions designed to curb many of the abuses attributed to tax-shelter investments. It is still the opinion in some quarters that these new laws were not sufficiently comprehensive and that more "reform" is needed. Further, the Internal Revenue Service has announced that it will make a concerted effort to examine the tax returns of investors in tax-shelter investments and the deductions claimed therein. This fact should be borne in mind when considering the advisability of participating in this investment.

Given this attitude toward tax-shelter investments, it is possible that new laws may be enacted severely limiting the tax benefits that might otherwise be derived by the Limited Partners. It would appear that any changes in the tax laws would not be retroactive; however, there can be no assurance on this point. It is also possible that the Limited Partners' individual tax returns may be subjected to close scrutiny by the Internal Revenue Service as a result of acquiring an interest in the Partnership.

Partnership Status

Although counsel believes that the Internal Revenue Service should treat the Partnership as a partnership for federal income-tax purposes, if the Service were to successfully contend that the Partnership should instead be taxed as a corporation, the tax consequences to the Limited Partners would be quite adverse. Specifically, the taxable income of the Partnership would be subject to corporate income tax at rates ranging up to 46 percent, tax losses incurred by the Partnership would not be deductible on the individual returns of the Limited Partners, and distributions from the Partnership to the Limited Partners would be taxable, in whole or in part, as dividends.

Taxation of Limited Partners

Each Limited Partner will be required to report on his federal income-tax return his allocable share of the income, gains, losses, deductions, and credits of the Partnership, whether or not any actual cash distributions are made to the Limited Partner during his taxable year. Any loss deduction, however, will be allowable only to the extent of his tax basis in his Partnership interest as determined at the end of the partnership year in which such loss occurred.

Basis in Partnership Interest

The tax basis of Limited Partner's interest in the Partnership will be equal to the cost of such interest, reduced by the Limited Partner's share of partnership distributions and losses and increased by his share of partnership income. In addition, the tax basis is increased by the Limited Partner's share of any so-called "nonrecourse liabilities" to which partnership property is subject. It is counsel's view that the Anytown National Bank liability to which the Project will be subject subsequent to the sale to the Partnership will qualify as a "nonrecourse liability," which should serve to increase the Limited Partner's basis in his partnership interest.

Accelerated Cost Recovery System Deductions

In 1981, Congress replaced the prior scheme of depreciation deductions with the accelerated cost recovery system (ACRS). As noted above, the Partnership will elect to claim straight-line ACRS deductions over a 15-year period. If the Partnership elects to claim ACRS deductions in this manner, all gain subsequently realized on the sale of the Project will be treated as capital gain.

Limited Partners should be aware that there is presently pending in Congress legislation that, if enacted, would require the Partnership to claim ACRS deductions under the straight-line method using a 40-year recovery period. It is presently unclear whether this legislation will be enacted, and, if enacted, whether the legislation will be applicable to the purchase of the Project by the Partnership.

As set forth in detail in the tax opinion, the Internal Revenue Service may allege that this investment lacks "economic substance." If the IRS were to make such an allegation, it would attempt to disallow all ACRS deductions claimed by the Partnership on the theory that the Partnership had no "investment" in the Project. In counsel's view, however, such an allegation, if asserted by the Service, would not be sustained by the courts.

In addition, the Internal Revenue Service could allege that the Partnership did not have an "economic interest" in the Project, and as a consequence, all claimed ACRS deductions should be disallowed. It is counsel's opinion, however, that the Partnership will acquire a sufficient economic interest in the Project so as to support the claimed ACRS deductions.

### Cash Distributions from the Partnership

A cash distribution received by a Limited Partner from the Partnership generally will not cause recognition of gain or loss for federal income-tax purposes. However, cash distributions in excess of a Limited Partner's adjusted basis in his Partnership interest will result in the recognition of gain to the extent of such excess. Any resulting gain will ordinarily be treated as the sale of a Partnership interest and taxed accordingly. Since a Partner can be taxed on his distributive share of partnership net income, whether or not distributed to him, a Limited Partner may have taxable income with no offsetting deductions or distributed cash with which to pay the resulting taxes.

### Allocation of Partnership Income and Losses

Under the Limited Partnership Agreement, allocations of Partnership income and loss will be made in proportion to the capital contributions of the respective Limited Partners. Although it is possible that the Internal Revenue Service could attempt to reallocate such allocations, it is counsel's opinion that these allocations will have a "substantial economic effect" and should therefore be respected for federal income-tax purposes.

### Investment Interest Limitation

Section 163(d) of the Internal Revenue Code sets forth certain limitations on the amounts of allowable deductions for interest paid by a taxpayer during any taxable year to acquire or carry investment property. Generally, interest paid on debts incurred to acquire or carry investment property is deductible only to the extent of $10,000 plus (1) the taxpayer's net investment income and (2) his out-of-pocket loss as the lessor of "net lease property." Any interest paid in excess of these amounts is carried forward to the following year subject to the same limitations. It is counsel's opinion that interest paid by the Limited Partners in connection with this transaction will fall within the scope of the section 163(d) investment interest limitations and therefore Limited Partners should consult with their personal tax advisors to determine the extent to which this investment interest limitation may adversely affect their personal tax situation.

Section 183

Section 183 of the Internal Revenue Code sets forth a limitation on the allowable deductions with respect to an "activity not engaged in for profit" and generally provides that a taxpayer will not be entitled to claim a loss deduction with respect to any such activity. Although counsel is of the opinion that the investment by the Partnership in the Project will constitute an activity engaged in for profit, it is possible that the Internal Revenue Service could contend otherwise. If the Service were successful in this contention, the Limited Partners would lose a significant portion of the tax benefits otherwise allowable in connection with this investment.

Sale or Disposition of the Project or Partnership Interest

If the Partnership were to dispose of the Project more than 12 months after acquisition, the gain realized, if any, would be taxed as long-term capital gain, except to the extent of any ACRS ordinary-income recapture as described above. The amount of the Partnership's gain realized from the sale would be allocated to the Limited Partners in the manner prescribed in the Partnership Agreement. Limited Partners should be aware that any gain so allocated may substantially exceed the distribution of capital proceeds, if any, resulting from the sale.

A Limited Partner who sells his interest in the Partnership will recognize gain or loss for federal income-tax purposes in an amount measured by the difference between his adjusted basis in his Partnership interest and the amount realized upon the sale. Assuming that the Limited Partner is not a "dealer" in either real estate or securities such as limited partnership interests, gain or loss realized on the sale will generally be treated as capital gain or loss.

Termination of the Partnership

A termination of the Partnership for federal income-tax purposes will occur if either (1) no part of the business of the Partnership continues to be carried on by the Partners, or (2) 50 percent or more of the total interest in the Partnership's capital and proceeds is sold or exchanged within a 12-month period. In either event, the taxable year of the Partnership will be treated as closed, and the property owned by the Partnership will be treated as distributed to the Limited Partners. Such a distribution might result in the recognition of taxable gain or loss by the Limited Partners.

Minimum Tax

Beginning in 1983, taxpayers will be subject to a revised minimum tax, which is generally computed by adding so-called "preference amounts" to adjusted gross income and then subtracting allowable deductions. This net amount is then further reduced by an exemption for the first $30,000 of minimum taxable income ($40,000 on joint or surviving-spouse income-tax returns). Minimum taxable income above the applicable exempt amount is then taxed at a 20-percent rate. A taxpayer is subject to the minimum tax only if and to the extent such tax exceeds his tax liability computed in the normal fashion.

Because the existence and amount of tax preference items subject to the minimum tax will necessarily vary with respect to each taxpayer, the extent to which any tax preference item resulting from an investment in the Partnership will be subject to the minimum tax cannot be predicted herein. Accordingly, prospective Limited Partners are urged to consult their personal tax advisors in this regard.

Internal Revenue Service Audits and Possible Penalties

Limited Partners should be aware that an audit by the Internal Revenue Service of the Partnership's tax return may lead to an audit of the returns of the individual Limited Partners. In addition, an audit of any Limited Partner's tax return could lead to an audit of the Partnership's tax return, which, in turn, could lead to audits of the returns of other Limited Partners. Limited Partners should also be aware that, under certain circumstances described in detail in the tax opinion, they may be foreclosed from any involvement in the administration or judicial resolution of disputes regarding items of income, loss, deduction, or credit of the Partnership.

Congress recently enacted Section 6661 of the Internal Revenue Code which imposes a penalty for a "substantial understatement of tax" for any taxable year. This penalty is equal to 10 percent of the amount of the underpayment of tax attributable to the understatement. An "understatement" is defined as the difference between the tax required to be shown on the return and the amount actually shown. A taxpayer may, however, convince the Service to abate or reduce such a penalty by showing that there is or was substantial legal authority for tax treatment set forth on the return and a reasonable belief that the tax treatment of the item was more likely than not the proper treatment.

Congress also recently enacted Section 6659 of the Code, which imposes a graduated penalty applicable to certain income tax "valuation overstatements." This penalty is imposed on the amount of an individual's underpayment of income tax attributable to a "valuation overstatement." A "valuation overstatement" generally exists if the value exceeds 150 percent of the amount subsequently determined to be the correct valuation. Counsel does not believe, however, that this valuation overstatement penalty should be imposed with respect to this transaction.

The abovementioned tax risks are by no means all-inclusive, and in order to better understand these risks as well as the other tax risks inherent in this transaction, it is imperative that each prospective Limited Partner read carefully the accompanying tax opinion and, in addition, discuss the transaction with his personal tax advisor.

Summary of Projected Operating Results and Federal Income Tax Consequences

Exhibit F, accompanying this Memorandum, contains estimates of projected operating results and federal income tax consequences based on information available as of the date of this Memorandum. These estimates, however, are for illustrational purposes only and no representation is or can be made as to future operations or the amount of any future income or loss of the Partnership. No assurances can be given that actual expenses and costs will not exceed projected expenses and costs, or that competitive factors in the local market will not limit the ability of the Partnership to achieve estimated resale price levels. The Summary does not take into account the effect, if any, of the alternative minimum tax and the investment interest limitation on the particular circumstances of a prospective investor and is subject to all of the tax risks discussed in "FEDERAL INCOME TAX CONSEQUENCES." The Summary contains merely projections that are based on the stated assumptions and are dependent upon occurrence or nonoccurrence of events and contingencies that may be beyond the control of the Partnership. No assurance can be given that the amounts reflected in the projections will in fact be realized by the Partnership or that the projected tax benefits will be available to the Limited Partners.

## SUMMARY OF CERTAIN PROVISIONS OF THE LIMITED PARTNERSHIP AGREEMENT

Introduction

The Limited Partnership Agreement is the governing instrument establishing the rights and duties of the General Partner and the Limited Partners and the terms governing the operation of the Partnership. In order to become a Limited Partner, each investor must complete and execute the Subscription Agreement. Certain provisions of the Limited Partnership Agreement are summarized elsewhere in this Memorandum under various headings. Certain other provisions are summarized below, but the summaries should be read in conjunction with the entire Limited Partnership Agreement.

Term

The Partnership will commence on or before December 31, 19 ____ and shall continue until December 31, 1999, unless earlier terminated upon:

(i) the retirement, expulsion, bankruptcy, or cessation to exist of the General Partner, unless the Limited Partners elect a successor within 120 days, which successor elects to continue the Partnership;

(ii) the vote of the Limited Partners holding a majority interest in favor of termination;

(iii) the disposition of all assets of the Partnership.

The Limited Partners, by vote of the holders of a majority interest, may extend the term of the Partnership.

Liability of Limited Partners

The Limited Partnership Agreement provides that Limited Partners shall not be liable for expenses, liabilities, or obligations of the Partnership. See "RISK FACTORS—Business Risks; Liability of Limited Partners."

Allocation of Income, Loss, and Distributions

The portion of net income, net loss, and distributions allocated to the Limited Partners will be apportioned among them in proportion to their interest in the Partnership on the last day of the calendar quarter, without regard to capital accounts. Net loss, net income, and any cash distributions from operations are allocated 100 percent to the Limited Partners and none to the General Partner.

Distributions from disposition of Partnership assets are distributed in the following order: first, to the General Partner in the amount equal to his fee; second, to the Limited Partners in the amount of the remainder of any gain on the disposition, the amount of contributed capital, and any remainder not otherwise required for the operation of the Partnership.

The General Partner's Authority

The General Partner has all authority required or appropriate to the management of the Partnership including the specific powers enumerated in Section 15.1 of the Limited Partnership Agreement. The General Partner, however, does not have authority to take the actions enumerated in Section 15.3.

Authority of the Limited Partners

The Limited Partners are prohibited from participating or interfering in any manner with the control or operation of the Partnership and have no authority to act for the Partnership. Limited Partners, however, have the right by vote of the holders of a majority of the interests in the Partnership to vote upon the following matters:

(i) removal of the General Partner;

(ii) election of a successor General Partner;

(iii) termination and dissolution of the Partnership;

(iv) amendment of the Limited Partnership Agreement, provided that such amendment is not for the purpose of reflecting the addition or substitution of Limited Partners or the reduction of capital accounts upon the return of capital;

(v) the sale of substantially all of the Partnership assets in a single sale, or in the same 12-month period, except in the liquidation of the Partnership upon its termination and dissolution;

(vi) the encumbrance of substantially all Partnership assets at one time;

(vii) the extension of the term of the Partnership.

The General Partner may call a meeting of the Limited Partners or for a vote without a meeting at any time in his discretion. The General Partner is required to call for such a meeting or vote upon written request of the Limited Partners holding a 25 percent or more interest in the Partnership. The General Partner must provide notice in accordance with the Limited Partnership Agreement.

Limited Partners do not have the right to:

(i) withhold or reduce their contributions except upon dissolution or in accordance with law;

(ii) bring an action for partition;

(iii) cause the termination and dissolution of the Partnership by court decree or otherwise except as provided in the Limited Partnership Agreement;

(iv) demand or receive property other than cash in return of their contributions.

Indemnification of the General Partner

The Partnership shall indemnify the General Partner from any liability incurred by reason of any act or omission of the General Partner in connection with the business of the Partnership, including attorneys' fees incurred in the defense of any action including an action brought by a Limited Partner. If a claim for indemnification is made by the General Partner, the Partnership will, unless in the opinion of counsel the matter has been settled by controlling precedent, submit to a court of appropriate jurisdiction whether the indemnification would be against public policy and will indemnify the General Partner unless contrary to public policy. The Partnership will indemnify the General Partner without submission to a court for expenses incurred in a successful defense by the General Partner of a claim against him.

Notwithstanding the indemnificaion provisions, the General Partner is not relieved from liability imposed by law, including liability for fraud, bad faith, willful neglect, or negligence. Moreover, as to liabilities arising under the Securities Act of 1933, it is the opinion of the Securities and Exchange Commission that indemnification is contrary to public policy and, therefore, is unenforceable.

The General Partner has the right to require that all contracts of the Partnership provide that the General Partner will not be personally liable such that the contracting party must look solely to the Partnership.

Appointment of General Partner as Attorney-in-Fact

Each Limited Partner irrevocably appoints the General Partner as his attorney-in-fact for the execution, acknowledgment, and filing of any documents that are required or the General Partner deems advisable, including the following:

(i) Certificates of Limited Partnership and amendments thereto;
(ii) other instruments or documents that may be required under the laws of any state;
(iii) amendments to the Limited Partnership Agreement;
(iv) any instruments or document that may be required to effect within the terms of the Limited Partnership Agreement, the continuation of the Partnership, the admission of Limited Partners, or the dissolution and termination of the Partnership.

## REPORTS TO LIMITED PARTNERS AND ADDITIONAL INFORMATION

The General Partner will cause to be prepared at the Partnership's expense, annual financial statements prepared on an accrual basis in accordance with generally accepted accounting principles and accompanied by a report of an independent certified public accounting firm. The financial statements will consist of a balance sheet, statement of income or loss, partners' equity, and changes in financial position. Copies of the financial statement and accountant's report shall be distributed to each Limited Partner within 90 days after the close of each taxable year of the Partnership. In addition, the General Partner will cause to be prepared and distributed to the Limited Partners the Partnership information necessary in the preparation of the Limited Partners' federal income-tax returns within 90 days of the close of the Partnership's taxable year.

The General Partner shall cause to be prepared and filed all required federal and state tax returns for the Partnership and all other reports required to be filed with governmental bodies. Upon written request, any Limited Partner will be provided with a copy of any such return or report.

The Partnership's books and records, the Partnership Agreement, Certificates of Limited Partnership, and copies of appraisals of Partnership assets shall be maintained at the principal office of the Partnership or such other place as the General Partner may determine and shall be open to inspection by any Limited Partner or his representative.

## DESCRIPTION OF THE UNITS

### General

Each unit represents a capital contribution of $50,000 in cash. All purchases of Units will be pursuant to a signed Subscription Agreement. The maximum number of Units to be sold is 35, and no Units will be sold after the closing of the offering. Each Unit entitles the holder to an interest in the net income, net loss, and distributions of the Partnership and the right to vote on certain matters set forth in the Limited Partnership Agreement. The Limited Partners as a group may be required to make additional capital contributions up to a maximum of 10 percent of the initial purchase price of the 35 units in the event the Partnership incurs operating deficits. The General Partner does not intend to purchase any Units but may do so if the offering is not otherwise fully subscribed. Unless he does purchase any Units, the General Partner will make no capital contribution to the Partnership and will not have a vote on matters subject to a vote of the Limited Partners.

### Restrictions on Transfer

No Units may be transferred except after approval by the General Partner. In addition, no Units may be assigned if such an assignment, when added to all other Units assigned within the 12 prior months, would result, in the opinion of counsel for the Partnership, in the termination of the Partnership under Section 708 of the Internal Revenue Code unless the holder of the Units obtains a private letter ruling to the effect that the proposed assignment will not terminate the Partnership.

No assignee may become a substituted Limited Partner without the consent of the General Partner, the adoption of the Limited Partnership Agreement by the assignee, and payment of a transfer fee.

The transfer of the Units is restricted by the Securities Act of 1933 (the "Act"). The Units have not been registered under the Act in reliance on an exemption from registration pursuant to Regulation D under the Act, which requires limitations on resale. The Partnership and the General Partner have no obligation or intention to register the Units under federal or state securities laws. An exemption for resales under Rule 144 under the Act is not available currently and the Partnership and General Partner have no intention or obligation to facilitate transfers under Rule 144 or any other exemption.

A legend will appear on the Subscription Agreement stating that the Units have not been registered and referring to the restrictions on transferability, and the investors will make representations as to their investment intent. A stop transfer notation will be made in the records of the Partnership restricting transfer.

The transferability of the Units may be further limited under the securities laws of various states.

## PLAN OF DISTRIBUTION

The Units will be offered to a limited number of persons by the General Partner. No brokers or dealers will be employed. The Units will be offered only to persons who the General Partner believes to be Accredited Investors as defined in Relgulation D under the Act. Potential investors will be required to establish that they meet the suitability requirements. Subscriptions will be effective only upon acceptance by the General Partner and the right is reserved to reject any subscription in whole or in part. The offering will be terminated upon receipt and acceptance of subscriptions for all 35 Units, but not later than December 31, 19 ____ unless extended by the General Partner. The proceeds will be placed in an escrow pending termination. The General Partner does not intend to purchase any Units but may elect to purchase up to ten Units if the offering is not otherwise fully subscribed. If the offering is not fully subscribed or the required approvals of the sale of the Project to the Partnership are not received prior to December 31, 19 ____ (unless extended as aforesaid), the escrowed funds will be refunded to the subscribers.

## EXHIBITS

The following exhibits are attached to this Memorandum:

A. financial statements of General Partner and Lessee
B. form of Subscription Agreement
C. form of Limited Partnership Agreement
D. form of Lease to Lessee by the Partnership
E. opinion of counsel to the Partnership and the General Partner, as to certain tax matters
F. summary of projected federal income-tax consequences
G. appraisal of the Project

The foregoing list of seven items appended as exhibits to the Private Placement Memorandum typifies the kinds of documents usually accompanying an offering. An indication of the syndicator's financial soundness is the first item. Its content, as described in the previous chapter, should be documented by supporting statements from accountants. The form of Subscription Agreement and the form of Limited Partnership Agreement for the ABC Limited Partnership described in the Private Placement Memorandum will be provided in the following pages. Since the property being syndicated is an office complex to be leased by prospective tenants, the fourth item consists of a typical lease agreement, which will not be illustrated here. The significance of the remaining three items pertaining to a legal assessment or opinion of tax status, probable income tax ramifications, and an appraisal of the asset is obvious beyond any need for comment or illustration.

Had the proposed syndication been more complex or structured to reach a wider market, the list of exhibits might well have been more extensive to the point of expanding the offering documentation beyond practicality. Special circumstances might have warranted disclosure as exhibits for such items as

- details of land transfer substantiated by appropriate deeds, purchase agreements, and other related documents;
- conditions of title insurance and other contractual obligations affecting the property;
- financial details involving mortgage encumbrances and loan-to-value ratios;
- architectural plans and construction specifications;
- partnership contracts with architects and general contractors;
- contractual arrangements with subsidiary companies of the general partner;

as well as a host of other documents relating to various aspects of the offering. When complexities actually or potentially exist in syndicating a property, judgment must be used in providing what is essential exhibit material and making overtures to provide additional exhibits to any potential investor wishing to review them. In this way one complies with requirements of full disclosure without overburdening the potential investors with excessive documentation. Additional exhibits not accompanying the offering package should be listed along with those supplied and preceded by a statement that they will be made available to any potential purchaser upon written request.

The Subscription Agreement is the next document. Investors interested in committing to the ABC Limited Partnership executed and returned it with their appropriate deposits. In Part III of this document the potential investors provided the financial information necessary to qualify themselves as limited partners. The syndicator had the option and obligation to disqualify any applicant who, in his opinion, lacked the means and stability to endure the potential financial strains inherent in this partnership.

SUBSCRIPTION AGREEMENT

THE LIMITED PARTNERSHIP UNITS SUBSCRIBED FOR HEREBY HAVE NOT BEEN REGISTERED UNDER THE SECURITIES ACT OF 1933 OR THE SECURITIES LAWS OF ANY STATE AND MAY NOT BE TRANSFERRED UNLESS, AMONG OTHER THINGS, THEY ARE SUBSEQUENTLY REGISTERED OR IN THE OPINION OF COUNSEL FOR THE PARTNERSHIP AN EXEMPTION FROM REGISTRATION IS AVAILABLE.

CONFIDENTIAL

Subscriber: ______________ Office Address: ______________
Number of Units: ______________ Residence Address: ______________
Office Telephone ( )______________
Residence Telephone ( )______________

This document should be read and responded to in its entirety.

ABC Limited Partnership
Anytown, U.S.A.

I. Subscription for Units

(a) I hereby subscribe to purchase the number of units of limited partnership interest ("Units") (the minimum purchase being one whole Unit) set forth at the top of this page in ABC Limited Partnership, a limited partnership organized under the Uniform Limited Partnership Act as enacted in (any state) (the "partnership"), the General Partner of which is Developer, at a subscription price of $50,000 per Unit.

(b) I am delivering herewith:

(i) A check in the amount equal to $50,000 multiplied by the number of Units subscribed, payable to the order of Anytown Bank as escrow agent for ABC Limited Partnership;

(ii) Three dated, completed, executed, and notarized copies of the Limited Partner Signature Page, in the form attached hereto, to the Partnership's Agreement of Limited Partnership (the "Partnership Agreement"), which signature page includes the grant of a special power of attorney by me to the General Partner pursuant to Section 20 of the Partnership Agreement.

(c) Except as may be provided under state securities law, this subscription is irrevocable, except that the execution and delivery of this Subscription Agreement will not constitute an agreement between the Partnership and me until this Subscription Agreement is accepted on behalf of the Partnership.

(d) I understand that the General Partner reserves the right, in his sole discretion, to allocate to me fewer Units than I have subscribed to purchase.

(e) I understand that the payment by me made under this Subscription Agreement will be held by an escrow agent for my benefit. If my subscription is rejected, if subscriptions for 35 Units (including any subscriptions by the General Partner) have not been accepted by December 31, 19____ (unless extended by the General Partner), or if certain other conditions as described in the offering are not satisfied, the amount of the payment tendered herewith will be returned to me. If this subscription is accepted and all other conditions are satisfied, the payment for the Units allocated to me will be applied as described in the Private Placement Memorandum dated January 31, 19____ (the "Memorandum") (and any amounts that I have tendered in excess of the payment for the Units allocated to me will be returned to me).

II. Access to Information; Understanding of Certain Matters

(a) I acknowledge that, prior to making this subscription, I and my advisors, if any, have received a copy of the Memorandum and Exhibits A through G thereto.

(b) I assure you that I have carefully reviewed the risks of, and other considerations relating to, investment in the Partnership.

(c) I understand that transfer of Units is subject to various restrictions; that, since the Units have not been registered under the Securities Act of 1933 or the securities laws of any state, the Units cannot be sold unless they are subsequently registered under said Act and applicable state laws or are exempt from registration thereunder; and that I must bear the economic risk of ownership of the Units for an indefinite period of time and am able to bear such risk.

(d) I understand that investment in the Partnership is illiquid, and I confirm that I have adequate means of providing for my current needs and possible future contingencies and that I have no need for liquidity in this investment.

(e) I assure you that after reviewing my entire investment portfolio, I and my advisors, if any, have concluded that my overall commitment to investments that are not readily marketable is not disproportionate to my net worth, and my investment in the Units will not cause such overall commitment to become excessive.

(f) Except for the information that my advisors or I have requested, as described in Sections II(a), II(g) and II(h), neither my advisors nor I have been furnished any other offering material or literature by the General Partner or any affiliates of the General Partner.

(g) My advisors, if any, and I have been furnished any material I have requested, including that relating to the Project (as defined in the Memorandum), the Lease of the Project to the Lessee, the proposed operation of the

Partnership, the General Partner and his affiliates, and any other matters relating to the business of the Partnership and the offering and sale of the Units, or anything set forth in the Memorandum, and have been afforded the opportunity to obtain any additional information necessary to verify the accuracy of any representation or information set forth in the Memorandum.

(h) My advisors, if any, and I have had the opportunity to have answered any questions concerning financial, business, or other information with respect to the Project, the Lease to the Lessee, the Partnership, the General Partner and his affiliates, and with respect to the merits and risks of investment in the Partnership, and the General Partner and his affiliates have given complete and satisfactory answers to all inquiries that my advisors and I have put to them concerning the matters listed above.

III. Financial Position and Experience of Individual Investors

I represent and warrant to the General Partner as follows:

(a) My own occupation is ______________________________.

(b) My individual net worth, or my joint net worth with my spouse, is as follows:

| | |
|---|---|
| Gross Assets: | |
| Liquid Assets .................................. | $________ |
| Illiquid Assets .................................. | $________ |
| Total.................................. | $________ |
| Gross Liabilities .................................. | $________ |
| Net Worth.................................. | $________ |

(Note: for purposes of this paragraph, you may show your joint net worth with your spouse. Net worth includes all of your assets, liquid or illiquid, including such items as home, home furnishings, automobiles and restricted securities, less any liabilities, including, for example, home mortgages and other debts and obligations.)

(c) I have had, during each of the past two years, individual income of at least $________.

(d) I reasonably expect to have, during 19_____, individual income of at least the following: $________.

(e) I have an ongoing relationship with an accountant and/or legal, tax, or business advisor with whom I review tax or financial matters (even though I may not have reviewed this investment with them).

(f) I am able to bear the economic risk of investment in the Units.

IV. Agreements of Investor

(a) I will make such representations and warranties and furnish such information and documentation as to my investment experience and financial position as the General Partner may reasonably require, and if there should be any material change in the information set forth herein prior to the closing of the sale of Units to me, I will immediately furnish such revised or corrected information to the General Partner.

(b) I hereby represent that I am acquiring Units for my own account, as principal, for investment and not with a view to the resale of such Units or any interest therein.

(c) I agree to be bound by all of the terms and conditions of the Partnership Agreement and to perform any obligations therein imposed upon a Limited Partner.

(d) I agree to indemnify the Partnership and the General Partner and his affiliates and hold such persons and firms harmless from and against any and all loss, damage, liability, or expense, including costs and reasonable attorneys' fees, to which they may be put or which they may incur by reason of or in connection with any misrepresentation made by me, any breach of any of my warranties, or my failure to fulfill any of my covenants or agreements under this Subscription Agreement. This Subscription Agreement and the representations and warranties contained herein shall be binding upon my heirs, executors, administrators, successors, and assigns.

(e) I am a permanent resident at the residence street address set forth at the top of page one.

IN WITNESS THEREOF, the undersigned has executed this Subscription Agreement as of the date indicated below.

Dated: ____________, 19____

______________________________

(Signature of Investor)

Accepted as of ____________, 19____

ABC LIMITED PARTNERSHIP

By its General Partner,

By ______________________________

(Authorized Signature)

The third and last of the documents we are presenting is the typical Limited Partnership Agreement, following the Uniform Limited

Partnership Act format, which cannot be completed until all the investment units are subscribed. We have slightly shortened it by omitting the usual Table of Contents. This lengthy document constitutes the basis from which the Certificate of Limited Partnership is drawn. Only this highly abridged certificate is filed in the name of the partnership with the secretary of state in the jurisdiction in which the partnership intends to operate and recorded in the county in which the partnership intends to transact business, so that syndication membership is fully disclosed with a minimal amount of information pertaining to the operation's financial affairs being available or open for public inspection.

## LIMITED PARTNERSHIP AGREEMENT

THIS PARTNERSHIP AGREEMENT ("Partnership Agreement") is entered into as of the ______day of __________, 19_____, by and between General Partner, and (any state) Corporation duly qualified to do business in (any state) ("General Partner"), as General Partner and

(List of Limited Partners)

as the original Limited Partners ("Limited Partners"), all of whom hereby form a Limited Partnership pursuant to the Uniform Limited Partnership Act of the State of (any state), upon the following terms and conditions:

### 1. Name and Place of Business

The name of the Partnership is ABC Limited Partnership, and its principal place of business is 1234 Ocean Drive, (any state), or such other place or places as the General Partner may hereafter determine.

(Table of Contents, omitted here.)

### 2. Definitions and Glossary of Terms

2.1 The following terms used in this Partnership Agreement shall (unless otherwise expressly provided herein or unless the context otherwise requires) have the following respective meanings:

2.1.1. "Adjusted Cash from Operations" shall mean the excess of cash revenue from operation of Partnership Property (including lease payments on net leases) over cash disbursements without deduction for depreciation and amortization of intangibles such as organization, underwriting, and debt placement costs but after a reasonable allowance for cash reserves for repairs, replacements, contingencies, and anticipated obligations (including debt service), as determined by the General Partner. Adjusted Cash from Operations shall not include Cash from Sales or Refinancings or Cash from Initial Financing.

2.1.2 "Adjusted Invested Capital" of a Holder shall be the Original Invested Capital paid for or attributable to his Units reduced by the total cash distributed to him and prior Holders of his Units from Cash from Sales or Refinancings and from Cash from Property Reserve Account (to the extent such cash distributed came from Net Proceeds).

2.1.3. "Assignee" shall mean a person who has acquired a beneficial interest in one or more Units from a third party but who is neither a substituted Limited Partner nor an Assignee of Record.

2.1.4 "Assignee of Record" shall mean an Assignee who has acquired a beneficial interest in one or more Units whose ownership of such Units has been recorded on the books of the Partnership and which ownership is the subject of a written instrument of assignment, the effective date of which assignment has passed.

2.1.5 "Cash from Sales or Refinancing" shall mean the net cash realized by the Partnership from the sale, refinancing, or other disposition of any Partnership Property after retirement of applicable mortgage debt and all expenses related to the transaction.

2.1.6 "Closing Date" shall mean such date designated by the General Partner, but not later than ____________, 19_____.

2.1.7 "Code" shall mean the Internal Revenue Code of 1954, as amended, or corresponding provisions of subsequent revenue laws.

2.1.8 "Cost of Partnership Property" means the total consideration paid for federal income-tax purposes by the Partnership in connection with the purchase of such Property, whether paid to the seller, the General Partner, or any other person, either in cash or by way of promissory notes, including financing charges.

2.1.9 "Distributions" shall refer to any cash or other property distributed to Holders and the General Partner arising from their interests in the Partnership, but shall not include any payments to the General Partner under the provisions of Paragraph 9 or Paragraph 10.

2.1.10 "General Partner" shall refer to General Partner, or to any other person or corporation who succeeds him in such capacity.

2.1.11 "Gross Proceeds" shall mean the aggregate total of the Original Invested Capital of the original and all of the additional Limited Partners.

2.1.12 "Gross Revenues" shall mean revenues from the operation of real property owned by the Partnership other than from security deposits paid by lessees thereof. The term "Gross Revenues" shall not include revenues from sale, refinancing, or other disposition of Partnership Property.

2.1.13 "Holders" shall refer to owners of Units who are either Partners or Assignees of Record, and reference to a "Holder" shall be to any one of them. The General Partner shall *not* be considered to be a Holder unless he shall have purchased any Unit as a Limited Partner.

2.1.14 "Limited Partners" shall refer to the original Limited Partners and to any other persons who are admitted to the Partnership as additional or substituted Limited Partners. Reference to a "Limited Partner" shall refer to any one of them.

2.1.15 "Majority Vote" shall mean the vote of Limited Partners who own more than 50 percent of the Total Outstanding Units.

2.1.16 "Net Income" or "Net Loss" shall mean the net income or net loss of the Partnership, as determined in accordance with the cash method of accounting.

2.1.17 "Net Proceeds" shall mean the total Gross Proceeds less expenses incurred and to be paid by the Partnership in organizing the Partnership and in offering the Units.

2.1.18 "Original Invested Capital" shall mean the amount in cash contributed by each Limited Partner to the capital of the Partnership for the Units, which amount shall be attributed to such Units in the hands of a subsequent Holder.

2.1.19 "Partners" shall refer collectively to the General Partner and to the Limited Partners, and reference to a "Partner" shall be to any one of the Partners.

2.1.20 "Partnership" shall refer to the Limited Partnership created under this Partnership Agreement.

2.1.21 "Partnership Property" or "Property" shall refer to the property acquired by the Partnership with Net Proceeds or Cash from Initial Financing.

2.1.22 "Total Outstanding Units" shall mean all Units issued at or before the Closing Date.

2.1.23 A "Unit" shall represent a capital contribution of $50,000 to the Partnership and shall entitle the Holder thereof to an interest in the Net Income, Net Loss, and Distributions of the Partnership, without regard to capital accounts.

3. Business and Purpose

The primary purpose (character of business) of the Partnership is to invest in, hold, and manage income-producing real estate.

4. Term

The Partnership commenced ____________, 19_____, and shall continue until December 31, 19_____, unless previously terminated in accordance with the provisions of this Partnership Agreement.

5. General Partner

The General Partner has not contributed any cash to the Partnership and at all times during the existence of the Partnership, has no interest in Net Income, Net Loss, and Distributions, except as set forth in the provisions of Paragraph 11. This shall not preclude participation by the General Partner as a Limited Partner.

6. Original and Additional Limited Partners

6.1 The original Limited Partners shall contribute the sum of $50,000 to the capital of the Partnership for each Unit to be issued.

6.2 The Partnership intends to sell and issue a total of 35 Units, and to admit as additional Limited Partners the persons who contribute cash to the capital of the Partnership for such Units.

6.3 Each person who acquires any such Units shall become a Limited Partner in the Partnership at such time as he has: (i) purchased at least one Unit, (ii) contributed the sum of $50,000 cash for each Unit purchased, and (iii) executed and filed with the Partnership a written instrument that sets forth an intention to become a Limited Partner and requests admission to the Partnership in that capacity, together with such other instruments as the General Partner may deem necessary or desirable to effect such admission, including the written acceptance and adoption by such person of the provisions of this Partnership Agreement, and the execution, acknowledgment, and delivery to the General Partner of a special power of attorney, the form, style, and content of which are more fully described herein.

6.4 The General Partner shall in timely fashion amend (but not later than the last day of the calendar month following the date of acceptance of the additional Limited Partner's subscription) this Partnership Agreement and any separate certificate of limited partnership filed for record to reflect the admission of a person as an additional Limited Partner.

6.5 The Partnership shall not issue any additional Units after the Closing Date.

6.6 All Original Invested Capital of Holders shall be received by the Partnership in trust and shall be deposited in an escrow account in any of the branches of the Anytown Bank or in any other banking institutions designated by the General Partner as escrow holder for the Original Invested Capital. Upon receipt of a minimum of $1.75 million in Original Invested Capital from purchasers of Units, the Partnership will admit such purchasers into the Partnership as additional Limited Partners not later than 15 days after the receipt of such minimum. At the time the purchaser is admitted as a Limited Partner, the escrow holder shall transfer such person's Original Invested Capital to the Partnership. If the $1.75 million minimum amount is not obtained within 180 days from the effective date of this Agreement, all Original Invested Capital will be promptly refunded to the purchasers with any interest earned on such Original Invested Capital.

6.7 The Limited Partners shall, upon demand of the General Partner, make contributions in proportion to their respective interests as Limited Partners to meet any operating deficit with respect to any Partnership property or expenses incurred in connection with the ownership or use and occupation thereof, which contributions in the aggregate shall be sufficient to satisfy the Partnership's estimated obligations not paid from Partnership income; provided, however, that such contributions shall be used solely for the purpose stated herein and provided further, the aggregate of such demands over the life of the Partnership shall not exceed 10 percent of the Original Invested Capital.

6.7.1 The Limited Partners shall be obligated to make the entire amount of each such contribution within 30 days after receipt of a mailed request therefor from the General Partner; a contribution when made shall be applied to the payment of Partnership obligations and shall be credited to the capital account of each contributing Limited Partner.

6.7.2 If a Limited Partner shall fail to pay his share of the contribution within 30 days of receipt of request therefor, the General Partner shall seek such share from the other Limited Partners who shall be collectively obligated to contribute the sum that the defaulting Partner failed to contribute and when such sum is received (a) the interest of a defaulting Partner shall be reduced by a fraction, the numerator of which shall be the amount of such contribution and the denominator of which shall be the sum of the contributions theretofor made by the defaulting Partner and the amount of such defaulted contribution; (b) the interest of the Partner making the contribution of a defaulting Partner shall be increased by that portion of the interest lost by the defaulting Partner; and (c) any increase or decrease in the interest of any Partner shall be entered on the schedule of Partners.

6.7.3 Neither the General Partner nor the Partnership may exercise any other right or remedy by the reason of failure of any Limited Partner to make a contribution hereunder, the provisions of this paragraph mean exclusive.

7. Status of Limited Partners

Limited Partners shall not be bound by, or be personally liable for, the expenses, liabilities, or obligations of the Partnership.

8. Status of Units

Each Unit shall be fully paid and nonassessable, except to the extent permitted by paragraph 6.7 hereof.

9. Compensation of General Partner

9.1 The General Partner will receive compensation only as specified by this Partnership Agreement.

9.2 The General Partner shall be entitled to a fee for services in providing continuing property management or supervision of the Partnership Property, and for services rendered as General Partner; provided, however, that such fee shall not exceed 15% of the net proceeds from the sale of the property. In the event the property shall be refinanced, the General Partner shall be entitled to a fee of 15% of the amount available for distribution to the Limited Partners from such refinancing. In the event the General Partner retains third parties to perform a portion or all of the services set forth below, the General Partner will be solely responsible for any fees charged by such persons which will be paid by the General Partner without cost to the Partnership. Property management services will include, but not be limited to: (i) review of the maintenance, repair, remodeling, and refurbishing of the Partnership Property; (ii) review of rental schedules and recommendations with respect to changes thereto; (iii) supervision of employees together with the establishment of procedures regarding the management of Partnership Property; (iv) preparation and review of rental surveys; (v) preparation and review of historical and projected performance; (vi) preparation and review of leases, management agreements, and maintenance agreements; (vii) review of replacement reserves and working capital and recommendations with respect to changes thereto; and (viii) preparation of income and expense statements and federal tax information for partners.

10. Partnership Expenses

10.1 Reimbursement (other than for organization and offering expenses) to the General Partner shall not be made, except for reimbursement of the actual cost to the General Partner of goods, materials, and services used for or by the Partnership. The reimbursement for expenses provided for in this Paragraph 10.1 shall be made to the General Partner regardless of whether any Distributions are made to the Limited Partners under the provisions of Paragraph 11.4.

10.2 The General Partner will pay: (i) salaries and other compensation of its officers and directors incidental to the organization of the Partnership, the sale of Units, and the acquisition of the Partnership Property; (ii) expenses incurred by the General Partner in connection with the administration of the Partnership, including the overhead expenses of the General Partner; (iii) expenses incidental to the organization of the Partnership and marketing of Units; (iv) expenses related to the performance of those services for which the General Partner is entitled to compensation by way of fee; and (v) all other expenses that are unrelated to the business of the Partnership.

10.3 Subject to Paragraphs 10.1 and 10.2 preceding, the Partnership shall pay all expenses of the Partnership not passed on to the Tenant of the Partnership Property through the lease(s), which may include, but are not limited to: (i) all costs of personnel employed by the Partnership and involved in the business of the Partnership, including persons who may also be officers or employees of the General Partner; (ii) all costs of borrowed money, taxes, and assessments on Partnership Property and other taxes applicable to the Partnership; (iii) legal, audit, accounting, and other fees; (iv) printing and other expenses and taxes incurred in connection with the issuance, distribution, transfer, and recording of documents evidencing ownership of an interest in the Partnership or in connection with the business of the Partnership; (v) fees and expenses paid to independent contractors, brokers and servicers, leasing agents, consultants, real estate brokers, insurance brokers, and other agents; (vi) expenses in connection with the disposition, replacement, alternation, repair, remodeling, refurbishment, leasing, refinancing, and operation of Partnership Property (including the costs and expenses of foreclosures, insurance premiums, real estate brokerage, and leasing commissions and of maintenance of such Property); (vii) the cost of insurance as required in connection with the business of the Partnership; (viii) expenses of organizing, revising, amending, converting, modifying, or terminating the Partnership; (ix) expenses in connection with Distributions made by the Partnership to, and communications and bookkeeping and clerical work necessary in maintaining relations with Unit Holders, including the cost of printing and mailing to such persons certificates for Units and reports of meetings of the Partnership, and of preparation of proxy statements, if required, and solicitations of proxies in connection therewith; (x) expenses in connection with preparing and mailing reports required to be furnished to Unit Holders for investor, tax reporting, or other purposes, or which reports the General Partner deems the furnishing thereof to Unit Holders to be in the best interests of the Partnership; (xi) costs of any accounting or bookkeeping necessary for the maintenance of the books and records of the Partnership; and (xii) the cost of preparation and dissemination of the informational material and documentation relating to potential sale, refinancing or other disposition of Partnership Property.

11. Allocation of Income, Loss, and Distributions

11.1 That portion of Net Income, Net Loss, and Distributions of the Partnership allocated to the Unit Holders shall be apportioned among the Holders, in the ratio in which the number of Units owned by each of them on the last day of each calendar quarter bears to the total number of Units owned by all of them as of that date, without regard to capital accounts or the number of days during such quarter in which a person was a Holder.

11.2 Allocation of net loss. Except as provided in Section 11.9 of the Partnership Agreement, Net Loss shall be allocated as follows:

11.2.1 None shall be allocated to the General Partner.

11.2.2 One hundred percent shall be allocated to the Unit Holders.

11.3 Allocation of net income. Net Income shall be allocated as follows:

11.3.1 None shall be allocated to the General Partner.

11.3.2 One hundred percent shall be allocated to the Unit Holders.

11.4 *Distribution of adjusted cash from operations.* Adjusted Cash from Operations shall be distributed as follows:

11.4.1 None shall be distributed to the General Partner.

11.4.2 One hundred percent shall be distributed to the Unit Holders.

11.5 *Distributions of cash from sales and refinancings.* Cash from Sales and Refinancings shall be distributed in the following order of priority after provision for expenses of the Partnership.

11.5.1 First, to the General Partner, in an amount equal to the fee to which he is entitled under Paragraph 9.2.

11.5.2 Second, the remainder to the Unit Holders.

11.6 The Partnership may be restricted from making Distributions under the terms of notes, mortgages, or other types of debt obligation that it may issue or assume in conjunction with borrowed funds, and Distributions may also be restricted or suspended in circumstances when the General Partner determines, in his absolute discretion, that such action is in the best interests of the Partnership.

11.7 The methods hereinabove set forth by which Distributions and allocations of Net Income and Net Loss are made and apportioned are hereby expressly consented to by each Partner as an express condition to becoming a Partner.

11.8 All Distributions are subject to the payment of Partnership expenses and to the maintenance of reasonable reserves for alterations, repairs, improvements, maintenance, and replacement of furniture, equipment, and fixtures.

## 12. Assignment of Partnership Units

12.1 Holders shall have the right to assign whole Units by a written instrument of assignment, only after prior approval of such transfer by the General Partner, the terms of which assignment are not in contravention of any of the provisions of this Partnership Agreement.

12.2 An Assignee of Record shall be entitled to receive distributions of cash or other property from the Partnership attributable to the Units acquired by reason of such assignment from and after the effective date of the assignment of such Units to him; however, anything herein to the contrary notwithstanding, the Partnership and the General Partner shall be entitled to treat the assignor of such Units as the absolute owner thereof in all respects, and shall incur no liability for allocations of Net Income, Net Loss, or Distributions, or transmittal of reports and notices required to be given to Holders hereunder that are made in good faith to such assignor until such time as the written instrument of assignment has been received by the Partnership and recorded on its books and the effective date of the assignment has passed. Provided the Partnership has actual notice of an assignment of Units, the effective date of such assignment on which the Assignee shall be deemed as Assignee of Record shall be the first day of the month set forth on the written instrument of assignment.

12.3 Except as provided in this Paragraph 12.3, no assignment of any Units by a Holder may be made if the Units sought to be assigned, when added to the total of all other Units assigned within the period of 12 consecutive months prior to the proposed date of assignment would, in the opinion of counsel for the Partnership, result in the termination of the Partnership under Section 708 of the Code. However, such assignment may be made if, upon the application and at the expense of the Holder desiring to assign his Units in the Partnership, there shall have been granted to the transferring Holder and the Partnership a private ruling by the Internal Revenue Service that the proposed assignment will not cause such termination.

12.4 No assignment, sale, transfer, exchange, or other disposition of any Units in the Partnership may be made except in compliance with the then applicable rules of any other applicable governmental authority.

12.5 Any assignment, sale, exchange or other transfer in contravention of any of the provisions of this Paragraph 12 shall be void and ineffectual and shall not bind or be recognized by the Partnership.

13. Substituted Limited Partners

13.1 No Assignee shall have the right to become a substituted Limited Partner in place of his assignor unless all of the following conditions are first satisfied:

13.1.1 A duly executed and acknowledged written instrument of assignment previously aproved by the General Partner shall have been filed with the Partnership, which instrument shall specify the number of Units being assigned and set forth the intention of the assignor that the Assignee succeed to assignor's interest as a substituted Limited Partner in his place;

13.1.2 The Assignor and Assignee shall have executed and acknowledged such other instruments as the General Partner may deem necessary or desirable to effect such substitution, including the written acceptance and adoption by the Assignee of the provisions of this Partnership Agreement as the same may be amended and his execution, acknowledgment, and delivery to the General Partner of a special power of attorney, the form and content of which are described herein;

13.1.3 The written consent of the General Partner to such substitution shall have been obtained, the granting or denial of which shall be within the absolute discretion of the General Partner;

13.1.4 A transfer fee shall have been paid to the Partnership that is sufficient to cover all reasonable expenses connected with such substitution; and

13.1.5 The provisions of Paragraph 12.3 and 12.4 of this Partnership Agreement are complied with.

13.2 By executing or adopting this Partnership Agreement, each Limited Partner hereby consents to the admission of additional or substituted Limited Partners by the General Partner and to any Assignee of his Units becoming a substituted Limited Partner.

13.3 The General Partner shall promptly cause the Partnership Agreement or any separate certificate of limited partnership to be amended to reflect the substitution of Limited Partners.

## 14. Books, Records, Accountings, and Reports

14.1 The Partnership's books and records, the Partnership Agreement and all amendments thereto, any separate certificates of limited partnership, and copies of each appraisal on Partnership Property shall be maintained at the principal office of the Partnership or such other place as the General Partner may determine and shall be open to inspection and examination of Limited Partners or their duly authorized representatives at all reasonable times. Upon written request, a Limited Partner or his duly authorized representative will be provided with a copy of the certificate or certificates of limited partnership containing the most recent listing Partners' names, addresses, and capital contributions. Each appraisal on Partnership Property will be maintained by the General Partner and available for such inspection and examination by any Limited Partner or his duly authorized representative.

14.2 The General Partner shall have prepared at least annually, at Partnership expense, financial statements (balance sheet, statement of income or loss, partners' equity and changes in financial position) prepared in accordance with generally accepted accounting principles and accompanied by a report thereon containing an opinion of an independent certified public accounting firm. Copies of such statements and reports shall be distributed to each Limited Partner within 90 days after the close of each taxable year of the Partnership.

14.3 The General Partner shall also have prepared at least annually, at Partnership expense, Partnership information necessary in the preparation of the Limited Partners' federal income-tax returns, as well as appropriate federal and state tax returns for the Partnership, and shall provide such information to the Limited Partners within 90 days of the close of each tax year.

14.4 The General Partner, at Partnership expense, shall cause to be prepared and timely filed, with appropriate federal and state regulatory and administrative bodies, all reports required to be filed with such entities under then current applicable laws, rules, and regulations. Such reports shall be prepared on the accounting or reporting basis required by such regulatory bodies. Any Limited Partner shall be provided with a copy of any such report upon request without expense to him.

14.5 The General Partner, at Partnership expense, shall maintain for a period of at least four years a record of the information obtained to indicate that a Limited Partner meets with the suitability standards set forth in the offering memorandum.

## 15. Rights, Authority, Powers, Responsibilities, and Duties of the General Partner

15.1 The General Partner shall have all authority, rights, and powers conferred by law and those required or appropriate to the management of the Partnership business, which, by way of illustration but not by way of limitation, shall, subject only to the provisions of Paragraph 15.3 following, include the right, authority, and power:

15.1.1 To acquire, develop, hold, and dispose of real property, interest therein, or appurtenances thereto, as well as personal or mixed property connected therewith, located at Anytown, U.S.A.;

15.1.2 To borrow money and, if security is required therefor, to mortgage or subject any Partnership investment to any other security device; to obtain replacements of any mortgage or other security device; and to prepay, in whole or in part, refinance, increase, modify, consolidate, or extend any mortgage or other security device, all of the foregoing at such terms and in such amounts as the General Partner, in his sole discretion, deems to be in the best interests of the Partnership;

15.1.3 To place record title to, or the right to use, Partnership assets in, the name or names of a nomineee or nominees, trustee or trustees for any purpose convenient or beneficial to the Partnership;

15.1.4 To acquire and enter into any contract of insurance that the General Partner deems necessary or appropriate for the protection of the Partnership and the General Partner for the conservation of Partnership assets, or for any purpose convenient or beneficial to the Partnership;

15.1.5 To employ persons in the operation and management of the business of the Partnership;

15.1.6 To prepare or cause to be prepared reports, statements, and other relevant information for distribution to Holders;

15.1.7 To open accounts and deposit and maintain funds in the name of the Partnership in banks or savings and loan associations, provided, however, that the Partnership funds shall not be commingled with the funds of any other person;

15.1.8 To cause the Partnership to make or revoke any of the elections referred to in Sections 108, 709, 754, or 1017 of the Internal Revenue Code of 1954 or any similar provisions enacted in lieu thereof;

15.1.9 To select as its accounting year a calendar year or such fiscal year as approved by the Internal Revenue Service;

15.1.10 To determine the apropriate accounting method or methods to be used by the Partnership (the Partnership intends initially to utilize the accrual method of accounting in maintaining its books and records);

15.1.11 To offer and sell Units in the Partnership to individuals who qualify as "accredited investors";

15.1.12 To amend this Partnership Agreement to reflect the addition or substitution of Limited Partners or the reduction of capital accounts upon the return of capital to Partners;

15.1.13 To require in all Partnership obligations that the General Partner shall not have any personal liability thereon but that the person or entity contracting with the Partnership is to look solely to the Partnership and its assets for satisfaction and in the event that any such obligations have personal liabiliity, the General Partner may require their satisfaction prior to contracts without such personal liability;

15.1.14 To execute, acknowledge, and deliver any and all instruments to effectuate the foregoing and to take all such action in connection therewith as the General Partner shall deem necessary or appropriate;

15.1.15 To reinvest all Cash from Initial Financing; and

15.1.16 To purchase Property in its own name or in the name of the nominee, a trust or a corporate "nominee," or otherwise (and assume loans in connection therewith) and temporarily hold title thereto for the purpose of facilitating the acquisition of such Property or the borrowing of money or obtaining of financing for the Partnership or completion of construction of the Property or any other purpose related to the business of the Partnership, provided that such Property is purchased by the Partnership for a purchase price no greater than the fair-market value of the Property as of the date of transfer from the General Partner to the Partnership, and further provided that there is no difference in interest rates of the loans secured by the Property at the time acquired by the General Partner and the time acquired by the Partnership, nor any other benefit arising out of such transaction of the General Partner apart from the compensation otherwise permitted by this Partnership Agreement.

15.1.17 The General Partner shall be the "tax matters partner" for purposes of Section 6221 of the Internal Revenue Code.

15.2 The General Partner shall, except as otherwise provided in this Partnership Agreement, have all the rights and powers and shall be subject to all the restrictions and liabilities of a Partner in a Partnership without Limited Partners.

15.3 The General Partner shall not have the authority to:

15.3.1 Enter into contracts with the Partnership that would bind the Partnership after the expulsion, adjudication of bankruptcy, or insolvency of the General Partner or continue the business with Partnership assets after the occurrence of such event;

15.3.2 Grant to it an exclusive listing for sale of Partnership assets, including Partnership Properties;

15.3.3 Sell substantially all of the assets of the Partnership in a single sale, or in multiple sales in the same 12-month period, except in the orderly liquidation and winding up of the business of the Partnership upon its termination and dissolution;

15.3.4 Pledge or encumber substantially all of the assets of the Partnership at one time, other than in connection with the acquisition or improvement of assets or the refinancing of previous obligations;

15.3.5 Alter the primary purpose of the Partnership as set forth in Paragraph 3;

15.3.6 Purchase Partnership Property without first having obtained an appraisal with respect to the value thereof, rendered by an independent appraiser who is a member of a nationally recognized society of apraisers that provides that the Cost of such Partnership Property equals or is less than the apraised value;

15.3.7 Make long-term secured loans to the Partnership and on short-term unsecured loans made to the Partnership receive interest or other financing charges or fees in excess of those amounts that would be charged by third-party-financing institutions on comparable loans for the same purpose in the same geographic area but in no event in excess of 2 percent above the prime rate of Anytown National Bank;

15.3.8 Redeem or repurchase Units on behalf of the Partnership;

15.3.9 Do any act in contravention of this Partnership Agreement or which would make it impossible to carry on the ordinary business of the Partnership;

15.3.10 Confess a judgment against the Partnership in connection with any threatened or pending legal action;

15.3.11 Admit a person as a General Partner except with the consent of the Limited Partners as provided for in this Partnership Agreement;

15.3.12 Perform any act (other than an act required by this Agreement or any act taken in good faith reliance upon counsel's opinion) that would, at the time such act occurred, subject any Limited Partner to liability as a general partner in any jurisdiction;

15.3.13 Employ, or permit to employ, the funds or assets of the Partnership in any manner except for the exclusive benefit of the Partnership;

15.3.14 Incur any nonrecourse indebtedness wherein the lender will have or acquire, at any time as a result of making the loan, any direct or indirect interest in the profit, capital, or property of the Partnership other than as a secured creditor;

15.3.15 Commingle the Partnership funds with those of any other person or entity;

15.4 The General Partner shall have the duty and responsibility for providing continuing administrative and executive support, advice, consultation, analysis, and supervision with respect to the functions of the Partnership as an owner of Partnership Property, including decisions regarding adjustments to rental schedules, the sale of refinancing or other disposition of property, and compliance with federal, state, and local regulatory requirements and procedures.

## 16. Rights, Powers, and Voting Rights of the Limited Partners

16.1 Limited Partners shall take no part in or interfere in any manner with the control, conduct, or operation of the Partnership and shall have no right or authority to act for or bind the Partnership.

16.2 Limited Partners shall have the right, by Majority Vote, to vote only upon the following matters affecting the basic structure of the Partnership:

16.2.1 Removal of the General Partner;

16.2.2 Election of a successor General Partner;

16.2.3 Termination and dissolution of the Partnership;

16.2.4 Amendment of the Partnership Agreement, provided such amendment is not for the purpose of reflecting the addition or substitution of Limited Partners or the reduction of capital accounts upon the return of capital to Partners;

16.2.5 The sale of all or substantially all of the assets of the Partnership in a single sale, or in multiple sales in the same 12-month period, except in the liquidation and winding up of the business of the Partnership upon its termination and dissolution;

16.2.6 The pledge or encumbrance of all or substantially all of the assets of the Partnership at one time;

16.2.7 The extension of the term of the Partnership.

16.3 In any such vote each Holder shall be entitled to cast one vote for each Unit which he owns and the procedures set forth in Paragraph 16.5 of this Partnership Agreement shall be applicable.

16.4 The General Partner may at any time call a meeting of the Limited Partners or for a vote, without a meeting, of the Limited Partners on matters that they are entitled to vote and shall call for such meeting or vote following receipt of written request therefor of Limited Partners holding 25 percent or more of the Units held by all Limited Partners as of the date of receipt of such written request ("notice date"). Within ten days of such notice date, the General Partner shall notify all Limited Partners of record as of the notice date as to the time and place of the Partnership meeting, if called, and the general nature of the business to be transacted thereat, or if no such meeting has been called, of the matter or matters to be voted upon and the date upon which the votes will be counted. Any Partnership meeting or the date upon which such votes, without a meeting, will be counted (regardless of whether the General Partner has called for such meeting or vote upon the request of Limited Partners or has initiated such event without such request) shall be no less than 15 nor more than 60 days following mailing of the notice thereof by the General Partner. All expenses of the voting and such notification shall be borne by the Partnership.

16.5 A Limited Partner shall be entitled to cast one vote for each Unit he owns: (i) at a meeting, in person, by written proxy, or by a signed writing directing the manner in which he desires that his vote be cast, which writing must be received by the General Partner prior to such meeting, or (ii) without a meeting, by a signed writing directing the manner in which he desires that his vote be cast, which writing must be received by the General Partner prior to the date upon which the votes of Limited Partners are to be counted. Only the votes of Limited Partners of record on the notice date, whether at a meeting or otherwise, shall be counted. The General Partner shall not be entitled to vote; provided, they shall not abridge his right to vote as a Limited Partner. The laws of (any state) pertaining to the validity and use of corporate proxies shall govern the validity and use of proxies given by Limited Partners.

16.6 No Limited Partner shall have the right or power to: (i) withdraw or reduce his contribution to the capital of the Partnership except as a result of the dissolution of the Partnership or as otherwise provided by law, (ii) bring an action for partition against the Partnership, (iii) cause the termination and dissolution of the Partnership by court decree or otherwise, except as set forth in this Partnership Agreement, or (iv) demand or receive property other than cash in return for his contribution. No Limited Partner shall have priority over any other Limited Partner either as to the return of contributions of capital or as to Net Income, Net Loss, or Distributions. Other than upon the termination and dissolution of the Partnership as provided by this Partnership Agreement, there has been no time agreed upon when the contribution of each Limited Partner may be returned.

16.7 In addition to any amendments otherwise authorized herein, this Agreement may be amended from time to time by the General Partner, without the consent of any of the Limited Partners (i) to add to the representations, duties, or obligations of the General Partner or surrender any right or power granted to the General Partner herein, for the benefit of the Limited Partners; (ii) to cure any ambiguity, to correct or supplement any provision herein that may be inconsistent with any other provision herein, or to make any other provisions with respect to matters or questions arising under this Agreement that will not be inconsistent with the provisions of this Agreement; and (iii) to delete or add any provision of this Agreement required to be so deleted or added by a State "Blue Sky" Commissioner or similar such official, which addition or deletion is deemed by such Commissioner or official to be for the benefit or protection of the Limited Partners. Notwithstanding anything to the contrary contained in this Partnership Agreement, the Agreement may not be amended without the consent of the Partners to be adversely affected by an amendment that:

16.7.1 Converts a Limited Partner into a General Partner;

16.7.2 Modifies the limited liability of a Limited Partner;

16.7.3 Alters the interest of the General or Limited Partners in Net Income or Net Loss or Distributions from the Partnership; or

16.7.4 Affects the status of the Partnership as a partnership for federal income tax purposes.

## 17. Expulsion, Bankruptcy, or Dissolution of the General Partner

17.1 The General Partner may be expelled from the Partnership upon a Majority Vote.

17.2 Written notice of the expulsion of the General Partner shall be served upon it either by certified or by registered mail, return receipt requested, or by personal service. Such notice shall set forth the date upon which the expulsion is to become effective.

17.3 Upon the retirement, expulsion, adjudication of bankruptcy, or dissolution of the General Partner ("Terminated Partner"), the interest of such Terminated Partner in the Net Income, Net Loss, and Distributions of the Partnership shall be purchased by the Partnership for a purchase price determined according to the provisions of Paragraph 17.4, following.

17.4 The Terminated Partner shall receive from the new General Partner or partners ("Acquiring Partner") the fair-market value of its interest in the Partnership, determined by agreement between the Terminated Partner and the Acquiring Partner, or if they cannot agree, by arbitration in accordance with the then current rules of the American Arbitration Association. For this purpose, the fair-market value of the interest of the Terminated Partner shall be deemed to be the amount the Terminated Partner would receive upon dissolution and termination of the Partnership under Section 19.2 assuming such dissolution or termination occurred on the date of the dissolving event and assuming the assets of the Partnership were sold for their then fair-market value without compulsion of the Partnership to sell such assets. Payment shall be made by a promissory note bearing 8% simple interest per annum on the unpaid principal amount of the promissory note, secured by assignment by the Acquiring Partner to the Terminated Partner of the future Distributions by the Partnership to the acquiring partner, which principal amount together with accrued interest shall be payable at the times and in the amounts equal to 75% of such Distributions until such time as the principal amount together with accrued interest is paid in full, but shall become due and payable in full by the Acquiring Partner at such time as the Partnership is finally wound up and liquidated. The Terminated Partner shall be required to sell and the Acquiring Partner shall be required to purchase the Terminated Partner's interest in the Partnership no later than the sixtieth day after the occurrence of one of the events specified in Section 19.1, or election of a new General Partner under Section 16.2, whichever occurs later.

## 18. Certain Transactions

The General Partner, any Holder, any shareholder, officer, director, or employee thereof, or any person owning a legal or beneficial interest therein, may engage in or possess an interest in any other business or venture of every nature and description, independently or with others including, but not limited to, the ownership, financing, leasing, operation, management, brokerage, and development of real property.

## 19. Termination and Dissolution of the Partnership

19.1 The Partnership shall be terminated and dissolved upon the earlier to occur of the following:

19.1.1 The retirement (provided there has been 90 days prior written notice to the Limited Partners), expulsion, adjudication of bankruptcy, insolvency, dissolution, or other cessation to exist as the General Partner, unless the General Partner elected in place thereof within 120 days of the date of such event by Majority Vote elects to continue the business of the Partnership. Expenses incurred in the reformation, or attempted reformation, of the Partnership shall be deemed expenses of the Partnership;

19.1.2 A Majority Vote in favor of dissolution and termination of the Partnership;

19.1.3 The expiration of the term of the Partnership; or

19.1.4 The disposition of all interests in real property and other assets of the Partnership.

19.2 Upon a dissolution and termination of the Partnership for any reason, the General Partner shall take full account of the Partnership assets and liabilities, shall liquidate the assets as promptly as is consistent with obtaining the fair value thereof, and shall apply and distribute the proceeds therefrom in the following order:

19.2.1 To the payment of creditors of the Partnership but excluding secured creditors whose obligations will be assumed or otherwise transferred on the liquidation of Partnership assets;

19.2.2 To the repayment of any outstanding loans made by the General Partner to the Partnership; and

19.2.3 To the General Partner and Holders pursuant to the provisions of Paragraph 11.5, "Allocation of Income, Loss and Distributions," of this Partnership Agreement.

20. Special Power of Attorney

20.1 Concurrently with the execution of written acceptance and adoption of the provisions of this Partnership Agreement, each Limited Partner shall execute, acknowledge, and deliver to the General Partner, or the designee of the General Partner, a special power of attorney in form acceptable to the General Partner in which the General Partner, or his designee, is constituted and appointed as the attorney-in-fact for such Limited Partner, with power and authority to act in his name and on his behalf to execute, acknowledge, and swear to in the execution, acknowledgment, and filing of documents, which shall include, by way of illustration but not of limitation, the following:

20.1.1 The Partnership Agreement and any separate certificates of limited partnership, as well as any amendments to the foregoing that, under the laws of (any state), are required to be filed or which the General Partner deems to be advisable to file;

20.1.2 Any other instrument or document that may be required to be filed by the Partnership under the laws of any state or by any governmental agency or that the General Partner deems advisable to file; and

20.1.3 Any instrument or document that may be required to effect the continuation of the Partnership, the admission of an additional or substituted Limited Partner, or the dissolution and termination of the Partnership (provided such continuation, admission or dissolution and termination are in accordance with the terms of this Partnership Agreement), or to reflect any reductions in amount of contributions of Partners.

20.2 The special power of attorney to be concurrently granted by each Limited Partner:

20.2.1 Is a special power of attorney coupled with an interest, is irrevocable, shall survive the death or legal incapacity of the granting Limited Partner, and is limited to those matters herein set forth;

20.2.2 May be exercised by the General Partner acting alone for each Limited Partner by a facsimile signature of the General Partner or by one of his officers, or by listing all of the Limited Partners executing any instrument with a signature of the General Partner or one of his officers acting as his attorney-in-fact; and

20.2.3 Shall survive an assignment by a Limited Partner of all or any portion of his Units except that, where the Assignee of the Units owned by a Limited Partner has been approved by the General Partner, the special power of attorney shall survive such assignment for the sole purpose of enabling the General Partner to execute, acknowledge, and file any instrument or document necessary to effect such substitution.

<u>21. Indemnification</u>

21.1 The Partnership, its receiver, or its trustee shall indemnify, save harmless, and pay all judgments and claims against the General Partner, from any liability or damage incurred by reason of any act performed or omitted to be performed by it in connection with the business of the Partnership, including attorneys' fees incurred by it in connection with the defense of any action based on any such act or omission, which attorneys' fees may be paid as incurred, including all such liabilities under Federal and State Securities Acts (including the Securities Act of 1933) as permitted by law. If a claim for indemnification (other than for expenses incurred in a successful defense, which expenses shall be reimbursed forthwith) is asserted against the Partnership by the General Partner under this Partnership Agreement or otherwise, the Partnership will, unless in the opinion of its counsel the matter has been settled by controlling precedent, submit to a court of appropriate jurisdiction the question whether such indemnification by it is against public policy and will be governed by the final adjudication of such issue.

21.2 In the event of any action by a Holder against the General Partner, including a Partnership derivative suit, the Partnership will indemnify, save harmless, and pay all expenses of the General Partner including attorneys' fees incurred in the defense of said action, in accordance with paragraph 21.1, above.

21.3 Notwithstanding the provisions of Paragraph 21.1 and 21.2, the

General Partner shall not be relieved from any liability imposed by law, including liability for fraud, bad faith, willful neglect, or negligence. All judgments against the Partnership and the General Partner, wherein the General Partner is entitled to indemnification, must first be satisfied from Partnership assets before the General Partner is responsible for these objectives.

21.4 The General Partner shall have the right and authority to require in all Partnership contracts that he will not be personally liable thereon and that the person or entity contracting with the Partnership is to look solely to the Partnership and its assets for satisfaction.

22. Miscellaneous

22.1 This Partnership Agreement may be executed in several counterparts and all so executed shall constitute one Partnership Agreement, binding on all of the parties hereto, notwithstanding that all of the parties are not signatory to the original or the same counterpart.

22.2 The terms and provisions of this Partnership Agreement shall be binding upon and shall inure to the benefit of the successors and assigns of the respective Partners.

22.3 In the event any sentence or paragraph of the Partnership Agreement is declared by a court of competent jurisdiction to be void, such sentence or paragraph shall be deemed severed from the remainder of the Partnership Agreement and the balance of the Partnership Agreement shall remain in effect.

22.4 All notices under this Partnership Agreement shall be in writing and shall be given to the Holder entitled thereto, by personal service or by mail, posted to the address maintained by the Partnership for such person or at such other address as he may specify in writing.

22.5 Paragraph titles or captions contained in this Partnership Agreement are inserted only as a matter of convenience and for reference. Such titles and captions in no way define, limit, extend, or describe the scope of this Partnership Agreement nor the intent of any provision hereof.

22.6 Whenever required by the context hereof, the singular shall include the plural, and vice versa; the masculine gender shall include the feminine and neuter genders, and vice versa; and the word "person" shall include a corporation, partnership, firm, or other form of association.

22.7 The name and address of the General Partner is:

____________________________

____________________________

____________________________

22.8 The names, addresses, and capital contributions of the Limited

Partners are set forth on Exhibit I attached hereto, which exhibit shall be maintained at the principal place of business of the Partnership.

22.9 Each undersigned Limited Partner does, by execution hereof, appoint and constitute the General Partner, his attorney-in-fact for the purposes and with all of the powers and authority set forth in Paragraph 20 hereof.

22.10 The Signature page of the Agreement may be executed in multiple counterparts by the several Limited Partners; each counterpart, when executed by at least one Limited Partner and the General Partner, shall become a part of this Partnership Agreement, shall constitute one agreement, and shall be binding on all Limited Partners so executing, notwithstanding that all parties are not signatories of the original of the same counterpart.

Dated: General Partner

______________________, 19____ By______________________

Limited Partner

______________________, 19____ ______________________

STATE OF )
)SS:
COUNTY OF )

The Foregoing was acknowledged before me by ______________________
______________________, Limited Partner, this ______ day of ____________,
19____.

______________________

Notary Public
My Commission expires: ____________

STATE OF )
) SS:
COUNTY OF )

The Foregoing was acknowledged before me by ______________________
______________________, officer of General Partner, this ______ day of
____________, 19____.

______________________

Notary Public ____________
My Commission expires: ____________

The foregoing document offering 35 units of the ABC Limited Partnership to investors are typical nuclear ingredients of a legitimate private offering meeting the full requirements of the Securities and Exchange Commission. Similar documents (and the appropriate exhibits) are used to interest potential investors in the many thousands of privately placed syndications offered each year in the United States. The offering is quite conservative in nature. Like other offerings meeting the SEC's requirements for full disclosure, it is hedged with warnings of risk, liability, and uncertainties about tax consequences. Yet it can be effectively used as a norm against other offerings or syndication documents.

Syndications in the real estate industry were born of economic necessity arising from fluctuating interest rates and decreasing loan-to-value ratios. Given their relative newness, they are now with us in a highly sophisticated form and promise to blossom even more profusely in the future. Without question, many offerings, both public and private, are being mismanaged and manipulated by syndicators to achieve questionable purposes and produce exorbitant profits. Our purpose has been to examine the positive aspects of syndications mutually beneficial to all partners. In the final chapter we will explore the proposals to regulate abusive syndication activity, particularly in the realm of tax-shelter offerings.

# 18

## The IRS Crackdown on Abusive Tax Shelters

Over the past decade, creation of tax shelters has been refined into an art whose effects are highly visible in today's economy. Given the present business climate, the real estate field, like so many other industries, has actively participated in pursuing elusive tax advantages so successfully that it has become the focal point of attention. Critics have charged, for example, that tax shelters in real estate syndications now account for twice the investment dollars formerly put into once-popular gas and oil offerings.

To put matters in perspective, public sales of real estate tax-shelter partnerships were estimated at approximately $100 million in 1971. As of 1980, this figure was approaching $1 billion, rising to $2.7 billion in 1982, and estimated to increase to over $4 billion in 1984. In addition to the public partnerships registered with the Securities and Exchange Commission in 1982, the private offerings, which are generally the subject matter of this book, were estimated to account for another $8 billion to $10 billion during the same year.

The 1981 Tax Reform Act significantly stimulated the real estate industry, leading to staggering tax implications. The effects of these changes alone are anticipated to have cost the U.S. Treasury in excess of $4 billion for the fiscal year ending September 30, 1984, and more than $10 billion for the fiscal year ending September 30, 1986. Given the current attitude on Capitol Hill and in the administration relative to methods for reducing the huge federal budget deficit, real estate tax shelters are a tempting quarry. As evidence of this, the Chairman of the House Ways and Means Committee, which is the principal tax-writing committee in Congress, predicted that the 15-year depreciation rule brought into the Code in 1981 might be one of the major targets of those who want to eliminate some of the substantive 1981 business tax incentives. Chairman Dan Rostenkowski indicated that rolling back this depreciable life from 15 to 20 years "is an option on a lot of lists." In fact, as we noted earlier, the Tax Reform Act of 1984 struck a compromise at 18 years.

Statistics regarding the dollar magnitude of the industry fail to convey the entire picture. The administration, Congress, the Treasury, and the Internal Revenue Service are all clearly concerned about the widespread proliferation of these "abusive" tax shelters during the past ten years. Statistics reveal that in 1973, when the IRS initiated its current tax-shelter program, 400 cases were under examination at the audit level. More than a decade later the IRS informs us that 325,000 tax shelter cases are under examination. At its current completion rate of about 70,000 examinations annually, four years would be required for IRS processing, assuming no new cases were added to the workload.

IRS auditing is only the initial step. Over the years individuals have taken their tax-shelter cases beyond the audit stage and into litigation, which has created significant problems in the administration of justice in the U.S. Tax Court. Currently this court has 58,000 income-tax cases pending, of which 18,000 are tax-shelter cases. According to the IRS, the lawyers for taxpayers are fighting these cases in many situations only to delay payment of large deficiencies.

By IRS definition, an abusive tax shelter is a promotional scheme involving transactions with little or no economic reality or substance, evidenced by inflated appraisals, excessive use of leverage, and unrealistic allocations of tax losses in which the claimed tax benefits are disproportionate to the economic benefits. In the opinion of the IRS, they are entered into solely to evade taxes, with little or no regard for a positive financial outcome.

Given the backdrop of these prevalent attitudes, it becomes imperative to analyze the probable future of the real estate tax-shelter industry. To examine this subject, we must first analyze what the Administration, the Congress, the Treasury, and the Internal Revenue

Service are currently considering. We will then offer a limited amount of speculation as to what we believe the future will bring for the industry

## HOW THE IRS IS PREVENTING ABUSIVE TAX SHELTERS

At the annual meeting of the American Institute of Certified Public Accountants held on October 4, 1983, the Commissioner of Internal Revenue, Roscoe L. Egger, Jr., unveiled a nationwide "coordinated field attack" designed to prevent abusive tax shelters in advance of syndication. This new program uses certain weapons against the promoters of abusive tax shelters that were added by the Tax Equity and Fiscal Responsibility Act of 1982 and enlarged by the Tax Reform Act of 1984. Specifically the promoter penalty under Section 6700 of the Code and the injunction provisions given to the IRS under Section 7408 permit the IRS to seek legal remedy by enjoining a promoter from further involvement in shelter activities. The field attack also adopts a rather novel technique that has become known as "prefiling letters." In advance of the syndication when an abusive tax shelter is suspected, letters are sent to the investors notifying or advising them that certain claims, deductions, and/or credits on federal income-tax returns will be scrutinized, the returns will be audited, and the deductions and/or credits potentially disallowed.

This "coordinated field attack" of 1983 was by no means the first stepped-up effort of the IRS. Ten years earlier the IRS initiated a coordinated program to examine the potentially abusive oil and gas industry schemes. Over the years, this program was expanded to cover tax-shelter promotions in the areas of real estate, cinema activities, and farming. Accompanying this was a campaign for legislation limiting the taxpayer's deduction of tax losses from an activity to the amount for which the taxpayer has actual risk or potential economic loss. All of this culminated in the addition of the so-called "at risk" provisions of the Code brought about by the Tax Reform Act of 1976. These at-risk provisions did not basically affect real estate tax shelters if they were appropriately structured.

Additional legislation was also enacted aimed strictly at curbing tax-shelter abuses. The Economic Recovery Tax Act of 1981 added penalties for evaluation overstatements and also amended Code Section 6654 to put more teeth in the negligence penalty. The Tax and Fiscal

Responsibility Act of 1982 provided the IRS with two additional new weapons, the first of which involves the promoter penalty:

1. As a result of the 1982 act, Section 6700 provides that a penalty of $1,000 or 10% of the gross income, whichever is greater, can be assessed against anyone who organizes, assists in the organization of, or participates in the sale of an interest in a partnership or any other plan or arrangement that has, or purports to have, an effect on federal-tax liability. The penalty is assessable only if the promoter makes a statement concerning the tax benefit of the offering and knows, or has reason to know, that the statement was false or fraudulent, or where the promoter makes a gross valuation overstatement. The Tax Reform Act of 1984 raised the ante by increasing the penalty from 10% to 20%.
2. The second provision of the act is implemented in Section 7408, which allows a civil action to be brought seeking to prohibit a promoter of an abusive tax shelter from further involvement in the promotion of any other abusive tax-shelter activity. Injunctive relief may be granted against any person found to be engaging in this type of conduct subject to the promoter penalty discussed herein, where an injunction is appropriate to prevent further violations. The Tax Reform Act of 1984 expanded this injunctive relief to cover individuals who aid and abet an understatement of tax liability.

This second section of the Internal Revenue Code has far-reaching ramifications in that it is one of the few areas of the tax code that gives the IRS the authority to attack a problem prior to the filing of a tax return. Departing from the historic approach of having to wait until the taxpayers have filed their returns claiming substantial tax benefits, the program, aimed at halting tax abuses before they are initiated, involves a front-end attack on both promoters and investors.

## HOW THE IRS IMPLEMENTS THE TAX-ABUSIVE STRATEGY

The first step in implementing the new IRS strategy is to identify the shelters that are considered abusive. To accomplish this, each IRS district now has a coordinator responsible for gathering information on tax shelters currently being promoted by means of leads obtained from federal, state, and local information agencies, other IRS investigations, and trade magazines and newspapers. Additionally, the IRS hopes to obtain information and assistance from lawyers, accountants, and other professionals who are knowledgeable individuals in these abusive tax-shelter programs. Once a tax shelter has been identified as abusive, the IRS will notify the promoter that his or her offering is the subject of an investigation that may lead to

- the imposition of the promoter penalty;
- injunctive relief prohibiting further promotion of the shelter, and
- the issuance of prefiling notification letters to investors.

The promoter will also be served with a list of documents to be submitted to the IRS within a ten-day period and will be advised that a summons may be issued if he or she fails to adequately provide such information.

Procedurally, the next step is for the IRS to schedule a meeting with the promoter of the supposedly abusive tax shelter, where one's case is presented to support the consistency of the tax benefits claimed with existing tax laws. The promoter has no administrative alternative to this confrontation. Upon its completion, the IRS decides whether or not to proceed with the assertion of the penalty against the promoter, whether injunctive relief is appropriate, and whether prefiling notices should be sent to the investors.

Since the prefiling letters sent to investors constituted such a novel departure from normal IRS practices, this procedure was tested on a limited basis before the program was adopted nationwide in the fall of 1983. A challenge to the notice procedure was rejected by the courts, which ruled that this practice falls within the broad discretion of the Treasury Department in adopting enforcement techniques. The prefiling letters are apparently here to stay, however repugnant they may be to promoters.

Continuing with its front-end attack, the IRS announced in January of 1984 that it was adopting new and tougher policies on pre-1981 tax-shelter cases in an attempt to reduce the mounting backlog to be handled by its administrators and the courts. The IRS will withdraw its administrative settlement offer, generally made in 1982, which allows investors to deduct first year out-of-pocket expenses attributable to investment tax shelters—that is, allow a deduction for the amount of the investment and disallow deductions arising from, for example, nonrecourse obligations. This withdrawal reflects the conclusion drawn by the IRS that this offer had not been effective in encouraging settlements and reducing legal caseloads. Now the inventory of IRS cases will be examined and grouped according to litigation potential, similarity of issue, and geographical location. By packaging a group of cases as a unit, the IRS will notify investors of the planned withdrawal of the out-of-pocket expense offer and of the Agency's intention to issue a statutory notice of deficiency and proceed to the tax court.

## HOW TREASURY ACTIVITIES AFFECT TAX-ABUSIVE OFFERINGS

In addition to the IRS concentration on abusive tax shelters, the Treasury Department has also been actively involved with the situation. In September of 1980 it issued proposed rules relating to the standards of practice before the Internal Revenue Service with respect to tax-shelter opinions, revising these proposed amendments to Circular 230 on December 15, 1982. Concurrent with this activity, the Committee on Ethics and Professional Responsibility of the American Bar Association issued Formal Opinion 346 expressing a preferred norm of proper professional conduct for lawyers who issue tax-shelter opinions. In this effort to regulate itself and perhaps avoid harsher federal regulation, the American Bar Association demonstrated that its position did not vary substantially from that of the Treasury Department.

By way of background, Circular 230 was originally proposed because the IRS perceived that many abusive tax shelters "depend for their successful marketing on the participation of professional tax advisors" and decided that it would be appropriate to explore the ethical and legal standards governing participation by those professional advisors. The original 1980 proposal would have charged a tax advisor with violation of the proposed regulations unless he or she concluded his or her opinion with the statement that "it is more likely than not that the bulk of the tax benefits on the basis of which the shelter has been promoted are allowable under the tax laws." It also required the advisor to exercise due diligence to assure that his or her opinion fully and fairly discloses the facts bearing significantly on each important federal tax aspect. Unless professionally inappropriate, his or her conclusion was to anticipate the likely tax audit outcome and verify that the tax portion of the offering material accurately described his or her opinion. Any violation of the 1980 proposal would have entailed disbarment or suspension from practice before the Internal Revenue Service.

The organized bar reacted immediately and vociferously to the

1980 proposal, subsequently generating ABA Formal Opinion 346. This states that a legal opinion on a tax-shelter promotion should, where possible, provide an overall evaluation of the extent to which the aggregate tax benefits are a significant feature of the investment and to what degree they are likely to be realized as contemplated by the offering materials. The opinion also permits the advisor to state that such tax benefits

- probably will be realized; or
- probably will not be realized;
- are equally likely to be realized or not; or
- in rare instances, that it cannot be predicted whether they are likely to be realized.

If the tax advisor's opinion is negative, its nature must be clearly stated and prominently noted in the offering materials.

Circular 230 as finally adopted, which was effective for opinions rendered after May 23, 1984, adopts in large part the guidelines set forth in Opinion 346. For example, under both, the professional advisor has a duty to review the facts necessary to issue a tax opinion and to discuss all material tax issues of the offering. Both also require that the tax practitioner render an opinion as to the outcome of each material tax issue if the issue is raised and litigated, unless inappropriate to the circumstances. Exceptions might involve, for example, a situation where the facts necessary for a proper opinion are not yet in existence or are unknown, or where the tax law surrounding the particular issue is unclear.

Opinion 346 and Circular 230 agree in defining a tax shelter as an investment where the deductions derived from the offering exceed the income therefrom or where the tax credits derived exceed the tax attributable to income from the investment. In either case, real estate syndications would not be excluded when tax benefits exceed the anticipated income from the property. Both also agree in defining a tax-shelter opinion as any advice relating to the federal-tax aspects of an offering that is referred to in the promotional material. Under this definition, the mere preparation of the tax-risk-factors section of an offering circular would be deemed an opinion regardless of whether or not the advisor rendered a separate tax opinion. On the other hand, a counselor who renders advice directly to the promoter of a tax shelter would not be liable for penalties provided that advice is not referred to in the offering materials or that the tax attorney does not prepare or become involved in the tax discussion of the offering circular.

## CONGRESSIONAL ACTIVITIES ON ABUSIVE OFFERINGS—THE TAX REFORM ACT OF 1984

As we indicated at the outset of this chapter, the uses and abuses of tax shelters are of great concern in today's political atmosphere of huge governmental budget deficits. Created as an incentive to industry, tax deductions have served their purpose well and, for the most part, legitimately. Yet, their effects on an industry as highly visible as real estate are bound to serve as a political temptation to Congress, especially since the so-called abusive areas have been identified.

We can only hope that corrective legislation is indeed intended and is limited to abusive situations and that Congress chooses not to throw out the baby with the bath water. Repeal or even a modest reduction of tax benefits could seriously undermine the real estate industry and threaten the clear economic benefits, including the increased employment, inherent in its vitality.

More than likely, Congress will continue to refine the taxpayer-compliance aspects of abusive tax shelters. The Tax Reform Act of 1984 enacted by Congress is an example of this approach and contains several provisions that purport to strengthen taxpayer compliance:

1. Under this Act, a promoter of a syndication selling directly to investors would be required to register the promotion with the IRS and to compile and maintain a "customer list" that may be examined by the Internal Revenue Service. Failure to maintain such a list would subject the promoter to penalties comparable to those imposed on income-tax-return preparers.
2. Another provision is designed to help reduce the tax-shelter cases under administrative examination by the IRS. The otherwise applicable interest rate will be increased by 120% with respect to substantial underpayments attributable to tax-motivated transactions, meaning that a taxpayer motivated by a desire to evade or avoid federal income taxes will have to pay a higher rate of interest if he or she is found to have underpaid his or her tax obligation.
3. The present penalty for promoting abusive tax shelters has been

doubled from 10% to 20% of gross income derived from the activity. The report of the Conference Committee indicates recognition of the fact that promoters of tax shelters operate on large profit margins and the belief that $2,000 or 20% of the gross income derived would reflect a penalty more in keeping with the nature of the offense.

The foregoing are just a few of the recent legislative steps taken by Congress, and the number will inevitably swell. Preliminary results of legislative and administrative attempts to thwart abusive tax shelters indicate some degree of success. The basic goal of the IRS as well as Congress appears to be to cleanse the system of heavily tax-oriented transactions lacking economic substance without eliminating economically viable, legitimate real estate tax-shelter offerings. We believe, nonetheless, that dramatic changes in the area of real estate tax syndication will occur during the remainder of this decade.

The American Bar Association's response was immediate and vigorous when the Treasury initially issued Circular 230. When the ABA shortly thereafter issued Opinion 346, which materially lightened the regulation of the original Circular 230 proposal, the Treasury largely backed off from its position and aligned itself with that of the ABA. This example indicates at the very least that the real estate syndication industry should begin to do some of its own soul searching. If the profession is not to be legislated out of existence or profit, we believe that the various trade associations within the industry should take note of its problems and seriously consider a certain degree of self-regulation.

## RONALD REAGAN ADMINISTRATION'S TAX SIMPLIFICATION PROPOSALS

The Treasury Department under the Reagan Administration, as well as both houses of Congress, in an apparent attempt to deal with the massive deficits of the federal government, have individually advanced proposals to be categorized as the Tax Simplification Plan. If enacted in whole or in part, this will have a major effect on the economics and the viability of tax-sheltered real estate-oriented syndications. Currently there are three proposals that are being advanced: the Treasury proposal, put forth by Secretary Donald Regan; the House version advocated by Representatives Bill Bradley of New Jersey and Richard Gephardt of Missouri; and the Senate bill sponsored by Senator Robert Kasten of Wisconsin and Representative Jack Kemp of New York.

The consensus of all three proposals is that the tax simplification plan will not raise substantial or additional revenues for the Treasury, but will simplify the complicated current system, which involves 13 individual tax brackets. The concept would substantially reduce their number, thus eliminating in many respects the artificial tax losses that many high-tax-bracket individuals are so accustomed to generating as an offset against their ordinary taxable income. The general proposal is designed to redistribute the overall taxable income obligations to lower tax brackets by reducing the maximum tax bracket for individuals from 50% to 30–35%, depending upon which proposal eventually filters into the IRS regulations.

By restructuring many of the major deductions for accelerated depreciation, eliminating capital gains treatment, and substantially reducing the maximum individual tax bracket, it is argued that the system or tax code will become simplified, producing a comparable net revenue result to the U.S. Treasury.

## CONCEPTS BEHIND TAX SIMPLIFICATION LEGISLATION

The Treasury proposal argues that the substantial growth in the tax shelter industry, and in many respects in the real estate syndication field, has played a major role in the erosion of the federal income tax base, particularly among affluent taxpayers. It is estimated that more than $30 billion a year is exempt from individual taxation due to the excessive tax-shelter opportunities readily available to high income individuals. Roughly 80% of the total partnership losses claimed by tax-sheltered returns filed by individuals, a figure in excess of $25 billion annually, were reported by those with gross incomes before tax losses of $100,000 or more, and that 60%, or over $21 billion, were reported by taxpayers with gross incomes before losses in excess of $250,000. This would be the most likely group to be most affected by the tax simplification legislation if it is eventually enacted.

One measurement of the current tax-shelter activity is reflected in the fact that between 1962 and 1982 the estimated number of taxpayers claiming partnership losses increased almost fivefold to over 2 million individuals. By comparison, the aggregate number of tax returns filed during that same period increased by less than half. Of these partnership returns that were filed showing net losses for tax purposes, over 50% were concentrated in the oil, gas, and mining industries, through farming ventures, and in the real estate syndication field. Most of these industries benefit substantially from opportunities created by a combination of deferred taxes, preferential treatment of long-term capital gains, and the unquestioned deductibility of interest. The tax deferral aspect surfaces when investors are in a position to accelerate deductions or defer their reportable income. Opportunities for such deferral in real estate syndications are achieved through depreciation rules that permit tax deductions in excess of economic depreciation generally front-loaded during the early years of a partnership offering.

Another important feature gained through tax-sheltered syndications is the conversion of ordinary income into that of tax-preferred capital gains. Tax deferral in this situation occurs when accelerated depeciation deductions are used to offset ordinary income, and where a major portion of the projected return on equity in the syndicated investment is realized and recognized on a long-term capital gains basis, taxed at a preferential tax rate. When these conditions exist in a syndication, that is, the taxation of income from a real estate asset which can be deferred or converted into tax-preferred income, investors then generally need to finance the acquisition of a syndicated holding through the vehicle of leverage, thus permitting an additional interest-related tax arbitrage. This arbitrage situation transpires when borrowed funds, the interest being fully deductible, are used to purchase the investments which earn either partially or entirely tax-exempt or tax-deferred income. These major tax advantages as they apply to affluent high-tax-bracket investors are applied to and often exempt other income from taxation.

The reasoning behind the Tax Simplication Act is that these tax-shelter-oriented real estate syndications are undesirable primarily because preferential tax treatment interferes with the market-determined allocation of resources, and artificially provides benefits to syndicated investors through these tax-sheltered ventures. This is basically the thrust behind the tax simplification proposals, even though they will not produce additional overall tax revenues to the United States Treasury. Elimination of the tax shelter provisions, however, will have a significant deficit reduction impact.

## MAJOR PROVISIONS OF THE TAX SIMPLIFICATION PROPOSALS

A partial motivation behind tax simplification is that the proliferation of tax-sheltered vehicles consumes valuable time of the IRS that could be devoted to other more productive auditing areas. It also complicates the auditing procedure, as these tax-sheltered syndications have a tendency to be confused or commingled with legitimate tax shelters, making it more difficult for the IRS to identify and audit these tax-abusive vehicles. The Treasury Department also reasons that lower and middle income taxpayers generally cannot benefit from these syndicated tax shelters, as they have neither the expertise nor the fiscal ability to be actively involved in investments that seldom provide an initial or substantial cash return on equity.

The majority of the Treasury Department's proposals and those of both houses of Congress generally relate to:

- lower individual tax rates;
- lower corporate tax rates;
- taxation of capital gains as ordinary income, coupled with an indexing feature;
- depreciation allowances that are realistic and determined in light of economic conditions;
- disallowance of most interest expense, with exception for mortgage interest on primary residences;
- matching expenses and receipts from multi-period production; and
- tax treatment of certain large partnerships as corporations.

The Accelerated Cost Recovery System (ACRS), which was incorporated into the 1981 tax bill, has had a major effect on the amount of the deductions that syndications have taken. It is anticipated that the elimination of the ACRS under tax simplification would materially affect syndications; depreciation deductions are an extremely important aspect of real estate offerings, especially in the initial years of a project where investor capital contributions can be staged. The benefits to investors in tax-oriented syndications could be substantially reduced by the eradication of this beneficial aspect.

The elimination of the ACRS could be softened somewhat, as the tax simplification plan calls for a maximum personal income tax in the range of 30% in contrast to the current ceiling of 50%. Changing this particular benefit could have a substantially larger effect on individuals with extensive amounts of income.

If the Treasury Department tightens the interest limitation rules, individuals would not be allowed deductions for interest expense in excess of the passive investment income that they receive. The proposal calls for this passive investment income to be inclusive of partnership interests, sole proprietorships, and Subchapter S corporations. The only possible exception would be for mortgage interest on one's primary principal residence. This is not expected to apply to the deduction of interest incurred in the conduct of one's trade or business. The proposed limitation on interest expense deductions would reduce the extent to which high-tax-bracket investors might engage in tax-motivated borrowing. If enacted, this would have a substantial effect on the amount of borrowed funds and corresponding investor equity that would be required in real estate syndications. This provision of the Tax Simplification Act, if enacted, could substantially alter the after-tax yields that syndications would have to offer.

The tax simplification proposal is also attempting to reduce the maximum individual tax bracket from 50% to about 30%. If this is accomplished, it will have a tendency to downplay or minimize the artificial tax advantages that are such an integral part of real estate syndications. If in fact the maximum tax bracket is substantially lowered, many real estate ventures will have to show a substantial cash flow providing a realistic and predictable return to the investors in order to offset the elimination of the major tax advantages currently offered in most syndications. This aspect, combined with the elimination of the ACRS, will have a major effect on the economics of syndicated projects, and will require that they compete directly with other forms of non-tax-sheltered investments. Real estate syndications after tax simplification will have to rely on cash flow and appreciation through the inflationary process to make real estate syndicatons viable. Future offerings will not be as leveraged if the major provisions of the Tax Simplification Bill are enacted, and substantially larger equities required up front, showing a positive cash-on-cash return, will be the wave of the future.

## HOW SIMPLIFICATION WILL AFFECT CAPITAL GAINS AND ITC

Another aspect of the tax simplification proposal is the elimination of the investment tax credit that was an important aspect of the 1981 tax law. Any syndicated real estate investors who are contemplating taking advantage of the investment tax credit should adjust their projections based upon the potential elimination of the ITC. Other tax-sheltered investments, specifically those with fixtures or equipment, will probably be more affected than the real estate syndications if the ITC is eliminated. However, in certain real estate investments the ITC deductions can be substantial, and its elimination could materially affect these investments, primarily in the initial years. It is conceivable that the elimination of the investment tax credit and the ACRS, if enacted, will be phased into law over a period of time, thereby minimizing its detrimental effects.

Another proposal under consideration in the tax simplification bill is the elimination of the preferential long-term capital gains treatment. Several concepts are being advanced, ranging from the total elimination of the preferential capital gains treatment to a plan that indexes the basis of capital gains with levels of inflation. The concept is to tax the gain on the sale of a real estate syndicated asset at an ordinary income level, and not at the preferred capital gains rate, with the possibility of allowing an adjusted deduction from the calculated gain based upon the rate of inflation during the holding period of the asset. If the preferential treatment on capital gains is eliminated, it could have a substantial effect on syndicated investments, especially in areas where long-term appreciation is a major contributing factor. Elimination of preferential capital gains treatment could be partially offset by the proposed drop in the maximum personal income tax rate from 50% to 30%. The reduction of maximum tax brackets would obviously reduce the detrimental effects caused by the elimination of the preferential treatment of capital gains on the taxable proceeds of sale.

The entire concept of the tax simplification package that reduces tax brackets across the board, substantially broadening the tax base, is a plan that will be discussed for many months within the Executive Branch, both houses of Congress, and among Treasury Department officials. It appears that in this battle many influential special interest groups will surface, and given the concept that the Tax Simplification Act will not generate additional monies to the Treasury, quick passage is unlikely, especially in light of the significant deficits that are currently being incurred by the federal government. However, due to the significant nature of the tax simplification program, it is extremely important to bear in mind the overall ramifications of this potential legislation, as it will significantly affect your tax-oriented syndications.

# Glossary

*Abusive tax shelter.* By definition of the Internal Revenue Service, a promotional scheme involving transactions with little or no economic reality or substance, evidenced by inflated allocations of tax losses in which the claimed tax benefits are disproportionate to the economic benefits of the investment.

*Accredited investor.* One meeting the financial suitability requirements of a syndication.

*Accrual accounting.* A method of keeping financial records whereby income and expenses are reported when obligations become due and not when cash is actually received or disbursed.

*ACRS (Accelerated cost recovery system).* A method of calculating depreciation for assets placed in service after December 31, 1980, established by the Economic Recovery Tax Act of 1981. Under this system, real property can be depreciated over 15 years.

*Advance ruling.* A nonbinding pronouncement by the Internal Revenue Service.

*Alternative minimum tax.* The minimum rate (20%) that investors in high tax brackets are required to pay, regardless of the tax shelters inherent in their investment portfolios.

*Asset management.* Supervision of the financial affairs of a group of partners, such as a syndication, as opposed to management of the physical properties owned by those partners.

*Assignee of record.* One acquiring beneficial interest in a partnership who is not formally a partner.

*Association.* By legal definition, a corporation subject to taxation at the entity or corporate level.

*At-risk provisions.* A term relating to and measuring the equity and mortgage exposure an investor has in a highly leveraged situation. The total amount of the at-risk funds puts a ceiling on the investor's total tax deductions that can be taken over the life of an investment.

*Back-end fees.* The compensation a general partner receives when a syndication is terminated, consisting potentially of such items as brokerage commissions and profit-sharing bonuses.

*Balloon mortgage payment.* A method of debt reduction that provides for systematic payments that do not fully amortize the loan over the committed period. A final lump sum payment is called upon prior to full amortization.

*Best-efforts offering.* An investment proposal in which an individual offers to raise the required equity for purchase of an asset, without a guarantee.

*Blind-pool syndications.* Investments in which the managing general partner has unilateral discretion in use of the funds, which are normally invested first in safe, high-yielding securities and later in real estate holdings.

*Blue-sky laws.* State legislation specifically regulating securities transactions.

*Book value.* The value of a real estate investment as reflected in the accounting records of the owner, not the fair-market value. Book value reflects the cost of the asset less the accrued depreciation.

*Broker.* As defined by the Securities Exchange Act of 1934, a person "engaged in the business of effecting transactions in securities for the account of others."

*Brokerage commission.* A fee payable to an agent who sells a property, generally amounting to a percentage of the value of the asset, usually set at a maximum of 6 percent.

*Cash accounting.* A method of keeping financial records in which income and expenses are entered as they are incurred, as opposed to accrual accounting.

*Cash-on-cash return.* The return on invested equity after operating expenses and debt service obligations.

*Certificate of limited partnership.* An abridged version of the partnership agreement filed in a recording office where partnership records are maintained.

*Churning.* Excessive trading of a customer's account by a broker or dealer, specifically prohibited by the National Association of Securities Dealers' guidelines.

*Consolidated tax return.* The joint return of a parent and a subsidiary company in which allotments of income and credits are reconciled between the two.

*Continuity of life.* A characteristic of a corporation, determined legally and not by a fixed date of termination.

*Corporation.* A publicly registered legal entity usually consisting of not less than three stockholders and a board of directors elected by them that allows for free transferability of shares, limited investor liability, and centralized management.

*Cost-of-living indexes.* A measurement of the average amount of money spent by consumers to acquire a predetermined list of goods and services. The index uses a base year as 100, as compiled by the U.S. Department of Labor.

*Dealer.* An individual who acquires real estate holdings as a full-time profession, therefore not qualifying for capital gains treatment on property used in the course of business.

*Debt service ratio.* Percentage of financial leverage to equity invested in a real estate asset.

*Direct Participation Program.* An educational course and license offered by the National Association of Securities Dealers. Successful completion entitles a participant who is a member of a real estate brokerage firm to market real estate syndications.

*Dissolution* The termination of authority of any partner or officer to act for the partnership or corporate entity. A notice of dissolution should be published.

*Distributive shares.* That portion of a syndication's income, gain, loss, deduction, credit, and items of tax preference allocated to a participating investor.

*Economy Recovery Tax Act of 1981.* Legislation substantially affecting depreciable building lives, investment tax credits, and the writeoffs obtained on older investment properties.

*Encumbrance.* Right, claim, or lien against a real estate holding, usually taking the form of a first mortgage.

*Equity build-up.* Regularly scheduled principal payoff of mortgage encumbrances.

*Equity interest.* Profit-sharing status in a syndication as opposed to fee-type compensation.

*Escalation clauses.* Provisions in leases or other agreements for increasing compensation to reflect decreased purchasing power of currency attributed to inflation.

*Exclusive intrastate exemption.* A provision of the Securities Exchange Act of 1934 exempting all issuers of securities except investment companies from registration when operations are conducted within one state or territory.

*Fair-market value.* The resale value an asset will command in a current market, as opposed to its book value.

*Fiduciary capacity.* The responsibility of the trustee of a syndication (corporate officer, general partner, and the like) to perform acts in the investors' best interests.

*Financing fee.* An assessment for arranging mortgage financing generally calculated as a percentage of the funds raised.

*Fiscal year.* The business year in which a syndication conducts activities, which may or may not correspond to the calendar year.

*Floating interest rates.* Financial interest charges for reducing a debt that rise or fall based upon the bank's cost of funds.

*Gap financing.* An additional loan obtained by a developer when the interim commitment is not sufficient to complete a project. This mortgage is normally short-term, and is repaid either from the permanent financing or from the proceeds of sale.

*General partnership.* An agreement among two or more investors to share their equity, skills, profits, and losses in a venture, with each member having a voice in its management.

*Gross income.* The total amount of funds received from a property, calculated prior to operating expenses, depreciation, and mortgage payments.

*HUD (Department of Housing and Urban Development).* An agency of the U.S. government specifically involved with urban renewal, low-income or subsidized housing, and other residential or commercial mortgage guarantees.

*Indemnification provision.* Assurance absolving the general partner from liability and loss provided in the limited-partnership agreement.

*Integrated offering.* A multifaceted investment backed by a single financial plan.

*Investor suitability requirements.* The financial standards an investor must meet to qualify for participation in a syndication. These qualifications are dictated by securities legislation to ensure that the illiquidity of an asset does not cause hardship to an investor.

*IRA (Independent Retirement Account).* A personal pension fund established with untaxed contributions that are normally subject to lower taxation when the contributor withdraws them at retirement.

*Joint venture.* An agreement among two or more individuals to pool their funds and skills in a project or development, sharing profits equally or at a predetermined level.

*Leaseback.* An arrangement by which the seller of a property leases it from the buyer, thereby subsidizing the rentals or providing management in exchange for receiving the selling price.

*Leverage.* A concept of utilizing borrowed funds when acquiring investment or residential real estate, where one achieves the maximum return and tax-shelter benefits with a minimum amount of personal equity funds.

*Limited partner.* An equity investor in a limited partnership who has minimum say in its management, shares profits and tax advantages, and is liable for its indebtedness only to the extent of his or her equity contribution.

*Limited partnership.* An entity not taxable at the corporate level, consisting of one or more general partners and one or more limited partners, each contributing equity or managerial skill, to share prorated profits and losses in a venture under the autonomous management of the general partner(s).

*Limited representative license.* A permit to market private real estate syndications, available to a member of a real estate brokerage firm who successfully completes the Direct Participation Program offered by the National Association of Securities Dealers.

*Liquidity restrictions.* Prohibitions against resale of units or shares, particularly applicable to limited partners' interests in syndications.

*Loan-to-value ratio.* A method of expressing the degree of financial leverage in which the outstanding mortgage amount is stated in terms of the appraised or market value of the property.

*Management fee.* Compensation for supervising the operation of a property or for overseeing the affairs of a syndication, usually payable to the general partner of a syndication or his or her agents.

*Market feasibility study.* An analysis based upon census reports and other demographic statistics to determine the need for a real estate venture within a given locality or region.

*Mortgage amortization.* The contractual period of time it takes to pay off the principal on a mortgage on an equal installment basis.

*Mortgage constant.* The amount of funds needed to repay the annual interest and principal on a mortgage. Normally this is expressed on a basis of constant dollars-per-thousand of the mortgage obligation.

*Multiclass syndication.* An arrangement by which the benefits, rewards, and risks of an offering are stratified so that the needs of various classes of investors are met in the form of cash flow, tax benefits, and appreciation potential.

*NASAA.* The North American Securities Administrators Association.

*NASD (National Association of Securities Dealers).* A self-regulatory agency of the securities industry, which is the only national association registered with the Securities and Exchange Commission. All brokers and dealers must belong and follow its rules, regulations, and guidelines.

*Offering statement.* A written document describing securities or partnership shares in a real estate syndication being offered for sale; a prospectus.

*Origination phase.* The first of three distinct periods in a syndication's life, beginning with its conception, continuing with its operation, and lasting through the disposition stage.

*Partnership.* As defined by the 1914 Uniform Partnership Act, "an association of two or more persons to carry on as co-owners, a business for profit"; for federal income-tax purposes, a group of two or more investors including "a syndicate, group, pool, joint venture, or other unincorporated organization through or by means of which any business, financial operation, or venture is carried on, and which is not . . . a corporation or a trust or estate."

*Partnership agreement.* The basic document defining the membership and business arrangements of a partnership.

*Prefiling letters.* A system initiated by the Tax Equity and Fiscal Responsibility Act of 1982, whereby the promoter of a syndication in which tax abuses are suspected is required to send letters to potential investors advising them of this possibility.

*Private-placement memorandum.* A document drafted by a syndicator and his or her consultants that describes all the details of a proposed syndication to potential investors.

*Property management.* Supervision of a physical property itself, including functions pertaining to income, expenses, maintenance, and resale, as opposed to asset management.

*Prospectus.* A written statement describing securities or partnership shares in a real estate syndication being offered for sale; an offering statement.

*Recapture tax provisions.* The amount of sales proceeds that are subject to ordinary income tax upon the sale of a real estate asset, reflecting the difference between the amount of accelerated deductions taken over and above those allocated under the straight-line method of depreciation or cost recovery system.

*Registration statement.* Information that must be filed with the Securities and Exchange Commission before securities can be marketed, consisting of a prospectus and supporting information and exhibits.

*Rehabilitation expenditures.* Capital disbursements designed to improve a property permanently, or for a minimum five-year period, subject to special tax credits under the 1981 Tax Reform Act.

*REIT (Real estate investment trust).* A highly regulated entity of at least 100 investors, which is usually publicly registered. REIT shares are transferable, investments are primarily in real estate, and excess tax losses cannot be distributed to shareholders.

*RESSI (Real Estate Securities and Syndication Institute).* A division of the National Association of Realtors, which offers professional instruction to those wishing to take the broker/dealer examination.

*RULPA (Revised Uniform Limited Partnership Act.)* A bill drafted in 1976 by the National Conference of Commissions on Uniform State Laws adopted or being considered for adoption by an increasing number of states.

*SEC (Securities and Exchange Commission).* A regulatory agency of the United States Government established in 1934 and charged with enforcing provisions of the Securities Act of 1933 and subsequent securities legislation.

*Securities Act of 1933.* The basic legislation in the United States regulating securities, supplemented and revised by subsequent legislation.

*Securities Exchange Act of 1934.* Legislation creating the Securities and Exchange Commission and designed to assure the availability of adequate information on companies with publicly traded stock to regulate their trading markets and to control the activities of those dealing in or selling these securities.

*SIPC (Securities Investor Protection Corporation).* An agency supported and backed by the U.S. government, whose chief purpose is to compensate investors for losses of deposits or securities when a broker or dealer firm declares insolvency.

*Staged equity payments.* Incremental contributions of capital, tailored to meet development needs in a project. Such payments are sometimes deposited in escrow accounts.

*Straight-line depreciation.* A method of reducing the tax basis of an asset by taking equal allowances yearly throughout that asset's total economic life, as opposed to less conservative accelerated depreciation.

*Subchapter S corporation.* An organization of no less than three and no more than 35 stockholders functioning as a corporation in all respects except that stockholders can elect to prorate income to themselves, thereby bypassing taxation at the corporate level.

*Subordinated participation.* A form of compensation in which a syndicator participates in the profits of a syndication only after his or her partners have received their equity investment in return plus a predetermined rate of interest.

*Subscription agreement.* The document contained in an offering package that an interested investor returns, along with a deposit, to the syndicator, indicating his or her desire to join the offering.

*Substantial economic effect.* A criterion used by the Internal Revenue Service to determine the substance of a syndication for purposes other than tax abuse or evasion.

*Suitability standards.* The financial requirements an investor must meet to qualify for participation in a syndication. Terms are dictated by securities legislation to ensure that the illiquidity of an asset will not cause hardship to an investor.

*Tax Equity and Fiscal Responsibility Act.* Legislation enacted in 1982 to prevent such abuses as tax shelters.

*Tax shelter.* An investment where the deductions derived from the offering generally exceed the income therefrom.

*Tax-shelter opinion.* Any advice relating to the federal tax aspects of an offering that is referred to in the promotional material of a syndication.

*Termination clause.* That portion of a contract or other working agreement specifying the time and conditions of the dissolution of the joint effort.

*UBTI (Unrelated business taxable income).* Business-related taxable income that a tax-exempt plan receives from its regular operations.

*ULOE (Uniform Limited Offering Exemption).* An official policy guideline adopted by the North American Securities Administrators Association in October of 1981, designed to create a basic framework of limited offering exemptions to apply uniformly at state and federal levels.

*ULPA (Uniform Limited Partnership Act).* Legislation enacted that, together with the Uniform Partnership Act, currently governs the workings of limited partnerships in the United States.

*Uniform Securities Agents State Law Examination.* An examination administered by the National Association of Securities Dealers to quality brokers and dealers to operate in states that do not have specific examinations of their own.

*Unspecified property offering.* A syndication or other real estate venture in which the specific property to be developed or acquired is not identified in the private placement memorandum, the choice being left to the managing partner after organization of the syndication.

*UPA (Uniform Partnership Act).* Legislation enacted in 1914 that is the principal element of current U.S. partnership law. Wording and interpretation vary from one state to another.

*Up-front fees.* Charges that a syndicator levies at the beginning of a syndication as recompense for structuring and marketing the investment.

*Warranty deed.* A conveyance of interest in real property in which the seller warrants or represents that he or she has merchantable title to pass on to the buyer.

*Wraparound mortgage.* A refinancing vehicle that permits the seller, or in some cases a lender, to increase the existing encumbrance by adding a second or wraparound mortgage.

*Yield.* The expected or actual income received on an investment property, expressed as a percentage return on the overall investment or on the equity portion of a leveraged syndication.

# Index